After the Bell – Family Background, Public Policy, and Educational Success

In the years since the publication of the controversial "Coleman report" in the U.S., a tacit consensus has evolved among scholars that the effects of various dimensions of background – family, community, genotype – are stronger influences on educational achievement than are specific school-based policies. Yet, in the four decades since the report first appeared, educational politics and policy have continued to focus almost exclusively on schools. That schools have an important role in education is beyond question, but this book demonstrates some of the crucial ways that non-school factors matter, covering such themes as:

- the impact of fathers on educational success
- socio-economic background and young children's education
- school–community relationships.

With contributions from such figures as Jere Behrman, Jeanne Brooks-Gunn, Doris Entwisle, and Richard Arum, this book is an important contribution to a debate that has implications across the board in social sciences and policy-making. It will be required reading for students and academics within sociology, economics, and education and should also find a place on the bookshelves of education policy makers.

Dalton Conley is the Director of the Center for Advanced Social Science Research, Professor of Sociology and Public Policy at New York University, and a Research Associate at the National Bureau of Educational Research. **Karen Albright** is a Ph.D. Candidate and Instructor of Sociology at New York University.

Routledge Advances in Sociology

This series aims to present cutting-edge developments and debates within the field of sociology. It will provide a broad range of case studies and the latest theoretical perspectives, while covering a variety of topics, theories and issues from around the world. It is not confined to any particular school of thought.

1 **Virtual Globalization**
Virtual spaces/tourist spaces
Edited by David Holmes

2 **The Criminal Spectre in Law, Literature and Aesthetics**
Peter Hutchings

3 **Immigrants and National Identity in Europe**
Anna Triandafyllidou

4 **Constructing Risk and Safety in Technological Practice**
Edited by Jane Summerton and Boel Berner

5 **Europeanisation, National Identities and Migration**
Changes in boundary constructions between Western and Eastern Europe
Willfried Spohn and Anna Triandafyllidou

6 **Language, Identity and Conflict**
A comparative study of language in ethnic conflict in Europe and Eurasia
Diarmait Mac Giolla Chríost

7 **Immigrant Life in the U.S.**
Multi-disciplinary persepectives
Edited by Donna R. Gabaccia and Colin Wayne Leach

8 **Rave Culture and Religion**
Edited by Graham St. John

9 **Creation and Returns of Social Capital**
A new research program
Edited by Henk Flap and Beate Völker

10 **Self-care**
Embodiment, personal autonomy and the shaping of health consciousness
Christopher Ziguras

11 **Mechanisms of Cooperation**
Werner Raub and Jeroen Weesie

12 **After the Bell – Family Background, Public Policy, and Educational Success**
Edited by Dalton Conley and Karen Albright

After the Bell – Family Background, Public Policy, and Educational Success

Edited by Dalton Conley and Karen Albright

Routledge
Taylor & Francis Group
LONDON AND NEW YORK

First published 2004
by Routledge
2 Park Square, Milton Park, Abingdon, Oxon, OX14 4RN

Simultaneously published in the USA and Canada
by Routledge

711 Third Avenue, New York, NY 10017

Routledge is an imprint of the Taylor & Francis Group

First issued in paperback 2012

Typeset in Times by Wearset Ltd, Boldon, Tyne and Wear

British Library Cataloguing in Publication Data
A catalogue record for this book is available from the British Library

Library of Congress Cataloging in Publication Data
A catalog record for this book has been requested

ISBN 978-0-415-30896-0 (hardback)

ISBN 978-0-415-64576-8 (paperback)

Contents

Contributors

Karen Albright is a Ph.D. Candidate in Sociology at New York University.

Karl L. Alexander is the John Dewey Professor of Sociology at The Johns Hopkins University.

Richard Arum is the Chair of the Department of Humanities and the Social Sciences in the Professions in New York University's Steinhardt School of Education. He is also an Associate Professor of Sociology at New York University.

Jere R. Behrman is the William R. Kenan, Jr. Professor of Economics and the Director of the Population Studies Center at the University of Pennsylvania.

Jeanne Brooks-Gunn is the Virginia and Leonard Marx Professor of Child Development and Education at Teachers College, Columbia University. She is also the Director of the Center for Children and Families, and Co-Director of the Institute for Child and Family Policy.

Emily Forrest Cataldi is a Research Scientist at MPR Associates, Inc. in Berkeley, California.

Dalton Conley is the Director of the Center for Advanced Social Science Research, Professor of Sociology and Public Policy at New York University, and a Research Associate at the National Bureau of Educational Research.

Doris R. Entwisle is a Professor Emerita of Sociology at The Johns Hopkins University.

Allison Sidle Fuligni is a Research Scientist at the Center for Improving Child Care Quality, in the Graduate School of Education and Information Studies at the University of California at Los Angeles.

Ariel Kalil is an Assistant Professor at the Irving B. Harris Graduate School of Public Policy Studies at The University of Chicago. She is also a Faculty Affiliate at the Northwestern University/University of

Chicago Joint Center for Poverty Research and a Faculty Associate at The University of Chicago Center on Parents, Children and Work.

Jennifer C. Lee is a Ph.D. Candidate in Sociology at the University of Minnesota.

Miriam Linver is a Senior Research Scientist at the Center for Children and Families at Teachers College, Columbia University, and an Assistant Professor of Family and Child Studies at Montclair State University.

Linda Steffel Olson is a Senior Research Assistant in the Department of Sociology at The Johns Hopkins University.

Mary Pattillo is an Associate Professor of Sociology and African-American Studies at Northwestern University. She is also a Faculty Fellow at the Institute for Policy Research at Northwestern University.

Monique R. Payne is a Graduate Fellow in the Department of Sociology at Northwestern University.

Brian Powell is the Allen D. and Polly S. Grimshaw Professor of Sociology at Indiana University.

Lala Carr Steelman is a Professor of Sociology at the University of South Carolina.

John Robert Warren is an Assistant Professor of Sociology at the University of Minnesota.

Sandra Way is a Ph.D. Candidate in Sociology at the University of Arizona.

Regina Werum is an Associate Professor of Sociology at Emory University.

W. Jean Yeung is a Research Scientist at the Center for Advanced Social Science Research at New York University. She is also an Adjunct Associate Professor of Sociology at New York University.

Introduction

American educational policy in historical perspective

Karen Albright and Dalton Conley

In 1966, sociologist James Coleman and his co-authors issued what is today considered a seminal report on inequality in schooling. While the document, which came to be known as the "Coleman report," drew attention to the effects of racial segregation as opposed to school resources on student outcomes, it also raised a surprising additional sociological insight: family background, not schools, was primarily responsible for differences in educational attainment.[1] While for minority students some school characteristics had minor to moderate effects, these were largely school composition effects (that is, their racial make-up); expenditures only seemed to matter for African-Americans in the South.[2] Such a conclusion was shocking, primarily because it implied that the indicators upon which educational policy had focused for most of the twentieth century, such as per-pupil expenditures and student-to-teacher ratios, did not matter nearly as much as policy makers had thought. Comprising information on over 600,000 students in 4,000 schools, the data indicated that the importance of family background dwarfs the role that school-based dynamics play in the educational experience.

The report was met with significant resistance in many quarters, and some scholars assailed it on methodological grounds.[3] Yet in the intervening decades since it first appeared, the fire that the Coleman report ignited has hardly been extinguished.[4] Numerous scholars have gone back to reanalyze Coleman *et al.*'s original data, and the overall pattern of their findings has held steady. Though there remains some disagreement regarding the degree of influence that should be accorded to schools, a tacit consensus has evolved across the ideological spectrum that the effects of various dimensions of background – family, community, genotype – are stronger influences on educational achievement than are specific school-based policies.

Of course, it would be foolish to argue that what goes on during the institutional confines of the school day is unimportant. Significantly, Coleman and his co-authors did not make such a claim; rather, they acknowledged the potential of school reform in their evaluation of school faculty, facilities, and curriculum. Indeed, there are a number of ways that schools can and should be improved, and these are deserving of attention; subsequent research has suggested that areas particularly worthy of examination are those that focus on the impact of peer cultures, teacher quality, instructional approaches, tracking and, certainly, the aforementioned student-to-teacher ratios.[5] But focusing our attention *only* on the school day has obvious limits. Thanks to Coleman's pioneering efforts and the efforts of those who have followed him, we have ample evidence that family background matters considerably for academic achievement. We must now use this evidence to reframe the educational policy debate. One way to do this is to examine more precisely *which* aspects of family background matter, as well as how much and why.

Reframing the discussion in this way is the goal of this volume. The following chapters, which began life as papers for the academic conference "After the Bell: Education Solutions Outside the School," held at the Jerome Levy Economics Institute at Bard College in June 2001, push the implications of the Coleman report further than any previous published work on the subject. Each explores the complex effects of family background on educational success, thus expanding the discussion regarding various educational solutions to those outside the school day itself. Together, these chapters reiterate the argument that there is much more to educational achievement than the school-based dynamics on which elected officials, educators, and the general public typically focus.

In order to put the current debate about educational policy in its proper context, however, a brief historical overview is in order. Though debate about the determinants of academic success hardly began with the Coleman report, the vast majority of contemporary political rhetoric regarding educational policy fails to recognize the historical salience of earlier debates or to acknowledge how they inform our current situation. Indeed, the way Americans have conceived of the role of schools has gone through a series of important changes since the late nineteenth century. A history of American educational policy, even before the publication of the Coleman report, is one rife with competing visions regarding the interpretation and meaning of national progress, and the institutional roles and forms most conducive for those visions.

Debate and dissent, progress and practicality: educational policy in historical context

For much of American history, there was little question that family background was the primary force behind a lack of academic success. Rather than using such a belief to propel more informed and developed educational and social policies, however, policy makers generally took this as permission to give up on poor children. As economic policy analyst Richard Rothstein notes, it was once conventional wisdom that "disadvantaged children could not learn under any circumstances."[6] Few gave sustained consideration to the educational development of children who came from poverty; those who stayed in school were typically directed into lower-achieving tracks and abandoned there. Further, because expectations regarding the potential of poor children were low, educators took little responsibility for their poor performance. The fact that one came from a disadvantaged environment was regarded as explanation enough for the trajectory that usually followed; the devastating impact of social inequality was not seen as something that could be addressed within the school, or even by academic achievement itself.

Over time, however, as the shape and character of the nation began to change with increasing industrialization and urbanization, many policy makers' thoughts turned to the issue of national progress and what role schools could – and should – play in its facilitation. With a mere 6.3 percent of seventeen year olds graduating from high school at the turn of the century,[7] there was reason (and room) to believe that increased educational achievement might hold the key to increased national performance. Yet exactly how to go about increasing national educational achievement was not clear. The first significant debate about the direction of future educational policy began to take shape with the emergence of two camps that were directly opposed on this issue. The first camp, headed by Charles W. Eliot, the president of Harvard University, believed that all students should have equal access to an advanced curriculum of concentrated academic subjects. Eliot and his supporters "argued that all high school students should be educated with equal seriousness in the major branches of human knowledge and that occupational decisions should be put off until after graduation."[8] Members of this camp were concerned that many school administrators were attempting to attract high school students by offering courses in more practical, occupational subjects, such as bookkeeping, typing, and mechanical drawing, and believed that this resulted in a dumbing-down of the academic curriculum. Eliot argued that few benefited from a system that cheated students out of the more rigorous intellectual development that they deserved, and which would likely help them succeed later in life.[9] Thus, he and his followers opposed the introduction and proliferation of what they considered a second-class curriculum.[10]

On the other hand, the president of Clark University, the psychologist G. Stanley Hall, adamantly opposed Eliot's view of the role of education in students' lives. Hall did not consider Eliot's position a practical one.[11] Rather than demand that all students adhere to a strict and demanding academic curriculum regardless of ability and inclination, Hall and his supporters argued that schools would best serve the students and the nation by recognizing and attempting to meet the diversified needs of students. From their perspective, curricula should be adapted to the majority of students, rather than to the elite few who would eventually attend college.[12] What the majority of students needed most, they argued, were practical skills.

Hall's camp eventually won the debate, aided in no small part by important structural changes that were impacting the nation's schools in the early 1900s: with the arrival of more and more waves of immigrants, school enrollments were doubling every decade, and a multi-tiered curriculum was simply more practical to execute.[13] By the 1930s, the strict core curriculum that Eliot had espoused had largely given way to one given by consumer choices, and high schools seemed to function as much to sort students as to educate them. In order for schools to keep up with the streams of new students, educators could not devote as much time or effort as some students required to learn the assigned material, but they were typically discouraged from failing their students even when it was evident that the material had not been sufficiently grasped. In all but the most challenging tracks, academic and performance standards were fairly low, and they reached a new depth in 1939, with the introduction of the "life course curriculum." This program, which extended the concept of practical education to include lessons in etiquette and primers on everyday activities such as housekeeping, was widely adopted in the 1940s.[14] It was espoused as the ideal curriculum in a 1944 report by the National Education Association, *Education for All American Youth*, in part because it addressed the "imperative needs of youth."[15] Marketing the educational experience to the consumer-student had won out; challenging students to aspire to a more demanding curriculum seemed not only impractical, but also unnecessary.

Not incidentally, the particular sorting function now inherent in public schools was very much in keeping with the movement towards the scientific management of education that had also begun around the turn of the century.[16] New forms of bureaucratic organization were appearing throughout American life, particularly in the workplace, and the reformers (and creators) of public education believed them to be appropriate for extension to the schools, both for rural schools, which were frequently considered inefficient, and for urban schools, whose growth had often been unruly in the face of increasing urbanization.

The underlying belief, termed the Cult of Efficiency by historian Raymond Callahan, was that America could best reach its potential if the talents of each generation were harnessed by educators in one common, bureaucratically organized institution.[17] A certain uniformity began to be imposed, particularly on the expanding urban schools. This included the introduction of the "eggcrate" school design, which consisted of one long corridor with a spine of classrooms. Such schools graded students by age, and taught them a uniform course of study by employing textbooks identified as grade-appropriate.[18] Curricula became increasingly specified, and teachers were encouraged to enforce the correctness of certain answers over others. With time, the value of testing increased dramatically, both for sorting and for checking to see how well (or if) the curricula was being followed; after being administered, tests became property of the school district's central bureaucracy.

This increasing trend towards bureaucratic organization was one of the main reasons that the debate between Eliot and Hall came to the fore when it did: not only was there reason to believe that America's destiny could be cemented through improved educational performance, it was deemed crucial that uniform decisions be made to maximize and control the educational process as effectively as possible. The historian David Tyack has termed this the search for the One Best System.[19] Inefficiency was considered undesirable, a relic of the pre-industrialized past, especially with regard to an issue so important to the nation's future. Thus, even though curricula might have been more "dumbed down" (at least according to Eliot's definition), they were more specified and, consequently, more measurable, and both criteria fit well with the goals of scientific management.

Not surprisingly, not everyone was pleased with such efforts to standardize public education. The application of the Cult of Efficiency to the educational domain spawned at least two distinct countermovements, which would ultimately work together to oppose the rigid systemization of public schools. Administrative progressives sought reform with regard to the particular approach to standardization. They opposed the hierarchical organization that both physically and figuratively characterized the eggcrate schools and argued instead for a more complex and differentiated school system, including better teacher training and more cooperative leadership. At the same time, pedagogical progressives, inspired by John Dewey, criticized public school officials for emphasizing what they saw as a disturbingly narrow focus on the school itself rather than emphasizing the interdependence of economic, social, and educational reforms, which they considered necessary for meeting individual needs and for ensuring the survival of democracy itself.[20] The alliance that formed between administrative and pedagogical progressives, cemented by their mutual opposition to a rigid hierarchical system within the public schools, would challenge bureaucratic educational efforts for more than half a century, and their unified concerns helped to pave the way for arguments that would arise more vociferously in the 1960s and 1970s in support of more "open" classrooms and more child-centered forms of teaching.[21]

In any case, other complaints about schools' organization and curricula were also beginning to take shape by the 1950s. Foremost among these were complaints about the content of the "life adjustment" curricula: a faint but growing chorus of voices began to question the substitution of less challenging lessons for a more rigorous academic education.[22] That chorus, however, was not strong enough to force a change in the dominant academic curricula or to significantly alter public consciousness about the issue. In general, most parents were happy with the education that their children were receiving; they (and the nation) were particularly proud of the ever-increasing rate of high school graduation, which was taken as evidence of individual and collective upward mobility, and as unlimited potential for the future. It was also difficult to make a case that adapting a curriculum to the desires of the consumer-student was harmful in any way, particularly since America was basking in a state of relative post-War isolation and international comparisons seemed largely irrelevant.[23]

Such domestic contentment was rudely shattered, however, with the launching of *Sputnik* on October 4, 1957. Immediately and exponentially, America's anxieties about possible domination by the Soviets, which had always existed as an undercurrent of social and political life in the early Cold War era, intensified. Further, these anxieties quickly found an outlet in criticism of the educational realm, and the logic was simple: the reason that the Russians were ahead of the Americans in the space race – in *anything* – was because American schools were just not rigorous enough. Demands abounded for substantial changes in academic standards and curricula, girded by the fear that if American youth did not increase their scholastic aptitude, the nation would remain forever behind in the space race and in all other competitions.[24]

These demands were acted upon almost immediately, for the government was also anxious. New and revitalized curricula in mathematics and the physical and biological sciences were developed, and the impact was phenomenal. By 1961, while general enrollment had grown by only about 50 percent since 1949, enrollment in advanced math, physics, and chemistry had increased by an impressive 2,000 percent.[25] With significant federal funds now dedicated to whipping state departments of education into shape and helping poor children in slums and rural areas came a reinvigorated belief in scientific management, this time encouraged by the attention of applied social scientists, whose enthusiasm about the possibilities of social engineering was profound.[26] This devotion to the design and evaluation of educational programs signaled a renewed belief in the centrality of the role of schools: whereas the ability of schools to address or correct inequality had once been regarded as severely limited at best, education was now enthusiastically embraced as the leading pathway to self-improvement – both for the individual student and for the nation itself. Some argument would continue to exist about exactly which specific kinds of school dynamics were most beneficial for optimal performance, but overall it was a heady, optimistic time, and the consensus regarding the inherent value of education and the definitive role that schools played in the achievement of life outcomes seemed untenable.

Yet, frustratingly, evaluations showed that children in the slums were not making the same kinds of educational inroads that their suburban counterparts were. To combat this, some schools experimented with other, more comprehensive management approaches, including a variety of techniques designed and implemented by the military,[27] but to little avail. In the face of this persistent inequality, the widespread explanation was that schools in concentrated poor areas, which were often overwhelmingly black, received fewer resources than did those in the largely white suburbs, and that this difference in resources was what made the difference in educational achievement.[28] Such an explanation, of course, did nothing to question the national conviction that schools themselves were what counted. Though the issues that were beginning to be raised about differential resources and racial inequality were certainly important ones, the particular way that the educational policy debate was framed meant that it could not yet address other factors that might also play a role in continuing inequality.

The educational turn: the arrival of the Coleman report

With the publication of the Coleman report in 1966, the consensus that school resources alone could affect educational success was abruptly shattered. Coleman and his colleagues, commissioned by the U.S. Congress, had originally intended their data to provide definitive evidence that differential resources were to blame for the disparities in educational outcomes. What their work showed, however, was that racial segregation and students' family characteristics were more explanatory of the variation in achievement than were school resources themselves.[29] Consequently, they argued that:

> [s]chools bring little influence to bear on a child's achievement that is independent of his background and general social context; and that this very lack of an independent effect means that the inequalities imposed on children by their home, neighborhood, and peer environment are carried along to become the inequalities with which they confront adult life at the end of school.[30]

The backlash was immediate. Many policy makers and scholars, offended at the suggestion that school reform had its limits, interpreted the report as implying that progress was not possible. Coleman and his colleagues were consequently accused of being overly conservative,[31] and a number of scholars set to work on rebutting their data. Indeed, a few problems with the report were uncovered; specifically, the statistical approaches used by Coleman and his colleagues are sometimes inadequate and, because the report focused on explaining variance rather than examining the effects of independent variables on educational and labor market outcomes, it underestimated their effects to some degree. Despite this, reanalyses of the data, in that report and in subsequent research, have been unable to topple their conclusion that schools are not the primary factor in student achievement.[32]

The tide slowly began to turn. Though many researchers and policy makers continued to focus exclusively on schools' efficacy (or lack of it, as was often the case) rather than incorporating the impact of family characteristics and other social factors into their analyses of learning outcomes, the discussion had effectively been expanded. In 1972, Christopher Jencks and his colleagues published *Inequality*, which presented an argument similar to that of the Coleman report.[33] Using data that showed that within-school variation was roughly equal to variation found in the educational attainment between schools, Jencks *et al.* argued that schools themselves had little effect on students. Instead, they argued that family background was the primary determinant of educational outcomes, followed by the closely related considerations of individual intelligence and aspirations. While some elements of the educational experience (particularly the interactions between students and teachers) might impact students more strongly than other elements, Jencks and his colleagues asserted that such elements were precisely the ones that defied change by educational policy makers.[34] Further, they argued that the issue of the specific effects of schooling was ultimately moot, since educational attainment (as well as cognitive ability) had only modest effects on occupational attainment and virtually zero effect on income. In other words, the equalization of schools' resources – or even of educational attainment itself, if such a thing were possible – could not affect adult inequality in any meaningful way, because it could not address inequality in the labor market, which is arguably what matters most.

Though *Inequality*, too, would meet with resistance, including some statistical criticism,[35] the floodgates had opened. New questions regarding the degree that education could actually affect life outcomes further expanded the debate about what the focus of educational policy should be. The sociologists, economists, historians, and other social scientists that were drawn to the study of education beginning in the late 1960s were influenced by these questions as well as by the continuing civil unrest in the nation. No doubt partly reacting to the determined refusal of many administrative officials and policy makers to address the inequality that went beyond the confines of the schools themselves, these newer social scientists continued to push the lines of inquiry, questioning the amount of real change that could take place in a capitalist social structure like America's. One of the most influential works to result from this more radical perspective was *Schooling in Capitalist America*, in which the economists Samuel Bowles and Herbert Gintis argued that the American educational system could never provide true equality of opportunity because it reflected the necessarily hierarchical structure of the capitalist economy.[36]

In recent years, the virulence of the academic debate has abated somewhat, though passionate and persuasive arguments continue to be made on both sides.[37] Recent research indicates that both sides of the debate have some legitimacy; thus, after a century of the argument that schools made all the difference and decades of the argument that schools made little to no difference, the swing of the pendulum seems to have stopped somewhere in the middle. To some degree, this is due to new analyses which give ground to both sides: while school quality, as measured by resources, does not seem to have an effect on test scores per se,[38] some research has shown that it does have an effect on educational attainment and labor market outcomes.[39] Perhaps more important to the resolution of this debate, however, are data that show that the *degree* of difference is what matters most: small differences in school quality appear to have little to no effect, but large differences have a significant effect.[40] Indeed, research on students who experience the extremes of the quality distribution – schools that have either extremely abundant or extremely depleted resources – has documented the profound impact that school quality can have.[41]

Despite this growing consensus in scholarly research, however, resistance to the findings and implications of the Coleman report continues in today's educational policy. Despite considerable evidence that family characteristics are the most crucial variable in academic achievement, the primary emphasis in the public debate concerning educational policy continues to be on schools themselves, particularly with regard to class size and, more recently, school voucher programs.[42] How can this be so? In the simplest terms, it has to do with politics. Because schools are a government responsibility, they represent an area about which campaign promises can be made and a realm where we can have a "valid" public debate. Further, schools are easy targets when the political climate is rough and/or complicated; indeed, the urgency of the public discussion about the state of our national education waxes and wanes according to larger economic and political forces. For example, attention to American educational attainment was strongly intensified in the 1980s, when Japan emerged as a formidable economic competitor. In an echo of the hysteria that had followed the *Sputnik* launch, reports such as *A Nation At Risk*, the product of Ronald Reagan's "Commission on Educational Excellence," argued that the reason America was losing ground in the economic competition with Japan was that American schools were simply not doing a good job of providing students with a solid education.[43]

Attributing the decline in the American economy primarily to a decline in American schools, however, is dubious at best. Of course, if we acknowledge that schools matter little, what is society to do? If parenting styles – or worse still, genetics – are really more important for kids than schools are, one can only imagine what kind of public policies that might potentially lead to, beginning with invasive home visits and extending to the domain of eugenics.[44] But we must remember that policy does not have to be limited to these rather sinister options; there are other non-school-based policy choices that are reasonable and well within our reach. For example, the United States could pursue a goal of universal day care for the critical early years before kids arrive at kindergarten – though of course, day care blurs the line between school and non-school factors by essentially increasing the number of years of "formal" schooling. Much research shows that rates of illness strongly affect academic performance, so we might improve the health care of school-aged children.[45] We could also expand the housing stock, for recent research also shows that when kids live in crowded conditions at home – and are unable to sleep well, have no privacy to do homework, and so on – they tend to concentrate poorly in school and perform worse overall.[46]

Unfortunately, however, these issues are not on the lips of educational policy makers and pundits, nor are they familiar in this context to the general public. And elected officials are hardly the only parties responsible for the lopsided emphasis in the "debate." Ultimately, numerous players – not just politicians, but also educational researchers, teachers unions, school voucher advocates, even custodians – have an institutional stake in keeping the debate focused on the time period between 9 a.m. and 3 p.m. Thus, while more and more scholars now agree that the most comprehensive and effective educational policy must address what happens both during and beyond the limited time a child spends in school, public discussion about education is still overwhelmingly, even stubbornly, focused on issues pertaining to school quality.

Family background, public policy, and educational success: new data, new perspectives

The chapters in this volume are meant as a corrective to this focus. Their intent is not to argue that schools are unimportant, but to present evidence that the emphasis placed on schools has been unduly heavy while the need for other important reforms has been largely ignored. *Both* school and non-school factors are important to educational success, and – even more importantly – to labor market outcomes. The main point of this volume is to demonstrate some of the crucial ways that non-school factors matter, in order to remind reformers to expand their vision of what allows for educational success. We must recognize that the belief that schools alone can be society's primary instrument of economic and social reform is extremely misleading. It creates a myopic focus on education that is neither accurate nor fair, and it sets goals that simply cannot be fulfilled. In fact, such a focus positions public schools for failure and ultimately leads to a withdrawal of support for schools. Similarly, we must also gain a better understanding of the complexities of the modern labor market.[47] While education certainly has considerable value beyond its labor market consequences, it is imperative that we recognize that an emphasis on school reform alone will not solve the significant problems that we currently face, either in our national economy or our educational attainment.[48]

So what will? Economic policy analyst Richard Rothstein has argued that we must extend cost-benefit analyses to a variety of policies beyond school interventions alone if we are to find out.[49] This would include examination of policies aimed at raising family income, particularly those that would increase the permanent income for the lowest income families. It would also include investigation of policies designed to improve national health care, since the vast inequalities that currently exist impact the educational performance of millions of children; this would include policies addressing inadequate nutrition, prenatal care, and dental care, as well as the effects of maternal smoking and lead exposure. Finally, it would include examination of policies addressing the frequent instability of living arrangements among the working poor, with particular attention to those policies that examine the beneficial impact of housing subsidies.[50]

The chapters in this volume follow in the spirit of these suggestions for policy interventions. Part I sets the stage for the discussion by demonstrating the importance of what happens after the bell. "How do parents matter?: Income, interactions, and intervention during early childhood," by Miriam Linver, Allison Sidle Fuligni, and Jeanne Brooks-Gunn, makes the case for the importance of family environment. This chapter examines how family environment might mediate the associations between both income and interventions with child cognitive and emotional outcomes. Using data from three large studies (The Infant Health and Development Project, the Panel Study of Income Dynamics – Child Development Supplement, and the National Longitudinal Study of Youth – Child Supplement), the authors argue that a stimulating home environment, positive parenting behaviors and maternal emotional health are all important when examining the links between income and child outcomes, and intervention and child outcomes. They find that exploring the processes linking SES and child development is especially critical in thinking about how poor children may or may not be "ready" for school. They argue that when considering how interventions are important in the lives of children and families, interventions should be designed to address the stated goals as directly as possible; parenting education should be offered when attempting to influence parenting behavior, whereas direct early childhood education should be provided when attempting to influence child behavior.

The second chapter in Part I, Jere R. Behrman's "Family background, education determination and policy implications: Some selected aspects from various countries," identifies a number of methodological and theoretical problems in the current literature on family background and child education. Behrman argues that most studies use imperfect measures of the key observable variables, including those for education and for family income. As a result, even the descriptions that they provide may be misleading, including those regarding the strength of the association between family background and education. Similarly, he argues that most studies do not provide convincing evidence of causality, particularly with regard to genetic endowments. Indeed, if there are intergenerational correlations in genetic endowments that facilitate learning and are rewarded in labor markets, much or even all of the associations between most of the primary family background variables that are used in the literature – income, schooling, occupation – may be due to such correlations, and not to the family background variables themselves. He also argues that most studies do not establish clearly the context of their results, such as how household behaviors in response to incentives created by markets, culture, and policies may differ substantially depending on the nature of markets, culture, and policies. Finally, he states that though most studies provide some information needed for the evaluation of policies, they typically neglect key elements of what is needed with regard to either the costs or the benefits. Behrman uses international data regarding family background, schooling determination, and policy implications to address each of these limitations.

The third chapter in Part I, "Young children's achievement in school and socioeconomic background," by Doris Entwisle, Karl L. Alexander, and Linda Steffel Olson, makes the claim that the importance of family background is evidenced by gains made through summer learning. As they report, a longitudinal study of about 800 young Baltimore children found that during their first three years of school, children enrolled in low-SES schools gained, on average, about the same number of points on standardized achievement tests as did children enrolled in higher-SES schools – when elementary schools were open. In the summer, however, when schools were closed, only children from better-off families made gains on these tests. The authors confirm through repeated analyses of variance that the divergence by SES in summer gains is coupled with an invariance by SES in winter gains; further, parents' psychological capital supported the achievement growth of high-SES children observed in summer. More simply put, summer gains occurred mainly among children of high-SES parents who held high expectations for their children's performance, while children of high-SES parents who held low expectations or children of low-SES parents (irrespective of parents' expectation levels) did not gain during summer periods. By contrast, in winter, neither family SES nor parental expectations mattered much: children of both SES levels gained the same amounts on standardized tests of reading comprehension and math reasoning. These findings contradict the common assumption that home resources supplement school resources during the school year. Rather, school resources underwrote the considerable progress made by all children in winter, especially those from disadvantaged families. However, during the summer, when the school's resources were unavailable, only the children in families with relatively plentiful economic and psychological resources continued to progress.

The chapters that comprise Part II of this volume examine particular components of "family background" more specifically. The first chapter in this section, "Macro causes, micro effects: linking public policy, family structure, and educational outcomes," by Brian Powell, Regina Werum, and Lala Carr Steelman, analyzes several common explanations for the association between sibship size and educational outcomes, with particular attention to the resource dilution hypothesis. Following this discussion, the authors then present research that examines the relationship between parental age and allocation of resources to offspring. Using data from the National Educational Longitudinal Study of 1988 and the National Longitudinal Survey of the High School Class of 1972, the authors identify parental age as a critical factor in determining the parental allocation of economic resources, social capital, and cultural capital to adolescents. They find that, at the bivariate level, the relationship is curvilinear, suggesting that having comparatively young or old parents is disadvantageous to teenagers, at least with regard to resource allocation. With controls for socioeconomic background and family structure, however, the pattern becomes positive and linear: as the age of the parent rises, so too does the transmission of resources to adolescent offspring. These results suggest that parental age may warrant attention similar to that given to, for example, family structure, race, and gender.

The next chapter, "Fathers: an overlooked resource for children's educational success," by W. Jean Yeung, makes the case for the importance of devoting specific attention to fathers when examining the impact of family background. Yeung uses data from the Panel Study of Income Dynamics to examine how different dimensions of fathering relate to children's cognitive abilities and behavior problems. Measures of paternal involvement include fathers' roles in economic provisioning, direct interaction, monitoring, coparenting, emotional support, and human capital. After controlling for mothers' involvement with children and other family characteristics, Yeung finds that various aspects of fathers' involvement are strongly associated with children's well-being: fathers' income is positively associated with both children's cognitive ability and behaviors, and the human capital of the father is positively related to children's cognitive ability. In addition, emotional support from fathers and fathers' monitoring of children's school activities are associated with fewer behavior problems in children.

The third chapter in this section, "Intergenerational assets and the black/white test score gap," by Ariel Kalil, Mary Pattillo, and Monique R. Payne, explores questions regarding family background by focusing specifically on the impact of intergenerational capital, as assessed by grandparents' education and contact with the present generation of adolescent children. The authors draw on both sociological and psychological perspectives to investigate the sources of black-white differences in young adolescents' standardized test scores, using survey data from the Maryland Adolescent Development in Context Study. Their results underscore the importance of studying intergenerational capital as domain specific: their conclusion stresses the endurance of discrimination against and unequal treatment of blacks across generations, particularly in the field of educational attainment and achievement, and directs attention to the importance of recognizing an extended family history when examining the present gap in black-white academic achievement.

Part III of this volume connects what we know about family background specifically to the labor market. The first chapter in Part III, "Teenage employment and high school completion," explores the relationship between family background and teenage employment, particularly with regard to the effect they have on students' likelihood of dropping out of school. Examining trends in the selectivity and consequences of adolescent employment, John Robert Warren, Jennifer C. Lee, and Emily Forrest Cataldi use five nationally representative data sets to answer three questions: First, how did rates of employment and the mean number of hours worked per week among high school students change during the thirty years between 1966 and 1997? Second, have changes in rates and intensity of student employment taken place primarily among students from particular socioeconomic or demographic groups during these years? Third, how did the effects of sophomore-year employment on high school dropout rates (net of socioeconomic background and academic factors) change during these years? The authors find that there have been few changes in overall rates of employment or hours worked per week since about 1980. In addition, important demographic changes have taken place over time in the populations of employed and intensively employed students, and the negative consequences of intensive employment for high school dropout rates have declined since at least the late 1960s.

The second chapter in Part III, and the final chapter in the volume, is "School-community relationships and the early labor market outcomes of sub-baccalaureate students," by Richard Arum and Sandra Way. This chapter goes beyond family background to give specific attention to the nature and function of school-business relationships, demonstrating the impact of both family and institutional mechanisms in shaping the long-term effects of the educational experience. The authors note that although school-assisted job placement is rarely used in U.S. schools, when schools do facilitate employment through institutional or network ties with employers, labor market benefits occur, particularly for women. These connections between schools and employers account for some of the labor market gains women receive from taking high school vocational business classes. Because entry-level jobs that are open to male high school graduates typically require job-specific occupational skills rather than academic prowess, however, men use school assistance less than women do in order to find employment, and therefore receive fewer benefits from these connections. These results support those by other sociologists who have suggested the substantive importance of focusing greater attention on the role of institutional environments in structuring young adult labor market outcomes, but indicate that previous research on this subject has neglected to take into account how such structuring varies by gender.

After the bell: a call for dialogue

The chapters in this volume span the wide expanse of important issues regarding our understanding of the role that family background plays in the interrelated education and labor markets. Each introduces a provocative line of inquiry that invites further research; though each chapter focuses on a unique aspect of the effects of family background, each is also very much in dialogue with the others, and the volume is best read in this way. There is much that we do not yet know about the effects of family background, but if we are to address the very real inequality that exists in our educational attainment and in our nation more generally, it is imperative that we engage the issue comprehensively. We hope this volume will help to expand the discussion about the myriad of factors that contribute to educational success, and that it will help to reinvigorate discussion regarding the future of educational policy. After the bell, the policy possibilities are endless.

Notes

1 "The first finding is that the schools are remarkably similar in the way they relate to the achievement of their pupils when the socioeconomic background of the students is taken into account. It is known that socioeconomic factors bear a strong relation to academic achievement. When these factors are statistically controlled, however, it appears that differences between schools account for only a small fraction of differences in pupil achievement." (J. S. Coleman, E. Q. Campbell, C. J. Hobson, J. McPartland, A. M. Mood, F. D. Weinfeld, and R. L. York, *Equality of Educational Opportunity,* Washington, DC: U.S. Government Printing Office, 1966, pp. 21–22.)

2 According to the report, "[w]hatever may be the combination of non-school factors – poverty, community attitudes, low educational level of parents – which put minority children at a disadvantage in verbal and nonverbal skills when they enter the first grade, the fact is the schools have not overcome it." (Ibid., p. 21; see also pp. 297–303 for a more detailed discussion about the impact of family background characteristics.)

3 Reanalyses of data from the Coleman report were generated by such methodological criticisms. (G. E. Thomas and F. Brown, "What does educational research tell us about school desegregation effects?," *Journal of Black Studies* 13, 1982, 155–174; M. T. Hallinan, "Equality of educational opportunity," *Annual Review of Sociology* 14, 1988, 249–268.) Among these reanalyses were those by the U.S. Commission on Civil Rights (*Racial Isolation in the Public Schools, Volume 1,* Washington, DC: Government Printing Office, 1967); J. McPartland (*The Segregated Student in Desegregated Schools: Final Report to the Center for the Study of the Social Organization of Schools*, Baltimore, MD: Johns Hopkins University Press, 1968); S. Bowles and H. M. Levin ("The determinants of scholastic achievement – an appraisal of some recent evidence," *Journal of Human Resources* 3, 1968, 3–24); and D. J. Armor ("The evidence on busing," *Public Interest* 28, 1972, 90–126); and T. F. Pettigrew and R. T. Riley ("Race and the outcomes of schooling," in F. Mosteller and D. P. Moynihan, *On Equality of Educational Opportunity*, New York, NY: Vintage, 1972).

4 Indeed, according to sociologist Barbara Heyns, the Coleman report and the

numerous reanalyses, critiques, and subsequent studies that followed it have fundamentally and permanently altered the discourse in the sociology of education. (B. Heyns, "Educational effects: issues in conceptualization and measurement," in J. C. Richardson, *Handbook of Theory and Research in the Sociology of Education*, New York: Greenwood, 305–340; Hallinan, op. cit.)

5 D. Kember and J. McKay, "Action research into the quality of student learning: a paradigm for faculty development," *Journal of Higher Education* 67, 1996, 528–554; I. Dawson, "The schools history project: A study in curriculum development," *The History Teacher* 22, 1989, 221–238; K. E. Eble and W. J. McKeachie, *Improving Undergraduate Education Through Faculty Development: An Analysis of Effective Programs and Practices*, San Francisco, CA: Jossey Bass, 1985; A. Gamoran, "The stratification of high school learning opportunities," *Sociology of Education* 60, 1987, 135–155; S. R. Lucas, "Effectively maintained inequality: educational transitions, track mobility, and social background effects," *American Journal of Sociology* 106, 2001, 1642–1690. Recent findings indicate that per-pupil expenditures are associated with achievement specifically because they typically result in reduced class size. (H. Wenglinsky, "How money matters: the effect of school district spending on academic achievement," *Sociology of Education* 70, 1997, 221–237.)

6 R. Rothstein, "Out of balance: Our understanding of how schools affect society and how society affects schools," paper presented at The Spencer Foundation 30th Anniversary Conference: Traditions of Scholarship in Education, 2002, p. 11.

7 U.S. Bureau of the Census, "Series H, Table 599: high school graduates, by sex: 1870 to 1970," *Historical Statistics of the United States: Colonial Times to 1970, Bicentennial Edition, Part 1*, Washington, DC: U.S. Bureau of the Census, 1975, p. 379. For a good review of the expansion of American education throughout the twentieth century, see L. A. Cremin, *American Education: The Metropolitan Experience, 1876–1980*, New York, NY: Harper and Row, 1988.

8 G. Grant, *The World We Created at Hamilton High*, Cambridge, MA: Harvard University Press, 1988, 209–210. See also H. Hawkins, *Between Harvard and America: The Educational Leadership of Charles W. Eliot,* New York, NY: Oxford University Press, 1972.

9 B. Bledstein, *The Culture of Professionalism: The Middle Class and the Development of Higher Education in America*, New York, NY: W. W. Norton and Company, 1976.

10 Eliot and his Committee of Ten have been typically viewed as conservative, accused of attempting to preserve a high school education for the college-bound elite while discounting the wide array of needs necessary for others. For a persuasive revision of this interpretation, see E. A. Krug, *The Shaping of the American High School, Volume I, 1880–1920*, New York, NY: Harper and Row, 1964 and E. A. Krug, *The Shaping of the American High School, Volume II, 1920–1941*, Madison, WI: University of Wisconsin Press, 1972. Of course, the history of secondary education reform is more complex than can be adequately addressed in this brief discussion. For a more comprehensive treatment of the multiple layers of this debate, see Grant, op. cit.; Bledstein, op. cit.; P. C. Violas, *The Training of the Urban Working Class: A History of Twentieth Century American Education,* Chicago, IL: Rand McNally, 1978; W. Feinberg and H. Rosemont Jr., *Work, Technology, and Education: Dissenting Essays in the Intellectual Foundations of American Education*, Urbana, IL: University of Illinois Press, 1975. For an excellent account of the Progressive movement in education and the obstacles it encountered, see M. Emirbayer, "Beyond structuralism and voluntarism: The politics and discourse of Progressive school reform, 1890–1930," *Theory and Society* 21, 1992, 621–664.

11 L. S. Feuer, "John Dewey and the back to the people movement in American thought," *Journal of the History of Ideas* 20, 1959, 545–568.
12 D. Ross, *G. Stanley Hall: The Psychologist as Prophet,* Chicago, IL: University of Chicago Press, 1972. See also Grant, op. cit.
13 Grant, op. cit.
14 D. K. Cohen, "Origins," pp. 233–308 in Powell, Farrar and Cohen (eds) *The Shopping Mall High School: Winners and Losers in the Educational Marketplace*, Boston, MA: Houghton Mifflin, 1985.
15 Educational Policies Commission, *Education for All American Youth*, Washington, DC: National Education Commission, 1944, p. 142.
16 The historians David Tyack and Elisabeth Hansot have characterized the push toward the creation of public education at this time as similar to that of a moral crusade. (D. B. Tyack and E. Hansot, *Managers of Virtue: Public School Leadership in America, 1820–1980*, New York, NY: Basic Books, 1982.
17 R. Callahan, *Education and the Cult of Efficiency*, Chicago, IL: University of Chicago Press, 1962.
18 Grant, op. cit. Scholars have noted that this type of school design isolated schoolteachers as well as pupils, to the benefit of few. (E. J. Haller, "Pupil influence in teacher socialization: A socio-linguistic study," *Sociology of Education* 40, 1967, 316–333; D. C. Lortie, "Teacher socialization: The Robinson Crusoe model," *The Real World of the Beginning Teacher*, National Commission on Teacher Education and Professional Standards, Washington, DC: National Education Association, 1966.)
19 D. B. Tyack, *The One Best System: A History of American Urban Education,* Cambridge, MA: Harvard University Press, 1974. See also J. Meyer, W. R. Scott, D. Strang, and A. L. Creighton, "Bureaucraticization without centralization changes in the organizational system of U.S. public education 1940–1980," pp. 450–462 in R. Arum and I. R. Beattie (eds), *The Structure of Schooling*, Mountainview, CA: Mayfield, 2000.
20 Emirbayer, op. cit. See also J. Dewey, *John Dewey on Education: Selected Writings*, Chicago: The University of Chicago Press, 1964.
21 W. Urban, "Organized teachers and educational reform during the progressive era: 1890–1920," *History of Education Quarterly* 16, 1976, 35–52; J. R. Raftery, *Land of Fair Promise: Politics and Reform in Los Angeles Schools, 1885–1941*, Stanford, CA: Stanford University Press, 1992; S. F. Semel, *The Dalton School: The Transformation of a Progressive School*, New York, NY: Peter Lang, 1992; Emirbayer, op. cit; Grant, op. cit.
22 Perhaps the most notable critic of the "life adjustment" curriculum during the 1950s was Arthur Bestor, author of the widely influential and well-known *Educational Wastelands: The Retreat from Learning in Our Public Schools* (Urbana, NY: University of Illinois Press, 1953). (J. Spring, *The Sorting Machine: National Educational Policy Since 1945*, New York, NY: David McKay Company, Inc., 1976.)
23 See R. L. Church, M. B. Katz, H. Silver, and L. A. Cremin, "Forum: The metropolitan experience in American education," *History of Education Quarterly* 29, 1989, p. 445; Grant, op. cit.; Spring, op. cit.
24 Books such as Arthur Trace's *What Ivan Knows That Johnny Doesn't* (New York: Random House, 1961) and Urie Bronfenbrenner's *Two Worlds of Childhood: U.S. and U.S.S.R.* (New York: Basic Books, 1970) both capitalized on and helped to flame this fear.
25 Grant, op. cit.; A. C. Gross, "On engineering education and engineering students," *The Journal of Higher Education* 40, 1969, 520–533. See also L. Tanguy, "Academic studies and technical education: new dimensions of an old struggle in the division of knowledge," *Sociology of Education* 58, 1985, 20–33, for a

critique of the separation between the institutionally constituted scientific knowledge emphasized in twentieth century schools and technical education.

26 R. P. Nathan, *Social Science in Government: Uses and Misuses*, New York: Basic Books, 1988; R. H. Haveman, *Poverty Policy and Poverty Research: The Great Society and the Social Sciences*, Madison, WI: University of Wisconsin Press, 1987. See also W. G. Bennis, "A new role for the behavioral sciences: effecting organizational change," *Administrative Science Quarterly* 8, 1963, 125–165; S. J. Fauman and H. Sharp, "Presenting the results of social research to the public," *Public Opinion Quarterly* 22, 1958, 107–111; P. M. Hauser, "The chaotic society: product of the social morphological revolution," *American Sociological Review* 34, 1969, 1–19.

27 For example, some schools brought in military experts to develop more orderly and efficient approaches to education. Similarly, the PPBS (Program Planning Budgeting System), developed by the Department of Defense, was an attempt to increase the cost efficiency of specific educational objectives (Grant, op. cit.).

28 F. Brown, "Assessment and evaluation of urban schools," *The Journal of Negro Education* 44, 1975, 377–384; J. E. Coons, W. H. Clune III, and S. D. Sugarman, *Private Wealth and Public Education*, Cambridge: Harvard University Press, 1970; J. W. Guthrie, G. B. Kleindorfer, H. M. Levin, and R. T. Stout, *Schools and Inequality*, Cambridge, MA: MIT Press, 1971.

29 Rothstein, op. cit.

30 Coleman *et al.*, op. cit., p. 325.

31 Not all scholars interpreted the report as conservative, however. Frederick Mosteller and Daniel Patrick Moynihan were among the few who recognized it as a radical document, citing its direct challenge to the exclusive and increasingly institutionalized focus on the school. (F. Mosteller and D. P. Moynihan, "A pathbreaking report," pp. 3–66 in F. Mosteller and D. P. Moynihan, *On Equality of Educational Opportunity*, New York, NY: Random House, 1972.)

32 Indeed, "no study has been able to attribute more than half the variation in student achievement to what schools do, and most find schools responsible for no more than a quarter." (Rothstein, op. cit., p. 11.) See, for example, D. W. Grissmer, A. E. Flanagan, J. H. Kawata, and S. Williamson, *Improving Student Achievement: What State NAEP Test Scores Tell Us,* Santa Monica, CA: RAND, 2000.

33 C. Jencks, M. Smith, H. Acland, M. J. Bane, D. Cohen, H. Gintis, B. Heyns, and S. Michelson, *Inequality: A Reassessment of the Effects of Family and Schooling in America,* New York, NY: Harper Press, 1972.

34 Recent research has also emphasized the importance of student-teacher interactions. In one study, David Card and Alan Krueger compared blacks and whites in North and South Carolina, demonstrating that as the gap in student-teacher ratios narrowed across states and racial groups, so did educational attainment and income. (D. Card and A. Krueger, "School resources and student outcomes: an overview of the literature and new evidence from North and South Carolina," *Journal of Economic Perspectives* 10, 1996, 31–50.) Similarly, the Tennessee Class Size Experiment, the only truly random experiment to be performed with regard to resources, indicated that class size affects student achievement. (F. Mosteller, *The Tennessee Study of Class Size in the Early School Grades*, Somerville, MA: The American Academy of Arts and Sciences, 1995.)

35 Among the statistical critiques that Jencks *et al.* faced was that they lacked controls for many of the important variables that could affect labor market outcomes, including age, work experience, family structure, and region, and that they underestimated the strength of some of the effects. Some critics also noted their employment of individual-level models to make societal-level arguments.

See H. F. Taylor, "Playing the dozens with path analysis: methodological pitfalls in Jencks *et al.*, *Inequality*," *Sociology of Education* 46, 1973, 433–450, for a thorough critique.

36 S. Bowles and H. Gintis, *Schooling in Capitalist America: Educational Reform and the Contradictions of Economic Life*, New York, NY: Basic Books, 1976.

37 In the past decade, the economist Eric Hanushek has been one of the most outspoken critics of the tendency to focus solely on school resources. He argues that the large increases devoted to public schools' resources have had little effect over the past century, and urges instead the improvement of student and teacher incentives in future educational policy. "Nobody would advocate zero spending on schooling, as nobody would argue for infinite spending on schooling. The issue is getting productive uses from current and added spending ... The most promising alternative policy to make current and additional resources more productive [is to] emphasiz[e] performance incentives." (E. A. Hanushek, "School resources and student performance," in G. Burtless (ed.) *Does Money Matter? The Effect of School Resources on Student Achievement and Adult Success*, Washington, DC: Brookings Institution Press, 1996, p. 69.) See also E. A. Hanushek, *Improving America's Schools: The Role of Incentives*, Washington, DC: National Academy Press, 1996; E. A. Hanushek, *Making Schools Work: Improving Performance and Controlling Costs*, Washington, DC: Brookings Institution Press, 1994; E. A. Hanushek and S. G. Rivkin, "Understanding the twentieth century growth in U.S. school spending," *The Journal of Human Resources* 32, 1997, 35–68; E. A. Hanushek, S. G. Rivkin, and L. L. Taylor, "Aggregation and the estimated effects of school resources," *The Review of Economics and Statistics* 78, 1996, 611–627.)

38 Card and Krueger, op. cit.

39 D. Card and A. Krueger, "Does school quality matter? Returns to education and the characteristics of public schools in the United States," *Journal of Political Economy* 100, 1992, 1–40; J. Grogger, "Does school quality explain the recent black/white wage trend?," *Journal of Labor Economics* 14, 1996, 231–253. For similar findings in studies of higher education, see T. Kane, "Racial and ethnic preferences in college admissions," pp. 431–456 in C. Jencks and M. Phillips, *The Black-White Test Score Gap*, Washington, DC: The Brookings Institute, 1998; W. Bowen and D. Bok, *The Shape of the River*, Princeton, NJ: Princeton University Press, 1998; E. T. Pascarella and P. Terenzini, *How College Affects Students: Findings and Insights from Twenty Years of Research*, San Francisco, CA: Jossey Bass, 1991.

40 For this reason, Kingston and Smart argue for the use of categorical selectivity variables in measuring school quality. (See P. W. Kingston and J. C. Smart, "The economic pay-off of prestigious colleges," in P. W. Kingston and L. S. Lewis, *The High-Status Track: Studies of Elite Schools and Stratification*, Albany, NY: State University of New York Press, 1990.

41 For example, Cookson and Persell document the advantages that students in elite institutions have with regard to college acceptance and increased occupational attainment and prestige, while Kozol documents the frequently insurmountable difficulties that greet students in many impoverished inner-city schools. (P. W. Cookson and C. H. Persell, *Preparing for Power: America's Elite Boarding Schools*, New York, NY: Basic Books, 1985; J. Kozol, *Savage Inequalities: Children in America's Schools*, New York, NY: Crown Publishers, 1991.)

42 While some data have indicated that black students benefit more from smaller class sizes than white students, Alan Krueger and Diane Whitmore find that when effects were estimated for white and black students who attended the same mix of schools, both whites and blacks benefited equally from smaller

classes. (A. B. Krueger and D. Whitmore, "Would smaller classes help close the black-white achievement gap?," in J. Chubb and T. Loveless, *Bridging the Achievement Gap*, Washington, DC: Brookings Institute Press, 2002.) Similarly, recent research suggests that school vouchers' positive effect on African American students' academic achievement is less robust than has previously been believed. This research indicates that the effect of vouchers is particularly sensitive to how racial and ethnic categories are defined; if children with African American fathers are included in the sample as well as children with African American mothers, the effect of vouchers is smaller and statistically insignificant at conventional levels. This was demonstrated in analyses of the New York City voucher experiment, one of three randomized voucher experiments that provide the most recent data on vouchers' effects. More broadly, data on school vouchers are not encouraging. The other two experiments, in Washington, DC and Dayton, Ohio, did even less to demonstrate vouchers' positive effects; in Washington, vouchers had a statistically insignificant, negative effect on black students' scores after three years, and in Dayton, vouchers had a statistically insignificant effect at the 0.10 level holding constant family background controls in the final year of the experiment. (A. B. Krueger and P. Zhu, "Another look at the New York City school voucher experiment," Working Paper No. 1, Education Research Section, Princeton University, 2003; W. G. Howell and P. E. Peterson, *The Education Gap: Vouchers and Urban Schools*, Washington, DC: Brookings Institute Press, 2002.)

43 National Commission on Excellence in Education, *A Nation at Risk: The Imperative for Educational Reform.* Washington, DC: Government Printing Office, 1983. Ironically, Terrel Bell, Secretary of Education during the Reagan administration, later regretted the emphasis that he had placed on school reforms in *A Nation at Risk*, observing that the more significant influences on educational achievement came from outside the school. (T. H. Bell, "Reflections one decade after *A Nation At Risk*," *Phi Delta Kappan* 74, 1993, 592–597.)

44 If such a perspective were over-emphasized, it also might encourage the erroneous argument that schools don't matter at all. This, of course, would be a mistake. What happens during the school day is, indeed, important – it's just that some other factors seem to be more so.

45 Research on this topic covers a broad array of illness types, though in recent years increased attention has been devoted to the particularly detrimental effects of asthma and poor nutritional health on educational performance. (See, for example, the project led by S. Mangione and funded by Schering-Plough, "Asthma in Philadelphia minorities: prevalence among middle-school children and the assessment of a multi-intervention self-management program," 1998–2000; and the report written by G. Woodward-Lopez, J. Ikeda, and P. Crawford, "Improving children's academic performance, health, and quality of life: a top policy commitment in response to children's obesity and health crisis in California," for the California Elected Women's Association for Education and Research, 1999, p. 13. http://www.cnr.berkeley.edu/cwh/PDFs/Cewaer Paper_Research.pdf.) Further, research has shown that the health problems of family members also affect children's well-being, particularly increasing their risk of severe behavioral problems. Such behavioral problems are often associated with poor academic performance. (F. B. LeClere and B. M. Kowalewski, "Disability in the family: the effects on children's well-being," *Journal of Marriage and the Family* 56, 1994, 457–468.)

46 Dalton Conley has argued that housing matters not only for the immediate well-being of families, but also for the life chances of the subsequent generation, and should thus be a standard variable in the conception of class back-

ground. (D. Conley, "A room with a view or a room of one's own? Housing and stratification," *Sociological Forum* 16, 2001, 263–280.)

47 Jennifer Hochschild has referred to 1973 as the year that "the quiet depression" of the modern, neo-liberal economy began. (J. L. Hochschild, *Facing up to the American Dream: Race, Class, and the Soul of the Nation*, Princeton, NJ: Princeton University Press, 1995, p. 94.)

48 C. A. Ray and R. A. Mickelson, "Restructuring students for restructured work: the economy, school reform, and non-college-bound youths," *Sociology of Education* 66, 1993, 1–20; J. Anyon, *Ghetto Schooling: A Political Economy of Urban Educational Reform*, New York, NY: Teachers College Press, 1997.

49 Rothstein, op. cit.; see also R. H. Haveman and B. Wolfe, "Children's prospects and children's policy," *The Journal of Economic Perspectives* 7, 1993, 153–174; V. Fuchs and D. Reklis, "America's children: economic perspectives and policy options," *Science* 255, 1992, 41–46.

50 One small but heartening step in this direction is the increasing popularity of certain after-school programs and community schools, which we may consider a direct effect of the growing awareness of the importance of reforms outside the school itself. Community schools are a growing phenomenon in the Northeast United States, particularly in Boston and New York City. These schools not only have the traditional day programs, they also provide free mental and physical healthcare to its students as well as various social services. For example, the community schools of the Children's Aid Society offer free dental and healthcare services to students, as well as family resource centers, after-school activities and other social services. Such schools are testimony to the fact that family background and socioeconomic issues of students should be a major part of the action and discussion involving school reform. (M. S. Johnson, "Alternate possibilities in education reform: the impact of non-school programs on school performance," unpublished manuscript, New York University, 2002.)

Part I

The case for family background

1 How do parents matter?

Income, interactions, and intervention during early childhood

Miriam R. Linver, Allison Sidle Fuligni, and Jeanne Brooks-Gunn[1]

The current political climate in the United States places a strong focus on the achievement of young people. At the heart of the concern is the well-documented and publicized discrepancy in school achievement outcomes for children from poor socioeconomic backgrounds compared to their more affluent counterparts. The difference between poor and non-poor children is often evidenced even earlier in life, before school entry, as young children from disadvantaged families exhibit lower scores on tests of school readiness and enter school less prepared to succeed. A related issue is the disparity between test scores of African American and European American children, which still persists, though diminished, after accounting for income and other family background differences.[2]

What is it about coming from an economically disadvantaged family that is driving these differences in young children's development and achievement? In the 1960s, the Coleman report brought the attention of the sociology field to the importance of the family context for school performance. At the same time, psychologists were focusing on the importance of early experience (and by definition, the family) on later development. Together, these two disciplines helped to shape the terms of President Johnson's War on Poverty, which directed attention to child and family interventions and how these might make a difference in lives of poor families.

In this chapter we discuss the importance of the family environment (including family income, parents' human capital, maternal emotional health, and parenting) as well as neighborhood context and how they may operate to link income and child outcomes. In our discussion, we draw upon our own and others' previous research from several different disciplines to illustrate these pathways. We provide several examples of how we have empirically examined these contextual components and their relation to children's development. We draw upon data from three large national datasets to address these issues: the Infant Health and Development Program (IHDP), the Panel Study of Income Dynamics – Child Development Supplement (PSID-CDS), and the National Longitudinal Study of Youth – Child Supplement (NLSY-CS).

The IHDP is a multisite clinical trial designed to test the efficacy of providing family and early-childhood intervention services to low birthweight (LBW) premature children, to reduce developmental delays. Services were provided to families randomized into an intervention or follow-up only group. Children received services from the time of their discharge from the neonatal nursery until they were 3 years of age. Home visits were provided throughout the 3 years, while center-based schooling was provided for the second and third years of life (ages 12 to 36 months). The sample was stratified according to site (8 medical centers) and birthweight (lighter LBW children were 2,000 grams or less, and heavier LBW children were 2,001 to 2,500 grams at birth). The program is further described in several publications.[3]

The PSID is an ongoing longitudinal survey of U.S. households begun in 1968. By following all members of its sample over time, including children as they leave their parents' homes, the PSID maintains a representative sample of the nonimmigrant U.S. population. In 1997, the PSID added the Child Development Supplement (CDS) to the existing longitudinal study, collecting information on parents and their children from birth to age 12.[4] This rich dataset includes a wide-range of family process measures as well as measures of child and mother cognitive and emotional well-being. Parents in the core PSID sample with children between birth and age 12 were recruited to participate in the CDS. If there were multiple children within the age range, two were randomly selected to be target children. The full CDS sample includes about 3,500 children. The integrated PSID-CDS dataset provides high-quality annual measurements of family income history and a wide range of family process measures and child assessments for a national sample of children.

The NLSY is a nationally representative sample of youth (14 to 19 years old) drawn in 1979; members are followed yearly. The Child Supplement (CS) was added to collect data on children of the study participants (beginning in 1986, with children seen in 1988, 1990, 1992, 1994, 1996, and 1998). The children are not a representative sample because children born to younger mothers are overrepresented. As the NLSY cohort ages, the child sample becomes more representative.[5] In addition, African Americans and low income European Americans were oversampled. Data from these three studies are used to set the stage for examining the cognitive and socio-emotional development of young children.

In response to the pattern of poorer cognitive, linguistic, social, emotional, and health outcomes of young children from low-SES families, intervention efforts have been designed and conducted in attempts to minimize or prevent these disparities early in life. In the second part of the chapter, we discuss various policy approaches to intervene in the course of development for disadvantaged children, and examine whether early childhood interventions make a difference for poor children. Here we review the literature on interventions and describe empirical tests of these links from 3 large studies. We focus on how the family environment may act as a mediator in the relation between intervention programs and children's outcomes.

Early experience and later educational outcomes and well-being

Although the recent interest in early family experiences and their connection to children's later well-being began in the 1960s, the past decade has also seen a renewed and expanded focus on this topic. The National Academy of Science's recent volume *From Neurons to Neighborhoods* reviewed the evidence from several areas of scientific inquiry including effects of early environments on brain development and the effects of numerous early settings on later development.[6] In this section, we review some of the evidence linking early experiences to later educational outcomes. We must note, however, that early experience and early development, while influential, do not set one upon an immutable course; change can certainly occur throughout the life course. Rather, we concur with the conclusions set forth in *Neurons to Neighborhoods* that early development "matters a lot, not because this period of development provides an indelible blueprint for adult well-being, but because it sets either a sturdy or fragile stage for what follows."[7]

Indeed, there is evidence for continuity in children's educational performance from before they enter school. The skills a child has when he or she begins formal schooling (popularly known as "school readiness") are of interest because they are predictive of how well children will fare as they progress through the school years. In a longitudinal examination of firstborn children born of low-income black teenage mothers in the late 1960s, early indicators of school readiness were associated with the children's later measures of school success and well being. For instance, lower scores on a preschool skills inventory were associated with a higher likelihood of having failed a grade by the high school years,[8] and higher likelihood of dropping out of high school or not going on to some college education.[9] Similarly, for these children, repeating a grade in middle childhood was associated with eventual high school dropout.[10] In fact, the cognitive and language scores exhibited in preschool were predictive of the children's levels of functional literacy when they were 19 to 21 years old.[11] These adverse consequences of poor cognitive and language scores at preschool age operated over and above the effects of having failed a grade in school. Thus, poor early development can set at-risk children on a course for ongoing difficulties in school and eventual failure both in school and in attaining the functional skills necessary to operate in today's society.

Studies of intellectual achievement in the form of intelligence test scores also suggest some continuity from early experience through the later school years. Some of the skills that underlie general cognitive ability seem to show continuity from infancy into middle childhood, and some information-processing abilities show continuity throughout the lifespan.[12] However, several studies illustrate the impact that family characteristics may have on IQ scores. For instance, psychologist Arnold Sameroff and his colleagues found that the number of adverse familial risk factors experienced by a child was more influential in affecting children's IQ scores than the type of risk factors experienced. The risk factors examined included characteristics such as parental mental health problems, membership in a racial minority group, low parental education, low levels of maternal warmth toward the child, absence of the father in the home, and experience of negative life events. Furthermore, early patterns of risk were predictive of later IQ (at age 13) even after taking into account the child's IQ at age 4.[13] These studies found great stability in children's IQ scores from age 4 to age 13, but also great stability in the number of risk factors experienced by families with multiple risks. Conclusions could be drawn regarding the stability of achievement and intelligence over childhood, that such continuity is due, at least in part, to the continuity in the family environment children are experiencing. In addition, the effects of poverty interact with cumulative risk to affect early IQ scores. Children aged 2 to 4 years who are not poor, but who have a large number of other risk factors, tend to have IQ scores resembling those of high-risk poor children.[14]

Family income and maternal education

Income enables parents to provide for their families in various ways. For example, parents with higher income levels are able to purchase materials, experiences, and services to invest in building the human capital of their children. These goods and services include schools, child care, food, housing, stimulating learning materials and activities, neighborhood environment, and medical care. Parents also may invest in themselves, for example by achieving a higher level of education, which in turn is associated with more positive outcomes for children. Terms for this perspective include human capital, financial resources, or investment model;[15] according to this perspective, children in families with lower income tend to fare worse because they have limited access to resources that help them develop. Economist Gary Becker and colleagues view children's economic success as a result of both the biological endowment that parents pass to their children, and the resources, in the form of money and time, that parents invest in their children.[16] Investment in children's learning environment is considered to be a main determinant of children's economic success, whereas investments in health care, quality home environments, advantaged neighborhoods, and other goods and services also enhance children's well-being.

We have examined the human capital effects of parents' education level on children's earnings and completed schooling 25 years later, using the PSID-CDS data.[17] These analyses also demonstrated effects of growing up in a clean, organized, and efficient home on subsequent education and earnings, and that these effects can be accounted for in part by parents' education level. We have also examined effects of parents' schooling experiences and their children's test scores using the NLSY-CS data.[18] In these analyses, we found that the mothers' experiences in school – specifically of proportion of African Americans in her classes (a limited measure of school segregation) – made a contribution to the gap in test scores between African Americans and European Americans. African American children whose mothers were in more highly segregated classrooms had lower test scores than other children. In addition, the test score gap was also influenced by the grandparents' level of education; if grandparents had more education, the gap was reduced. These human capital effects were found over and above the effects of maternal education, verbal ability, and other traditional demographic characteristics such as family income and marital status. Intergenerational effects are addressed in greater detail in Chapter 6.

Investigators of family environment's influence on early development often focus primarily on family income, or more generally on family socioeconomic status (SES) which is usually defined by family income and education levels. Maternal education levels have been consistently linked with child outcomes. Strong associations have been found between mother's education and child language, achievement, and IQ scores for children from 2 to 8 years of age in two of the datasets we discuss later in this chapter. Even after accounting for the effect of family income, maternal education levels still exert a measurable effect on children's IQ.[19,20]

Family income shows even stronger associations with cognitive outcomes for young children. In the NLSY-CS and the IHDP data, income associations were found with several different cognitive indicators, using several different measures of income.[21] Even after controlling for mothers' education, family income has an additional effect on 3- to 8-year-old's verbal, achievement test, and intelligence test scores.[22] Children living in persistent poverty had cognitive scores 6 to 9 points lower than those of children who had never lived in poverty.[23]

Recent evidence suggests that significant numbers of young children experience mental health problems.[24] The incidence of mental health disorders in 3- to 5-year-old children is consistent with that found in older children,[25] a fact that is not surprising given the moderate stability of aggression and anti-social behavior throughout childhood and adolescence.[26] Higher rates of mental health problems in children are often associated with low maternal education and family income. Data from IHDP and NLSY illustrate associations of maternal education with children's emotional health. Both studies assessed behavior problems using items derived from the Child Behavior Checklist (CBCL).[27] This measure is often divided into two subscales, one assessing externalizing or aggressive behavior and the other assessing internalizing, withdrawn, or sad behavior. In both samples, higher maternal education is related to fewer internalizing problems; maternal education is associated with fewer externalizing problems in the IHDP sample only.[28] Family income has been linked to externalizing behavior in these studies as well: higher family income-to-needs ratio is associated with lower levels of externalizing problems in the IHDP and NLSY samples at ages 3 through 6.[29] Similarly, family poverty is associated with parent reports of emotional and behavior problems among children aged 3 to 17 years in the 1988 National Health Interview Survey Child Health Supplement.[30]

Family income and human capital each have independent associations with child cognitive, emotional, and health outcomes. Maternal education tends to be strongly associated with all types of cognitive assessments (cognitive, verbal, and school achievement measures), but is more strongly associated with internalizing than externalizing behavior problems. Family income also affects cognitive assessments, but is more predictive of externalizing problems than internalizing.

Maternal mental health and child development

Children of mothers with depressive symptoms are more likely to have higher levels of behavior problems;[31] similar findings are reported for adolescents with conduct disorder,[32] and depressive symptoms or disorders in older children as well as adolescents.[33] In addition, many studies report significant associations between maternal depressive symptoms and children's cognitive and school competence.[34] Thus, in addition to families' material and educational resources, parents' psychological well-being should be considered in models of family effects on children's school readiness and school success.

Links between parenting and child development

Parental emotional support, especially sensitivity, is a major dimension believed to contribute to secure infant–parent attachment as well as to later child well-being.[35] Within the infant–parent relationship, sensitivity refers to two dimensions: the parent's awareness of the infant's needs and accuracy in reading of the infant's cues; and the parent's contingent responsiveness to the infant's cues and needs. Parental insensitivity can take a number of forms, including intrusiveness, detachment, and negative regard or hostility.

Provision of learning experiences in the home has been associated strongly with child cognitive and school competencies.[36] Many studies use the Home Observation of Measurement of the Environment (HOME)

Inventory, to assess the home environment; the HOME is based on observation and interview during a home visit (i.e. types of play materials in the home are observed, and mothers are asked about reading materials and amount of time spent reading to the child). In addition, the ways in which parents read to their children have been found to be associated with their preschooler's language skills, over and above the amount of reading that occurs in the home.[37] In a related vein, help and support provided by mothers during a problem-solving assessment have been associated with young children's enthusiasm and persistence toward the task.[38] Sensitive and involved parenting is therefore important at an early age to promote children's emotional and cognitive development.

Neighborhoods and child development

Measures of a family's neighborhood often include SES indicators such as income, percentage of poor residents, percentage of working professionals, percentage of residents with high school or college degrees, percentage of female headed households, and percentage of employed (or unemployed) individuals. Although neighborhood effects are usually small (especially after accounting for family level SES measures), living in a neighborhood with a high SES level is positively associated with children's school readiness, as well as educational and achievement outcomes.[39] Living in a neighborhood with a low SES level is negatively associated with children's emotional and social outcomes.[40]

Neighborhood SES effects may operate through other realms such as families, peers, and schools.[41] Also, because a majority of evidence linking neighborhood SES to child development is based on non-experimental studies, the data may be biased because families have some choice in where they live.[42] Other factors, such as literacy, motivation, and mental health, may account for neighborhood effects, so studies may be over- or underestimating the effects (depending on the situation). For example, parents who are depressed may be less likely to move out of poor neighborhoods than non-depressed parents; this could result in an overestimation of neighborhood effects. Or, parents who are saving money to pay for their children's education or extracurricular activities may remain in poorer neighborhoods (instead of moving to a more affluent neighborhood) leading to an underestimation of neighborhood effects.

The research presented thus far provides evidence of the importance of early developmental well-being for children's subsequent cognitive and socio-emotional outcomes, and the influence of both family environments (including family economic resources, maternal education, maternal emotional health) and neighborhood context on early development. Data from studies of adoption provide a unique opportunity to explore how children's intellectual abilities are affected by a dramatic change in the family environment and the economic resources it affords. Michael Duyme has conducted a series of longitudinal analyses of a sample of French children's IQ scores before and after adoption. In this study, children with low IQs who were adopted between 4 and 6 years of age showed improved IQ scores in adolescence, and the amount of improvement was related to the SES of the adoptive family. The children's IQ scores before and after adoption were correlated, illustrating the continuity of individual differences, but the scores were higher after adoption, and rates of increase were correlated with SES, illustrating the effect of moving into a more affluent family environment, even after the preschool years.[43] The importance of the family and neighborhood contexts on both early and later development is clear for children's developmental and school success. The question now becomes: How do family and neighborhood environments influence children's development?

Putting it all together – our research models

Much of the research examining family and neighborhood effects on children's well-being focuses on one or two spheres in isolation, for example focusing on how parenting practices affect children's emotional or cognitive well-being, or how family income is correlated with school success. In this chapter we are particularly concerned with combining multiple domains in order to understand how these contexts may work together to influence children's development; specifically, we are interested in the family processes that may serve as the links between family economic and human capital indicators and child outcomes.

The role of family processes in SES disparities in young children's cognitive and socio-emotional development has been studied extensively. Two major perspectives have emerged in the literature to explain these processes. The first is the human capital model that we described earlier; to reiterate, this model posits that income enables families to purchase materials, experiences, and services (including schools, childcare, food, housing, stimulating learning materials and activities, neighborhood environment, and medical care) to invest in the human capital of their children.[44]

The second perspective has been termed the family stress model.[45] In general, the family stress model (and other related models) hypothesize that low income (as well as the specific experience of job loss) is associated with family financial strain, which in turn influences parental mental health and parenting behavior.[46] The proposed pathways differ somewhat from scholar to scholar: some believe that parenting behavior may be directly influenced by financial strain while others believe that such associations are usually mediated through the influence of financial strain on parents' mental health. Social support is often thought to be a moderator of the link between financial strain and parental mental health.[47] This general model is presented in Figure 1.1.

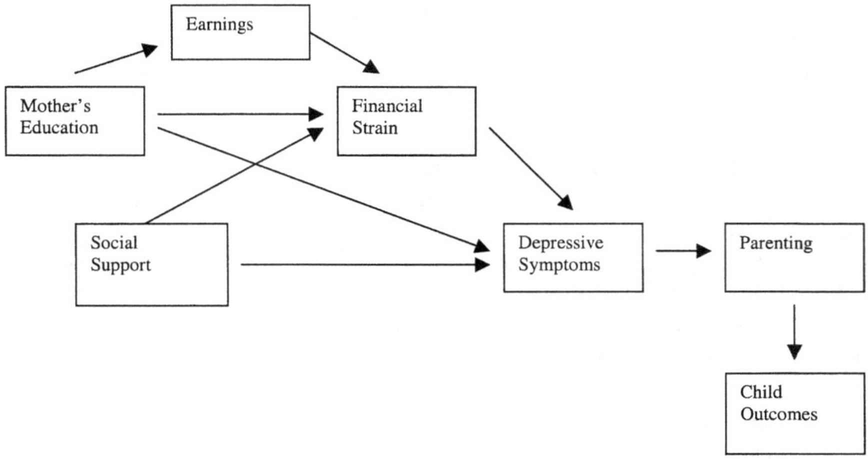

Figure 1.1 One possible model for examining SES effects on parental mental health, parenting, and child outcomes.[48]

While most of the research related to the family stress model has focused on adolescents, our group focuses on young children's achievement and cognitive outcomes.[49] About one-third to one-half of the effects of income on achievement and cognition seem to operate through maternal mental health and parenting behavior. For example, a study of low-wage-earning single African American mothers in New York City found some support for the model in Figure 1.1.[50] Specifically, maternal education and earnings were directly related to financial strain, which in turn was associated with maternal depressive symptoms. Depressive affect was associated with mothers' provision of cognitive stimulation, and emotional support to their 3- to 5-year-old children. Completing the link, preschoolers' scores on a school readiness measure are directly related to these parenting practices; however, an indirect pathway from financial strain to depression to parenting and then to school readiness was not found.[51] The breakdown of the model here may be due to a small sample size in the study; we conducted similar models with a larger sample size and found that indeed these pathways are found with a large nationally representative sample.[52] Researchers who have focused on adolescents have found links between financial strain, depression, parenting, and children's school achievement.[53]

We have investigated further the link between income and young children's outcomes with two large datasets: IHDP and PSID-CDS.[54] Using IHDP data, we examined constructs from both the parental investment and family stress perspectives as mediators of the relation between income and child cognitive ability and behavior problems outcomes.[55] Income was measured broadly and included persistent poverty (percent of child's life spent in poverty), family income, and income-to-needs. Cognitive ability was assessed by standardized test scores (IQ) and child behavior problems with the CBCL (maternal report) when the children were 3 and 5 years of age. Two potential mediators were included from the family stress perspective: maternal emotional distress and parenting behavior. Maternal emotional distress was measured when the children were 1 and 2 years of age. Parenting behavior was observed during a free play situation when the children were 2 and a half years (coded via videotape for warm and firm controlling authoritative and punitive authoritarian behavior, as conceptualized by Diana Baumrind.[56] An additional potential mediator from the parental investment perspective was included; cognitively stimulating home environment was measured during a home visit when the children were 3 years of age.[57]

In these analyses, we employed a number of family background characteristics to reduce the likelihood that the findings are not totally accounted for by unmeasured characteristics (i.e. selection bias).[58] In our study, we can control for some alternative explanations of income associations, for example that income affects child outcomes largely due to other parental characteristics, such as intelligence or education. Unlike most of the studies of adolescents, the IHDP has a measure of maternal receptive ability (the Peabody Picture Vocabulary Test – Revised) as well as years of maternal education. Our results, therefore, represent the effect of income (including persistent poverty, family income, and income-to-needs) over and above the effects of maternal education and maternal receptive ability.

Our analyses revealed that the income was linked with child behavior outcomes through the family stress model constructs, and income was linked with both cognitive and behavioral outcomes through the parental investment construct.[59] In other words, maternal depressive affect and parenting practices can be said to mediate the relation between family income and child behavior problems, whereas a stimulating home environment can be said to mediate the relation between income and children's achievement and behavior problems. Additional analyses revealed that these findings were robust; models were similar for boys and girls, for heavier and lighter low birthweight infants, for married and single mothers, and for European American and African American mothers.

We examined similar models for children ages 3 to 5 years old in the PSID-CDS, with a more extensive set of potential mediators for both the family stress and parental investment perspectives. Potential mediators of the parental investment perspective included the physical environment of the home, child care costs, cognitively stimulating materials provided to children in the home and neighborhood, and parents' activities with the child. Potential mediators of the family stress model in these analyses included economic pressure, maternal depressive affect, warm parenting, and parents' spanking of their children. Child outcomes examined were Woodcock Johnson Achievement test scores (both letter-word and applied problems subscales) and the externalizing behavior subscale of the behavior problem index.

Our income measure included total pre-tax income of all family members,[60] from the child's birth until one year prior to the time child well-being was assessed. We used income from multiple years because single-year measures of income are not particularly reliable given yearly fluctuations.[61] In all our analyses, we controlled for other family background constructs including maternal education and maternal cognitive ability (the passage comprehension test of the Woodcock Johnson Achievement Test – Revised).

Our results revealed that different mediating mechanisms are at work for different child outcomes. Much of the income association with children's cognitive test scores was mediated by the family's investment in providing an environment that is beneficial to children's learning, and not by maternal emotional distress or parenting behavior. Cognitively stimulating materials and activities are the most important mediators of the association between income and children's letter-word scores, and the physical environment of the home is the most important mediator in the association between income and children's applied problem scores. In contrast, results for children's behavior problems demonstrated that maternal emotional distress was the primary mediator of income associations with children's behavior. Although human capital mediators did not have direct associations with children's behavior problems, a stimulating home environment is indirectly related to lower behavior problems through its association with lower maternal distress and better parenting practices.[62]

In summary, we found that warm parenting, harsh parenting, parental mental health, and the environment that parents provide for their children all act as significant mediators of the association between income and child developmental outcomes (both cognitive and emotional), even when taking into account a host of family demographic characteristics. We have found that the provision of a stimulating environment is most consistently a mediator of this relation, across datasets and across child development outcomes, for preschool aged children.

In the remaining sections of this chapter, we evaluate research on five spheres of influence on child developmental outcomes: family income, human capital, maternal mental health, parenting, and neighborhood characteristics. We examine each of these spheres as policy levers, describing how evaluation research demonstrates the extent to which these areas affect children's cognitive and behavioral outcomes.

Policy extensions – levers of change for child outcomes

As we have described above, research has demonstrated how children's family and neighborhood environments are important in their development. Policy makers to some extent have taken advantage of this literature in designing and implementing programs and policies to promote positive developmental outcomes for children and their families. Such programs can be seen as policy levers that, when activated, have a direct impact on specific components in the lives of families and children. For example, the Earned Income Tax Credit (EITC) and other such programs provide low income families with more disposable income because they pay less in taxes. Other programs, such as the Infant Health and Development Program, the Teenage Pregnancy Intervention Program, and the Yale Child Welfare Project, have focused on (among other targets) the human capital available in a family by promoting parental education.[63] Improving parent mental health is also a goal of these same intervention programs.[64] Some programs (such as the Nurse Home-Visiting Program) have demonstrated positive effects on parenting practices, for example promoting more sensitive and less harsh parenting.[65] Other interventions, such as the Moving to Opportunity for Fair Housing Demonstration (MTO), have been successfully undertaken to move families to more desirable neighborhoods.[66] Evaluations and reviews of these programs and policies provide valuable data in determining the differential effects of each sphere on the lives of children. Figure 1.2 illustrates the inter-connectivity of the

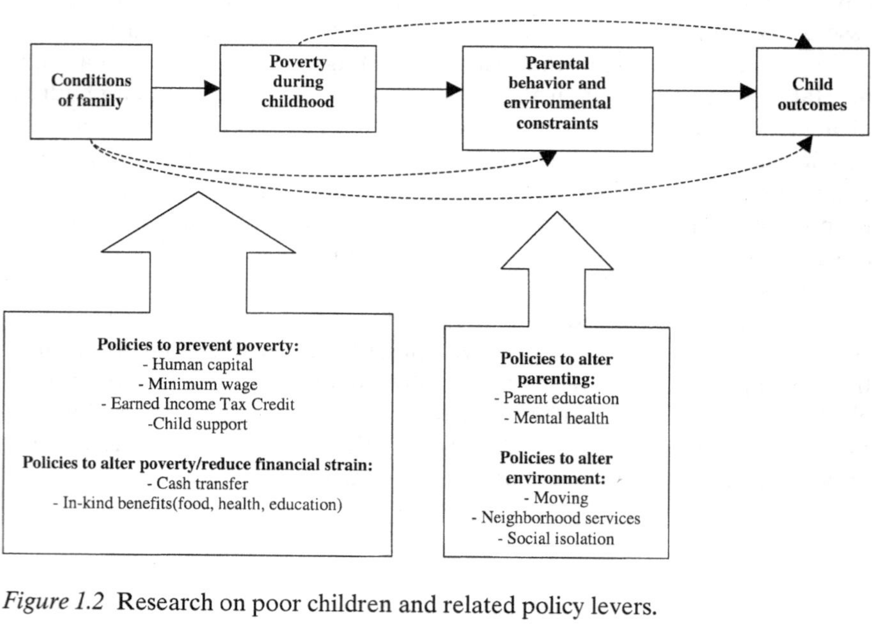

Figure 1.2 Research on poor children and related policy levers.

spheres of family influence and related policy levers. Below, we summarize evaluation reports from many of these programs.

Income and human capital

Although the welfare reform act of 1996 had an impact on who receives income assistance, and how that assistance is received, many families receive government income assistance, for example, in the form of EITC, the former Aid to Families with Dependent Children (AFDC), and its replacement Temporary Assistance for Needy Families (TANF). A major change of welfare reform is that of time limits; most families, even if they meet eligibility requirements, have a lifetime limit of 5 years on cash benefits. Although the assistance programs are nationally mandated, states are given much latitude in how they distribute money to poor families. For example, some states mandate the recipient must participate in employment-related activities, in order to receive benefits. Families who participate in these programs essentially trade their benefits for employment income, so their total family income remains unchanged although employment status is different. Other programs allow income benefits to continue to some extent even after employment is secured. So called "income supplement" programs change family income level as well as employment status. In a study of impacts of both types of programs, Pamela Morris found that participating in income supplement programs (compared to the mandatory employment with no income supplement programs) was positively related to children's achievement and negatively to children's behavior problem scores.[67]

The strong effects found for income supplement programs were unique. Some state level programs mandated participation in education as well as employment activities. The effects seemed stronger at first for programs where maternal education level was increased compared to those programs that focused on job searching. However, unless family income increased, such as through income supplement programs, the effects of education and employment were not significant. Sharon McGroder and her colleagues analyzed data from the National Evaluation of Welfare-to-Work Strategies (NEWWS); her findings concur with Morris' report.[68] Although there was limited evidence linking maternal education with children's achievement outcomes, other factors, such as maternal mental health and parenting, may also play an important role.

Parenting and maternal mental health

Several types of prevention efforts that focus on the family as the mechanism by which low income affects young children have been developed. These include home visiting programs, intergenerational or family literacy programs, and family support programs. Often, these programs focus their service delivery on the mother or family rather than the child, while others may include a direct child component. Effects on child outcomes reflect this variation, and tend to be mixed. Some programs show beneficial effects on mothers but weaker effects on children.

Family literacy programs have documented modest improvements in parents' own literacy skills and on the number of reading materials they provide for children in the home.[69] A national evaluation of the Federal Even Start family literacy program found no differences between program and control families on measures of parent–child reading interactions or parental educational expectations for their children, and no changes over time for program families' maternal depression, locus of control, or family income and resources.[70] Family-focused interventions that include a center-based component (such as the IHDP, Teenage Pregnancy Intervention Program, and the Yale Child Welfare Project) have found positive effects on maternal mental health.[71]

Home visiting programs provide the services of a professional (often a nurse) or paraprofessional who visits the home regularly. Home visiting services may begin during pregnancy, and continue through the first months or years of the child's life. Home visiting curricula tend to focus on improving parental functioning and promoting preventive health care usage. A well-known example is the Nurse Home Visitation Program (NHVP),[72] aimed at promoting children's health and development. Other home visiting programs include components to show parents intellectually stimulating ways of interacting with their young children. For example, the Parents as Teachers (PAT) program serves parents of diverse socioeconomic backgrounds with children up to the age of 3 and focuses on supporting parents as their children's "first teachers."[73] The Home Instruction Program for Preschool Youngsters (HIPPY) was designed specifically for low-income parents of preschoolers, to guide them in the use of specific educational activities with their preschool aged children.[74]

When home visiting programs do not provide direct services for children, they tend to report few effects on children's cognitive and linguistic outcomes. Comprehensive reviews of home-visiting programs have found that only a fraction (some 30–60 percent of programs) have documented immediate positive gains in children's cognitive scores.[75] The well-known NHVP reported no intervention effects on children at age 3 and 4 years, except for the children of mothers who were heavy smokers during pregnancy. These children exhibited significant gains in IQ at 3 and 4 years of age.[76] Although HIPPY is designed specifically to enhance the cognitive skills and school readiness of preschool children, the program provides its treatment only to the parent (through weekly lessons on activities to engage in with children). Recent evaluation of HIPPY has revealed modest and sometimes no effects on children's cognitive measures.[77] Similarly, the PAT program, which provides monthly home visits to teach mothers about parenting and stimulating their children, found only modest and inconsistent effects on child cognitive outcomes in two recent demonstrations.[78]

Home-visiting programs have documented some impacts on children's social and emotional development. For instance, short-term gains in children's social skills, reduction of problem behaviors, and improved quality of mother–infant and mother–child interactions have been reported.[79] The IHDP reported significant impacts on problem behavior when children were aged 2 and 3, though these effects were sustained at age 5 only for the heavier group of low birthweight children.[80] The IHDP provided center-based child services in addition to home-visiting.

Family literacy programs are intergenerational programs designed to enhance the skills of both the young child and one or more adult family members in order to improve the family's well-being.[81] Thus, impacts are expected to occur for both children and adult participants. These programs tend to offer a combination of early childhood education, adult education, and parenting education, provided either exclusively in center-based settings, or via a combination of center- and home-based services. Children are expected to benefit directly from the child-focused component, as well as indirectly from program impacts on parenting and the home environment. Adult education is expected to improve the occupational potential of parents, improving family resources and well-being. Educating in the area of parenting is also included, to enhance the cognitive stimulation available in the child's home environment.[82]

Although many evaluations of family literacy programs lack experimentally rigorous designs in comparison with the home-visiting program evaluations described above, positive program impacts have been documented for preschool cognitive outcomes and school readiness.[83] Family literacy program evaluations to date have not focused on social or emotional outcomes for children, nor have they followed the children longitudinally to assess the stability of the cognitive gains over time. Typically, evaluations of these programs have not included systematic tests of full mediated models of expected influence.

A recent review has focused specifically on the effects of early intervention programs on parents, and has found variation in program effects based on program type.[84] Home-visiting programs for infants and toddlers have documented program effects on mothers. For example, these programs were associated with more supportive and less harsh parenting,[85] as well as more stimulating home environments in some programs and more developmentally appropriate child-rearing attitudes.[86] 6 out of 7 studies reporting on parenting behaviors found that program participation improved the quality and sensitivity of parent-child interactions, but only 2 of 4 studies assessing children's home environment found positive effects of program participation.[87]

Neighborhoods

The largest neighborhood-focused intervention that has been conducted to date is MTO, a 5-site program initiated by the Department of Housing and Urban Development to examine the impact of residential relocation on child and family outcomes. The experimental design of MTO allows researchers to estimate neighborhood effects without the bias of omitted variables. Evidence from MTO suggests that moving from high poverty, more dangerous neighborhoods to safer, lower poverty neighborhoods had positive effects for parental mental health, children's achievement test scores, and children's lowered behavior problems.[88] Few economic effects were found for children and their families. Although the specific underlying mechanisms of influence at work in MTO are not identifiable, we have framed our MTO findings in terms of a Collective Efficacy model, where the capacity of residents to monitor the behavior of others in accordance with social norms maintains the public order.[89]

Pathways of intervention effects

Although family-focused intervention programs aim to affect children both directly and indirectly through improving outcomes for parents and families, few evaluations have directly tested these pathways.[90] However, an analysis of Abecedarian and Project CARE programs tested both the quality of the home environment and parental authoritarian attitudes as possible mediators of program effects on children. The analysis showed a direct effect of the quality of the home environment on children's cognitive test scores, although none of this effect was mediated through the effect of the intervention upon the home environment (no treatment effect on the home environment was found). Futhermore, no direct association was found between parent's authoritarian attitudes and child outcomes, so this pathway was ruled out.[91] Evaluation research explicitly testing these types of pathways is important for assessing the effects of interventions that seek to influence children's development through affects on the family. When possible, program evaluations should address the question of mediation empirically.

Our research group has conducted analyses of the IHDP specifically to examine the mediating effects of the home environment on the association between the intervention and child outcomes at ages 3 and 5 years.[92] Our analyses revealed that for the heavier low birthweight group (weighing between 2,001 and 2,500 grams at birth), home environment (measured with the learning environment subscale of the HOME Inventory at age 3 years[93]) indeed mediated the association of the IHDP treatment for 3 outcomes: child cognitive ability at age 3 and at age 5, and child behavior problems at age 3.

Overall, the research on intervention programs points to strong effects of programs that provide high-quality center-based child care services to economically disadvantaged children. Effects are found in children's cognitive, literacy, emotional, and behavioral domains, and long-term effects are seen for participating children in their later related adult outcomes such as high school graduation, employment, less welfare use, and less delinquent behavior. Many researchers have therefore concluded that in order to achieve effects on economically disadvantaged children, direct early childhood education is needed, in addition to the provision of comprehensive services to the family.[94]

Conclusions

In this chapter, we have discussed the importance of considering the interaction of multiple contexts (both family and neighborhood) of children's lives that can affect young children; we provided examples of explicit empirical tests of such complex models. Our research findings underscore the importance of trying to understand the process of how family – and wider – contexts are associated with children's outcomes. In particular, parenting stands out in our statistical models as a strong mediator, often explaining much of the association between income and child developmental outcomes. W. Andrew Collins and his colleagues,[95] in an extensive review of parenting research, conclude that parenting is of crucial importance to how children end up, even after taking into account the effects of heredity. The connection between parenting and children's well-being, they caution, is not straightforward. Instead, other contexts, such as conditions in the home (including how many parents live with the child, whether or not the parent works, or parent mental health), individual characteristics (such as ethnicity and cognitive functioning), and neighborhood and societal factors must be taken into account when examining parenting and child outcomes.

One such characteristic is that of race; we control for race in all our analyses reported in this chapter. However, controlling statistically for race does not specifically address how race matters for children's development. We have also participated in another line of research, trying to understand racial test score gaps. European American and African American children in the United States have vastly different experiences in school and the broader society. Gaps in test scores are found as early as 3 years and persist at least through age 8 (we have not yet analyzed data of older children and adolescents). One factor that may be operating here is quality of the parents' schooling; controls for parental education and verbal ability do not capture variation in parents' schooling. In our research, we found the black-white test score gap was influenced by quality of maternal high school, over and above maternal education, maternal verbal ability, and a host of demographic characteristics (including grandparent characteristics).[96] When such characteristics were controlled, the gap in scores is decreased by 40 percent–85 percent.

Numerous studies support the statement that living in poverty is associated with poorer children's outcomes, but fewer try to address why and how this connection is so strong. Exploring the processes linking income and child development is especially critical when thinking about how poor children may or may not be "ready" for school and ways to improve their "readiness." Previously, many program developers have not addressed their theoretical assumptions regarding how they expect their interventions to influence children. More recently, some prevention scholars have begun to outline their "theories of change," articulating program goals and the ways in which specific program components are thought to relate to these goals.[97]

The design of effective (and fundable) intervention programs will be greatly enhanced if program goals and the means for achieving them are spelled out from the outset. The "theory of change" approach will also aid evaluators in documenting the successes of such programs. An example of links between services and outcomes is found in the Early Head Start (EHS) Research and Evaluation Project, a randomized study of 17 of the first Early Head Start sites (conducted by Mathematica Policy Research; Brooks-Gunn is a co-PI of the national evaluation). Early Head Start serves pregnant women and children up to age 3, with individual EHS programs offering different packages of services to women and their children. In one set of analyses, the sites were divided into those that offered center based early childhood education to the infants and toddlers (4 sites) and those that offered home-based and case management services (13 sites). Outcomes have been examined when children were age 2. In general, the center-based programs exhibited treatment effects on an early intelligence test score (Bayley Scales of Infant Development) while the more home-based programs found treatment effects on parenting behavior (maternal report of lowered stress, videotaped observations of more maternal sensitivity).[98] Theories of change would predict such a pattern of results, where home-based components focusing on parenting behavior and family functioning have effects on families, and center-based components emphasizing child competencies have effects for children's development. We expect that efforts like these to match interventions with desired effects will continue in the next decade; providing enhanced understanding of the mechanisms by which intervention programs can help prepare children for success in school and beyond.

Notes

1 This chapter is based on a paper presented at, "After the Bell: Education Solutions outside the School," June 4th and 5th, 2001, The Jerome Levy Economics Institute of Bard College, Annandale-on-Hudson, New York. Funders for this paper include the NICHD Research Network on Child and Family Well-Being; the National Institute on Early Childhood Development and Education, the Office of Educational Research and Improvement, U.S. Department of Education; the Office of the Assistant Secretary of Planning and Evaluation,

U.S. Department of Health and Human Services; and the National Institute for Child Health and Human Development. We would like to thank W. Jean Yeung for her invaluable contributions, and Nitika Tolani for her expert assistance in the preparation of this chapter. Address correspondence via e-mail to Miriam Linver, MRL23@columbia.edu.

2 For a more complete discussion of racial differences in test score performance, see C. Jencks and M. Phillips, *The Black/White Test Score Gap*, Washington, DC: Brookings, 1999.

3 J. Brooks-Gunn, C. M. McCarton, P. H. Casey, M. C. McCormick, C. R. Bauer, J. C. Berenbaum, J. Tyson, M. Swanson, F. C. Bennett, D. T. Scott, J. Tonascia, and C. L. Meinert, "Early intervention in low birth weight, premature infants: results through age 5 years from the Infant Health and Development Program," *Journal of the American Medical Association* 272, 1994, 1257–1262; Gross, Spiker and Haynes 1997; Infant Health and Development Program (IHDP), "Enhancing the outcomes of low-birth-weight, premature infants," *Journal of the American Medical Association* 263, 1990, 3035–3042; M. C. McCormick, C. M. McCarton, J. Brooks-Gunn, P. Belt, and R. T. Gross, "The Infant Health and Development Program: interim summary," *Journal of Developmental and Behavioral Pediatrics* 19, 1998, 359–370.

4 S. L. Hofferth, P. E. Davis-Kean, J. Davis, and J. Finkelstein, "The child development supplement to the Panel Study of Income Dynamics 1997 User Guide," 1997. http://www.isr.umich.edu/src/child-development/usergd.html.

5 P. L. Chase-Lansdale, F. L. Mott, J. Brooks-Gunn, and D. A. Phillips, "Children of the National Longitudinal Survey of Youth: a unique research opportunity," *Developmental Psychology* 27, 1991, 918–931.

6 J. P. Shonkoff and D. A. Phillips (eds), *From Neurons to Neighborhoods: The Science of Early Childhood Developmental Science*, Washington, DC: National Academies Press, 2000.

7 Ibid., p. 5.

8 F. F. Furstenberg Jr., J. Brooks-Gunn, and S. P. Morgan, *Adolescent Mothers in Later Life*, Cambridge: Cambridge University Press, 1987, p. 143.

9 J. Brooks-Gunn, G. Guo, and F. F. Furstenberg Jr., "Who drops out of and who continues beyond high school? A 20–year follow-up of black urban youth," *Journal of Research on Adolescence* 3, 1993, 271–294.

10 Ibid.

11 N. Baydar, J. Brooks-Gunn, and F. F. Furstenberg, "Early warning signs of functional illiteracy: predictors in childhood and adolescence," *Child Development* 64, 1993, 815–829.

12 R. A. Weinberg, "Intelligence and IQ: landmark issues and great debates," *American Psychologist* 44, 1989, 98–104.

13 A. J. Sameroff, R. Seifer, A. Baldwin, and C. Baldwin, "Stability of intelligence from preschool to adolescence: the influence of social and family risk factors," *Child Development* 64, 1993, 80–97; A. J. Sameroff, R. Seifer, R. Barocas, M. Zax, and S. Greenspan, "Intelligence quotient scores of 4-year-old children: social and environmental risk factors," *Pediatrics* 79, 1987, 343–350.

14 F. Liaw and J. Brooks-Gunn, "Cumulative familial risks and low-birthweight children's cognitive and behavioral development," *Journal of Clinical Child Psychology* 23, 1994, 360–372.

15 G. S. Becker and N. Tomes, "Human capital and the rise and fall of families," *Journal of Labor Economics* 4, 1986, S1–S139; R. H. Haveman and B. S. Wolfe, *Succeeding Generations: On the Effects of Investments in Children*, New York, NY: Russell Sage Foundation, 1994; S. E. Mayer, *What Money Can't Buy: Family Income and Children's Life Chances*, Cambridge, MA: Harvard University Press, 1997.

16 G. S. Becker, *A Treatise on the Family* (2nd edn). Cambridge, MA: Harvard University Press, 1991; Becker and Tomes, op. cit.
17 R. Dunifon, G. J. Duncan, and J. Brooks-Gunn, "As ye sweep, so shall ye reap," *American Economic Review* 91, 2001, 150–154.
18 M. Phillips, J. Brooks-Gunn, G. J. Duncan, P. K. Klebanov, and J. Crane, "Family background, parenting practices, and the black-white test score gap," pp. 103–145 in *The Black-White Test Score Gap*, edited by C. Jencks and M. Phillips, Washington, DC: Brookings Institution Press, 1998.
19 G. J. Duncan, J. Brooks-Gunn, and P. K. Klebanov, "Economic deprivation and early childhood development," *Child Development* 65, 1994, 296–318; J. R. Smith, J. Brooks-Gunn, and P. K. Klebanov, "Consequences of living in poverty for young children's cognitive and verbal ability and early school achievement," pp. 132–189 in *Consequences of Growing Up Poor* edited by G. J. Duncan and J. Brooks-Gunn, New York, NY: Russell Sage Foundation, 1997.
20 Both these studies also controlled for child gender, ethnicity, birthweight, and marital status, and duration of poverty.
21 Smith *et al.*, op. cit.
22 Ibid.; Duncan *et al.*, op. cit.; P. K. Klebanov, J. Brooks-Gunn, C. M. McCarton, and M. C. McCormick, "The contribution of neighborhood and family income to developmental test scores over the first three years of life," *Child Development* 69, 1998, 1420–1436.
23 Smith *et al.*, op. cit.
24 K. Keenan, D. S. Shaw, B. Walsh, E. Delliquadri, and J. Giovannelli, "DMS-III-R disorders in preschool children from low-income families," *Journal of the American Academy of Child and Adolescent Psychiatry* 36, 1997, 620–627; J. V. Lavigne, R. D. Gibbons, K. K. Christoffel, R. Arend, D. Rosenbaum, H. J. Binns, N. Dawson, H. Sobel, and C. Isaacs, "Prevalence rates and correlates of psychiatric disorders among preschool children," *Journal of the American Academy of Child and Adolescent Psychiatry* 35, 1996, 204–214.
25 Lavigne *et al.*, op. cit.
26 R. E. Tremblay, "The development of aggressive behaviour during childhood: what have we learned in the past century?," *International Journal of Behavioral Development* 24, 2000, 129–141.
27 T. M. Achenbach and C. S. Edelbrock, "Behavioral problems and competencies reported by parents of normal and disturbed children aged four through sixteen," *Monographs of the Society for Research in Child Development* 46, 1981, No. 188; T. M. Achenbach and C. S. Edelbrock, "Psychopathology of childhood," *Annual Review of Psychology* 35, 1984, 227–256.
28 J. Brooks-Gunn, G. J. Duncan, T. Leventhal, and J. L. Aber, "Lessons learned and future directions for research on neighborhoods in which children live," pp. 279–297 in *Neighborhood Poverty: Vol. 1. Context and Consequences for Children*, edited by J. Brooks-Gunn, G. J. Duncan, and J. L. Aber, New York: Russell Sage Foundation, 1997; P. L. Chase-Lansdale, R. A. Gordon, J. Brooks-Gunn, and P. K. Klebanov, "Neighborhood and family influences on the intellectual and behavioral competence of preschool and early school-age children," pp. 79–118 in *Neighborhood Poverty: Vol. 1. Context and Consequences for Children* edited by J. Brooks-Gunn, G. J. Duncan, and J. L. Aber, New York, NY: Russell Sage Foundation Press, 1997.
29 J. Brooks-Gunn, G. J. Duncan, P. K. Klebanov, and N. Sealand, "Do neighborhoods influence child and adolescent development?," *American Journal of Sociology* 99, 1993, 353–395; Chase-Lansdale *et al.*, op. cit. 1997
30 J. Brooks-Gunn and G. J. Duncan, "The effects of poverty on children," *The Future of Children* 7, 1997, 55–71.

31 G. Downey and J. C. Coyne, "Children of depressed parents: an integrative review," *Psychological Bulletin* 108, 1990, 50–76; B. Egeland, M. Kalkoske, N. Gottesman, and M. F. Erikson, "Preschool behavior problems: stability and factors accounting for change," *Journal of Child Psychology and Psychiatry* 31, 1990, 891–909; K. Lyons-Ruth, D. Zoll, D. B. Connell, and H. U. Grunebaum, "The depressed mother and her one-year-old infant: environmental context, mother–infant interaction and attachment, and infant development," pp. 61–82 in *Maternal Depression and Infant Disturbance*, edited by E. Tronick and T. Field, San Francisco, CA: Jossey Bass, 1986; NICHD Early Child Care Research Network, "Chronicity of maternal depressive symptoms, maternal sensitivity, and child functioning at 36 months," *Developmental Psychology* 35, 1999, 1297–1310.

32 D. M. Fergusson, M. T. Lynskey, and L. J. Horwood, "The effort of maternal depression on maternal ratings of child behavior," *Journal of Abnormal Child Psychology* 21, 1993, 245–269.

33 Downey and Coyne, op. cit.; C. Hammen, D. Burge, and C. Adrian, "Timing of mother and child depression in a longitudinal study of children at risk," *Journal of Consulting and Clinical Psychology* 59, 1991, 341–345.

34 P. A. Brennan, C. Hammen, M. J. Andersen, W. Bor, J. M. Najman, and G. M. Williams, "Chronicity, severity, and timing of maternal depressive symptoms: relationships with child outcomes at age 5," *Developmental Psychology* 36, 2000, 759–766; Downey and Coyne, op. cit.; NICHD, op. cit.; C. Zahn-Waxler, R. J. Iannotti, E. M. Cummings, and S. A. Denham, "Antecedents of problem behaviors in children of depressed mothers," *Development and Psychopathology* 2, 1990, 349–366.

35 M. Ainsworth, M. C. Blehar, E. Waters, and S. Wall, *Patterns of Attachment*, Hillsdale, NJ: Lawrence Erlbaum, 1978; J. Belsky and J. Cassidy, "Attachment: theory and evidence," pp. 373–402 in *Developmental Principles and Clinical Issues in Psychology and Psychiatry*, edited by M. Rutter, D. Hay, and S. Baron-Cohen, Oxford: Blackwell, 1994; R. A. Thompson, "Sequelae of early attachment experiences," in J. Cassidy and P. Shaver (eds), *Handbook of Attachment Theory and Research*, New York: Guilford Press, 1998.

36 R. H. Bradley, "Environment and parenting," pp. 235–261 in *Handbook of Parenting,* edited by M. H. Bornstein, Mahwah, NJ: Lawrence Erlbaum Associates, 1995; R. H. Bradley, B. M. Caldwell, S. L. Rock, C. T. Ramey, K. E. Barnard, C. Gray, M. A. Hammond, S. K. Mitchell, A.W. Gottfried, L. Siegel, and D. L. Johnson, "Home environment and cognitive development in the first three years of life: a collaborative study involving six sites and three ethnic groups in North America," *Developmental Psychology* 25, 1989, 217–235; A. E. Gottfried, J. S. Fleming, and A. W. Gottfried, "Role of cognitively stimulating home environment in children's academic intrinsic motivation: a longitudinal study," *Child Development* 69, 1998, 1448–1460; Mayer, op. cit.

37 For example, C. E. Snow, "Conversations with children," pp. 69–89 in *Language Acquisition: Studies in First Language Development,* edited by P. Fletcher and M. Garman, Cambridge: Cambridge University Press, 1986; G. J. Whitehurst, D. S. Arnold, J. N. Epstein, A. L. Angell, M. Smith, and J. E. Fischel, "A picture book reading intervention in day care and home for children from low-income families," *Developmental Psychology* 30, 1994, 679–689; G. J. Whitehurst and C. J. Lonigan, "Child development and emergent literacy," *Child Development* 69, 1998, 848–872.

38 M. H. Bornstein, "Between caretakers and their young: two models of interaction and their consequences for cognitive growth," pp. 197–214 in *Interactions in Human Development*, edited by M. H. Bornstein and J. S. Bruner Hillsdale, NJ: Lawrence Erlbaum, 1989; J. A. Crowell and S. S. Feldman,

"Mothers' internal models of relationships and children's behavioral and developmental status: a study of mother–child interactions," *Child Development* 59, 1988, 1273–1285; D. Spiker, J. C. Ferguson, and J. Brooks-Gunn, "Enhancing maternal interactive behavior and child social competence in low birth weight, premature infants," *Child Development* 64, 1993, 754–768.

39 T. Leventhal and J. Brooks-Gunn, "The neighborhoods they live in: the effects of neighborhood residence upon child and adolescent outcomes," *Psychological Bulletin* 126, 2000, 309–337.

40 Ibid.

41 D. S. Elliot, W. J. Wilson, D. Huizinga, R. J. Sampson, A. Elliott, and B. H. Rankin, "The effects of neighborhood disadvantage on adolescent development," *Journal of Research in Crime and Delinquency* 33, 1996, 389–426; P. K. Klebanov, J. Brooks-Gunn, P. L. Chase-Lansdale, and R. Gordon, "Are neighborhood effects on young children mediated by features of the home environment?," pp. 119–145 in *Neighborhood Poverty: Context and Consequences for Children,* edited by J. Brooks-Gunn, G. Duncan, and J. L. Aber, New York, NY: Russell Sage Foundation Press, 1997; R. J. Sampson, "The embeddedness of child and adolescent development: a community-level perspective on urban violence," pp. 31–77 in J. McCord (ed.), *Violence and Childhood in the Inner City*, New York, NY: Cambridge University Press, 1997.

42 M. Tienda, "Poor people and poor places: deciphering neighborhood effects on poverty outcomes," pp. 244–262 in *Macro-Micro Linkages in Sociology,* edited by J. Huber, Newbury Park, CA: Sage Publications, 1991.

43 M. Duyme, *Focus on Naturally Occurring Changes in Development After Varied Early Life Circumstances,* paper presented at the Well-Being and Dysfunction Across the Generations: Change and Continuity Conference, Zurich, Switzerland, 2001.

44 Becker and Tomes, op. cit.; Haveman and Wolfe, op. cit.; Mayer, op. cit.

45 R. D. Conger and G. H. Elder Jr., *Families in Troubled Times: Adapting to Change in Rural America*, New York, NY: Aldine de Gruyter, 1994; R. D. Conger, M. A. Rueter, and G. H. Elder Jr., "Couple resilience to economic pressure," *Journal of Personality and Social Psychology* 76, 1999, 54–71.

46 R. D. Conger, K. J. Conger, and G. H. Elder Jr., "Family economic hardship and adolescent adjustment: mediating and moderating processes," pp. 288–310 in *Consequences of Growing Up Poor,* edited by G. J. Duncan and J. Brooks-Gunn, New York, NY: Russell Sage Foundation, 1997; G. H. Elder Jr., *Children of the Great Depression: Social Change in Life Experience*, Chicago, IL: University of Chicago Press, 1974; V. C. McLoyd, "The impact of economic hardship on black families and children: psychological distress, parenting, and socioeconomic development," *Child Development* 61, 1990, 311–346; V. C. McLoyd, "Socialization and development in a changing economy: the effects of paternal job and income loss on children," *American Psychologist* 44, 1989, 293–302.

47 A. P. Jackson, J. Brooks-Gunn, C. Huang, and M. Glassman, "Single mothers in low-wage jobs: financial strain, parenting, and preschoolers' outcomes," *Child Development* 71, 2000, 1409–1423; McLoyd, op. cit. 1989.

48 Adapted from A. S. Fuligni and J. Brooks-Gunn, "The healthy development of young children: SES disparities, prevention strategies, and policy opportunities," in B. D. Smedley and S. L. Syme (eds), *Promoting Health: Intervention Strategies From Social and Behavioral Research*, Washington, DC: National Academy Press, 2000.

49 Jackson *et al.*, op. cit.; Klebanov *et al.*, op. cit. 1998; M. R. Linver, J. Brooks-Gunn, and D. E. Kohen, "Family processes as pathways from income to young children's development," *Developmental Psychology* 38, 2002, 719–734; W. J.

Yeung, M. R. Linver, and J. Brooks-Gunn, "How money matters for young children's development: parental investment and family processes," *Child Development* 73, 2002, 1861–1879.

50 Jackson *et al.*, op. cit.

51 Ibid.

52 Yeung *et al.*, op. cit.

53 Conger and Elder, op. cit.

54 Linver *et al.*, op. cit.; Yeung *et al.*, op. cit.

55 Linver *et al.*, op. cit.

56 D. Baumrind, "Effects of authoritative control on child behavior," *Child Development* 37, 1966, 887–907.

57 Provision of stimulating experiences and environment was measured with the HOME scale of B. M. Caldwell and R. H. Bradley, "*Home observation for measurement of the environment*," Little Rock, AR: University of Arkansas at Little Rock, 1984.

58 D. C. Rowe, *The Limits of Family Influence: Genes, Experience, and Behavior*, New York, NY: Guilford Press, 1994; D. C. Rowe and J. L. Rodgers, "Poverty and behavior: are environmental measures nature and nurture?," *Developmental Review* 7, 1997, 358–375; D. C. Rowe, K. C. Jacobson, and E. Van den Oord, "Genetic and environmental influences on vocabulary IQ: parental education level as moderator," *Child Development* 70, 1999, 1151–1162.

59 We tested our models with a structural equation modeling (SEM) approach, which allows simultaneous testing of all model constructs (R. E. Schumacker and R. G. Lomax, *A Beginner's Guide to Structural Equation Modeling*, Mahwah, NJ: Lawrence Erlbaum Associates, 1996). The direct and indirect associations of all predictors can be assessed while taking into account any number of control variables. Mediated effects were tested using Sobel's test for indirect effects. (M. E. Sobel, "Asymptotic confidence intervals for indirect effects in structural equation models," pp. 290–312 in S. Leinhart (ed.), *Sociological Methodology 1982,* San Francisco, CA: Jossey Bass, 1982.) We found that the family stress model constructs mediated the association between income and child behavioral outcomes, and the parental investment construct mediated the association between income and both cognitive and behavioral outcomes.

60 Income was inflated to 1997 price levels using the Consumer Price Index (CPI-UX1) and averaged over all of the years since the child's birth through 1996.

61 Duncan *et al.*, op. cit.

62 Yeung *et al.*, op. cit.

63 S. R. Andrews, J. Blumenthal, D. L. Johnson, A. J. Kahn, J. C. Ferguson, T. M. Lasater, P. E. Malone, and D. B. Wallace. "The skills of mothering: a study of parent child development centers," *Monographs of the Society for Research in Child Development* 47, 1982, No. 198; J. Brooks-Gunn, M. C. McCormick, S. Shapiro, A. A. Benasich, and G. W. Black, "The effects of early education intervention on maternal employment, public assistance, and health insurance: the Infant Health and Development Program," *The American Journal of Public Health* 84, 1994, 924–931; T. M. Field, S. M. Widmayer, R. Greenberg, and S. Stoller, "Effects of parent training on teenage mothers and their infants," *Pediatrics* 69, 1982, 245–269; V. Seitz and N. H. Apfel, "Parent-focused intervention: diffusion effects on siblings," *Child Development* 65, 1994, 677–683.

64 P. K. Klebanov, J. Brooks-Gunn, and M. C. McCormick, "Maternal coping strategies and emotional distress: results of an early intervention program for low birth weight young children," *Developmental Psychology* 37, 2001, 654–667; L. J. Schweinhart, H. V. Barnes, D. P. Weikart, W. S. Barnett, and A. S. Epstein, *Significant Benefits: The High/Scope Perry Preschool Study Through Age 27,* Ypsilanti, MI: High/Scope Press, 1993.

65 M. E. Barrera, P. L. Rosenbaum, and C. E. Cunningham, "Early home intervention with low-birth weight infants and their parents," *Child Development* 57, 1986, 20–33; T. M. Field, S. M. Widmayer, S. Stringer, and E. Ignatoff, "Teenage, lower-class, black mothers and their preterm infants: an intervention and developmental follow-up," *Child Development* 51, 1980, 426–436; S. W. Gray and K. Ruttle, "The family-oriented home visiting program: a longitudinal study," *Genetic Psychology Monographs* 102, 1980, 299–316; C. P. Larson, "Efficacy of prenatal and postpartum home visits on child health and development," *Pediatrics* 66, 1980, 191–197; A. F. Lieberman, D. R. Weston, and J. H. Pawl, "Preventive intervention and outcome with anxiously attached dyads," *Child Development* 62, 1991, 199–209; J. Madden, J. O'Hara, and P. Levenstein, "Home again: effects of the mother–child home program on mother and child," *Child Development* 55, 1984, 636–647; D. L. Olds, C. R. Henderson Jr., R. Chamberlin, and R. C. Tatelbaum, "Improving the life-course development of socially disadvantaged mothers: a randomized trial of nurse home visitation," *American Journal of Public Health* 78, 1988, 1436–1445; D. L. Olds, C. R. Henderson Jr., and H. J. Kitzman, "Does prenatal and infancy nurse home visitation have enduring effects on qualities of parental caregiving and child health at 25–50 months of life?," *Pediatrics* 93, 1994, 89–98.

66 J. Goering, J. Kraft, J. Feins, D. McInnis, M. J. Holin, and H. Elhassan, *Moving to Opportunity for Fair Housing Demonstration Program: Current Status and Initial Findings*, Washington, DC: U.S. Department of Housing and Urban Development, 1999; T. Leventhal and J. Brooks-Gunn, "Moving on up: neighborhood effects on children and families," pp. 209–230 in M. Bornstein and R. H. Bradley (eds), *Socioeconomic Status, Parenting, and Child Development*, Mahwah, NJ: Erlbaum, 2003.

67 P. A. Morris, "Effects of welfare reform policies on children," *Social Policy Report* 16, 2001, 1–20.

68 S. M. McGroder, M. J. Zaslow, K. A. Moore, and J. L. Brooks, *Impacts of a Mandatory Welfare-to-Work Program on Children at School Entry and Beyond: Findings from the NEWWS Childs Outcomes Study*, Washington, DC: Child Trends, 2002.

69 J. Heberle, "PACE: parent and child education in Kentucky," pp. 136–148 in *The Intergenerational Transfer of Cognitive Skills: Vol. I. Programs, Policy, and Research Issues,* edited by T. G. Sticht, M. J. Beeler and B. A. McDonald, Norwood, NJ: Ablex, 1992; D. C. Richardson and M. Brown, *Family Intergenerational Literacy Model: Fact Sheet and Impact Statements,* Oklahoma City, OK: National Diffusion Network, 1997; R. G. St. Pierre and J. P. Swartz, "The even start family literacy program," pp. 37–66 in *Advances in Applied Developmental Psychology: Vol. 9. Two Generation Programs for Families in Poverty: A New Intervention Strategy,* edited by S. Smith, Norwood, NJ: Ablex Publishing Corporation, 1995; F. Tao, J. Swartz, R. St. Pierre, and H. Tarr, *National Evaluations of the Even Start Family Literacy Program,* Washington, DC: U.S. Department of Education, 1997.

70 R. G. St. Pierre, J. P. Swartz, B. Gamse, S. Murray, D. Deck, and P. Nickel, *National Evaluation of the Even Start Family Literacy Program: Final Report*, Washington, DC: U.S. Department of Education, 1995.

71 Klebanov, *et al.*, op. cit. 2001; Schweinhart *et al.*, op. cit.

72 D. L. Olds, C. R. Henderson Jr., H. J. Kitzman, J. J. Eckenrode, R. E. Cole, and R. C. Tatelbaum, "Prenatal and infancy home visitation by nurses: recent findings," *The Future of Children* 9, 1999, 44–65.

73 M. M. Wagner and S. L. Clayton, "The parents as teachers program: results from two demonstrations," *The Future of Children* 9, 1999, 91–115.

74 A. J. Baker, C. S. Piotrkowski, and J. Brooks-Gunn, "The effects of the home

instruction program for preschool youngsters (HIPPY) on children's school performance at the end of the program and one year later," *Early Childhood Research Quarterly* 13, 1999, 571–588.

75 A. A. Benasich, J. Brooks-Gunn, and B. C. Clewell, "How do mothers benefit from early intervention programs?," *Journal of Applied Developmental Psychology* 13, 1992, 311–362; D. L. Olds and H. J. Kitzman, "Review of research on home visiting for pregnant women and parents of young children," *The Future of Children* 3, 1993, 53–92.

76 Olds *et al.*, op. cit.

77 Baker *et al.*, op. cit.

78 Wagner and Clayton, op. cit.

79 Olds and Kitzman, op. cit.

80 Brooks-Gunn *et al.*, op. cit. 1994.

81 St. Pierre and Swartz, op. cit.

82 Ibid.

83 W. W. Philliber, R. E. Spillman, and R. King, "Consequences of family literacy for adults and children: some preliminary findings," *Journal of Adolescent and Adult Literacy* 39, 1996, 558–565; R. G. St. Pierre, A. Ricciuti, and C. L. Creps, *Synthesis of State and Local Even Start Evaluations: Draft,* Cambridge, MA: Abt Associates, 1998; St. Pierre *et al.*, op. cit. 1995; F. Tao, B. Gamse, and H. Tarr, *National Evaluation of the Even Start Family Literacy Program: 1994–1997 Final Report*, Washington, DC: U.S. Department of Education, Planning and Evaluation Service, 1998.

84 J. Brooks-Gunn, L. J. Berlin, and A. S. Fuligni, "Early childhood intervention programs: what about the family," pp. 549–588 in *Handbook on Early Childhood Intervention,* edited by J. P. Shonkoff and S. J. Meisels (2nd edn), New York, NY: Cambridge University Press, 2000.

85 Barrera, *et al.*, op. cit.; Field, *et al.*, op. cit. 1980; Gray and Ruttle, op. cit.; Larson, op. cit.; Lieberman *et al.*, op. cit.; Madden *et al.*, op. cit.; D. L. Olds, C. R. Henderson Jr., R. Chamberlin, and R. C. Tatelbaum, "Improving the life-course development of socially disadvantaged mothers: a randomized trial of nurse home visitation," *American Journal of Public Health* 78, 1988, 1436–1445; D. L. Olds, C. R. Henderson Jr., and H. J. Kitzman, "Does prenatal and infancy nurse home visitation have enduring effects on qualities of parental caregiving and child health at 25–50 months of life?," *Pediatrics* 93, 1994, 89–98.

86 For example Barrera *et al.*, op. cit.; M. F. Erickson, J. Korfmacher, and B. Egeland, "Attachments past and present: implications for therapeutic intervention with mother–infant dyads," *Development and Psychopathology* 4, 1992, 495–507; Field *et al.*, op. cit. 1980; Gray and Ruttle, op. cit.; Larson, op. cit.; Olds *et al.*, op. cit. 1994; J. D. Osofsky, A. M. Culp, and L. M. Ware, "Intervention challenges with adolescent mothers and their infants," *Psychiatry* 51, 1988, 236–241; G. S. Ross, "Home intervention for premature infants of low-income families," *American Journal of Orthopsychiatry* 54, 1984, 263–270.

87 Brooks-Gunn *et al.*, op. cit. 2000.

88 Leventhal and Brooks-Gunn, op. cit. 2003.

89 Ibid.

90 Brooks-Gunn *et al.*, op. cit. 2000; B. C. Clewell, J. Brooks-Gunn, and A. A. Benasich, "Evaluating child-related outcomes of teenage parenting programs," *Family Relations* 38, 1989, 201–209.

91 M. R. Burchinal, F. A. Campbell, D. M. Bryant, B. H. Wasik, and C. T. Ramey, "Early intervention and mediating processes in cognitive performance of children of low-income African-American families," *Child Development* 68, 1997, 935–954.

92 M. R. Linver and J. Brooks-Gunn, "Parenting as mediating early intervention effects upon young children," unpublished manuscript, 2001.
93 Bradley, op. cit.
94 W. S. Barnett, "Long-term effects of early childhood programs on cognitive and school outcomes," *The Future of Children* 5, 1995, 25–50; L. J. Berlin, C. R. O'Neal, and J. Brooks-Gunn, "What makes early intervention programs work? The program, its participants, and their interaction," in L. J. Berlin (ed.), *Opening the Black Box: What Makes Early Child and Family Development Programs Work*? [Special Issue] *Zero to Three* 18, 1998, 4–15; D. M. Bryant and K. L. Maxwell, "The effectiveness of early intervention for disadvantaged children," pp. 23–46 in *The Effectiveness of Early Intervention*, edited by M. J. Guralnick, Baltimore, MD: Brookes, 1997; H. Yoshikawa, "Long-term effects of early childhood programs on social outcomes and delinquency," *The Future of Children* 5, 1995, 51–75.
95 W. A. Collins, E. E. Maccoby, L. Steinberg, E. M. Hetherington, and M. H. Bornstein, "Contemporary research on parenting: the case for nature and nurture," *American Psychologist* 55, 2000, 218–232.
96 Phillips *et al.*, op. cit.
97 C. H. Weiss, "Nothing as practical as a good theory: exploring theory-based evaluation for comprehensive community initiatives for children and families," pp. 65–92 in *New Approaches to Evaluating Community Initiatives: Vol. 1. Concepts, Methods, and Contexts,* edited by J. P. Connell, A. C. Kubisch, L. B. Schorr, and C. H. Weiss, Washington, DC: The Aspen Institute, 1995; see also K. E. Barnard, "Developing, implementing, documenting interventions with parents and young children," in L. J. Berlin (ed.), *Opening the Black Box: Understanding How Early Intervention Programs Work* [Special Issue], *Zero to Three* 18, 1998, 23–29.; Berlin *et al.*, op. cit.
98 J. M. Love, E. E. Kisker, C. M. Ross, P. Z. Schochet, J. Brooks-Gunn, K. Boller, D. Paulsell, A. S. Fuligni, and L. J. Berlin, *Building Their Futures: How Early Head Start Programs are Enhancing the Lives of Infants and Toddlers in Low-Income Families*, Washington, DC: U.S. Department of Health and Human Services, 2001.

2 Family background, education determination, and policy implications

Some selected aspects from various countries

Jere R. Behrman[1]

Family background has long been observed to be strongly associated with the determination of education. Children with "better" family backgrounds who choose to live in "better" neighborhoods, for example, have more and better education in most societies. And yet the literature on family background and child education is subject to some major limitations.

First, most studies use imperfect measures of the key observable variables – including those for education and family income. The most common measures of education, for example, are the highest grade completed, current enrollment, and years of schooling. None of these incorporate directly that school quality and family background are generally heterogeneous. Income, likewise, is generally represented by recent annual income or consumption, without consideration of the longer-run income that would seem critical for schooling investment decisions that are made over a number of years. As a result, even the descriptions that most studies provide may be misleading, including regarding the strength of the association between family background and child education.

Second, most studies do not provide convincing evidence of causality, particularly with regard to controlling for possible unobserved determinants such as genetic endowments and for behaviorally-determined proximate determinants of child education, such as child health/nutritional status. Indeed, if there are intergenerational correlations in genetic endowments that facilitate learning and are rewarded in labor markets, much or even all of the associations between most of the family background variables that are used in the literature – income, schooling, occupation – may be due to such correlations, not to the family background variables themselves. This question of causality is further complicated because marriage markets may sort individuals – mothers and fathers – not only in terms of observed characteristics such as completed schooling, but on unobserved characteristics such as innate abilities. For such reasons the estimated impact of family background variables such as income and parental schooling on child education in most of the literature may be biased, perhaps substantially, and – at least for this reason – probably upward. Likewise, child health and nutritional status is likely to be determined by behaviors, perhaps in part in response to the same factors that determine child education. If so, the association between child education and child health and nutritional status may be in part or in whole spurious regarding causality, and yield a biased estimate of unknown direction in estimates of causal effects.

Third, most studies do not establish clearly the context of their results and how, for example, household behaviors in response to incentives created by markets, culture, and policies may differ substantially depending on the nature of this context. If mother's time is a critical input into child education, for example, the impact of mother's schooling on child education may depend substantially on what is the nature of the time-use options that women face, including those in labor markets, and whether more schooling for a woman changes the relative rewards for different uses of her time. The extent of the impact of family background on education, for another example, may vary substantially depending on school policies pertaining to the accessibility and quality of schooling – and to what extent the availability of high quality schooling is correlated with family background.

Fourth, most studies provide some information needed for the evaluation of policies, but not other key elements of what is needed with regard to either the costs or the benefits. Often, for example, studies suggest that all that is needed is to show that schooling is positively associated, or better yet, causes some "good" outcome(s) to justify public subsidies for schooling. But, from an efficiency or distributional perspective, this is a non sequitur. Schooling might have a large impact on some outcomes, but the gains from that impact may be entirely private, so that there is no efficiency reason for subsidizing schooling. Or schooling may have a modest impact on an outcome, but there may be differences between the private and the social effects, so that there is an efficiency reason for subsidizing schooling. The size of the impact of schooling on an outcome simply does *not* necessarily indicate anything about the efficiency argument for subsidizing schooling. Likewise it does not necessarily tell much about the distributional argument for subsidizing schooling as opposed to alternatives. For both the efficiency and distributional motives for policy, information about direct and indirect costs, for example, is essential.

This chapter addresses these four points in turn. The studies that are summarized focus primarily on schooling in the United States but they are supplemented with international studies. After briefly summarizing frameworks for analysis, I consider selected empirical evidence and the implications of the frameworks for analysis for each of these four points, and then conclude. The conclusions emphasize that much of the literature currently available on impacts of family background on child education is likely to misrepresent – in some cases overstate and in others, understate – the true impacts because of measurement and analytical problems. Most of this literature, moreover, is inattentive to the basic policy motives of distribution and efficiency. Therefore there is considerable scope for improving our understanding of what are the impacts of family background on child education and how might related policies be improved.

Frameworks for analysis

Frameworks for analysis are essential for clarifying thinking about what we know and what we do not know about the determinants of education. This is the case in important part because we cannot conduct double-blind experiments with random assignment to treatment and control groups for the questions of interest. And even if we could conduct such experiments, they would reveal only the gross changes induced by the experimental treatment conditional on a particular situation, not what would happen in somewhat different circumstances. Those who are not clear about their framework of analysis are not revealing underlying truths unconstrained by such frameworks, but are usually making implicit assumptions that may upon examination not be very plausible.[2]

In the following pages, I eschew Greek letters and equations. Instead, I rely on verbal explanations of what such frameworks imply for the considerations of this chapter. I consider first the determination of household behaviors related to education and then the basic motives for policies.

Determination of household behaviors related to child education

The proximate determinants of education are decisions made by households, or individuals within households, given their objectives and the constraints that they face with regard to factors such as resources, markets, culture, policies, and genetic endowments. On a fairly abstract level, households can be characterized as acting as if they maximize their welfare subject to a number of constraints.[3] This need not be a conscious act. But for the purposes of this discussion, it suffices to assume that when households make conscious decisions they make those that they perceive to further their welfare even though there are substantial imperfections in their knowledge and for many repeated behaviors it is not desirable to make fresh decisions every time they are under consideration, but instead to follow "rules of thumb" or past patterns.

The welfare function depends in part on time use of the household members (e.g. working in economic activities, going to school, leisure, working in household production), in part on human resources per se including education of each household member, in part on consumption of goods and services consumed by each household member that are obtained through the returns on the household assets (including human resources), as well as other factors. Welfare is likely to increase directly and indirectly (through income to purchase more goods and services) through more education, all else being equal. The welfare function is likely to be defined not only over current values of the variables that affect it, but also over expectations regarding future values. There may be a trade-off between, say, increasing leisure today and being more educated tomorrow. The welfare is conditioned by culture, though typically there also is heterogeneity within a culture. The direct impact on welfare of more education or of using time to go to school, for example, may differ substantially across cultures, for different household members (e.g. by sex), and among different households within cultures.

The constraints subject to which welfare is maximized at any point of time include household resources, prices, kin and social networks, political systems, and production functions.

Household resources include physical, capital, and human resources of each household member. Among the human resources are the time of each individual, education to date, innate genetic endowments (including innate abilities and innate health).

Prices include the prices in all markets that may affect household decisions. Important examples include markets for schooling and other inputs into education (with prices depending on quality and perhaps on individual characteristics such as race, age, and sex), for labor (with wage rates conditional on education, work experience, sex, age, race, ethnic group, or whatever else affects wages) and for capital (including the extent to which education can be financed through these markets). The prices include those for public schools, pre-school and post-school programs, as well as public services related to other human resources and to financing human resource investments. These latter prices often include large subsidy elements (as do some of the prices for privately-provided goods and services), but conceptually the relevant constraint is what price does the household have to pay for a given good or service (e.g. fourth-grade schooling of a certain quality and proximity) independent of whether the provider is public or private. The prices of relevance include not only current prices, but also future prices (or the distributions of them) because they also affect current decisions. For example, future prices (wages) expected for different educational levels (perhaps conditioned on individual characteristics such as race, sex, age, and ethnic group) affect current allocations of time and other resources to education.

Kin and social networks also constrain household choices. Households are embedded in kin and social networks that may provide insurance (e.g. "home is where you go when there is no place to go"), loans (implicit or explicit) for investments (including in education), information, and support. It generally is thought that such networks have important roles relative to markets and public services in less developed contexts, but that many of these roles are diminished or disappear with development.[4]

Political systems also constrain the choices of households. Households can attempt to affect policies for what they consider important by using their resources, including time and money.

Production functions are technical relations that indicate what output can be obtained given current technology and the inputs, some of which reflect household decisions that are used to produce that output. Outputs can range from rice to information to health and nutritional status to education. The production function for education, for example, might include inputs such as time in school, quality of schooling,[5] pre-school experiences, genetic endowments, time spent doing homework, time spent in and quality of formal training programs, time spent learning in interaction with other family members, health and nutrition status, and experiences of various types. Three points about such an educational production function merit emphasis.

First, time spent in school is not likely to be the only relevant, nor necessarily the most important, input into education. Many other factors, including what happens in the household and genetic endowments, may be important. Therefore equating time in school with education may be quite misleading.

Second, because other inputs to education are likely to be associated with time in school, if they are not controlled in estimates of the impact of schooling, time in school will represent in part these other inputs so empirical estimates of the causal effect of time in school on education are not obtained. For example, suppose that there is a good measure of education (e.g. cognitive achievement); that education increases positively with time in school, school quality, parents' schooling and income (through improving the home and neighborhood learning environment) and innate ability; and that time in school, quality of school and parents' schooling and income all are positively correlated with innate ability (time and quality of schooling because the child's ability is a determinant of these; parents' schooling and income because these are determined positively in part by their abilities and ability endowments are intergenerationally correlated).

Third, even if a good estimate of the production function effect of time of schooling is obtained, that is not necessarily a good estimate of the total effect of some factor that affects the time spent in school on education. For example, suppose that time in schooling is increased through a new subsidy (voucher, scholarship) for time spent in school. Such a reduction in the price of schooling in general engenders a host of changes in household behaviors because of the lowered price and increased real income of the household, so many adjustments in time use and other inputs into education might occur. As a result, the gross effect on education might differ, perhaps substantially – and in either direction, from the direct production function impact of increased time in school on education holding all else constant.[6]

Social science estimates of relations that determine schooling or education in some cases may be production functions. But more often they are approximations to "demand relations" or "dynamic decision rules" in which schooling (or some aspect of schooling) or education is the dependent variable and the right-side variables include in principle ALL the predetermined variables and parameters underlying the above discussion – all the constraints imposed by the welfare function, prices, kin and social networks, political systems, and production functions. This includes, *inter alia*, all the education to date of all household members, all the genetic endowments of all household members, all other family background variables, all demographic characteristics of all household members, all current and expected future prices and how they depend on demographic characteristics, all other resources of the household, all relevant aspects of kin and social networks and political systems, all preference and production function parameters, and all relevant aspects of culture.

Two additional points about these relations should also be noted. First, they capture the gross effects of some change because in the background are all the behavioral adjustments that the household makes to, say, a reduction in the price of schooling. Second, there may be omitted variable biases akin to those discussed in the second point above for production functions if variables not included in the relation should be there and are correlated with some of the right-side variables. For example, if parents' schooling and income are included and there is not control for genetic ability endowments, the estimated impacts of parents' schooling and income are likely to be biased because they include the true effects plus any correlated effects of the unobserved endowments.[7] Therefore it may be difficult to obtain unbiased estimates of the impact of such variables on schooling.

Basic policy motives

At a general enough level of abstraction, policy should be chosen in order to maximize social welfare. That begs, of course, the critical political economy question of how the social welfare function is determined. Even if that difficult question is put aside, the practical guidance offered by the injunction to maximize social welfare may seem quite limited. For that reason it is useful to think separately of two related policy motives: efficiency and distribution, first in isolation and then together.

An intervention increases efficiency if it enables society to produce and consume more with the same resources and technology. Under a set of conditions, free markets would lead to efficient provision of productive inputs, efficient allocation of resources among production alternatives and efficient composition of production and consumption. Under these conditions private incentives at the margin for all activities, given by market prices, are identical to socially desirable incentives. There are no "market failures," no *distortions* between private and social marginal incentives. If there is efficiency, no person can be made better off without making at least one other person worse off. Or, equivalently, if there is not efficiency, everyone could be made better off with the same given resources. All else equal, efficiency thus obviously seems desirable.

The conditions for free markets to result in efficiency are stringent.[8] Nevertheless, efficiency remains an ideal against which to measure a critical dimension of policies. Lessening distortions between private and social marginal incentives is likely to lead to increased efficiency in the absence of explicit countervailing distortions. And the less are such distortions, the more market prices convey information about social marginal costs and benefits and provide guidance for private behaviors to be more efficient. Therefore, at least in a probabilistic sense, there is an efficiency argument for considering policy interventions that reduce market failures.

But that still leaves open the question of whether, from an efficiency perspective, there are policy interventions that it makes sense to undertake in the presence of a market failure and, if so, what policy intervention should be undertaken. Policies have costs – direct resource costs and indirect or distortion costs.[9] There can be – and often have been – "policy failures" that are worse than the market failures that they are ostensibly introduced to counterbalance. Many policy options, for example, have widespread effects on many markets and induce "rent-seeking" in which individuals privileged by policies (whether employed in the public or the private sector) seek returns on that policy-determined privilege. It is useful, therefore, to consider an *efficiency policy hierarchy* in which policy intervention alternatives to address to the same degree a specific market failure are ordered with the first-best option being the one with the least marginal resource and distortion cost. Generally (again this is a probabilistic statement), policy interventions that are more directed at the market distortion that is being addressed and that use price rather than quantitative means have less distortionary costs.

Thus, from an efficiency perspective in isolation, it is desirable to consider policy interventions that are possible to address a given market failure or distortion and to choose the intervention among those that is as high as possible in the efficiency policy hierarchy if the expected social marginal costs of that policy intervention are less than the social marginal costs of the market distortion being addressed.

The distributional motive for policy is distinct from the efficiency motive. Even if an economy were efficient, it might be possible to attain higher levels of social welfare with the same resources were the distribution of consumption altered from the efficient outcomes. Societies, and members of societies, may have many differing distributional concerns. Individuals and groups, for example, usually prefer redistribution toward themselves, their friends and relatives, and others with whom they associate or who provide support, including political support. A widespread distributional concern relates to lessening the probabilities that members of the society live in poverty that is motivated by a shared sense of altruism and justice. This is the distributional concern that probably is most relevant to this paper.

As for the efficiency motive, there are many policies that might address any particular distributional objective. Also as for efficiency concerns, such policies have both direct resource costs and distortionary costs, with the latter likely to be greater the less focused are the policies on the targeted distributional objective. And again, for any particular distributional concern, the possible policy interventions can be ordered in a *distributional policy hierarchy* in terms of increasing marginal resource and distortionary costs. From the point of view of distributional concerns alone, the best policy intervention is the one that is feasible and is highest in the distributional policy hierarchy.

Policies almost always have both efficiency and distributional implications. Therefore policies that maximize the social welfare function may not be "first-best" for either the efficiency or the distributional hierarchies. If so, attention to only one or the other of these hierarchies is likely to lead to less social welfare than might be possible with the same resources. In some cases there are policy changes that are "win-win" in the sense that an intervention both improves efficiency and improves distribution. Because many markets are most distorted for the poor, for example, interventions that improve such markets not only are likely to increase efficiency but also help attain distributional goals that weight heavily the welfare of the poor. But there also are many cases in which there may be trade-offs between efficiency and distribution. In such cases, if the intent is to attain some distributional goal, for instance, it is desirable to attain it at as little efficiency cost as possible.

Limitations in the literature

I noted at the start of this chapter four main limitations in many studies on family background and child education. I will now turn to more extensive discussions of these limitations.

Imperfect variable measures

Empirical work in the social sciences always is plagued by measurement errors. The relation between child education and family background is no exception. Random measurement errors in variables, as is well known, mask their true associations with other variables so that their estimated correlations are biased toward zero, as are their coefficient estimates if they are right-side variables in multivariate regressions. While random measurement errors are most emphasized in the social science literature, systematic measurement errors may be important, perhaps more important, in many cases. The biases introduced by systematic errors may be in either direction, depending on the exact nature of the errors.[10] I now consider illustrations related to two key variables – education and family resources.

Some studies in the social sciences use a direct measure of education, such as cognitive achievement. Some question whether such an indicator, leaving aside questions of measurement errors, captures fully the concept of education. They suggest that education is a multidimensional concept for which multidimensional indicators are needed for empirical work. If so, then focusing on a subset of these indicators may be misleading regarding the determinants of education more broadly defined.

However, most studies in the social sciences equate education with formal schooling, usually represented by completed years of schooling. Years of schooling as reported by survey respondents is likely to have measurement error. Various studies for the United States that use multiple reports on the schooling of an individual to estimate this measurement error and find that the noise to signal ratio in reported schooling is of the order of magnitude of ten percent.[11]

If the desired concept is education and years of schooling is used to represent it in empirical studies, in addition to random measurement error, there may be systematic measurement error that is tied into omitted variable bias. As is emphasized in the discussion of the production function for education, if education is produced by a number of inputs of which time in schooling is only one and if time in schooling is correlated with other inputs, the result will be biases (probably upward if the omitted inputs are complements with time in schooling in producing education and are positively correlated with years of schooling) in the estimated impact of schooling that may be substantial. Studies for a number of societies report results that are consistent with such effects.[12] For Brazil, for example, the impact of grades completed of schooling on market wages is over estimated by about two-thirds if school quality is omitted, the estimated rate of return in terms of wages is at least as high for school quality as for years of schooling, and the impact of school quality on child school enrollment is overestimated significantly if family background determinants are excluded. For Pakistan, years of schooling again is an imperfect representation of education (cognitive achievement) that results in misleading understanding of the trade-offs among school effects versus family background effects on both cognitive achievement and, among school effects, the impact of completed grades versus school quality. For the United States, both completed schooling and school quality have significant effects on wage rates and both respond to family background and genetic endowments so their effects are likely to be misunderstood (probably overestimated) if there is not control for family background and genetic endowments.

What are the implications of using years of schooling to represent education in studies of the determination of child schooling? Random measurement error in years of schooling causes the true association between child's and parent's schooling to be underestimated by about the same order of magnitude as the noise-to-signal ratio in measured schooling, so by about ten percent and thus – if a causal interpretation is warranted – underestimating by about this proportion the impact of parental schooling on child schooling. Systematic error/omitted variable bias in the representation of education by years of schooling means that the dependent variable in most (but not all) studies of the determinants of child schooling is only an input into education, albeit an important input, so important aspects of the process may be missed.[13] Systematic error/omitted variable bias in the right-side variables (e.g. in child years of schooling in relations for the determination of direct measures of educational outcomes such as cognitive achievement; in parental schooling in relations in which the dependent variable is child education or child years of schooling) tends to cause biases, perhaps considerable biases, in the estimated impact of schooling effects versus family background effects and in the decomposition of each between years of schooling and school quality measures.

As a result of these problems in measuring child and parental education, even the descriptions that most studies provide – to say nothing of causal interpretations – may be misleading, including regarding the strength of the association between family background and child schooling. While a number of studies suggest that the effects of years of schooling are overstated and of family background effectively downplayed if observed indicators of family background are not included among the right-side variables in reduced-form demand relations/dynamic decision rules for child years of schooling, most other aspects of these measurement problems remain almost unexplored. My conjecture is that they result in the role of family background and genetic endowments in child education to be perceived to be less than they actually are.

Family resources or income are emphasized in the literature as being one of the more important aspects of family background. To the extent that schooling is purely an investment, if markets – particularly capital and insurance markets for human resource investments – functioned perfectly, the standard economic model[14] implies that family background has no causal effects on child education or schooling. Within this framework, nevertheless, there may be significant associations between family income and child education if, for example, both family income and child education are affected by genetic endowments that are correlated between parents and children. Many think, however, that the relevant markets are sufficiently imperfect so that family resources are a major causal factor in child education because only better-off families can afford to self-finance substantial education for their children. This also is a major rationale for subsidizing schooling. Note that this rationale is doubly strong for public subsidies for education of children from poor families because there is a distributional motive if alleviating poverty is of concern and an efficiency motive if the poor are more affected by imperfect markets – a "win-win" situation. Note also, however, that this is a rationale for subsidizing schooling, and not for subsidizing only or subsidizing differentially public schooling – which is not likely to be as high in the efficiency hierarchy that is discussed above as general subsidies targeted more towards the poor because limiting such subsidies to one class of schooling providers introduces distortions regarding the distribution of resources among schools.

How associated is family income with child education? This is a question of interest from the perspective of the distributional motive for policies discussed even if inferences can not be comfortably made from these associations about the causal effect of family income on child schooling. There have been numerous studies of associations between indicators of household income and child schooling. Elsewhere, a co-author and I have reviewed the 42 studies (for 21 countries) we could locate. Estimates for about three-fifths of the schooling indicators used in these studies yield significant associations between household income and schooling. The median response of schooling with respect to income in these studies from all 21 countries suggests that doubling income increases schooling attainment by about 7 percent. For the United States the value is slightly smaller, about 4 percent, though with some variation among the estimates (see Figure 2.1). These estimates therefore suggest that children from higher-income households tend to do better in schooling than children from poorer households, though the magnitude of this effect is small. The estimates tend to be higher for poorer samples and a number of the studies find small inverse associations of the estimates with income. The literature on associations between schooling and income, in summary, finds that such associations often are significantly positive, probably somewhat larger for poorer populations, but generally are not all that large – probably much smaller than many people seem to perceive.

However most of the existing literature on associations between child

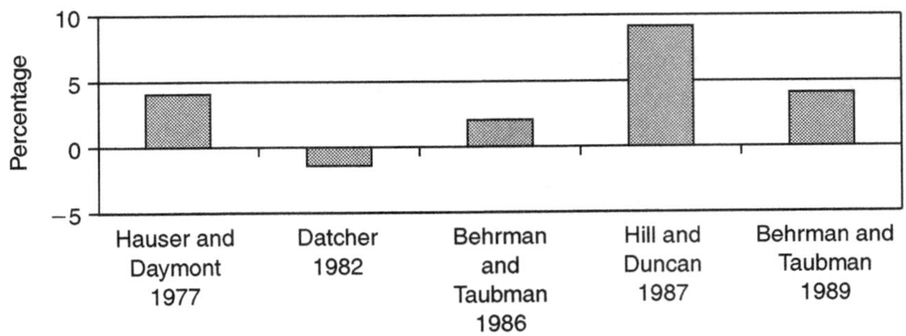

Figure 2.1 Percentage changes in years of schooling in response to 100 percent increase in income, various estimates for the U.S. (see Table 2.A.1).

schooling and parental household income suffers from the following four limitations:[15]

- The income measures used in most of these studies probably are contaminated by measurement error as well as possible endogeneity of schooling with other decisions. If there is random measurement error in the income indicator used as would be the case if annual income is used when the relevant household resource constraint really is longer-run, as noted above, the estimated association between family income and child schooling is biased toward zero.[16] If households adjust their income and expenditures simultaneously with the schooling decisions, there may be a bias toward or away from zero.[17]
- Most previous studies are limited to one schooling indicator, usually students' time input in school or their grade attainment. This narrow focus, as discussed above with regard to measuring child education, misses the possibility that there may be important associations between income on the one hand and, on the other hand, a broader set of inputs into education, such as age of starting school, grades passed per year in school, and examination performance conditional on grade completed that are separate from and additional to the completed grades of school.
- Many studies that use data on children of school age do not control in their estimates of schooling-household income associations for the fact that at the time of the sample some such children may not have yet started schooling and others may not have yet completed their schooling or for other aspects of sample censoring. Because of sample censoring, in fact, means or simple graphs or other nonparametric summaries of the data may not be very revealing regarding the extent of the associations with income.
- The true association between schooling and income may be masked in a number of previous studies because they include a number of other household, community and school controls that are correlated with income and may be proxying in part for the income association.[18]

These factors may make a considerable difference. In previous research, a co-author and I have illustrated this by exploring the extent of associations between household income and four indicators of progress in school for Vietnam in 1996, using data from a cross-sectional household survey linked with community and schooling surveys that we collected in collaboration with the Vietnamese General Statistical Office that deal with these limitations as compared with alternatives. In a number of cases there are considerable differences, with our preferred estimates substantially larger than the alternatives (Figure 2.2 gives some examples). The estimates indicate that the income associations for child school success are fairly considerable – e.g. the income elasticity of completed grades is five

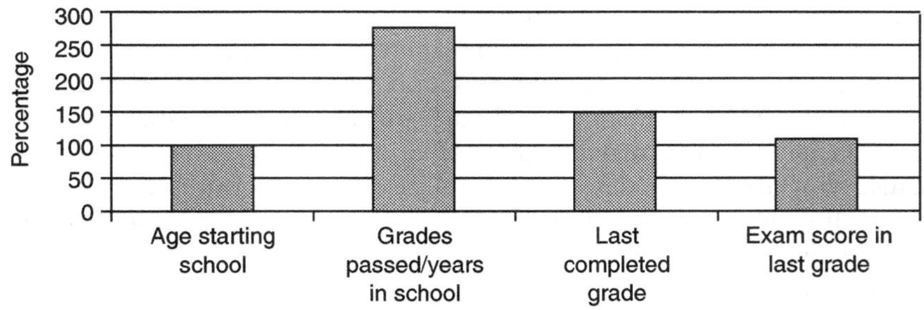

Figure 2.2 Impact of family income in preferred estimates relative to standard estimates, Vietnam 1996 (see Table 2.A.2).

times the median in the 42 earlier studies mentioned above. This association, moreover, is strongest *not* for completed grades on which most of the previous literature had focused, but for grades completed successfully per year of school. Exploration of the sensitivity of the estimates indicate that the estimated associations with income are significantly larger with predicted income to represent longer-run income, with control for censoring, and with representation of additional channels through which there may be effects beyond just the number of completed grades.

These estimates are for a particular context, but in some ways an especially interesting one because the government of Vietnam has publicly emphasized the importance of equality as a motive for policy and yet there appear to be substantial inequalities in schooling (and in schooling policies) associated with family income. These results also suggest that much of the previous literature may understate the true associations of household income with child school success and overstate true intergenerational social mobility and equality of opportunity in other countries. Of course the family-income association, while being of interest for the policy concern about distribution, does not necessarily carry over to the question of the causal effect of family income on child schooling progress. But it appears that the literature that is interpreted to provide evidence on the causal effects is subject to these same limitations (as well as others that are discussed immediately below), so such studies also tend to underestimate the role of family income on child education.

Associations versus causality

Most studies on child education and family background do not provide convincing evidence of causality, particularly with regard to genetic endowments and other components of family background that are not usually observed in available data sets. Indeed, if there are intergenerational correlations in genetic endowments that facilitate learning and are rewarded in labor markets, much or even all of the associations between most of the primary family background variables that are used in the literature – income, schooling, occupation – may be due to such correlations and not to the causal effects of these family background variables themselves. Most studies of the impact of other out-of-school activities on child education also do not provide persuasive evidence regarding causality because they treat right-side behaviorally-determined variables, such as child health and nutritional status, as if they are predetermined rather than dealing with the estimation problems that arise because these variables are also determined by household behaviors. I review selected studies that relate to these problems in this section with reference to evidence regarding the impact of endowments on schooling and the returns to schooling – including the impact of mother's schooling on child schooling – and the impact of pre-school health and nutrition status on child schooling.

Most of the large number of estimates of the impact of schooling – whether on wages or on other outcomes including that of parents' schooling on child education – assumes (usually implicitly) that schooling is predetermined and is independent of any relevant unobserved variables that might affect child education such as innate ability. Nevertheless, there has been considerable concern about ability bias in estimates of the wage returns to schooling. One important component of this literature has used data on identical twins to control for genetic endowments at conception and for other family endowments shared by twins.[19] This literature dates back at least a quarter century,[20] but has had a revival in recent years with focus on how random measurement error in years of schooling may be bias toward zero estimates using within twins data because the noise-to-signal ratio is much larger in such estimates than in the usual estimates.[21] Estimates for the United States and Australia suggest that in most cases there is substantial ability bias that may range over 100 percent (Figure 2.3).[22]

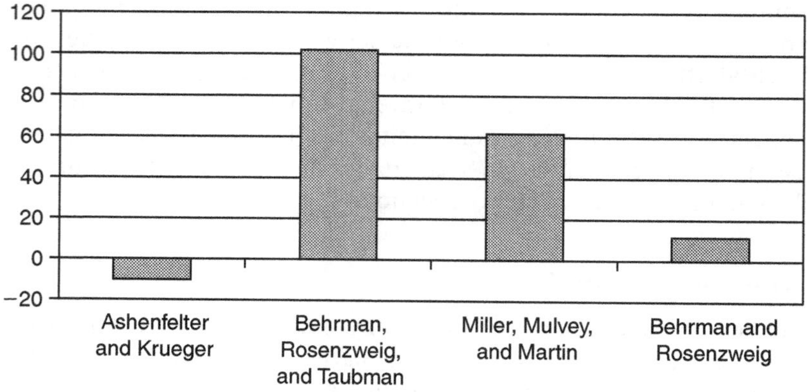

Figure 2.3 Estimated "ability bias" as percentage using twins data for U.S. and Australia (see Table 2.A.3).

These effects are consistent with endowments playing a substantial role in determining school. But what are these endowments? Elsewhere I demonstrate that there may be "ability" bias even if endowed ability does not affect schooling decisions directly, as long as ability is correlated with other family characteristics such as income that do affect schooling and that it is not possible to identify separately these individual components of "ability bias."[23] Thus the appropriate conclusion is that family background inclusive of the effects of genetic endowments has a substantial affect on child schooling and that if it is not controlled (including the unobserved components), not only will the impact of schooling be overestimated, but the determinants of schooling will be misunderstood.

Most of these twins studies do not address directly, however, the determinants of schooling. Several of our studies are exceptions to this generalization. In previous research, colleagues and I have used a combination of identical and fraternal twins to estimate how individual endowments affect years of schooling and quality of schooling.[24] Our estimates indicate that not only years of schooling, but also quality of schooling are allocated to reinforce endowment differences. This has important implications in terms of understanding the determinants of schooling and possible biases in estimated impacts of schooling. But because these are the individual-specific endowments that are examined, they do *not* include common family background shared by siblings. Instead, they are basically genetic endowments. So the policy implications do not point to a variable through which policy might work, but rather point to the limitations of policy effectiveness because of the importance of genetic determinants that policy is not likely to be able to affect.

In subsequent research, a co-author and I have examined directly the role of mother's schooling in determining child schooling. Widely held conventional wisdom is that an important return to investments in women's schooling is manifested in the increased schooling of the next generation. Moreover, it is also believed that increasing women's schooling has a greater beneficial educational impact on children than increasing men's schooling.[25] This is at times viewed as an important spillover or externality of women's schooling that justifies on efficiency grounds public subsidies (see p. 57). However, there are two fundamental problems with the findings on these intergenerational schooling relations. First, more "able" mothers may obtain more schooling, consistent with the literature on ability bias summarized in part above. If schooling or earnings ability is genetically transmitted to their children, the intergenerational schooling association may merely reflect that more able women, who have more schooling, have more able children, who obtain more schooling.[26] Second, even among mothers with the same abilities, those with higher levels of schooling may have children with greater academic and labor-market performances due to assortative mating. More schooled women in almost all societies marry more schooled men, and they thus marry more able men as well, given own ability-schooling correlations. Cross-sectional estimates are consistent with previous studies of the impact of parental schooling on child schooling attainment.[27] There is a significantly positive impact of mother's schooling that appears smaller if there is also control for father's schooling – indeed smaller than the coefficient estimate for father's schooling.[28] However, when twinning is exploited to estimate intergenerational schooling effects, the results are strikingly different. Controlling for women's earnings and child-rearing endowments and husbands' endowments and schooling leads to a marginally negative rather than a significantly positive coefficient for mother's schooling in the determination of child schooling (Figure 2.4). Our results thus suggest that the positive cross-sectional relationship between the schooling of mothers and their children is substantially biased upward due to correlations between schooling and heritable "ability" as well as assortative mating. Indeed our results indicate that an increase in the schooling of women would not have beneficial effects in terms of the schooling of children. We also find that increased maternal schooling leads to reduced home time for mothers. These findings together are consistent with the notion that the time of women is a significant factor in child-rearing.

There is a considerable literature on the impact of health and nutrition, particularly prior to school but also while at school, on child education. Most of this literature, however, reports associations between child schooling and health and nutritional status, without addressing that health and nutritional status also reflect behavioral decisions and that both schooling and health/nutritional status may respond to common factors such as endowments and therefore be correlated even if there are no causal effects. Recently I have been involved in studies that address these weaknesses in the literature by using statistical techniques or twins data to control for these possibilities.[29]

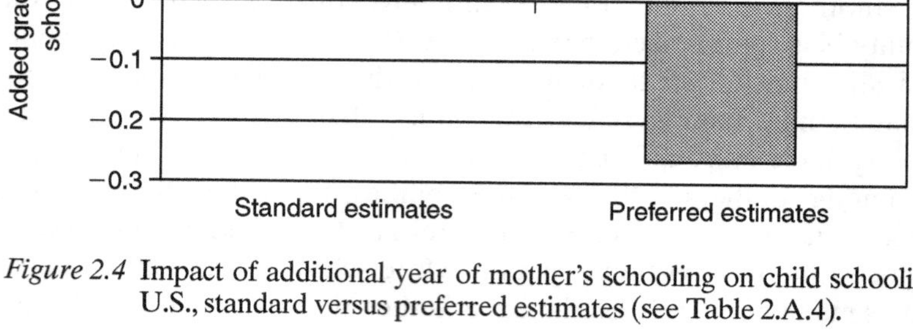

Figure 2.4 Impact of additional year of mother's schooling on child schooling in U.S., standard versus preferred estimates (see Table 2.A.4).

In one such study[30] we explore the impact of health and nutritional status at age five on whether there is school enrollment when age six or seven. This study employs longitudinal data to investigate the impact of child health (as indicated by nutritional status) on school enrollments in rural Pakistan using an explicit dynamic model for the preferred estimates. These estimates use price shocks when children were of pre-school age to control for behavior determining the child health stock measure.[31] Within the framework of the above discussion, the price shocks are past variables that determine child health, but that are not correlated with current decisions, including those regarding the age of initiating schooling. "Naive" estimates are compared with "preferred" estimates (that assume that child health/nutritional status is behaviorally determined and controlled for measurement error).[32] Separate estimates are presented for girls and boys because of alleged strong gender differences in this society. The preferred estimates indicate that the effect of health/nutritional status is significantly and substantially greater for girls than for boys – more than seven times larger for girls than for boys (0.51 compared to 0.07). The naive estimates yield estimates for both girls and boys that are about half of those obtained in the preferred procedure, with that for boys not significantly different from zero (Figure 2.5). If our preferred estimates are the true estimates, these naive estimates may be quite misleading – and, most of the estimates in the literature make the assumptions of the naive estimates. These results therefore reinforce strongly the importance of using estimation methods that are consistent with sensible models of the underlying household behaviors. In this case, they must recognize that households make decisions that affect child health and nutritional status as well as schooling enrollment, all possibly in the presence of unobservable variables such as innate health and ability endowments – in order to explore the impact of some choice variables on others using socioeconomic behavioral data.

In a second such study[33] we use data on adult female twins to estimate

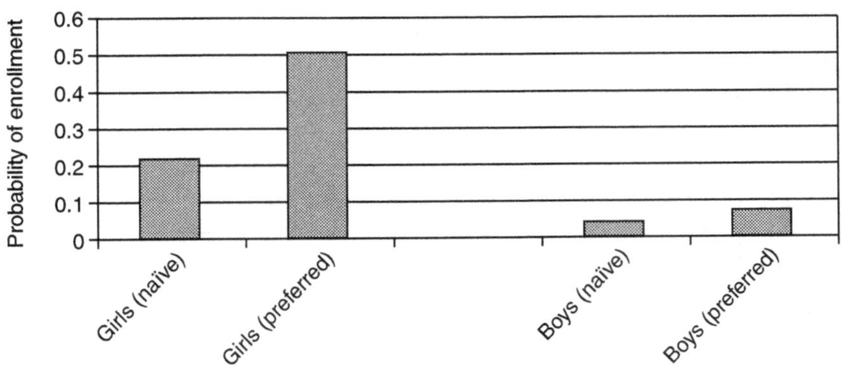

Figure 2.5 Impact of one standard deviation increase in health/nutritional status on school enrollment in rural Pakistan (see Table 2.A.5).

the relationships among fetal growth (i.e. birth weight/gestation), adult physical characteristics and adult schooling and wages. We develop a simple model of life-cycle resource allocations incorporating endowment heterogeneity to show in particular the difficulties in identifying the effects of adult physical characteristics on labor market outcomes. However, we also demonstrate that differences in birth weights between identical twins can be used to identify the life-cycle consequences on physical attributes, schooling and earnings of increasing fetal nutrient intake, for given endowments. We consider the estimated impact of fetal growth on such outcomes, both just using "standard" cross-sectional data and using "preferred" within-twins estimates to control for unobserved endowments (Figure 2.6). Our empirical results suggest that there are real payoffs to increasing body weight at birth. Increasing birth weight increases adult schooling attainment, adult height, and earnings. The estimates also imply that correlations between birth weight or adult body mass and adult outcomes that do not account for endowment heterogeneity:

1 understate considerably the beneficial returns to early interventions that increase fetal growth
2 overstate the consequences of higher birth weight for adult obesity
3 overstate the negative consequences of increased adult body mass on earnings.

These biases arise evidently because the genetic and family environmental factors associated with body mass are negatively correlated with both human capital investments and with endowments that augment earnings and human capital.[34]

These estimates have some important implications for policy. The significantly positive effects of fetal growth on schooling and adult height

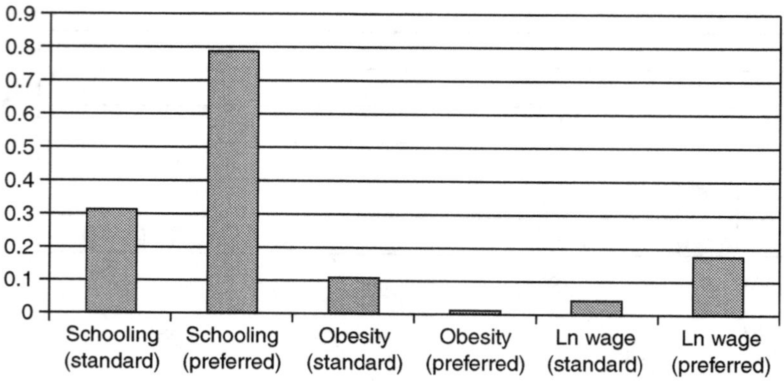

Figure 2.6 Estimated impact of fetal growth on schooling, obesity, and in wage for women in U.S., standard versus preferred estimates (see Table 2.A.6).

support programs that serve to increase weight at birth, such as Medicaid,[35] and the use of public resources to do so from an efficiency perspective if schooling has positive externalities as usually is assumed. In particular, the discouragement of smoking while pregnant would have real benefits for children that extend beyond survival chances – our estimates suggest, for example, that a mother who smokes one pack of cigarettes per day reduces the lifetime earnings of her child by over 10 percent. Finally, the incidence of twin births (and other multiple births) is growing with the increased use of medical procedures that augment fertility among older women. Our findings suggest that such procedures to the extent that they increase multiple births impose non-trivial costs on children's subsequent development. On average twins have 28 ounces less birth weight than single babies, which our estimates indicate translates into a reduction in schooling and then in lifetime earnings for such children of over 12 percent.

Context may be critical

Most studies do not establish clearly the context of their results and how, for example, household behaviors in response to incentives created by markets, culture, and policies may differ substantially depending on these and other aspects of context. The best social science empirical work makes this context explicit by modifying general frameworks to reflect the specific context and by interpreting the estimates in light of that context.

As noted above, we find that – once there is control for endowments and for assortative mating – there is no evidence of a positive impact of mother's schooling on child schooling for our sample from the United States. It appears that more schooling for women in this context increases their time in the labor market and thus reduces their time educating their children. Of course that does not mean that more schooling for women is necessarily bad. There may be many gains from increasing women's schooling. It is just that one of those gains is not more child schooling – in fact there may be a reduction in child schooling. Our findings, however, must be interpreted with care because they are outcome- and context-specific. It is possible that increased mother's schooling in the same environment leads to other improved outcomes for children, such as their health, particularly if improvements in these other outcomes are relatively information-intensive rather than time-intensive. And it is also possible that in other labor market contexts and cultures increased women's schooling leads to increased child schooling. Indeed, elsewhere[36] we report strong evidence of that effect in rural India in recent decades, a context in which more schooled women did not appreciably increase their participation in market activities outside the home. Anticipating the consequences of investments in women's schooling thus requires attention to the role that schooling plays in the marriage market as well as to opportunities in the labor market for women.

Another important example of the importance of context is reflected in the estimates of "ability bias" that are summarized above. As noted, these range from 11 to 102 percent (Figure 2.3), putting aside the one negative estimate for reasons noted above. As also noted, these estimates reflect not only the effects of ability, but of various other aspects of family background that may be correlated with ability and that affect both schooling and subsequent earnings. This means that if, for example, policies change over time so the association of child schooling attainment with family background is weakened (all else being equal), the estimated "ability bias" will fall. The two extreme estimates of positive "ability bias" are both for the U.S., with 102 percent for a cohort born in 1917–1927 and 11 percent for a cohort born in 1936–1955. This decline is consistent with a considerable decline over time in the correlation between policies that facilitate schooling attainment and family background. Thus it would appear that in this case the changing schooling policy context over time has weakened the influence of family background on schooling.

The estimates in the other studies summarized above also are context dependent in a fairly straightforward manner. The relatively great impact of nutrition on the age of school enrollment of girls in rural Pakistan, for instance, is in the context of a relatively poor and malnourished population with strong gender differentiation favoring males. These strong effects would not be expected to carry over to better-nourished populations, nor would the strong gender differentials be expected to carry over to populations with less gender differentiation.

Policy motives and policy implications

Putting aside questions addressed above regarding obtaining good estimates of causal effects, most empirical studies related to the topic of this chapter providing some information useful for evaluating the efficiency and distributional policy motives for policies related to schooling. But this information usually is limited and insufficient to provide a basis for policy decisions – often on the benefits or impact side and even more often on the cost side. Most studies related to this chapter only assess what the impact is of some policy directly or indirectly on schooling or of schooling on some outcome. Better estimates of these effects are an input, probably an important input, into better assessments of policy, but are only an input and thus not sufficient in themselves to provide policy guidance. It certainly is not sufficient to demonstrate that, say, schooling has a big effect on wages or health or nutrition to make the analytical case for subsidies for schooling. It likewise is not enough to demonstrate that, say, better prenatal, perinatal, and infant nutrition have large effects on schooling to make the analytical case for subsidies for such nutrition. To make an analytical case for policies and to place them in the efficiency and distributional policy hierarchies defined above more information is often needed on the benefit/impact side and almost always on the cost side.

On the benefit/impact side, the problem is that studies in the literature typically only address part of the benefits. This is perhaps most striking with regard to the efficiency motive for policies. Fundamental to this motive is that the social returns to some action, such as attending school, are different from the private returns. But most studies address only the private returns, not the difference between the social and the private returns.[37] Just because the private returns are high to schooling, for example, does not mean that the social returns are higher yet so that public subsidies are warranted on efficiency grounds. What is central to the assessment of the efficiency motive is the estimation of the difference between the private and the social returns. Such discrepancies are referred to as knowledge spillovers, externalities, or external benefits in terms of more responsible political and social participation. But these are very difficult to measure, though a few studies have made some progress, and have indeed found evidence of positive externalities to schooling.[38]

It is perhaps useful to mention one widely claimed spillover or externality of schooling – the nonmarket effects of schooling on fertility and human resource investments (health, nutrition, education) of other family members. Often these are alleged to be considerable, particularly for women's schooling (though the estimates discussed suggest that at least for the impact on child education in the United States, the empirical basis for this argument may be a lot weaker than generally assumed). But if more schooling for a woman means that her children are better educated (or better nourished), does that mean that there is an efficiency argument for subsidizing women's schooling? In this case there is a spillover on another individual that is not mediated by the market. Is that sufficient for the efficiency argument? If a worker in a firm or a farm has positive spillover benefits on other workers through increasing their marginal productivities, is that an argument for subsidizing the schooling of such workers from an efficiency perspective? Generally in the worker/firm case, the answer is thought to be no; such a worker is thought to be rewarded for spillover effects within the firm through higher wage rates, so there are private incentives for greater investment in the worker's schooling to account for such intra-firm spillovers. Why does not the same logic hold for spillovers in the family? Why do marriage markets not reward more-schooled women if there are spillovers of their schooling in the family? That these questions are posed to suggest that that there are nonmarket effects of schooling on other family members does not obviously mean that there is an efficiency argument for public subsidies for schooling. Further thought needs to be given as to why, in a particular context, those intra-familial spillovers are not internalized in the family in the same way that intra-firm spillovers are thought to be internalized in the firm.

For the distributional motive for policies, there also are some aspects of the benefits/impacts that are not addressed thoroughly in many empirical studies. One such aspect is how well benefits are targeted to the intended recipients given the distributional goal. For example, if the distributional concern is poverty alleviation, how well are the benefits targeted toward the poor? There is a literature on such targeting, which emphasizes particularly developing countries and includes concerns about mistargeting and the political economy of targeting given the desire for program sustainability.[39] But the targeting concerns are not central in many studies. Yet many programs that are ostensibly directed in part toward the poor may shift considerable resources, perhaps more resources, to those who are better off than to the poor. In the study on schooling and income associations in Vietnam discussed above for example, we explore some dimensions of how schooling policies relate to household incomes. School fees are progressive, but school fees are only about a third of what households pay directly to schools, and a much smaller proportion of total household school-related expenditures. All household expenditures paid directly to schools increase with household income much less proportionately than do school fees alone, so the overall structure of such payments is much less progressive than is the structure of school fees alone. Because school enrollments are positively related to household income, moreover, the extent of progressivity in school fee structures is less for the entire population than it is for the selected subset that has children enrolled in school. Further, the two school quality measures that are most strongly positively associated with child school success are allocated so that they are significantly more available for higher-income households, which means that part of the higher household school expenditures of higher-income households is because they are obtaining higher-quality schooling and not because of progressive charges for the same quality schooling across income classes. Such analysis suggests that in this case, and perhaps in others, many aspects of schooling subsidies are not well targeted to the poor despite rhetoric to that effect. The same results on a general level may hold for many school-related policies in other countries, including the United States, but such possibilities are not considered in many studies.

Information to guide policy choices also is limited on the cost side, probably even more so than on the benefits/impacts side. In order to assess where particular policies stand in the efficiency or the distributional hierarchy, it is essential to have cost as well as benefit estimates. A policy with small benefits and smaller costs may be much more desirable than a policy with much greater benefits – but also with even larger costs. Whether a particular intervention has a large or a small impact on schooling or on some outcome affected by schooling alone obviously does not provide information with which to judge the merit of the policy. Yet there are substantial limitations in regard to the evaluation of costs in this literature. First of all, many studies do not address the cost side of policy interventions at all, just the impact side. While the latter provides useful inputs for policy evaluation, as noted, it is not sufficient. Second, studies that do assess the costs often limit their assessment to the direct costs or to governmental budgetary costs. But the distortion costs may be large – in some cases larger than the direct costs. So, while it is true that they are harder to measure, the failure to do so may lead to quite misleading inferences about the policy hierarchies. Third, the efficiency motive for policy interventions pertains to differences in social versus private costs in addition to differences in social versus private benefits. Indeed, some of the efficiency arguments made for public subsidies related to schooling are based on such possible differences in social versus private costs. Capital markets, for example, are said to be imperfect for human capital investments with the result that private costs exceed social costs. Insurance markets do not permit private pooling of the uncertainties for such investments. Yet empirical estimates of possible differences between social and private costs are scarce indeed.

Thus, our informational bases for informing policies choices in this area are, in many respects, weak or almost nonexistent. Policies have been, are being, and will be made in the absence of good estimates of such effects. The a priori considerations that are discussed above (and in back-of-the envelope calculations) often might improve the evaluation of alternative policies prior to and subsequent to implementation. But social scientists potentially could contribute to strengthening the foundation for such policies through better and more complete estimates of the critical empirical magnitudes.

Conclusions

Making inferences in the social sciences is difficult, including regarding the effects of family background on child education. To advance our understanding of such possible effects – before the school-starting bell as well as after the school-closing bell – a skillful combination of better data and better analysis is needed. Much of the work to date has substantial measurement problems and confuses associations with causality. More careful considerations of some of these factors suggests that in some ways the existing literature understates the importance of family background on child education – particularly regarding some of the measurement issues for education and income, as well as related estimation issues.

However, in other ways, the existing literature may overstate or misstate in an indeterminate direction the causal effects of components of family background on child education. The usual failure to control for genetic endowments and assortative mating on unobserved characteristics in marriage markets, for example, appears to result in substantial upward biases in estimates of the impact of mothers' schooling on child schooling in the United States. Similarly, the effects of early nutrition starting at conception may not be well represented by conventional estimates that do not control for endowment effects and behavioral choices that affect health and nutrition. Further, the context regarding such factors as market development and gender roles may make a substantial difference. Therefore, as illustrated, though there may not be evidence of important causal impact of mother's schooling on child schooling once there is control for genetic endowments and assortative mating in the United States, there is evidence of an important effect in a rural Indian context in which women do not receive much in the way of returns to more schooling in labor markets. For another example, it would appear that the schooling policy context has changed over time in the United States so as to reduce the association between family background and schooling attainment. Finally, more clarity regarding policy motives and more attention to gaps in our information concerning critical benefits and costs would be beneficial. Most of the available studies provide no or very little information about efficiency motives for educational-related policy interventions. They neither provide sufficient guidance about how the impacts relate to distributional motives nor place such interventions into the distributional policy hierarchy. And most studies provide little or no information about costs, particularly distortion costs, that must be incorporated in order to fit possible policy interventions into either the efficiency or the distributional policy hierarchies.

Appendix

Table 2.A.1 Estimated income elasticities for the United States[a]

Year	*Schooling indicator*	*Income elasticity*	*Source*[b]	*Notes*
1957	Years of schooling	0.04*	Hauser and Daymont (1977)	Wisconsin high school graduates; parental income; control for household characteristics.
1978	Years of schooling	−0.03 to 0.00	Datcher (1982)	Income; control for household and community characteristics.
1981	Years of schooling	0.02*	Behrman and Taubman (1986)	Income; control for household characteristics.
1982	Years of schooling	0.09*	Hill and Duncan (1987)	Income averaged over three years; control for household and community characteristics.
1981	Years of schooling	0.04*	Behrman and Taubman (1989)	Income; control for household characteristics.
1979–1986	Negative or insignificant for college grades and graduation probabilities		Datcher-Loury and Garman (1995)	Income; control for individual test scores, race, and college mean test scores.

Notes

a Income elasticities give the percentage change in the schooling indicator relative to a given percentage change in income. For example the income elasticity of 0.04 in the first row means that years of schooling increases by 4 percent if income doubles (increases by 100 percent). These are the estimates for the United States only as extracted from Behrman and Knowles (1997) as reproduced in Behrman and Knowles (1999). Income elasticities calculated at point of sample means for what appears to be preferred estimates.

b Sources for this table are as follows: J. R. Behrman and P. Taubman, "Birth order, schooling and earnings." *Journal of Labor Economics* 4, 1986, S121–S145; J. R. Behrman and P. Taubman, "Is schooling 'mostly in the genes'? nature–nurture decomposition with data on relatives," *Journal of Political Economy* 97, 1989, 1425–1446; L. Datcher, "Effect of community and family background on achievement," *Review of Economics and Statistics* 64, 1982, 32–41; L. Datcher-Loury and D. Garman, "College selectivity and earnings," *Journal of Labor Economics* 13, 1995, 289–308; R. M. Hauser and T. N. Daymont, "Schooling, ability, and earnings: cross sectional findings 8 to 14 years after high school graduation," *Sociology of Education* 50, 1977, 182–206; M. S. Hill and G. J. Duncan, "Parental family income and the socio-economic attainment of children," *Social Science Research* 16, 1987, 39–73.

* Indicates that the underlying point estimates are significantly nonzero at the 5 percent level.

Table 2.A.2 Ratio of estimated elasticities of individual school progress indicators with respect to preferred income indicator (predicted income per household member with control for censoring but without control for school and commune characteristics) to alternatives, Vietnam 1996[a]

Individual school progress indicators	*Basic estimate as percentage of estimate with*		
	Annual income, no control for censoring	*Predicted income, no control for censoring*	*School/ commune fixed effects*
1 Age when started school	100	102	128
2 Grades passed/years since started school	276	164	144
3 Last completed grade	148	200	101
4 Exam score in last completed grade	108	100	106

Note

a See note a in Table A.2 for definition of elasticity. Excerpted from J. R. Behrman and J. C. Knowles, "Household income and child schooling in Vietnam," *World Bank Economic Review* 13, 1999, 211–256, Table 3. For the basic estimates (a) predicted income based on a number of household assets is used to represent longer-run income without short-run transitory income components and (b) censored normal regressions are used for age when started school and for last completed grade because of right censoring and upper limit tobits are used for grades passed/years since started school because of the mass point at 1.0.

Table 2.A.3 Summary of recent Ln earnings relations for identical twins with control for measurement error in schooling

Source[a]	*Sample size, year, gender and race composition, and mean age*	*Preferred estimates*[b]		*"Ability Bias"*[c]
		IV Level	*IV within MZ*	
1 Twinsburg, Ohio annual twins festival sample, Ashenfelter and Krueger (1994, Tables 3 and 9)	147 MZ twins at 1991 Festival – 54 percent female, 94 percent white, mean age 36.5	0.116	0.129	−10%
2 United States' National Academy of Science–National Research Council twins sample of white veteran males born in 1917–1927, Behrman, Rosenzweig, and Taubman (1994, Table 4)	141 white male MZ twins, 1973, mean age 51	0.101	0.050	102%
3 Australian Twins Register 1980–1982 and 1988–1989, Miller, Mulvey, and Martin (1995, Table 5)	602 MZ twins – 51.4 percent female, mean age 36.8[d]	0.073	0.045	62%
4 Minnesota Twins Registry based on all twins born in the state in 1936–1955, with survey in 1994, Behrman and Rosenzweig (1999, Table 3)	720 MZ twins – 65.6 percent female, mean age 46.8	0.118[b]	0.104	11%

Source: Behrman and Rosenzweig (1999, Table 1) with addition of their estimates in their Table 3.

Notes

a Sources used in this table are as follows: O. Ashenfelter and A. Krueger, "Estimates of the economic return to schooling from a new sample of twins," *American Economic Review* 84, 1994, 1157–1174, Tables 3 and 9; J. R. Behrman and M. R. Rosenzweig, "The returns to schooling: new evidence from twins data," *Economics and Education Review* 18, 1999, 159–167, Table 3; J. R. Behrman, M. R. Rosenzweig, and P. Taubman, "Endowments and the allocation of schooling in the family and in the marriage markets the twins experiment," *Journal of Political Economy* 102, 1994, 1131–1174, Table 4; P. Miller, C. Mulvey, and N. Martin, "What do twin studies tell us about the economic returns to education? A comparison of US and Australian findings," *American Economic Review* 85, 1995, 586–599, Table 5. An earlier version of this table appeared as Table 1 in Behrman and Rosenzweig 1999, op. cit.

b All the estimates reported here use schooling reports for each twin by another respondent as an instrument to control for measurement error. Behrman, Rosenzweig, and Taubman (1994) use the report by each twin's oldest child. The other studies use a report by the co-twin and find significant positive correlated measurement errors across reports by each respondent (i.e., for own and for co-twin's schooling).

c This is the percentage difference between the IV within MZ estimates and the IV level estimates relative to the latter.

d Use average income of full-time workers in each two-digit occupational group from the 1986 Census of Population and Housing for earnings variable.

Table 2.A.4 Estimates of the effects of mother's and father's schooling on children's schooling: married female MZ twins

Variable/estimation procedure	*Cross-section*	*Cross-section*	*Within-MZ*	*Within-MZ*	*Within-MZ, IV*
Mother's schooling	0.332	0.137	−0.245	−0.274	−0.263
	(6.88)[a]	(2.73)	(1.69)	(1.89)	(1.82)
Father's schooling	–	0.286	–	0.133	0.141
		(6.01)		(1.87)	(1.97)

Source: J. R. Behrman and M. R. Rosenzweig, "Does increasing women's schooling raise the schooling of the next generation?," *American Economic Review* 92, 2002, 323–334, Table 4.

Note

a Absolute value of t-statistic in parentheses.

Table 2.A.5 Impact of increase of one standard deviation in health/nutritional status on probability of school enrollment in rural Pakistan[a]

	"Naive" estimates	*Preferred estimates*
Girls	0.22[b]	0.51[b]
Boys	0.04	0.07[b]

Notes

a Source: H. Alderman, J. R. Behrman, V. Lavy, and R. Menon, "Child nutrition, child health, and school enrollment: A longitudinal analysis," *Journal of Human Resources* 36, 201, 185–205, Table 2. The "Naive" estimates assume that child health/ nutritional status is predetermined in the statistical sense (i.e., not correlated with any unobserved variables such as innate endowments and not subject to measurement error). The preferred estimates use the past price shocks as instruments to purge the measured child health/nutritional estimates of any correlation with unobserved variables and of measurement error. Child health/nutritional status is measured by Z scores for height (Z scores measure how many standard deviations an observation is above or below the gender-specific international references).

b Significantly nonzero at 5 percent level.

Table 2.A.6 OLS and within-MZ twin estimates of fetal growth on own schooling attainment, BMI, height and the Ln wage

Variable	*Schooling*		*BMI*[c]		*Height*		*Ln wage*	
Estimation procedure	*OLS*	*Within-MZ*	*OLS*	*Within-MZ*	*OLS*	*Within-MZ*	*OLS*	*Within-MZ*
Fetal growth	0.309	0.786	0.110	0.0109	1.49	1.48	0.0437	0.178
	(2.09)[a]	(3.29)[b]	(2.16)[a]	(0.13)[b]	(7.66)	(6.04)	(1.51)[a]	(2.37)[b]

Source: Excerpted from J. R. Behrman and M. R. Rosenzweig, "Returns to birthweight," *Review of Economics and Statistics*, forthcoming 2004, Table 2. Fetal growth is birth weight/gestation.

Notes

a Absolute value of robust t-statistic with clustering by individuals.

b Absolute value of robust t-statistic.

c BMI is divided by 100 so coefficient estimates are of the same order of magnitude as for the other columns.

Notes

1 Thanks to J. Lawrence Aber, Dalton Conley, Eric Hanushek, Giorgio Topa, and other conference participants for helpful questions, comments, and suggestions for improving this revision. Behrman alone is responsible for all interpretations.

2 Rosenzweig and Wolpin provide a number of interesting illustrations. (M. R. Rosenzweig and K. I. Wolpin, "Natural 'natural experiments' in economics," *Journal of Economic Literature* 38, 2000, 827–874.)

3 Households are usually collections of individuals who, in addition to many commonalities, may have different preferences and resources. There therefore may be (often implicit) bargaining among household members, including between parents and children, about the use of household resources. For simplicity, these possibilities are ignored in what follows. This does not affect any of the points that are made at this level of generality except that the resources, preferences, etc. would have to be included for each of the individuals rather than for "the household." Likewise, there is a related question of what determines the make-up of households – family formation, separation, fertility, morality, co-residence with non-nuclear family members, etc. These may be critical questions for analysis of some problems, but can be abstracted from for most purposes of this paper.

4 See, for example, Ben-Porath or Pollak (Y. Ben-Porath, "The f-connection: families, friends, and firms and the organization of exchange," *Population and Development Review* 6:1, 1980, 1–30; R. A. Pollak, "A transaction cost approach to families and households," *Journal of Economic Literature* 23, 1985, 581–608).

5 I use "school quality" throughout this paper as a shorthand way of summarizing all school inputs (e.g. books, computers, classrooms, teachers, organization, management skills). Of course there is considerable controversy about exactly which of these are important for child education (e.g. Hanushek), but that is a side issue for the purpose of this chapter. (E. Hanushek, "The economics of schooling," *Journal of Economic Literature* 24, 1986, 1141–1177; E. Hanushek, "Interpreting recent research on schooling in developing countries," *The World Bank Research Observer* 10:2, 1995, 227–246.)

6 This point is related to what good experiments can and cannot reveal. A good experiment can estimate the gross effect, conditional on all the other constraints facing the household being fixed. But it cannot give the gross effect under conditions in which some of these constraints change. Nor can it give the direct production function effect even if the other constraints remain the same. Good estimates of structural models of household behavior could do both of these, conditional on the validity of maintained hypotheses about the structure. But that is another story, one that is beyond the scope of this chapter.

7 Among the right-side variables are ones that were determined in the past, such as previous education or health. Because these variables were determined in part by unobserved variables such as genetic endowments, to avoid bias in their estimated coefficients, statistical procedures can be used (that depend on there being past variables such as price shocks that do not persist to the current period). Also note that these relations do not include on the right-side variables that are currently determined together with the dependent variable, so they generally cannot be used to estimate the effect say, of, the current change in health and nutritional status on the current change in education. Finally, note that some variables that may be predetermined from the point of view of a single household may not be predetermined when a number of households are affected. For example, consider again a drop in the price of schooling. From the

point of view of a single household, this means that the cost of attending school of a fixed quality has declined. But if that is the case for a number of a households in the same school catchment area, school quality also might change if, for example, a number of additional students are induced to attend and school quality deteriorates due to congestion.

8 They include: no entity having sufficient market power to affect prices, no externalities the effects of which are transmitted other than through markets, no scale economies for production ranges that are high relative to market sizes, all entities are net revenue maximizers, a complete set of markets including future and insurance and information markets. These conditions are not observed in the real world, so efficiency is not attained. Among the critical shortcomings of real world markets are lacking or incomplete insurance, futures and information markets – shortcomings that relate centrally to the concerns of the present paper because they affect investments, including those in human resources. Not only are the conditions for efficiency not nearly satisfied in the real world, but a change that would lead to efficiency if it were reducing the only distortion between private and social marginal incentives does *not* necessarily lead to greater efficiency in the presence of multiple distortions between private and social incentives (one aspect of the "theory of the second best"). The intuitive reason for this fact can be seen by considering that two distortions may be partially offsetting each other, so that removing one while the other persists may reduce rather than increase efficiency.

9 The most obvious costs, and those to which many governmental officials and some analysts tend to give primary (some times, exclusive) emphasis, are the direct governmental budgetary costs. These include program design, implementation, monitoring, and evaluation costs in addition to the costs of the services provided by the program. While public officials often focus on the direct costs in evaluating the cost side of potential or actual programs, the indirect or distortionary costs may be large. These include the distortions that are introduced in markets by policies. Some of these might be the direct result of the nature of the policies. For example, policies that subsidize some schools but not others on the basis of ownership (e.g. public but not private schools), all else equal, are likely to introduce distortions that unduly shift resources to that type of school. Yet another aspect of distortions pertains to the effects of raising resources for financing the public expenditures required by the policy. For the United States, for example, it has been estimated that the distortionary cost (often called the "deadweight loss") of raising a dollar of tax revenue ranges from $0.17 to $1.00, depending on the type of tax used (e.g. M. Feldstein, *A Tax Avoidance and the Deadweight Loss of the Income Tax*, Cambridge, MA: National Bureau of Economic Research Working Paper No. 5055, 1995).

10 There is some arbitrariness in whether some measurement problems are systematic measurement errors or omitted variable biases. For the points made in this chapter, this is not an important issue. So I consider what might arguably be called different forms of omitted variable bias in this section as well as the next.

11 See W. T. Bielby, R. M. Hauser, and D. L. Featherman, "Response errors of non-black males in models of the stratification process," in *Latent Variables in Socio-Economic Models*, edited by D. A. Aigner and A. S. Goldberger, Amsterdam: North Holland Publishing Co., 1977; O. Ashenfelter and A. Krueger, "Estimates of the economic return to schooling from a new sample of twins," *American Economic Review* 84:5 (December), 1994, 1157–1174; J. R. Behrman, M. R. Rosenzweig, and P. Taubman, "Endowments and the allocation of schooling in the family and in the marriage market: the twins experiment," *Journal of Political Economy* 102:6, 1994, 1131–1174; O. Ashenfelter and

C. Rouse, "Income, schooling and ability: evidence from a new sample of identical twins," *Quarterly Journal of Economics* 113:1 (February), 1998, 253–284; J. R. Behrman and M. R. Rosenzweig, "The returns to schooling: new evidence from twins data," *Economics of Education Review* 18, 1999, 159–167.

12 The examples mentioned in the rest of this paragraph are: Behrman and Birdsall, Behrman, Birdsall, and Kaplan, and Birdsall for Brazil; Alderman, *et al.* (1996a, 1996b) and Behrman, Ross, Sabot, and Tropp for Pakistan; and Behrman, Rosenzweig, and Taubman (1994, 1996) for the United States. While a number of other studies give more mixed results (e.g. Hanushek), in a number of these studies interpretation is more difficult because of lack of clarity about what is being estimated (e.g. including income in what is purported to be an education production function) or estimation problems due to failures to control for right-side variables that are choices of the household or for unobserved factors. (J. R. Behrman and N. Birdsall, "The quality of schooling: quantity alone is misleading," *American Economic Review* 73, 1983, 928–946, J. R. Behrman and N. Birdsall, "The quality of schooling: reply," *American Economic Review* 75, 1985, 1202–1205; J. R. Behrman, N. Birdsall, and R. Kaplan, "The quality of schooling and labor market outcomes in Brazil: some further explorations," in N. Birdsall and R. Sabot (eds) *Opportunity Foregone: Education in Brazil*, Baltimore, MD: The Johns Hopkins University Press for the Inter-American Development Bank, 1996, 245–266; N. Birdsall, "Public inputs and child schooling in Brazil," *Journal of Development Economics* 18:1, 1985, 67–86; H. Alderman, J. R. Behrman, D. Ross, and R. Sabot, "Decomposing the gender gap in cognitive skills in a poor rural economy," *Journal of Human Resources* 31:1 (Winter), 1996a, 229–254, H. Alderman, J. R. Behrman, D. Ross, and R. Sabot, "The returns to endogenous human capital in Pakistan's rural wage labor market," *Oxford Bulletin of Economics and Statistics* 58:1 (February), 1996b, 29–55; J. R. Behrman, D. Ross, and R. Sabot, "Improving the quality versus increasing the quantity of schooling: evidence for rural Pakistan," Topics in the Economics and Growth of Developing Areas of the B.E., *Journal of the Economics and Growth of Developing Areas*, forthcoming 2004; J. R. Behrman, M. R. Rosenzweig, and P. Taubman, "Endowments and the allocation of schooling in the family and in the marriage market: the twins experiment," *Journal of Political Economy* 102:6, 1994, 1131–1174; J. R. Behrman, M. R. Rosenzweig, and P. Taubman, "College choice and wages: estimates using data on female twins," *Review of Economics and Statistics* 73:4, 1996, 672–685; Hanushek, op. cit.)

13 As is well known, random error in a dependent variable does not cause biases in the estimated coefficients, so random error in years of schooling for children is not a problem here. But systematic errors in the child years of schooling measure may cause biases in the estimated coefficients of the determinants, which may (or may not) be large.

14 Such as that presented by G. S. Becker, 1967, "Human capital and the personal distribution of income: an analytical approach," Ann Arbor, MI: University of Michigan, Woytinsky Lecture, republished in Gary S. Becker, *Human Capital*, New York, NY: NBER, 2nd edition 1975, 94–117.

15 A minority of previous studies had addressed one or more of these limitations. I note here some examples, though not an exhaustive set of references. To address the first limitation regarding using current annual income or expenditure, Glewwe and Jacoby, Montgomery and Kouame and Tansel instrument household expenditure and Alderman, Behrman, Ross, and Sabot instrument household income. With regard to the second limitation of focusing narrowly on completed schooling, Alderman, Behrman, Lavy and Menon, Glewwe and Jacoby, and Glewwe, Jacoby, and King explore the relation of income with the

age of starting school and Alderman, Behrman, Ross, and Sabot (1996a, 1996b) and Alderman, Behrman, Khan, Ross, and Sabot investigate the relation between income and cognitive achievement. With regard to the third limitation of censored data, King and Lillard and Alderman, Behrman, Ross, and Sabot control for right-censoring in years of completed schooling data. But, again, these examples and other studies that address one or a few of these limitations noted in the text are a small proportion of the literature. (P. Glewwe and H. Jacoby, "An economic analysis of delayed primary school enrollment and childhood malnutrition in a low income country," *Review of Economics and Statistics* 77:1, 1995a, 156–169; P. Glewwe and H. Jacoby, *School Enrollment and Completion in Viet Nam: An Investigation of Recent Downward Trends*, Washington, DC: World Bank, mimeo, 1995b; M. R. Montgomery and A. Kouzme, *Fertility and Child Schooling in Cote d'Ivoire: Is There a Tradeoff?*, Stony Brook, NY: SUNY, mimeo, 1993; A. Tansel, "School attainment, parental education and gender in Cote d'Ivoire and Ghana," *Economic Development and Cultural Change*, 1997; H. Alderman, J. R. Behrman, D. Ross, and R. Sabot, "Decomposing the gender gap in cognitive skills in a poor rural economy," *Journal of Human Resources* 31:1 (Winter), 1996a, 229–254; H. Alderman, J. R. Behrman, V. Lavy, and R. Menon, "Child nutrition, child health, and school enrollment: a longitudinal analysis," *Journal of Human Resources* 36:1 (Winter), 2001, 185–205; Glewwe and Jacoby, op. cit.; P. Glewwe, H. Jacoby, and E. M. King, "Early childhood nutrition and academic achievement: a longitudinal data analysis," *Journal of Public Economics* 81, 2001, 345–368; Alderman, Behrman, Ross and Sabot, op. cit.; H. Alderman, J. R. Behrman, S. D. Ross, and R. Sabot, "The income gap in cognitive skills in rural Pakistan," *Economic Development and Cultural Change* 46:1 (October), 1997, 97–122; E. M. King and L. A. Lillard, "Education policy and schooling attainment in Malaysia and the Philippines," *Economics of Education Review* 6:2, 1987; Alderman, Behrman, Ross, and Sabot, op. cit.)

16 The same point holds for intergenerational income mobility. Behrman and Taubman (1990), Solon, and Zimmerman, for example, report estimates of intergenerational income correlations for the United States that are about twice as high (suggesting much less mobility) than previous estimates because they use longitudinal data to eliminate the transitory component in annual income. (J. R. Behrman and P. Taubman, "The intergenerational correlation between children's adult earnings and their parents' income: results from the Michigan panel survey of income dynamics," *The Review of Income and Wealth* 36:2, 1990, 115–127; G. R. Solon, "Intergenerational income mobility in the United States," *American Economic Review* 82:3, 1992, 393–408; D. J. Zimmerman, "Regression toward mediocrity in economic stature," *American Economic Review* 82:3, 1992, 409–429.)

17 This bias may be in either direction, depending in part on what income measure is used. It may be upward, for example, if total income is used and households reduce their total income (and possibly therefore their expenditure) when they have school-aged children through reduced child labor in order to increase schooling. But even if total income falls, expenditures may increase through dissavings to cover schooling costs, possibly with the opposite bias. Likewise the bias may be in the opposite direction if adult (head, father) income dominates in household income and parents increase their work efforts and income when children are of school age to finance their children's schooling.

18 The authors include these other variables because they are interested in obtaining the estimated causal impact of family income net of these other factors (as observed in a previous note). To answer the question regarding the extent of

the associations between child schooling and parental household income, however, it is desirable that there is not to be control for other characteristics that are correlated with income because the true association with income is likely to be misunderstood if such characteristics are included.

19 The within-twins estimates are conditional on the assumption that the within-twins schooling difference is due to stochastic shocks that do not directly affect earnings and that unobserved endowments enter into the specification used linearly (though in the determination of level variables, they may interact with other variables if, for example, a semilog or log specification is used, as is standard for wage functions). Bound and Solon present a critique of the twins approach. Behrman, Rosenzweig, and Taubman present estimates that indicate that within-twins variations in birth weight (due to chance events such as location in the womb) significantly predict within-twins schooling differences, but not within-twins earnings differences net of schooling effects (also see below). There are other components of this literature that use instrumental variable methods to attempt to abstract from ability bias (e.g. see Card and Rosenzweig and Wolpin). Controversy continues about the importance of this bias. (J. Bound and G. Solon, "Double trouble: on the value of twins-based estimation of the return to schooling," *Economics of Education Review* 18:2, 1999, 169–182; J. R. Behrman, R. Rosenzweig, and P. Taubman, "Endowments and the allocation of schooling in the family and in the marriage market: the twins experiment," *Journal of Political Economy* 102:6, 1994, 1131–1174; D. E. Card, "New developments in the economics of schooling," in O. Ashenfelter and D. Card (eds) *Handbook of Labor Economics*, Vol. 4, Amsterdam: North Holland Publishing Co., 1999; Rosenzweig and Wolpin, op. cit.)

20 See, for example, J. R. Behrman and P. Taubman, "Intergenerational transmission of income and wealth," *American Economic Review* 66:3, 1976, 436–440.

21 O. Ashenfelter and A. Krueger, "Estimates of the economic return to schooling from a new sample of twins," *American Economic Review* 84:5 (December), 1994, 1157–1174.

22 See Table 2.A.3. The exception is Ashenfelter and Krueger, op. cit. However the Rouse (1999) replication with three times as large a sample (including the subsample used by Ashenfelter and Krueger) and the Ashenfelter and Rouse study using twice as large a sample suggest that this aspect of the Ashenfelter and Krueger results is an artifact of their sample, though in neither of these more recent studies are individual estimates presented with control for measurement error for direct comparison with the within-MZ estimates with control for measurement error. (C. Rouse, "Further estimates of the economic return to schooling from a new sample of twins," *Economics of Education Review* 18:2, 1999, 149–157; O. Ashenfelter and C. Rouse, "Income, schooling and ability: evidence from a new sample of identical twins," *Quarterly Journal of Economics* 113:1 (February), 1998, 253–284.)

23 J. R. Behrman and M. R. Rosenzweig, "The returns to schooling: new evidence from twins data," *Economics of Education Review* 18, 1999, 159–167.

24 Intuitively, we use the MZ twins to generate the correct estimates of the earnings function parameters (i.e. not contaminated by ability bias) and then we estimate the individual-specific endowments for the fraternal twins as the component of the unobserved earnings residual that also is consistent with the unobserved schooling determinant residual. (Behrman, Rosenzweig, and Taubman, op. cit.)

25 See, for example, Haveman and Wolfe, Heckman and Hotz, Hill and King, Schultz, Thomas *et al.* However standard empirical estimates are not as consistent with conventional wisdom on this point as usually is assumed. I review all of over 300 estimates that I could locate from a number of countries in

Behrman: in 52 percent of the cases in which comparisons could be made, the estimated association between child's schooling and mother's schooling is larger than for father's schooling – which does not seem overwhelming. (R. Haveman and B. Wolfe, "The determinants of children's attainments: a review of methods and findings," *Journal of Economic Literature* 33, 1995, 1855; J. J. Heckman and V. J. Hotz, "The sources of inequality for males in Panama's labor market," *Journal of Human Resources* 21:4, 1986, 532; A. M. Hill and E. M. King, "Women's education and economic well-being," *Feminist Economics* 1:2, 1995, 25; T. P. Schultz, "Returns to women's education," in E. M. King and M. A. Hill, (eds) 1993, *Women's Education in Developing Countries: Barriers, Benefits, and Policies*, Baltimore, MD and London: The Johns Hopkins University Press, published for the World Bank, 1993, 74; D. Thomas, R. F. Schoeni, and J. Strauss, *Parental Investments in Schooling: The Roles of Gender and Resources in Urban Brazil*, Santa Monica, CA: RAND, mimeo, 1996, 14; J. R. Behrman, *Women's Schooling and Child Education: A Survey*, Philadelphia, PA: University of Pennsylvania, mimeo, 1997.)

26 Heritability variance decomposition estimates based on twins and other kin indicate that the variance in genetic endowments is consistent with a large share of the variance in years of schooling in the United States (e.g. Behrman *et al.*, Behrman and Taubman 1989). But such variance decompositions do not indicate whether the impact of changing some other variable such as other aspects of family background would be large or small. (J. R. Behrman, Z. Hrubec, P. Taubman, and T. J. Wales, *Socioeconomic Success: A Study of the Effects of Genetic Endowments, Family Environment and Schooling*, Amsterdam: North Holland Publishing Co., 1980; J. R. Behrman and P. Taubman, "Is schooling 'mostly in the genes'? Nature–nurture decomposition with data on relatives," *Journal of Political Economy* 97:6, 1989, 1425–1446.)

27 J. R. Behrman and M. R. Rosenzweig, "Does increasing women's schooling raise the schooling of the next generation?," *American Economic Review* 92, 2002, 323–334.

28 As observed in a previous note, the evidence to support the conventional wisdom that mother's schooling has a larger impact in cross-sectional estimates than father's schooling is not overwhelming. For the United States, in fact, for 33 sets of estimates from 11 studies that I could find (Behrman), the median estimate of the association between child and mother's schooling is 0.12 years of child schooling for every additional year of mother's schooling (in the study discussed in the text we get 0.14) and 0.15 years of child schooling for every additional year of father's schooling (we get 0.29). (J. R. Behrman, *Women's Schooling and Child Education: A Survey*, Philadelphia, PA: University of Pennsylvania, mimeo, 1997.)

29 There also have been a few other recent related studies. For example, Glewwe, Jacoby, and King also use statistical techniques (also instrumental variables, but with different instruments) and Coney and Bennett (2000) use sibling data to control for the common family genetics and other endowments (though not the individual-specific endowments). (P. Glewwe, H. Jacoby, and E. M. King, "Early childhood nutrition and academic achievement: a longitudinal data analysis," *Journal of Public Economics* 81, 2001, 345–368; D. Conley and N. G. Bennett, "Is biology destiny? Birth weight and life chances," *American Sociological Review* 65, 2000, 458–467.)

30 H. Alderman, J. R. Behrman, V. Lavy, and R. Menon, "Child nutrition, child health, and school enrollment: a longitudinal analysis," *Journal of Human Resources* 36:1 (Winter), 2001, 185–205.

31 In technical terms, the previous price shocks are used as identifying instruments for instrumental variable estimates.

32 See Table 2.A.5. The "naive" estimates assume that child health/nutritional status is not behaviorally determined and is not subject to measurement error. The "preferred" estimates assume that child health/nutritional status is behaviorally determined and controlled for measurement error.

33 J. R. Behrman and M. R. Rosenzweig, "Returns to birthweight," *Review of Economics and Statistics*, forthcoming 2004.

34 The negative correlation also is consistent with the result in Alderman *et al.* that the preferred estimates are larger than the naive estimates, though random measurement error also could account for this result in part or in whole. (Alderman *et al.*, op. cit.)

35 J. Currie and J. Gruber, "Saving babies: the efficacy and cost of recent changes in the medicaid eligibility of pregnant women," *Journal of Political Economy* 104, 1996, 1263–1296.

36 Behrman *et al.*, op. cit.

37 A central example is the summary of social versus private returns to schooling in the well-known surveys of Pscharapolous. These estimates of the private returns use the impact on wage rates for the benefits and private costs for the costs. For the social returns, the only adjustment is to add in public subsidies to the costs. With such a procedure, the social returns are always less than the private returns if there are any public subsidies, so that the implications for efficiency would seem to be that public subsidies should be zero. But there is no effort in these estimates to adjust the benefits so that they incorporate social benefits beyond private ones, so the essence of the efficiency justification for public subsidies is ignored. (G. Psacharopoulos, "Returns to investment in education: a global update," *World Development* 22:9, 1994, 1325–1344.)

38 See, for example, Foster and Rosenzweig on the diffusion of new technologies given imperfect information markets. (A. Foster and M. R. Rosenzweig, "Learning by doing and learning from others: human capital and technical change in agriculture," *Journal of Political Economy* 103:6, 1995, 1176–1209.)

39 For example, D. van de Walle and K. Nead (eds) *Public Spending and the Poor: Theory and Evidence*, Baltimore, MD and London: The Johns Hopkins Press for the World Bank, 1995; J. R. Behrman, *Targeting Social Protection to the Poor: What are the Tradeoffs?,* Philadelphia, PA: University of Pennsylvania, prepared for Inter-American Development Bank, mimeo, 2001.

3 Young children's achievement in school and socioeconomic background

Doris R. Entwisle, Karl L. Alexander, and Linda Steffel Olson

Family economic status strongly predicts school outcomes. Income and other measures of family economic status influence the amount of schooling children obtain,[1] with youth living in poverty for at least one year 6 percent less likely than those not raised in poverty to graduate from high school.[2] Moreover, family economic status predicts scores on standardized tests very early.[3] Children from advantaged homes have verbal and math skills in first grade already at a higher level than children from disadvantaged homes.[4] Longitudinal data are thin, but family background probably matters more for young children's test scores than it does for older children's.[5]

This chapter aims to shed light on the ways in which family resources affect young children's achievement in reading and math. It examines data from a longitudinal study of children in Baltimore, the Beginning School Study (BSS), in order to understand why family socioeconomic status so strongly predicts children's school success.

The correlation between parents' economic status and children's cognitive growth can be explained in many ways. One is that better-off families have more economic resources. Baltimore data[6] and other data,[7] however, suggest that learning *during the school year* does not vary much by family economic status when children are in the early grades; it is students' learning during the summer, when school is closed, that co-varies with economic and other resources in the home.[8] These observations suggest that the school achievement of better-off children exceeds that of poorer children because families and neighborhoods of better-off children supply resources in summer periods to support cognitive growth while families and neighborhoods of poorer children cannot. For this reason, as found in the famous Coleman report, children from better-off families in first grade have higher scores on achievement tests than poorer children because the better off children have had more access to out-of-school resources before they start school. Then, after formal schooling begins, children from better-off families gain more ground over summer vacations when schools are closed, while poor children's cognitive growth slows down, stops, or even retrogresses during summer.

This variation in achievement growth by family economic status in summer has been clear for some time.[9] Not so clear, however, are the relative contributions of resources provided by home and school in winter or the kinds of resources that support summer growth. These two issues are the main topics of this chapter. After describing the Beginning School Study (BSS), we present summaries of *seasonal* gains by better-off and not-so-well-off children on standardized tests in reading and math over the first three years of school for several hundred Baltimore children. We then describe parents' attitudes and behaviors in relation to their children's academic growth over that same period, distinguishing between parents' socioeconomic resources and their "psychological support" resources. We conclude that elementary schools are probably better than they have been given credit for at leveling the playing field between children of better-off and not-so-well-off families: it is in summer, when students are not in school, that the real gap in achievement opens up between disadvantaged and higher SES students.

The effectiveness of schools in promoting achievement in children from *all* SES groups during winter in the early grades squares well with a longstanding impression that schooling helps disadvantaged more than it helps advantaged children and is also consistent with the finding that children's achievement differs less across schools than within schools. But also apparent is the critical importance of family resources *in summer*. The Coleman report and many subsequent large-scale studies concluded that home influences were far more important than school influences for determining differences in children's achievement, but these studies overlooked the seasonality of these family effects. The challenge for policy then becomes how to boost the out-of-school resources available to poor children during the summer when they are not in school, and/or prior to the time their formal schooling begins.

The Beginning School Study (BSS)

In 1982 a representative sample of children who were beginning first grade in Baltimore City Public Schools was chosen to participate in the Beginning School Study (BSS). First, a sample of 20 schools, stratified by racial mix (six predominantly African-American, six predominantly white, eight integrated) and by socioeconomic status (14 inner-city or working class and six middle class) was randomly selected. The percentage of African-American students averaged 99.5 percent in the six African-American schools, 6 percent in the six white schools, and 48 percent in the eight integrated schools (range 17 percent to 87 percent). Second, within each school, students were randomly sampled from every first-grade classroom. Three percent of parents refused to have their children participate. The final sample consisted of 790 students beginning first grade for the first time (non-repeaters) in the fall of 1982. While the City school system enrolled about 77 percent African Americans at that time,[10] the BSS oversampled whites (45 percent of BSS students are white), in order to be able to compare ethnic groups. BSS parents' educational levels ranged from less than eighth grade to graduate and professional school degrees, averaging just under 12 years (11.9). School records indicated that 67 percent of BSS families qualified for free or reduced price meals at school.

Though the BSS is still ongoing, the data in this chapter come mostly from the first three years of the study. Our choice of time frame reflects the belief that family economic resources have the greatest impact on achievement in early childhood, especially in low-income families. The first three years of school are a period of rapid cognitive growth – yearly achievement score gains of children in third grade are about half as large as gains in first grade. The rapidity of cognitive growth during this period makes it easier to see differences in growth rates among students. Finally, early in elementary school children's performance forecasts educational outcomes in high school and beyond. For this reason the earliest years of school are the point at which any intervention is likely to have maximum effectiveness.

Beginning in the summer and fall of 1982, as children began first grade, data were collected by face-to-face interviews with students and parents. Teachers also responded to questionnaires, and school records were examined for data on marks, test scores and the like. In later years, most of the parent questionnaires were answered by mail or by phone but students were always individually interviewed.

Parents and children were surveyed in early fall before the end of the first marking period. Children's spring interviews took place between the third and fourth (final) marking periods. The timing of student and parent questionnaires ensured measurement of parents' and children's expectations for forthcoming marks before report cards were issued. Teachers filled out three questionnaires at various times in each of the first two years. In the third year, teachers filled out a single questionnaire.

In the next few paragraphs we explain how variables were measured. Student academic achievement was measured by California Achievement Test (CAT) scores obtained in October and May of each school year. Two subtests, Reading Comprehension and Mathematics Concepts and Applications,[11] provide an assessment of students' cognitive growth in reading and math.

The socioeconomic status of families in the BSS was determined by a composite index based on mother's and father's education, mother's and father's occupational status, and whether or not the student was eligible for the Federal meal subsidy program. Students were divided into low, medium, and high SES categories – approximately 50 percent of the sample fell into the low category, 26 percent into the medium, and 24 percent into the high. Category boundaries were drawn so that the mean educational level of both mothers and fathers was around 10 years for the low group, 12 years for the medium group, and 15 years for the high SES group. In this chapter comparisons are made between the high SES and low SES groups.

In addition to economic resources, families also possess psychological resources such as the aspirations they have for their child's education. To capture the level of psychological support available to students, we devised an index that combines information on parent's expectations for student's reading and math marks as well as the parent's aspirations for how far in school the student would go. (See Appendix for a more complete description of these and other variables.)

Seasonal learning

The main school outcomes we need to consider are the seasonal gains in BSS children's California Achievement Test scores (CAT) in reading comprehension and math concepts/applications. Since these tests were administered to BSS students in fall (October) and spring (May) of each school year, we can measure gains over "winters" (school in session) by subtracting fall scores from subsequent spring scores. Similarly, by subtracting spring scores from scores of the following fall, we can measure gains over "summers" (school vacation).

The school-year gains of BSS children in math and reading when school was open (winters) compared to the gains they made when school was closed (summers) show clear patterns of learning by seasons. Children from both high and low SES homes moved ahead substantially in the first winter and gained about the same number of points (see top half of Table 3.A.1). However, in the summer between first and second grades the low SES children lost ground, while students from high SES families continued to gain. All children's growth tended to decelerate as they progressed through the first three years of school, because gains or losses grew smaller each year, but the seasonal patterns continued.

Adding up test gains over all three summers shows that when schools were closed the low SES students lost six points in reading comprehension and 12 points in math. By contrast, over the same three summers high SES children *gained* 38 points in reading and 13 points in math (lower panel, Table 3.A.1). However, test gains over all three winters (upper panel, Table 3.A.1), when schools were open, are almost equivalent. The low and the high SES children gained almost the same number of points (136 points for low SES versus 135 points for high SES children in reading and 128 versus 123 points respectively in math). Figure 3.1 depicts these cumulative seasonal gains.

Family resources and children's schooling

The most obvious explanation for why a family's socioeconomic status can promote children's summer learning is that the resources parents need to

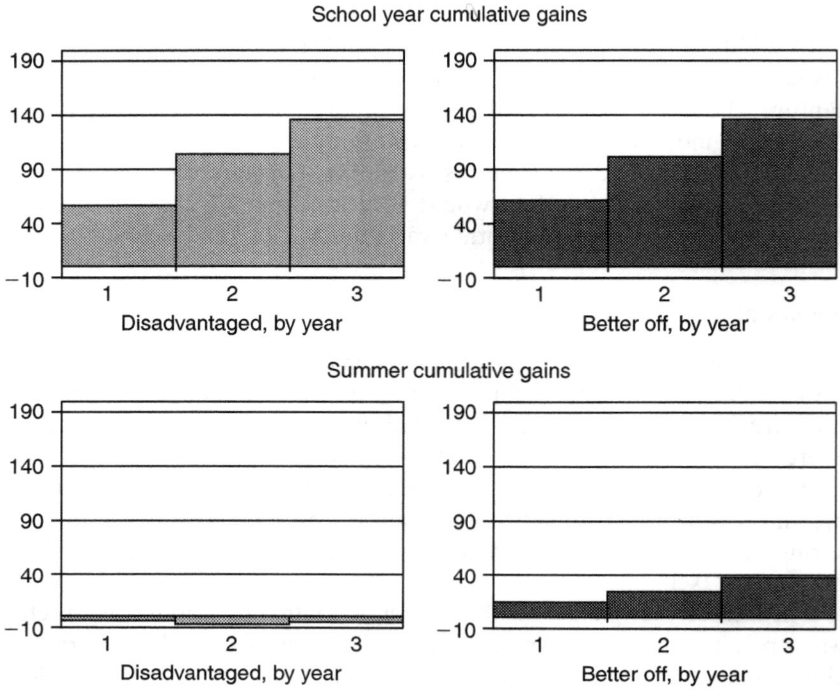

Note
Cumulative gains on California Achievement Test in reading over first three school years and summers. Sample consists of Baltimore public school students who entered first grade in 1982. Test "scale scores" are California Achievement Test scores calibrated to measure growth over a student's 12-year school career.

Figure 3.1 Cumulative school year and summer gains on CAT reading scores over the first three years of school by SES level.

promote children's learning require expenditure. Higher SES families have more income to purchase things like books, games, and computers, while lower SES families do not. Family trips to museums, zoos, science centers, historical sites, and sporting events, summer camp attendance and tutoring, as well as the purchase of bicycles, musical instruments, and hobby equipment are also things that better-off families are more able to provide in summers.[12]

The BSS data reveal that this coupling of economic resources and specific learning materials does occur in the high SES homes.[13] Compared to those who were less well off, BSS children in higher income households (i.e. those who did not receive subsidized school meals) were more likely to have a daily newspaper, magazines, encyclopedias, or an atlas in the home, and twice as likely to have a computer (38 percent versus 17 percent). In summers, BSS children in higher income households were also more likely to go to state or city parks, the zoo or science center, fairs or carnivals, or to take trips or vacations, and also more likely to play sports, go to the library and take books home, or to take music or dance lessons. The number of books BSS children read in summer correlated strongly with family socioeconomic status and predicted summer gains,[14] as did library use in the summer, summer day trips and overnight vacation trips.

But the lower SES parents also possessed less "psychological capital." Before their children started first grade, compared to the better-off parents, the poorer BSS parents expected their children to get marks about half a grade lower in reading and math. They also did not expect their children to get college degrees or to get higher status jobs whereas the better-off parents did. In addition, BSS parents of higher SES tended to express warmer feelings toward their children and held more positive views of their children's personality than did parents of lower SES (bottom panel, Table 3.A.2). When the BSS parents rated their children's favorable and unfavorable qualities on three scales (see Zill scales, Appendix) assessing whether children were "enthusiastic and liked to do things," "high-strung or fidgety," "happy and well-liked," "cooperative," "aggressive," and so on, the high SES parents rated their children at almost the top of these scales, while the low SES parents rated their children considerably lower (see Table 3.A.2). In essence, parents of higher SES viewed their children's personalities and behavior more positively, while poorer parents saw their children as considerably less appealing.

Parents' expectations for their children's first grade marks correlated with many things about their children's first grade experience. Their expectations predicted absences, children's academic self-esteem and self-image; work habits and many other measures (see Table 3.A.3). We therefore conjectured that parents' expectations and their correlates could be a major force in creating differences in children's summer-time gains in addition to the benefits children derived from their parents' economic resources.[15]

To investigate this question we used the measure of psychological capital that combined parents' expectations for their children's marks in reading and math with their expectations for children's long-term school attainment, the "Parent Psychological Support Index." We then used this Index to divide the sample in half, so that those below the midpoint were classified as having "low parent psychological support" and those above the midpoint as having "high" support.

When we tabulated children's seasonal gains by family SES *and* parent support level over winter periods, children from high or low SES families gained about the same amount on reading and math tests (see Table 3.A.4). As for psychological support, those with high support tended to gain more over the first winter in reading, while those with low support gained more in the second winter. Also high support helped overcome low SES while high SES helped overcome low support. In the first two years then, having either one of these resources alone appears to be advantageous.

In summers patterns were much simpler. Over the first three summers low SES children mainly lost ground whether parents provided high or low psychological support. For instance, in reading comprehension, low SES children lost two points over the summer if their parents provided high psychological support and four points if their parents provided low psychological support. The level of parents' support did not matter much for summer gains of children in low SES families.

Among children in high SES families, however, summer gains varied strikingly according to parents' psychological support. High SES children of low-support parents generally had summer losses. High SES children whose parents provided high support, however, gained much more in reading comprehension over the first summer than children in any of the other three categories. In subsequent summers these relatively high gains continued. The critical resources for summer gains thus appear to be high SES coupled with high parent psychological support.

We conclude from the statistical analyses of seasonal gains for reading and separately for math that the differences described above did not arise by chance (see Table 3.A.5).[16,17] When the seasonal gains on the reading and math CAT tests are analyzed by whether the student came from a high or low SES family *and* whether the student had low or high parents' psychological support, it becomes clear that family SES does not predict winter gains in either reading or math. Parents' psychological support over the first two winters does boost reading gains, but the direction of this effect reverses from one year to the next, suggesting that it does not matter much. This lack of a consistent pattern in winter gains suggests that parental resources play a less crucial role in promoting student achievement when schools are in session. In summer, however, the picture looks much different. When school resources are absent, students need both kinds of support. The only students who gain in summer are those from higher SES homes who also have supportive parents.

These analyses extend earlier findings in an important respect. Not only do parents' economic resources predict children's summer gains,[18] but high psychological capital is necessary as well. Perhaps the biggest surprise is how effectively schools are able to promote achievement in children from *all* SES groups during winters in the early grades – in other words, they help disadvantaged students the most. But it also has not been clear previously that a high level of psychological support is needed along with economic advantage for growth to occur when school is not in session.

The faucet analogy

The evidence from the BSS shows that schools can provide children from low SES families the resources they need to learn. Schools turn on a faucet of resources that support children's achievement independent of their family resources, either economic or psychological – all SES groups tend to move ahead during the school year at roughly the same rate. Any differences that emerge are relatively small and tend to favor the less advantaged. In winter low income students whose families provide them with strong psychological support even make up for some of their summer losses and gain as much or more than their higher income classmates. Overall, the big advantage in summer achievement gains made by higher income students with supportive families disappears when the resource faucet is turned on by schools. Schools confer benefits on all students, but especially on those most in need. This chapter points up the power of schools to prompt achievement gains by children irrespective of family SES.

The answer to the other key question – whether summer gains of high SES children differ by level of parent psychological support – is "yes" (see lower panel of Table 3.A.5). Children from high SES families who also have parents with high expectations for their academic performance consistently gained more over the summer than did children of the other groups in the first two years in both reading and math and in reading in the third year. This chapter thus qualifies our earlier research showing that parents' economic resources predict children's summer gains[19] because we see that high psychological capital is necessary as well. High SES children make large gains in summer only when their parents have high psychological capital (see Table 3.A.4). Similarly, during the summer, when resources of the school are cut off, parental psychological capital is not fungible for children from low SES homes.

Why? We suspect that parents from low SES backgrounds are less able to help their children live up to their high expectations in summer, not only because they lack economic resources, but also because they are not in tune with their children's developmental level. Other BSS research on children's expectations[20] shows that high SES parents are better at forecasting their children's school performance than are low SES parents. When asked at the beginning of the fourth year to recall their children's marks at the end of the third year, the high SES parents' recollections were more accurate than those of low SES parents' and their expectations also predicted their children's future performance better. Their greater awareness of children's school progress could lead them not only to provide learning materials in summer but also to select materials that are developmentally appropriate in terms of children's individual capabilities.

Implications

The sawtooth pattern of seasonal test gains for low SES children – moving smartly ahead in winter but stopping or retrogressing in summer – is far different from patterns seen when students are tested only once a year. Annual test data make it appear that children's social backgrounds predict their progress in school at a steady rate. Seasonal test scores, however, show that annual gains have two components. In one component (winter), the relationship between children's social background and test score gains is essentially nil or maybe even inverse. In the other component (summer), the relationship between social background and test score gains is strong and positive, especially during the first three years of school. These seasonal patterns agree with similar data for children in Atlanta,[21] New Haven,[22] and many other places[23] as well as with national data.[24]

Typically, school achievement is researched either in terms of single snapshots, by cross-sectional studies in which all the variables are measured at a single point in time, or by longitudinal studies tied to annual or biennial testing schedules over periods of two or more years (High School and Beyond). Because *seasons* are disregarded, either approach misses the substantial seasonal variation in children's summer learning rates and obscures the relative invariance by SES in children's winter learning rates. We argue that, at least in Baltimore, SES accounts for very little of the difference in children's levels of tested achievement in winters because when schools are open, they furnish sufficient resources so the poorer children can learn as much or more than the better-off children. In other words, schools are *not* unimportant. Rather, they are so effective that, as sociologist Barbara Heyns[25] argues, when schools are open, differences among students' home resources are much less consequential for children's learning than in summer periods.

A major implication of seasonal learning patterns is that the process of schooling has been misconceptualized, at least for young children. When elementary school children's cognitive gains are measured annually or less often, researchers "see" relatively slower progress of the poorer children and then conclude that poor youngsters derive less from school than do their better-off classmates. This conclusion leads to the mistaken notion that family SES boosts school performance by helping children do better during the school year as well as during the summer.[26] Instead, we believe SES and psychological capital both play a role. Poorer families that provide high levels of psychological capital may enable children to profit from school resources in winter, but only the better-off children have access to the needed economic or other resources to mobilize high parent capital in summer. Most encouraging is that when schools are open, the resources they provide tend to overcome deficits in family resources, whether economic or psychological.

As in Baltimore, Heyns'[27] study of seasonal differences in gains on word knowledge tests for sixth- and seventh-graders in Atlanta shows home resources are not predictive uniformly throughout the year. She says "Schooling consistently dampens the impact of parental status [for both blacks and whites]" and later:

> Unless one assumes quite implausible correlations among the residual determinants of income, it is not possible to replicate the observed correlations between income and achievement by assuming that the true effect [of income] is constant and of equal magnitude in the fall [after summer] and spring [after school year] ... family income is more highly related to fall achievement than to spring scores.

There is no question that family economic status strongly predicts all school outcomes in the long run: children's achievement, whether measured by test scores, marks, retention, or dropout; teachers' opinions of children, whether indicated by conduct marks, group placement, class interest/participation, or attention span/restlessness ratings. The seasonal patterns in achievement growth, however, argue that family resources *can* matter for achievement gains when school resources are absent if parents also provide the psychological support needed to make the home resources pay off. For parents' psychological support to be useful, however, it must be linked to necessary resources of the kinds money can buy, whether those of the school or those of the family.

Faucet imagery is useful to describe seasonal differences: schools turn on a "resource" faucet in winter and turn it off in summer. A major implication of this pattern is that schools are doing a far better job than they have been credited with. Until now family resources have been identified mainly as the games, books, computers, sports equipment, and the wherewithal to take children on trips or visit libraries, zoos, and museums. But because high parent psychological capital appears to boost poorer children's achievement in winter and because only higher SES children who also have high levels of parental psychological capital show substantial summer gains, apparently parents' psychological resources can condition the benefits conferred by their financial resources. Unless parents have sufficient psychological capital, their financial capital seems ineffective in promoting summer growth. Economic resources, whether found in family or school, are necessary but apparently not sufficient.

Even though low SES children gained as much on standardized tests over the winter as did children from higher SES families, in summer they fell behind. But also, at the beginning of first grade, low SES children's test scores on average were a little lower than those of high SES children.[28] These initial test scores then served as the continuing benchmark against which children's later progress was judged. In other words, children were evaluated in terms of absolute scores that continued to reflect where they started rather than what they had gained during the school year. One consequence is that low SES children received lower marks and were retained more often in first grade than were high SES children even though the test score gains made over the academic year by both groups were equivalent.[29] Their marks were based on the instructional level of their reading texts and not on how much progress they made. This mismatch between the amount of progress made by low SES children and the evaluations of that progress must tend to vitiate poorer parents' psychological capital.

The widespread perception that children's gains during the school year are proportional to their starting scores (Coleman's[30] notion of "fan-spread") now seems incorrect. To be fair, however, we must stress that Coleman's conclusion about families is correct – families matter more than schools in predicting differences in children's achievement. This insight was a landmark in educational research, and it has stood up to strenuous challenges. The temporal details of children's learning trajectories are now being established as a direct consequence of his pioneering work. Still, when gains calculated on the basis of gains when school is open (winters) show that on average children of high *or* low SES make equal progress, it is worrisome that, despite this equal growth, the schools attended by low SES children in Baltimore awarded lower marks than the schools attended by high SES children. Children whose progress in terms of yearly gains on standardized tests was equivalent were treated, not on the basis of those gains, but on the basis of their family resources.

This chapter suggests that more economic resources alone will not be likely to close the achievement gap between better-off children and their less advantaged counterparts. Financial resources are necessary but not sufficient. High expectations, or high psychological capital more generally, also seem to be required. But we need a level playing field at the start: If test scores were on average the same for high and low SES children when they started first grade, the parity between the two groups in gains over the school year would be more apparent, and hopefully would modify parents' and teachers' perceptions. Providing preschool programs to help bring poorer children up to speed before they start school is an essential element in closing the achievement gap. A number of robust randomized experiments have demonstrated that high quality preschools *can* raise disadvantaged children's scores by the start of first grade. Thus the field *could* be made more level at the start.[31] Good preschool and kindergarten programs also prepare disadvantaged students to successfully weather the crucial first-grade transition.

The good news is that despite poverty, young children's ability to learn during the school year seems little impaired by a scarcity of family financial resources. Even so, children are perceived as though the more advantaged groups are better able to benefit from school, and the less advantaged are seen as less capable. These perceptions need to be revised.

Appendix

Individual Child And Family Variables[32]

California Achievement Test Scores (CAT)

As children's grades in school increases, reliability of these tests increases. In the standardization sample the test-retest (two–three weeks) correlations for reading are reported as 0.50 at the beginning of grade one, 0.73 at the beginning of grade two, and 0.81 at the beginning of grade five. Correlations from fall to spring are reported as 0.45 in first grade, 0.71 in second grade, and 0.83 in grade five. Corresponding fall-to-spring correlations for the Beginning School Study sample in reading are 0.44, 0.66, and 0.86.

Measures of reliability for the standardization sample are somewhat higher for the math than for the reading subtest, particularly in grade one – the test-retest (two–three weeks) correlations for math are 0.80 at the beginning of grade one, 0.80 at the beginning of grade two, and 0.83 at the beginning of grade five. Fall-to-spring correlations in math also are higher, 0.69 in the first grade, 0.81 in the second grade, and 0.83 in grade five. Similarly, the corresponding fall-to-spring correlations for the BSS sample are 0.63, 0.78, and 0.86 on the math subtest.

Kuder-Richardson 20 (homogeneity) reliabilities for the two subtests are patterned in the same way as the test-retest reliabilities.[33]

Race

Race was coded 0 for *White*, 1 for *African American.*

Sex

Sex was coded 0 for *boys*, 1 for *girls.*

Meal Subsidy Eligibility

Children were eligible for free or reduced price meals (breakfast and lunch) based on family income and size as of July 1, 1984. A family of four with a yearly income at that time of up to $13,260 was eligible for full subsidy; one with an income between $13,261 and $18,870 was eligible for partial subsidy (1 = *no subsidy*, 0 = *full or partial subsidy*).

Parent educational attainment

Obtained directly from parent questionnaires, this is a measure of the number of school years completed by the parents. Using pooled parent education data over the first eight years of the study, the mean years of education completed by mothers (for 95 percent of students) is 11.7 years; by fathers (for 67 percent of students) is 12.2 years.

Parent occupation

Specific information on parent occupation was gathered for both mother and father (if both lived with the student) beginning in year two. Beginning in year nine parental occupation was asked for parents who had any regular contact with the student. Parent responses were classified into three-digit U.S. Bureau of the Census (1970) occupational codes, and these were transformed into updated Featherman-Stevens TSE12[34] occupational status scores. Pooling data over the first nine years, information is available on mother's occupation for 77 percent students and for father's occupation for 66 percent of students.

Home possessions

Beginning in year nine, parents were asked a series of 20 questions[35] about possessions in the home: newspaper, magazine subscription, encyclopedia, atlas, dictionary, typewriter, computer, telephone, refrigerator, dishwasher, clothes dryer, washing machine, microwave oven, over 50 books, VCR, pocket calculator, radio, color TV, black and white TV, and gun or rifle.

Marks

Student marks in reading, math, and conduct were obtained from report cards. Reading and math marks were coded 4 for *excellent*, 3 for *good*, 2 for *satisfactory*, and 1 for *unsatisfactory*. Coding for conduct marks was 2 for *satisfactory* and 1 for *needs improvement.*

Work habits

Teacher assessments of children's study habits were obtained from report cards and covered five areas: effort, attention, class participation, completes assignments, and works independently. Coding for each area was 2 for *satisfactory* and 1 for *needs improvement.* The sum of these five study habit assessments is the work habits scale score. Internal reliability (Cronbach's alpha) for this scale was 0.85 or better.

Absences

The total number of absences for the school year was taken from the end-of-year report cards.

The Zill[36] Scales

A scale developed by Zill and colleagues for use with a national sample (NSC) of children ages seven to 11 measured the child's "behavioral and emotional adjustment to the learning and deportment demands of elementary school." Homeroom teachers and parents rated students on 13 items, each with a six-category choice frame ranging from "exactly like" to "not at all like."

Factor analyses of teachers' responses in grades one through four identified three sub-scales: *Cooperation-Compliance* (five items), *Interest-Participation* (four items), and *Attention Span-Restlessness* (four items). Alpha reliabilities range from 0.74 to 0.85 for years one, two, four, and six. Over these years the factor structure does not differ by race, gender, or economic status.[37] Items are as follows:

INTEREST-PARTICIPATION (I-P)

1 Very enthusiastic, interested in a lot of different things, likes to express his or her ideas.
2 Usually in a happy mood; very cheerful.
3 Is creative or imaginative.
4 Keeps to himself or herself; spends a lot of time alone.
5 Very timid, afraid of new things or new situations.

COOPERATION-COMPLIANCE (C-C)

1 Fights too much; teases, picks on, or bullies other children.
2 Tells lies or fibs.
3 Has a very strong temper; loses it easily.
4 Is polite, helpful, considerate of others.

ATTENTION SPAN-RESTLESSNESS (A-R)

1 Doesn't concentrate, doesn't pay attention for long.
2 Rather high strung, tense, and nervous.
3 Acts too young for his or her age, cries a lot or has tantrums.
4 Is awfully restless, fidgets all the time, can't sit still.

Alpha reliabilities for the same three scales involving parents' responses ranged from 0.51 to 0.64. The higher reliabilities for the teacher data are consistent with the view that teachers hold more unitary views of children than parents do, perhaps because teachers see students mainly in a single setting (the classroom).

Student's expectations for marks

Every year, in fall and spring before receipt of the first and fourth quarter report cards, students were asked to "guess the marks you are going to get on your next report card" in reading, math and conduct. The expectations (mark estimates) given by students were coded in the same way as were marks (see above).

Academic self-esteem

This scale is the sum of five items taken from Dickstein's[38] self-esteem scale. During the spring of each year, students rated themselves on a five-point scale. Scoring is from 1 ("I am very bad at ") to 5 ("I am very good at "). The items for academic self-image include:

- Reading
- Doing arithmetic
- Being a good student
- Learning new things quickly
- Writing

The scale score is the sum of children's responses to these five items. The alpha reliability of this scale in the first year was 0.59.[39]

Harter Scholastic Competence Scale

Beginning in year two students completed the six-item Scholastic Competence subscale from the Harter Self-Perception Profile for Children.[40] It measures the child's perception of his/her competence or ability within the realm of scholastic performance. For each item, a child states whether he or she is more like the kids described in one of two statements. For example, students are asked to choose between:

> Some kids feel that they are very good at their schoolwork
> BUT
> Other kids worry about whether they can do the schoolwork assigned to them.

After making a first choice, the child is then asked whether the statement selected is "sort of true for me" or "really true for me." Thus four possible responses are available for each item with scoring from 1 (least adequate self-judgment) to 4 (most adequate self-judgment). Published internal consistency reliability is 0.80.[41] The Cronbach alpha for the BSS sample is in the 0.51 to 0.59 range.

Parent variables

Parents' mark expectations

Each year before issuance of the first report card, parents guessed their child's first report card mark in reading and math (4 for *excellent*, 3 for *good*, 2 for *satisfactory* and 1 for *unsatisfactory*), and in conduct (2 for *satisfactory* and 1 for *unsatisfactory*).

Parents' educational aspirations for student

Beginning in year one parents were asked "How far do you expect your child will go in school?" They responded on a five-point scale:

1 = Not finish high school
2 = Finish high school
3 = Finish one or two years college
4 = Finish four years college
5 = More than college (M.D., etc.)

Parent's job aspirations for child

Beginning in year one, parents were asked, "What kind of job would you like your child to have when he/she grows up?" Parent's responses were classified into three-digit U.S. Bureau of the Census occupational codes, and these were transformed into an updated version of the Duncan SEI scale, the TSEI2 which is based on education and income data for the total workforce (both men and women).[42]

School tracking variables

Reading instructional level

Taken from report cards, this indicates the instructional level of the reader the student was using in a given quarter.

Retention

Grade retention status is available every year from school records, and is coded 1 for *retained* and 0 for *promoted.* A cumulative measure of grade retention in grades one through three was also created that indicated whether student was ever retained through the first three grades. Coding was 1 for *retained at least once* and 0 for *never retained.* Retention rates are highest in grades one and two – nearly 17 percent in first grade and 10 percent in second grade – and the cumulative rate through year three was 35 percent.

Special Education placement.

Receipt of Special Education services was determined from school records. Coding is 1 = *receipt of any Special Education* or 0 = *no Special Education services.*

Table 3.A.1 School year and summer gains on CAT subtests in reading and math over elementary school by SES Level[a] (Ns in parentheses)[b]

	Reading *Family SES level*		*Math* *Family SES level*	
	Low (327)	*High (161)*	*Low (340)*	*High (158)*
School year gains (Winter)				
Year 1	57	61	49	45
Year 2	48	40	43	42
Year 3	31	34	36	36
Pooled school year gains	136	135	128	123
Summer gains				
Year 1	−4	15	−5	9
Year 2	−4	8	−5	3
Year 3	2	15	−2	1
Pooled summer gains	−6	38	−12	13

Notes

a Composite family SES measure for students in "low" category mean mother's education is ten years; for high category, 14.6 years. Students in "medium" category are not included in the table.

b Sample sizes vary year to year, Ns in parentheses represent the maximum in each SES category.

Table 3.A.2 Parent's educational and occupational aspirations for children, expectations for children's marks, and estimates of children's personality and disposition, year one, by family SES level

	Low SES Mean		*High SES Mean*
Parent educational aspirations for child[a]	2.7	**	3.9
Parent's job aspirations for child[b]	56.6	**	70.3
Parent's expectation for math mark	2.5	**	3.0
Parent's expectation for reading mark	2.5	**	3.0
Parent's ratings of child's personality/disposition			
Interest-participation	24.2	+	24.8
Cooperation-compliance	18.7	**	20.0
Aggression-restlessness	18.9	**	20.4

Notes

a Parent's educational aspirations are coded 1–5, with 2 = high school graduate, 3 = one or two years of college, 4 = college degree.

b Occupational status scores (Featherman and Stevens 1982) are based on earnings and educational characteristics of both men and women workers. Typical job scores are: clergy = 66.0, dentist = 89.6, librarian = 65.6, social worker = 66.1, elementary teacher 70.9, nurse = 46.4, police = 38.0, waiter = 18.9.

** Difference significant at or beyond 1 percent level.

\+ Difference significant at or beyond 10 percent level.

Table 3.A.3 Correlations of parent's expectations for the child's first reading mark in fall of first grade with student characteristics and teacher ratings of students, years 1–3

	Years in school			
	1	*2*	*3*	*1–3*
Student characteristics and performance				
Absences	−0.14[a]	−0.10[a]	−0.09[a]	
Referrals for academic or other problems	−0.28[a]	−0.18[a]	−0.26[a]	
Academic self-esteem (Dickstein)	0.18[a]	0.10[a]		
Academic self-image (Harter)		0.11[a]		
Student's own reading expectations	0.12[a]	0.01		
Retentions in years 1–3				−0.38
Special education placement, years 1–3				−0.29
Teacher's ratings of students				
Reading marks	0.42[a]	0.40[a]	0.30[a]	
Conduct marks	0.14[a]	0.17[a]	0.09[a]	
Work habits	0.32[a]	0.24[a]	0.23[a]	
Reading level (instructional level of reading)	0.33[a]	0.40[a]	0.40[a]	

Notes

a $p \leq 0.05$; + $p \leq 0.10$

Table 3.A.4 Winter and summer test score gains by family SES level and level of parent psychological support (high versus low SES with medium SES excluded)

	Mean test score gains (Winter)					
	Reading			*Math*		
	W1[a]	*W2*	*W3*	*W1*	*W2*	*W3*
Low family SES						
Low parent psychological support	48	49	29	47	41	34
High parent psychological support	75	46	36	53	45	39
High family SES						
Low parent psychological support	64	56	33	53	46	35
High parent psychological support	59	34	35	42	41	36
	Mean test score gains (Summer)					
	Reading			*Math*		
	S1[a]	*S2*	*S3*	*S1*	*S2*	*S3*
Low family SES						
Low parent psychological support	−4	−4	0	−4	−5	−3
High parent psychological support	−2	−3	4	−6	−5	0
High family SES						
Low parent psychological support	−5	−4	7	−3	−8	0
High parent psychological support	21	13	19	12	8	2

Note
a "W1" means first winter, "W2" means second winter, etc.

Table 3.A.5 Seasonal test score gains by family SES and parent psychological support: Significance levels from repeated measures MANOVAS

	Significance levels from repeated measures MANOVAS of winter test score gains					
	Reading			*Math*		
	W1[a]	*W2*	*W3*	*W1*	*W2*	*W3*
Family SES (high versus low)	n.s.	n.s.	n.s.	n.s.	n.s.	n.s.
Parent psychological support (high versus low)	*	**	n.s.	n.s.	n.s.	n.s.
SES X parent psychological support	**	*	n.s.	**	+	n.s.
	Significance levels from repeated measures MANOVAS of summer test score gains					
	Reading			*Math*		
	S1[a]	*S2*	*S3*	*S1*	*S2*	*S3*
Family SES (high versus low)	*	+	*	**	n.s.	n.s.
Parent Psychological Support (high versus low)	**	*	+	*	*	n.s.
SES X parent psychological support	**	+	n.s.	**	*	n.s.

Notes
a "W1" means first winter, "W2" means second winter, etc.
** $p \leq 0.01$
* $p \leq 0.05$
+ $p \leq 0.10$
n.s. not significant

Notes

1 G. H. Elder Jr., *Children of the Great Depression: Social Change in Life Experience*, Chicago, IL: University of Chicago Press, 1974; I. Garfinkel and S. S. McLanahan, *Single Mothers and Their Children: A New American Dilemma*, Washington, DC: Urban Institute Press, 1986; R. H. Haveman and B. L. Wolfe, *Succeeding Generations: On the Effects of Investments in Children*, New York, NY: Russell Sage Foundation, 1994; V. McLoyd, "Socialization and development in a changing economy: the effects of paternal income and job loss on children," *American Psychologist* 44, 1989, 293–302; V. C. McLoyd, "The impact of economic hardship on Black families and children: Psychological distress parenting, and socioemotional development," *Child Development* 61, 1990, 311–346.

2 Haveman and Wolfe, op. cit.

3 K. L. Alexander and D. R. Entwisle, "Educational tracking during the early years: first grade placements and middle school constraints," in A. C. Kerckhoff (ed.) *Generating Social Stratification: Toward a New Research Agenda*, New York, NY: Westview Press, 1996; K. Marjoribanks, *Families and Their*

Learning Environments, London: Routledge, 1979; R. J. Murnane, *The Impact of School Resources on the Learning of Inner City Children*, Cambridge, MA: Ballinger, 1975.

4 D. R. Entwisle and K. L. Alexander, "Beginning school math competence," *Child Development* 61, 1990, 454–471; A. C. Huston, "Children in poverty: designing research to affect policy," Social Policy Report, *Society for Research in Child Development* 8, 1994, 1–12; M. S. Smith, "Equality of educational opportunity: the basic findings reconsidered," in F. Mosteller and D. P. Moynihan (eds) *On Equality of Educational Opportunity*, New York, NY: Vintage Books, 1972; U.S. Department of Education, *America's Kindergarteners: Findings from the Early Childhood Longitudinal Study, Kindergarten Class of 1998–99, Fall 1998,* NCES 2000–070 by J. West (Project Officer), K. Denton, and E. Germino-Hausken, Washington, DC: U.S. Department of Education, National Center for Education Statistics, 2000.

5 D. F. Alwin and A. Thornton, "Family origins and the schooling process: early versus late influence of parental characteristics," *American Sociological Review* 49, 1984, 784–802; G. J. Duncan, W. J. Yeung, J. Brooks-Gunn, and J. K. Smith, "How much does childhood poverty affect the life chances of children?," *American Sociological Review* 63, 1998, 406–423; Marjoribanks, op. cit.

6 D. R. Entwisle, K. L. Alexander, and L. S. Olson, *Children, Schools and Inequality*, Boulder, CO: Westview Press, 1997.

7 B. Heyns, *Summer Learning and the Effects of Schooling*, New York, NY: Academic, 1978.

8 D. R. Entwisle and K. L. Alexander, "Summer setback: race, poverty, school composition, and mathematics achievement in the first two years of school," *American Sociological Review* 57, 1992, 72–84; D. R. Entwisle and K. L. Alexander, "Winter setback: school racial composition and learning to read," *American Sociological Review* 59, 1994, 446–460; Entwisle, Alexander, and Olson, op. cit; Murnane, op. cit.

9 Entwisle and Alexander 1992, op. cit.; Entwisle and Alexander 1994, op. cit. See also Barbara Heyns' analysis of Klibanoff and Haggart's 1981 data. (B. Heyns, "Schooling and cognitive development: is there a season for learning?," *Child Development* 58, 1987, 1151–1160; L. S. Klibanoff and S. A. Haggart, *Report No. 8: Summer Growth and the Effectiveness of Summer School,* technical report to the Office of Program Evaluation, U.S. Department of Education, February, Mountain View, CA: RMC Research Corporation, 1981.)

10 U.S. Census Bureau, *Census of Population: 1980 Vol 1. Characteristics of the Population*, Washington, DC: U.S. Government Printing Office, 1983.

11 See California Achievement Test and Appendix for more detail. (California Achievement Test, *Technical Bulletin 1, Forms C and D, Levels 10–19*, Monterey, CA: McGraw-Hill, 1979.)

12 D. R. Entwisle and K. L. Alexander, "A parent's economic shadow: family structure versus family resources as influences on early school achievement," *Journal of Marriage and the Family* 57, 1995, 399–409; Heyns 1978, op. cit.; G. B. Saxe, S. R. Guberman, and M. Gearheart, "Social processes in early number development," *Monographs Social Research Child Development* 52, 1987, No. 216; B. L. Schneider and J. S. Coleman, *Parents, Their Children, and Schools*, Boulder, CO: Westview, 1993.

13 Entwisle, Alexander and Olson, op. cit.

14 Ibid.; Heyns 1978, op. cit.

15 D. R. Entwisle and K. L. Alexander, "Family type and children's growth in reading and math over the primary grades," *Journal of Marriage and the Family* 58, 1996, 341–355.

16 In most research on educational attainment, the test scores used to measure

gains in children's school achievement are separated by two or more years (e.g. High School and Beyond). With data points at such wide intervals, analysts customarily assume that any structural disturbance associated with a later test score is uncorrelated with the structural disturbance of an earlier test score. Such an assumption is not appropriate, however, when test scores are procured in fall and spring of the same academic year, as here. Under these conditions, structural disturbances may not be independent, especially when students are often taking the same test on successive occasions. See Winer for a good explication of the varieties of repeated measures and MANOVA designs, including how the various error terms are derived. (B. J. Winer, *Statistical Principles in Experimental Design*, New York, NY: McGraw-Hill, 1971.) See Hertzog and Rovine for a review of the use of repeated measures in developmental research. (C. Hertzog and M. Rovine, "Repeated measures analysis of variance in developmental research: selected issues," *Child Development* 56, 1985, 787–809.) See SPSS for software used in this chapter. (SPSS, *SPSS for Windows Advanced Statistics*, Chicago, IL: SPSS, 1993; SPSS, *SPSS for Windows Based System User's Guide*, Chicago, IL: SPSS, 1993.) The *Advanced Guide* (p. 125) discusses the use of linear combinations of score differences and how contrasts are constructed.

17 The reading comprehension subtest in the California Achievement Test battery is relatively short in grades one and two (20 items), and the correlations between fall and spring scores in grade one are relatively low. To investigate how sensitive the MANOVA analyses are to floor and ceiling effects see Entwisle and Alexander 1992, op. cit.

18 Entwisle and Alexander 1992, op. cit., 1994, op. cit.; K. L. Alexander, D. R. Entwisle, and L. S. Olson, "Schools, achievement and inequality: a seasonal perspective," *Educational Evaluation and Policy Analysis* 23, 2001, 171–191.

19 Ibid.

20 K. L. Alexander, D. R. Entwisle, and S. D. Bedinger, "When expectations work: race and socioeconomic differences in school performance," *Social Psychology Quarterly* 57, 1994, 283–299.

21 Heyns discusses a linear model that captures the same relationship for data provided over a single year. She also comments at length on the nature of summer programs. (Heyns 1978, op. cit., 82–83.)

22 Murnane shows effects of summer learning for disadvantaged children in New Haven. His work is among the earliest on this topic. (Murnane, op. cit.)

23 See, for example, J. David, "Follow through summer study: a two-part investigation of the impact of exposure to schooling on achievement growth," Ed. D. Dissertation, Harvard Graduate School of Education, 1974; J. David and S. H. Pelavin, "Secondary analysis: in compensatory education programs," *New Directions for Program Evaluation* 4, 1978, 31–44.; P. A. Hammond and J. A. Frechtling, "Twelve, nine and three month achievement gains of low and average achieving elementary school students," paper presented at AERA Annual Meeting, San Francisco, 1979; D. P. Hayes and J. Grether, "The school year and vacations: when do students learn?," paper presented at the annual meeting of the Eastern Sociological Association, New York, 1969. Subsequently published in *Cornell Journal of Social Relations* 17, 1983, 56–71; D. P. Hayes and J. P. King, *The Development of Reading Achievement Differentials During the School Year and Vacations*, Ithaca, NY: Cornell University, 1974, mimeo; Murnane, op. cit.; S. H. Pelavin and J. L. David, *Evaluating Long-Term Achievement: An Analysis of Longitudinal Data from Compensatory Educational Programs,* prepared for Office of the Assistant Secretary for Education, Department of Health, Education and Welfare, EPRC 4537-15, Washington, DC: SRI International Educational Policy Research Center, 1977.

24 Heyns 1987, op. cit. In this review of seasonal learning Heyns examines carefully the Sustaining Effects Study, one of the largest ever undertaken on the topic of summer learning.
25 Heyns 1978, op. cit.
26 K. L. Alexander and B. K. Eckland, "School experiences and status attainment," in S. E. Dragastin and G. H. Elder Jr. (eds) *Adolescence in the Life Cycle*, New York, NY: Wiley, 1975.
27 Heyns 1978, op. cit., pp. 82, 92.
28 Just as higher SES children progress at a faster rate in summer when school is closed than do low SES children, we would expect that, before children's formal schooling begins, those from higher SES homes would have learned more. The preschool period, like summer, is a time when children are not in formal schooling and therefore also a time when home resources may have strong effects. At the beginning of first grade, BSS children's CAT scores corresponded to family SES level. (D. R. Entwisle and K. L. Alexander, "Entry into schools: the beginning school transition and educational stratification in the United States," in *Annual Review of Sociology*, Palo Alto, CA: Annual Reviews, Inc., 1993.) With BSS children divided into three groups by mother's educational level (10 years, 12 years, and 14.6 years) their average reading comprehension scores when they began first grade are 273, 280, and 300, respectively, and their average math scores are 282, 297, and 312, respectively.
29 See Table 3.7, p. 47 in Entwisle, Alexander, and Olson, op. cit.
30 J. S. Coleman, E. Q. Campbell, C. J. Hobson, J. McPartland, A. Mood, F. D. Weinfeld, and R. L. York, *Equality of Educational Opportunity*, Washington, DC: U.S. Government Printing Office, 1966.
31 W. S. Barnett and S. S. Boocock, *Early Care and Education for Children in Poverty: Promises, Programs, and Long-Term Results*, Albany, NY: SUNY Press, 1997.
32 These variables are limited to BSS variables specifically referred to in this chapter.
33 California Achievement Test, op. cit.
34 D. L. Featherman and G. Stevens, "A revised socioeconomic index of occupational status: application in analysis of sex differences in attainment," in R. M. Hauser, D. Mechanic, A. O. Haller, and T. Hauser (eds) *Social Structure and Behavior: Essays in Honor of William Hamilton Sewell*, New York, NY: Academic Press, 1982.
35 National Opinion Research Center, *Eighth Grade Questionnaire NELS:88*, prepared for U.S. Department of Education, Center for Education Statistics, Chicago, IL: University of Chicago, 1988.
36 N. Zill, "American children: happy, healthy, and insecure," report on Foundation for Child Development's National Survey of Children, New York, NY: The Foundation for Child Development, 1981.
37 K. L. Alexander, D. R. Entwisle and S. L. Dauber, "First grade classroom behavior: its short- and long-term consequences for school performance," *Child Development* 64, 1993, 801–814.
38 E. B. Dickstein, "The development of self-esteem: theory and measurement," unpublished doctoral dissertation, The Johns Hopkins University, 1972.
39 Additional psychometric detail is available in A. M. Pallas, D. R. Entwisle, K. L. Alexander and P. Weinstein, "Social structure and the development of self-esteem in young children," *Social Psychology Quarterly* 53, 1990, 302–315.
40 S. Harter, *Manual for the Social Support Scale for Children*, Denver, CO: University of Denver, 1985.
41 Ibid.
42 Featherman and Stevens, op. cit.

Part II

Exploring family effects

4 Macro causes, micro effects

Linking public policy, family structure, and educational outcomes

Brian Powell, Regina Werum, and Lala Carr Steelman[1]

As indicated by the theme of this volume, social scientists increasingly have appreciated the pivotal role that agents outside the school – more specifically, family and community – play in children's educational development. These scholars owe a great debt to the groundbreaking work by James Coleman and his colleagues, who firmly established the pattern that is by now familiar: the more favorable a family's socioeconomic standing, the brighter its children's educational prospects. Coleman's signature finding that families and communities may be more consequential than schools with respect to children's educational attainment still commands the attention of academicians, policy makers, and the public-at-large. Scholars have crafted volumes of research illustrating how family dynamics in combination with background factors help shape individual-level educational outcomes. Coleman's impression on policy makers spurred a host of educational reforms designed to encourage families' greater involvement in their children's education. His influence has been demonstrated, for instance, by the "community control" movement, while perhaps also inhibiting ongoing efforts to implement structural reforms, such as desegregating the nation's public schools. Public commentary continues to reflect the stance, held at both conservative and liberal ends of the political spectrum, that for educational reforms to accomplish their goals, attention also must be directed to the familial conditions that favorably (or unfavorably) affect children's educational progress.[2]

We too have been influenced by this research tradition and for over a decade, along with others, have examined whether (and if so, how) family composition is tied to the distribution of educationally profitable resources, which in turn affects access to educational and other opportunities. In previous research, our focus has typically been on the educational implications of sibship structure – namely, number of children, birth order, age-spacing between children, and gender composition of the family/sibship – and, to a lesser degree of parental structure, e.g. the presence of one or two parents for educational outcomes.[3]

In this chapter, we review our and other scholars' research on the educational consequences of family and sibling structure. Our chapter is comprised of five sections. We begin by discussing and evaluating several explanations for the consistently found association between sibship size and a host of educational outcomes (e.g. academic ability, achievement, and attainment). We next explore in greater detail what we consider to be the most persuasive explanation for the aforementioned pattern: the resource dilution hypothesis that proposes the family structure (in particular, sibship size) shapes resource allocation and thus affects individual-level educational outcomes. We follow this discussion by assessing the utility of this hypothesis in our understanding of the effects of other sibship and parental structural parameters (spacing, birth order, sex composition, number of residential parents). The next section focuses on our ongoing research that addresses the impact parental age has on how educational resources are allocated to children. We demonstrate the need to incorporate parental age as an important factor, not just as a control or background variable, when studying children's academic outcomes.

Detailing the influence of the family on educational outcomes and children's welfare carries profound policy implications. Thus, our final – and most comprehensive section – outlines how social context (i.e. at the macro level) may alter the impact of family structure on children's educational trajectories (i.e. at the micro level). To that end, we take an explicitly comparative perspective on the connection between status attainment/resource dilution factors and educational outcomes. We are not alone in detecting a glaring failure to encompass and learn from research conducted outside the United States. This oversight applies in particular to the way in which social policy and institutional parameters *shape* family structure itself as well as *mediate* the effects of family dynamics on educational outcomes.[4]

Ironically, one of the strengths of work by James Coleman and like-minded scholars – i.e. its crisp theoretical and empirical focus on the link between family structure and educational outcomes – inadvertently may have blinded social scientists to the need to look beyond normative patterns in the United States and other industrialized, usually Western European, countries. We recognize this shortcoming not only with respect to our own work on resource allocation but also with respect to studies in the status attainment tradition more generally. Given the repeated exhortations by our own peers, it is difficult to believe that researchers remain unaware of this omission. But this blind spot leads social scientists to underestimate the contributions cross-cultural comparisons can make to our understanding of domestic social policy, including education. Moreover, continuing to neglect existing inquiries of other societies may limit knowledge about how families can and do affect children's educational growth. We contend that to understand more precisely how the family affects children requires a fuller, more inclusive examination of the influence of the family on children in varying social contexts.

Theoretical explanations for family structure effects

Theorizing how family structure, in particular sibship structure, affects children's intellectual development and life chances appears to have originated in the late nineteenth century with Sir Francis Galton's proclamation of the "superiority of the eldest born child" in his *English Men of Science* (1874) and demographer Arsene Dumont's "law of capillary action" (1890) that siblings reduced resources linked to social mobility. Since then, interest in the implications of sibship size and birth order has intensified, with arguably the most programmatic and comprehensive work centering on the link between sibship size and educational outcomes.[5]

The inverse relationship between number of siblings and educational progress has been one of the most robust patterns reported in the social scientific literature – indeed, until recently one of the few patterns that social scientists appeared to agree upon. This pattern holds regardless of the type of educational outcomes, from ability as measured by standardized test scores to school grades to the likelihood of graduating high school and college enrollment and completion. Nevertheless, some scholars have noted that sibship size is more strongly related to educational attainment (e.g. college matriculation) than to ability, while others have shown that sibship size's link to educational attainment is net of its relationship to academic ability. The regularity of these patterns is matched by their strength. Sociologist Judith Blake suggested that the magnitude of the link between sibship size and educational attainment exceeds the impact of any other familial parameter (such as farm background, the presence of one versus two parents in the household, and paternal socioeconomic status) with the exception of parental education.[6]

With the inverse relationship between sibship size and educational outcomes firmly documented, most scholars in this area have turned their attention to accounting for this relationship. We can distinguish between several major approaches. Rooted in the biological framework, the *heritability argument* maintains that parents transmit their talents to children genetically and, therefore, any seeming effect of sibship size is actually a proxy for genetics: that is, the genetically fittest parents consciously choose to have fewer children in order to maximize their ability to produce superior offspring. Alternatively, but still under the rubric of the biological frame, the so-called *uterine fatigue hypothesis* holds that the more children women bear, the greater the likelihood that later-born children and, by extension, children from larger families endure birth traumas (e.g. low birth weight) that ultimately undermine school performance and educational outcomes at large. Evidence for these genetic and physiological claims, however, is scarce and contradictory. In addition, it is difficult to reconcile these biological claims with the many studies that show that sibship size's link to educational attainment remains even upon taking into account children's educational ability.[7]

Putting a different spin on *rational choice theory,* some researchers argue that an explicit difference exists between people who choose to bear or not to bear many children. For some parents, "quality" of children is preferred to "quantity": that is, those who opt to have fewer children presumably have more intensive concerns about their children's long-term success and choose to forego additional offspring in order to invest more in their few children. In contrast, other parents will select "quantity" over "quality." Judith Blake's work offers several challenges to this explanation, some persuasive, some not. Unfortunately, the painstaking, longitudinal data required to test this explanation is one reason that scholars have steered away from this perspective. If it could be shown that differences in motivations behind parent's fertility decisions also predict parental investments in their children, this evidence would bolster the rationality perspective.

A competing sociological explanation holds that family size influences *socialization strategies* that, in turn, may affect children's academic performance. This argument relies on the underlying premise that families become more bureaucratic, authoritative, and disciplinarian as they add members. Such child rearing practices are believed to discourage intellectual initiative and creativity and stifle educational advancement. A variant of this argument suggests that larger families are more insular than smaller ones, which limits their understanding of role behavior and reduces their capacity to "take the role of the other," qualities that may be critical in intellectual development and school performance. We find these ideas provocative, but unfortunately most scholars have not seriously considered them and empirical evidence to support this hypothesis remains sparse. And when empirically tested, the support for this hypothesis has been equivocal. For example, some research suggests that the relationship between sibship size and parental values (i.e. regarding the importance of obedience and self-direction) merely reflects socioeconomic characteristics of the family.[8]

Many scholars still surmise that family size effects are, in fact, spurious, reflecting some unmeasured factor. This argument overlaps to some degree with the rational choice and heritability claims outlined above, but typically focuses on others ways (e.g. socioeconomic differences between small and large families) in which the link between sibship size and educational outcomes may be artifactual. While this argument had been discounted by many, the recent analysis of sibling pairs by sociologists Guo Guang and Leah Van Wey has revived this proposition and has offered a compelling challenge to the conventional wisdom that family size dampens a child's ability. They argue that methodologies used in prior studies that affirm the negative impact of family size on ability are fundamentally flawed because they do not account for longitudinal changes in children's ability as their family grows in size and do not adequately resolve the issue of unmeasured heterogeneity. The authors' insightful use of change models and fixed effect models may correct for this flaw and, in so doing, they conclude that the sibship size effect on intellectual ability of young children may be entirely artifactual. Elsewhere we have identified methodological limitations and theoretical reservations about their analysis and have questioned whether their analysis, which is restricted to short-term changes in intelligence test performance by young children, can be generalized to older children, other educational outcomes (most notably, educational attainment), or to effects over a longer period of time. Nonetheless, their core argument serves as a healthy reminder that when it comes to family size, the issue of causality versus correlation is far from settled.[9]

Of the explanations that explicitly assume a causal relationship between sibship size and educational outcomes, the most popular are the *confluence model* and the *resource dilution hypothesis,* which often are pitted, perhaps unnecessarily, as rivals in the literature. According to the *confluence model*, a child's intelligence is seen as a function of the intellectual milieu in which the child is reared. This environment is operationalized as the average intellectual level of all family members. Unlike IQ scores, however, the intellectual level is not adjusted for age in the confluence model. As a result, the presence of children, especially very young ones, necessarily depresses the intellectual environment of the household. Thus, the larger the family, the lower the academic ability of the child. The model also proposes an intellectual disadvantage for later-born children and children who are closely spaced in age. When first presented in the mid-1970s, the confluence model was lauded for its originality and its inventive use of mathematical models; however, subsequent work challenges the degree to which the empirical data match the model, especially in regard to the effects of birth order. Equally important, the confluence model is unsuccessful in explaining why a significant relationship between sibship size and educational attainment endures even upon accounting for intellectual ability.[10]

Sibship size and the dilution of resources

Many social scientists now embrace the *resource dilution hypothesis* as the most palatable explanation for the relationship between sibship size and educational outcomes, be they intellectual ability, school performance, or especially educational attainment. As noted earlier, Arsene Dumont's "law of capillary action" posited that as the number of siblings increases, resources required for social mobility diminish. This classic proposition has persisted and been revamped by psychologist Anne Anastasi and Judith Blake, the latter labeling it the "resource dilution hypothesis." According to this hypothesis, the family is seen as a delivery system that dispenses educationally relevant resources, or for that matter other types of resources, to children. The nature of this distribution may stall or facilitate a child's academic progress. The negative impact of family size on educational outcomes is attributed to the dilution of resources accompanying the addition of new members to the family. Figure 4.1 illustrates the resource dilution sequence.

This proposition has proven to be exceptionally robust and appealing, capturing attention from sociologists, economists, demographers, sociobiologists, family therapists, and psychologists. Part of its appeal lies in its simplicity, for it is based on three basic and testable premises. First, resources are diluted as a function of family size. Second, resources are positively linked to a child's intellectual ability, school performance, and educational attainment. Finally, the negative link between sibship size and derivative family structure variables occurs vis-à-vis the allocation of resources to children.

Although the resource dilution hypothesis has been entertained by scholars for over a century, not until the past few decades did researchers begin to test it directly. A key to addressing this hypothesis is the definition and identification of those resources that may influence educational outcomes. We define resources very broadly: they are interpersonal or material, are measurable (at least for the purposes of testing the hypothesis), are possessed by families, and can be differentially distributed to children. This definition is in line with that of scholars across various disciplines who have differentiated between types of resources and have highlighted the occasionally overlapping concepts of cultural capital, social capital, and economic capital.[11]

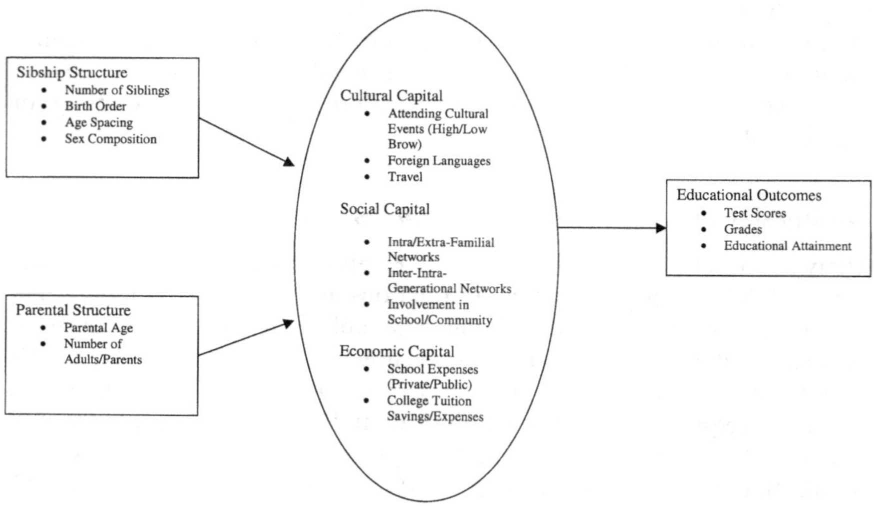

Figure 4.1 Modeling inter-generational effects of family structure on educational outcomes.

Areas of conceptual overlap notwithstanding, operationalizing something as amorphous as resources remains important to those of us interested in examining empirical links between family structure and educational outcomes. Social scientist Pierre Bourdieu and others emphasized how the cultural capital that parents impart to their children affects subsequent educational success. Cultural resources typically considered in empirical analysis include access to educational materials that parents may provide to their children (e.g. computers, books, encyclopedia, chemistry sets, etc.) and to "highbrow" activities (e.g. attending the opera, visiting museums, taking music or dance lessons). Regarding the latter, it is not that these resources are necessarily thought to be intrinsically valuable in improving academic outcomes (although they may be), but rather that members of the dominant culture (e.g. teachers) are impressed by youths' cultural knowledge. Similarly, it has been suggested that standardized tests often include class-biased questions related to elements of elite culture. Consequently, cultural capital is positively associated with school performance, independently of related variables like socioeconomic status.

In contrast, James Coleman rooted social capital in the notion that interpersonal relationships and connectedness in the community shape access to information and promote positive behavior. He distinguished between different dimensions of social capital, most notably intra- and extra-familial as well as intra- and inter-generational ties. In studying social capital, scholars thus have examined such indicators as the amount of time parents spend with the child, the degree to which parents encourage their children to do well in school, and the extent to which parents develop ties to educational institutions or "gatekeepers" (e.g. attending parent/teacher conferences or PTO meetings). One set of indicators popularized by Coleman centers on closure or embeddedness, often operationalized as the degree to which parents knew their children's friends and their friends' parents.[12]

Economic capital is the most concrete and in turn most easily measured of these three categories of resources. Very simply, it involves the monetary resources parents have and are willing to invest in their children's educational activities. The degree to which economic resources matter, of course, may vary across the life cycle. In other work, we (Brian Powell and Lala Carr Steelman) suggest that parental economic resources may be most salient when children and parents are making decisions regarding college attendance. This observation is not to deny the importance of economic resources in childhood or early adolescence. Indeed, having readily available financial assets enables parents to provide many forms of cultural capital and educational materials to children that, in turn, may yield long-term educational dividends.

The evidence that family size is inversely related to resource allocation to children is overwhelming. Examining a series of national data sets, we, along with sociologist Douglas Downey, have shown a negative relationship between sibship size and nearly every indicator of parental social, cultural, and economic resources, such as the degree to which parents know their eighth grader son or daughter's friends, parental participation in school-related activities, travel and participation in dance lessons, other cultural activities and lessons, maternal reading to pre-school children, the presence of educational resources such as books, encyclopedias, and computers, and even financial inputs into a child's post-secondary education.[13]

Still, the forms of these negative relationships do vary. For many resources, each additional child in the household has the same negative effect. For other resources (especially economic ones), however, each additional child bears a decreasingly negative effect. Still, for other resources (usually cultural resources), there may be a threshold pattern in which resources are slowly reduced or even constant until a certain "breaking point" at which the resources are dramatically reduced. That is, additional children may have less of a dampening impact on the pool of resources past a certain critical mass of children. Douglas Downey also locates a potential double disadvantage for children growing up in large families: not only are they less likely to have a computer in the home, but even if they do, access is necessarily restricted. Regardless of these variations, in American society, where resources that potentially could be devoted to children abound, it appears that family size, independent of other background factors such as social class, constrains the flow of educationally profitable resources to offspring.[14]

The evidence that the negative link between educational outcomes, especially educational attainment, and sibship size is due to resource dilution is quite strong. In arguably the most systematic analysis of the resource dilution hypothesis, Douglas Downey demonstrates not only that sibship size is negatively linked to a wide range of resources but also that this link explains most of, if not all of, the relationship between sibship size and schools grades and standardized test scores. Even stronger patterns have been found for educational attainment. In related work, we also show that increased sibship size deleteriously affects the likelihood and amount of financial assistance to children, which in turn negatively affects whether children matriculate, continue and graduate from college. This pattern persists even with children's ability, familial income and other socioeconomic factors held constant.

Despite its ostensible simplicity, there is still a great deal to be learned regarding the resource dilution hypothesis. One of the most intriguing yet untested possibilities, proposed by Douglas Downey, is that sibship size also dilutes negative (i.e. unfavorable) resources. While the concept of resources usually evokes positive connotations, this imagery need not necessarily be the case. We think of parents spending time with their children, investing in educational materials that may help them in school, supervising homework, setting high standards for their child's school work, representing exemplary role models and actively engaging in school related activities. Yet, just like ions, resources can be positively or negatively charged. Underpinning the debate about the family's role is the tacit presumption that a child always profits from interaction with his/her family and that outside interference with that interaction occurs at the child's expense. Accepting this assumption is naive. Not all mothers read enthusiastically to their children or encourage them to aspire to higher academic levels. Nor do all fathers offer warmth and support. Indeed, in some situations, interaction with parents may be more harmful than other alternatives in which children might engage. To the extent that interaction spent with a hostile parent is harmful, if that interaction is diluted among siblings, the unfavorable consequences of these interactions may lessen. Unfortunately, research to date on resource dilution research largely has focused on positive and left out negative resources.[15]

Though each of the foregoing explanations we have outlined remains viable, the resource dilution hypothesis enjoys the most empirical support and acceptance among social scientists. It makes common sense. It fits existing data nicely. It is parsimonious. It even encapsulates the confluence model, if we construe "collective intellect" as one type of resource families can provide. And it is pliable enough to encompass other family structure variables, for example one versus two-parent households, under its rubric. While public debate over the implications of divorce and single parenthood for children tends to feature cultural explanations, such as the need for children (especially boys) to have access to fathers as male role models and disciplinarians, some social scientists have identified more structurally based accounts for the connection between family dissolution and negative educational outcomes. In very basic terms, one less parent may reduce the social and economic resources available to children.[16]

Focusing on the distribution of resources within and across families also has compelling social and educational policy implications, which become more apparent when comparing international data. After providing an overview of the empirical literature on the impact of other components of sibship structure and parental age in the United States, we discuss evidence from comparative international studies to draw conclusions about these implications.

Beyond sibship size: spacing, birth order, and sex composition

There is, of course, more to sibship structure than its size. To the extent that sibship size shapes the allocation of educationally lucrative resources to children, the logic of the resource dilution hypothesis (or, for that matter, the other explanations for the link between sibship size and educational outcomes) easily can be augmented to incorporate related parameters of the sibship matrix such as age-spacing (i.e. the number of years separating the births of each sibling), sex composition (i.e. the relative number of brothers and sisters), and birth order. That relatively little attention has been directed to some of these features, especially age-spacing and sex composition, is due in part to the, until recently, infrequent presence of these items in the large national data sets typically used in the study of educational outcomes. With the inclusion of a more extensive (albeit still not as comprehensive as we would like) set of sibship (and parental) variables in recent data sets, however, social scientists are now in a position to rigorously explore the educational implications of these structural features of the family. At this point, it appears that age-spacing, which in the United States may now vary more than sibship size, behaves in a similar fashion to sibship size. That is, close spacing is negatively linked to children's educational outcomes such as test scores, grades, and educational outcomes. Close spacing is also negatively related to the allocation of resources and this link effectively explains a great deal of the negative relationship between spacing and educational progress, especially educational attainment.[17] We believe that these patterns comport well with the resource dilution model although others have proposed spuriousness or the confluence model as an alternative accounts.

The evidence regarding sex composition remains puzzling and contradictory. While some researchers find little difference between children of same-sex and mixed-sex sibling groups our earlier research leads us to conclude that having any brothers or having more brothers than sisters creates a disadvantage for both boys and girls, at least as far as the academic milieu of the household, parental support for post-secondary education, test scores, and educational attainment are concerned. Yet, recent analyses have found that having sisters deleteriously affects educational attainment, but only for females. And other studies suggest that having opposite-sex siblings impedes educational attainment success more than having same-sex siblings does. It should be apparent from these widely divergent patterns that any attempt to draw firm conclusions about the consequences of gender composition of sibling groups remains, at best, premature.[18]

As for birth order, before the early 1980s, research suggested that first-born children excel in terms of ability/intelligence over their later-born siblings. Since then, a sizeable body of literature disputes this claim. Often these critiques have made the simple observation that birth order and sibship size are so highly correlated (approximately 0.70) that what appears to be a birth order effect is, upon closer examination, a sibship size effect. An illustration here may be useful. Imagine a child who is the fourth-born in his family and has performed poorly in school. While one initially (and probably incorrectly) might attribute academic failure to the child's ordinal position, one would also have to recognize that a fourth-born child by definition comes from a large family (i.e. at least four children). Psychologist

Joseph Rodgers refers to the tendency to assume a birth order effect when other explanations are more likely as "the birth order trap." He contends that the public's fascination with birth order stems from the fact that everybody has a birth order and most people identify with it (much like with astrological signs). Therefore, it is not surprising that media efforts often place the spotlight on birth order, regardless of skepticism voiced by scholars and empirical evidence to the contrary.[19]

This line of thought does not automatically discount the possibility of birth order effects in the United States but rather suggests that these effects are much more circumscribed than previously posited. Moreover, the effects need not always be more beneficial for firstborns. As our own research shows, younger children are more likely than their elder siblings to receive financial support for their college education from their parents. This pattern is consistent with the resource dilution model because many later-born children enter college at a point in their parents' life cycles at which parents are nearing their professional and income peak and when their parents have less financial responsibility for their older children who have reached adulthood. Indeed, that birth order and family size are so closely linked to parental age has compelled us to further examine whether (and, if so, how) parental age influences the allocation of resources to children and, in turn, children's educational outcomes.

Parental age and resource allocation

Although scholarly interest in the life course and aging has reached or perhaps surpassed the level of interest in sibship structure, surprisingly little research has examined whether parental age affects the allocation of educational resources to children. To be sure, some studies have focused on the difference between children of teen mothers and children of older mothers, but such comparisons ignore the variation among non-teenage mothers and ultimately leave the impression that, for example, a child whose mother gave birth at the age of 20 has roughly equivalent experiences as a child whose mother gave birth at the age of 35.

It has been over a decade since sociologists Robert Mare and Meei-Shenn Tzeng demonstrated that parental age may strongly influence children's educational attainment. More specifically, they observe, at the bivariate level, a curvilinear relationship between paternal age and son's educational attainment; however, with the inclusion of socioeconomic background in multivariate models, this pattern transforms into a strong positive relationship. That is, the older the father, the greater the son's educational attainment. Unfortunately, data restrictions prevented the authors from identifying the mechanisms by which parental age wields its influence, although they suggest that the provision of educational resources may be a key explanatory factor. Nor did they explore the implications of maternal age or the effects of parental age (maternal or paternal) on daughters. Yet, despite the questions raised by this analysis and the promise of this line of inquiry, few scholars have followed Mare and Tzeng's lead and fewer have examined the link between parental age and children's educational progress. This gap seems astonishing in light of the attention, discussed above, devoted to the effects of other family variables, such as sibship size, spacing, and birth order, which may well be confounded with parental age.

A few years ago, we recognized this research gap on parental age as an excellent chance not only to build on our existing work but also to clarify further which family factors affect the distribution of educationally valuable resources to children. The result was another distinct, but related, stream of research with interesting results that suggest that parental age deserves a more central place in the study of family and education. In hypothesizing how parental age could be linked to resources to children, we saw five possibilities. First, the relationship between parental age and resources might be spurious, that is an artifact of parental age's connection to some other family feature (e.g. sibship size, parental education, parental income). We suspect that one of the reasons that parental age has been so understudied is that social scientists might assume that its impact stems entirely from its close association with socioeconomic indicators. Second, having an older parent may be beneficial with respect to resource allocation. If children are born to older parents, they may reap the benefit at least in terms of economic considerations. Earlier work by several research teams finds that even when parents express favoritism in terms of sponsoring their first child's education, in reality the later-born child more likely receives parental support, a pattern we attribute to later-born children arriving at a more opportune time when parent's income trajectory is close to or at its peak. But parental age may reflect much more than just financial assets. With age, parents may mature in ways that prompt them to give more to their children. To the extent that economic standing, social wisdom, and priorities shift with age in ways that favor children, we would expect resource allocation to children to trend upward as parental age rises.

Third, later parental age could have drawbacks that reduce resource allocation to children. Surely, physical and functional impairment may constrain how much parents can actually do for their children. Moreover, the larger age gap between parents and children may disrupt communication across generations. Younger parents also may have more energy to expend on their children and may relate more easily to children. In addition, older parents may curtail financial investments as retirement approaches or as the need to care for their own aging parents nears. Fourth, the relationship between parental age and resources might be curvilinear – that is, the advantage (or disadvantage) of having a much younger or much older parent could occur simultaneously. Fifth and finally, the effects of parental age might vary contingent on the type of resources evaluated – for example, younger parents might spend more time with their children while older parents may be more likely to value and invest in cultural resources.[20]

Despite the scholarly neglect of parental age, several extant data sets (the National Educational Longitudinal Study of 1988; the Early Childhood Longitudinal Survey 1998; High School and Beyond, the National Longitudinal Survey of the High School Class of 1972; and the National Household Education Household Survey) provide solid information on parental age. These data sets provide the empirical basis of our analysis of parental age. Not only do these data cover several different decades (the 1970s, the 1980s, and the 1990s through 1998), thus reducing the likelihood that any patterns are the result of a period or cohort effect. They also enable us to test whether parental age operates similarly for investments in young children and in adolescents. These data also amply cover social, cultural, and economic types of resources that have been linked to educational success. In addition, the inclusion of a wide range of socioeconomic variables in these data sets allows us to assess the possibility of spuriousness.

In our ongoing study, we have examined over 40 resources. For example, using data from the National Educational Longitudinal Study of 1988, we have investigated the effect of maternal age on cultural classes, that is, whether the youth (in eighth grade) attended classes outside the school in art, music, dance, language, or computers. We initially discern a curvilinear pattern: that is, children's participation in these classes rises with maternal age up to a certain point at which children's participation declines. However, once socioeconomic background and family structure (factors also linked to both resources and parental age) are also taken into account, the relationship becomes strictly linear and positive: that is, the older the mother, the greater the child's participation in these classes.[21]

The aforementioned patterns are strikingly consistent with the patterns for nearly all other parental resources we have studied. At the bivariate level (i.e. before taking into account other factors), the relationship usually is curvilinear; however, upon controlling for socioeconomic background and family structure, as the age of the parent rises so does the transmission of resources to children. The pattern holds across economic, social and cultural resources but is most pronounced for financial ones. The only exception to the general pattern is that older compared to younger parents express less willingness to go into debt for their children. Moreover, these patterns hold across the different U.S. data sets, suggesting that the results are not period or cohort specific (at least between the early 1970s and the late 1990s), and the results apply to both young children and adolescents. Perhaps the most impressive evidence besides the startling consistency of the findings is that parental age exhibits more pronounced effects on resource allocation to children than do other commonly relied upon social and familial factors such as race, gender, and marital disruption. We also find that the effects of some features of the sibling structure lessen or magnify when parental age is taken into account. Of the many variables we incorporate in this analysis, only parental education and income consistently outweigh parental age in significance. Stepping back from the details of resource allocation for a moment, it is indeed interesting that socioeconomic status, family size, and parental age almost always affect the allocation of resources to children in predictable directions, be they economic, cultural, or social. While there is still much to discover about the link between parental age and children's educational outcomes, these results are provocative and hint that parental age is implicated in children's development.

Comparative international evidence on family structure and resource allocation

The preceding discussion on how family structure influences educational outcomes via resource allocation focused almost entirely on the families in the United States. However, U.S.-based findings are shaped by underlying assumptions concerning access to education, the importance of a nuclear family structure, financial resources, and standardized indicators of achievement and attainment. Thus, while useful as a heuristic tool for within-country analyses, Figure 4.1, which earlier in this chapter delineated the links between family structure, resource allocation, and educational outcomes at individual levels, raises two questions that can best be addressed by means of comparative-international research:

1 Are family structure effects universal?
2 How does the public policy context shape the relation between family structure and educational outcomes?

The two sections below consider these questions.

Are family structure effects universal?

First, our very definitions of concepts like "family," "resources," and "outcomes" remain culturally bound. Definitions and empirical measures that are too narrowly conceived may miss the most important trends that determine educational attainment and achievement across the world, as they may lead researchers to underestimate (or, in some cases, overestimate) actual effects of family structure on resource allocation and educational outcomes. Alternative family structures in Latin America and West Africa, including principles of polygyny and child fosterage defy western definitions of household or family units, while also challenging our notion of intra-familial resources.

To give more specific examples, had sociologists Yossi Shavit and Jennifer Pierce disregarded extended families as a source of financial (and other forms of) support, they might have concluded erroneously that family structure affects attainment among Israeli Jews but not among Israeli Arabs. In this study, the authors also illustrate that different, ethnically specific types of family structure co-exist within countries. In his overview of tests of the resource dilution hypothesis, Douglas Downey and his colleague Stephanie Neubauer conclude that the detrimental impact of number of siblings attenuates when there are cultural norms supportive of higher fertility. Several examples support this position, even for some groups in the United States. Among Brigham Young University (mostly Mormon) students, for example, there is no relationship between family size and ACT scores. Similarly, family size has a less pronounced impact on test scores and educational attainment of Mormon children as compared to their Protestant counterparts. Judith Blake also observes a less steep effect of sibship size among Catholic than Protestant students. It appears that in subcultures, both in and outside of the United States, that encourage high fertility, there may well be alternative forms of support that compensate for the dilution of finite resources parents have at their disposal.[22]

While research conducted within the United States has examined at length the effects of family size and structure on a series of educational outcomes, comparative-international research predominantly focuses on issues related to attainment (enrollments, drop out rates, years of schooling) and has mostly ignored individual performance (grades, test scores). This focus might occur because it is possible that in most countries, family structure and resources do indeed play a greater role in determining individual access to education than in shaping academic performance. Academic performance only becomes an issue in societies in which education is easily accessible and affordable. Moreover, the popularity and frequent usage of standardized achievement tests in countries such as the United States and Japan remain rather unique. Few countries devise and implement comparable achievement indicators. Such data availability issues provide one more reason why comparativists have focused on how family structure shapes attainment. In this chapter, we provide just a few examples to illustrate that patterns are often similar but not identical across countries. The existing research shows that, persistent questions involving conceptualization and operationalization notwithstanding, some of the family structure patterns observed for the United States may be indeed generalizable.[23]

For instance, even across different ethnic groups, family size has a negative impact on high school track placement, which is often regarded as an indicator of both attainment as well as achievement. This seems to hold true for immigrants and non-immigrants in the United States and in Germany, though such effects weaken once family resources are taken into account. In addition, kindergarten attendance rates are higher among

German families, in which only children are more common. This pattern creates long-term consequences, because kindergarten serves as the main springboard for track placement at secondary levels. In Israel, such differences in educational attainment among Iraqi Jews (Sephardim) and Romanian Jews (Ashkenazim) are attributable to group-specific differences in family size. Similarly, family size effects on educational attainment seem strongest among Australians of Italian origin and weakest among Anglo-Australians.

In the Philippines the number and sex composition of siblings influences children's likelihood of being enrolled in school, and this relationship depends in part on the child's sibling position (birth order). In Thailand, a child's likelihood of attending secondary school also strongly depends on family size, especially in rural areas. In contrast, in Colombia the direct effects of family size on educational attainment may be limited to the largest families. In Vietnam, an underlying set of factors related to urban/rural residence and family SES explains most of the empirical association between family size and educational attainment. This pattern is further corroborated by case studies of Middle Eastern and North African countries, where population size and growth rate continue to impact children's access to, and the quality of, educational facilities. These factors appear to have a more detrimental effect on the educational attainment of girls, for whom family size and socialization practices continue to influence enrollment and continuation, even in countries like Ghana.[24]

However, the negative sibship size effect does not seem to be universal. In some countries, sibship size even exhibits positive effects. In the Netherlands, for example, children in immigrant families receive school-related help from older siblings. This is especially the case among Turkish and Moroccan children who profit from interaction with older siblings who help with schoolwork and other school-related matters. By serving as mentors, older siblings become a resource themselves. Positive effects of family size also have been documented among Kenyan and American Samoan children, although that evidence is not entirely conclusive.[25]

A related body of comparative-international research has investigated the specific mechanisms through which family size affects – positively or negatively – educational outcomes. Not surprisingly, resource allocation has emerged as a key factor. In countries as diverse as Taiwan, Malaysia, and Columbia, size, birth order, and gender composition of children per family have a direct, negative effect on parental investment in children's education, which in turn is known to affect attainment patterns. In fact, many researchers have employed the term "parental resources" more loosely, using it to refer to indicators related to family background (parental education, income, age), social and cultural capital, and even parental aspirations. Research on Europe, Africa, and the Middle East has shown that some types of resources are, in fact, more easily available in extended families and families with several children – including adult help with child care and socio-emotional support and guidance by older siblings. Non-family based parental resources include ties to the community-at-large, which can also provide added benefits to educational outcomes. Correspondingly, demographer Jay Teachman and his colleagues propose that different types of resources can have compensatory effects on educational attainment and achievement.[26]

Finally, even one of our fundamental assumptions about how parental structure influences educational outcomes is currently under challenge. Research on the United States and on Western Europe frequently shows that growing up in a nuclear family with two parents present benefits children's educational outcomes, presumably because it shapes the availability of financial as well as social support for children's education. But while single parenthood is strongly associated with lower achievement and attainment in most industrialized countries, the reverse may happen in developing countries. For instance, children in sub-Saharan Africa who live in female-headed households appeared to be advantaged: that is, they are more likely to be enrolled in school and complete more years of education. Similarly, in Russia, resources alone do not necessarily benefit children's educational trajectories. Instead, controlling for family SES, growing up with a single parent actually may have a positive impact at key educational transitions. In contrast, growing up with a step-parent as the second adult present has a negative impact on children's likelihood of continuing at secondary and higher levels, possibly due to the stress associated with living with a step-parent. In addition, we already mentioned that extended family systems like the "hamulas" (patrilineal systems based on kinship) common among Israeli Muslims may buffer the effects of sibship size on attainment by providing alternative types of resources to families. A similar pattern exists for children of widows in Malaysia, who seem to benefit from extended family resources.[27]

The next section focuses explicitly on the direct effects of social policy on family size/structure, followed by a discussion of the ways in which educational and social policy at large mediate both the effects of family structure on the distribution of resources to children as well as the effects of resource allocation on individual educational outcomes. The fundamental question remains whether and how much we can extrapolate from studies conducted mostly on large-scale U.S. data sets and, to a lesser extent, on data from industrialized European countries.

How does the public policy context shape the relation between family structure and educational outcomes?

Earlier, we alluded to a second criticism of Figure 4.1: It pays insufficient attention to how the social context can influence family structure itself as well as resource allocation and eventual educational outcomes. Figure 4.2 outlines this macro-to-micro link schematically. Essentially, we propose

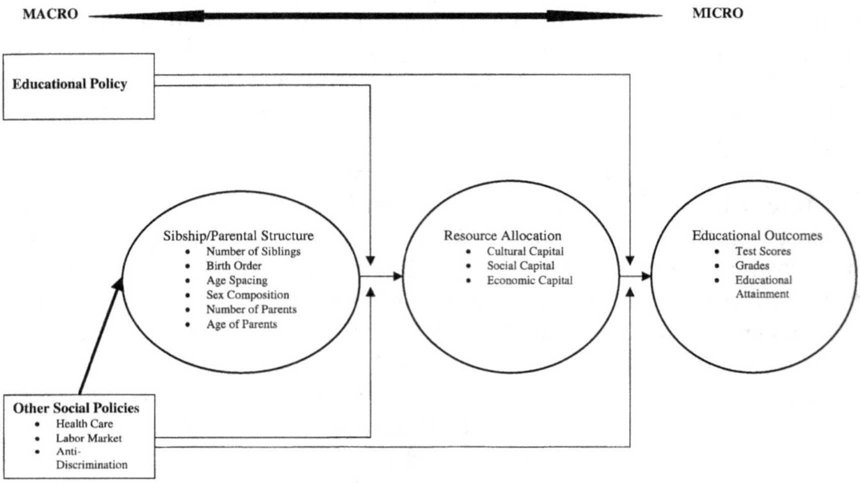

Figure 4.2 Modeling the macro-micro link.

that social policy can have direct as well as indirect effects. Some policies have a direct effect on family structure. Moreover, social policy, including educational policy, may mediate effects of both family structure on resource allocation and resource allocation on individual educational outcomes.

Most U.S.-based research assumes that family-level processes operate independently of the public policy context. Especially analyses based on cross-sectional data tend to overlook the importance of policy developments precisely because they lack historical as well as comparative-international perspective. But, in fact, country-specific social and educational policy environments have direct effects on family structure while also mediating the impact of both family structure and resource allocation on a variety of educational outcomes.

How does public policy affect educational outcomes, at both individual and aggregate (group or geographic) levels? Several researchers have pointed to the way in which macro-level developments related to demographic and economic transitions shape the above mentioned patterns. A growing literature indicates that the negative impact of family size should materialize only after the demographic transition has occurred.[28] Similarly, macro-economic policies make the negative relationship between family size and educational outcomes country-, cohort-, period-, and ethnically-specific. Moreover, basic infrastructural issues that are taken for granted in many industrialized countries (e.g. roads, public transportation) may dramatically affect access to education, especially in rural areas. Even supranational developments, including cultural and economic globalization processes, are thought to influence parental decisions about educating their children and shape children's educational outcomes.[29]

State theorists, as well as other social scientists focusing on politics, have concentrated mostly on the way in which social policies have shaped children's general welfare as well as their academic attainment and achievement. In particular, social policies related to regulating labor markets (e.g. protective labor legislation, unemployment and pension benefits), parental leave, and health care/population growth have direct effects on family structure. Moreover, they can mediate the effects of family structure on resource allocation and on individual-level educational outcomes.

Direct social policy effects

The direct effects of social policy on family structure are best illustrated by pointing toward population, labor market, and parental leave practices. For example, countries with explicitly anti-natalist policies (e.g. China) have curtailed population growth sharply by limiting the number of children per family. While this rule has been relaxed in recent years (especially for rural families and cases in which the firstborn child is female), limiting family size by restricting fertility should, in turn, enable parents to maximize the effect of financial and other available resources. At the same time, changes in economic policy can lead to period-specific gender differences in education. In China, gender differences in access to post-elementary education were greater during pro-capitalist periods (i.e. during the "Great Leap" in the late 1950s and again in the early 1990s) and declined during the period of the Cultural Revolution.

Policies designed to elevate birth rates and increase family size can also take various forms, such as tax incentives, parental leave policies, or state-sponsored day care. Most importantly, different social policies may have countervailing effects on birth rates and on family structure more generally. For example, pro-natalist policies such as generous parental leave regulations and financial incentives for families with children may have minimal effect on family size in countries with socialized health care systems (e.g. Northern Europe), which are more likely to offer extensive reproductive health care, including access to birth control and abortion services. Similarly, post-World War Two policies aimed at economic transformation led to a steady decline of children born to married couples in Japan, despite a generally pro-natalist stance expressed through laws that sponsored a traditional gender division of labor, discouraged the participation of married women in the labor force, and made divorce difficult to obtain. In contrast, similar pro-natalist social policies may influence family structure and size in countries where reproductive services are scarce (even if health care is socialized, like in Poland, Romania, or Italy). In that case, classic resource dilution problems may become exacerbated over time.[30]

Indirect social policy effects

To illustrate the indirect effects of social policy as it mediates family structure effects on resource allocation, we turn to the work of political sociologists and political scientists. For example, political scientist Suzanne Mettler shows how the principle of "dual federalism" in the United States has created gendered eligibility criteria for public assistance programs administered under federal versus state auspices. By regulating how single-parent families (most of whom are led by women) can access cash benefits as well as services, ranging from health care to child care and housing subsidies, governments constrain the primary care takers' ability to "invest" in their children's education. Such investments take different forms. While parents' personal involvement in their children's education tends to affect academic achievement, parents' ability to provide financial support most likely affects educational attainment, especially post-secondary education.

In countries where access to such services is means-tested, as it is in the United States, children whose parents have limited access to resources (cultural, social, economic capital) are most likely to experience competition for resources and, in turn, are most likely to experience lower levels of achievement and attainment. In contrast, when access to services is socialized, or at least widely available and affordable, we should expect to see weaker effects of factors like large family size or single parenthood on resource allocation. Empirical research on a number of countries confirms this pattern.

The way in which governments structure access to early childhood programs influences children's long-term cognitive and educational outcomes in virtually all industrialized and industrializing countries (including Colombia, India, Singapore, Turkey). While attendance at such programs generally benefits children, those from families with few resources stand to gain the most. Sociologist Savane Boocock suggests that governmentally subsidized programs with clearly specified goals and equitable resources (staff, facilities, materials) are most likely to ensure overall improvements in educational attainment and achievement. By extension, one may assume that differences in how families allocate educational resources to small children are bound to exacerbate differences in educational outcomes in those countries where access to and the quality of day care and pre-school programs remains unregulated and susceptible to socio-economic background.

Even in developing countries, where governments provide few if any public services, similar issues come into play, though they are likely to affect an even greater proportion of the population. For instance, female-headed households tend to distribute available resources differently. More specifically, household consumption, nutrition/health, and school enrollment patterns indicate that female-headed households invest more resources into children. The debt crisis of the 1980s and 1990s has led governments to cut back on social service (including nutrition programs) which, in turn, is likely to impact families' ability to invest financially into their children's education. A case study of Poland shows that governmental policies during the socialist era (especially 1965–1986) helped reduce the direct effect of family size on the allocation of food resources by raising living standards in general. The impact of such policies was particularly noticeable for large families (i.e. with five or more children).[31]

Whether governments subsidize the elderly population may also enter into if and how parents invest in children. The United States' social security and medicare systems reduce children's responsibility to care for aging parents. However, in other nations, a traditional "social contract" exists between generations. Those held responsible for elderly parents may have more legitimate claims on familial resources. In the Philippines, for example, daughters are obliged to care for aging parents, which may induce parents to invest into their daughters' education. In contrast, East Asian girls are often expected to sacrifice their own educational goals, enter the labor force, and help subsidize their brother's education. In that case, parents invest more heavily into male progeny because sons (and daughters-in-law) are expected to take care of parents in later years.[32]

Indirect educational policy effects

In their well-known book, sociologists Bruce Fuller and Richard Rubinson also note that educational policy represents one of the key factors shaping access to education (e.g. via enrollment patterns). As Figure 4.2 illustrates, educational policy does help determine whether and how family structure matters by mediating effects on both resource allocation within families as well as individual educational outcomes. Put differently, the effects that family structure and resource allocation have on educational outcomes should differ from the United States experience in countries where education is neither compulsory nor government-sponsored, as well as in contexts where access to (at least the most prestigious) educational opportunities favors specific ethnic groups or males. The significance of such policy differences becomes clear once we realize that, even in the United States, family size exerts its most pronounced impact on post-secondary educational outcomes.[33]

A recent review by sociologists Claudia Buchmann and Emily Hannum discusses the effects of educational policy on a variety of educational outcomes at individual and aggregate levels. Yet, our primary interest lies in the macro-micro links among educational policy, resource allocation, and individual educational achievement/attainment.[34] Gender differences in educational outcomes offer a clear-cut illustration of these patterns. Researchers usually attribute gender-specific educational outcomes to the influence of a priori legislative constraints, which circumscribe governmental resource allocation (funding for facilities, teachers) as well as eligibility criteria for schools as well as students. Lest readers infer that access to education in the United States historically has been gender-neutral, note that neither the concept of a "gendered state" nor the phenomenon of institutional discrimination (whereby seemingly gender-neutral educational policies produce gender-specific outcomes) occurs just in countries currently undergoing industrialization. As an illustration, the U.S. federal government historically has restricted women's access to higher education through its support for largely sex-segregated land grant colleges as well as vocational programs and grant programs that heavily benefit men (GI Bill, National Merit Scholarships). Thus, educational policies designed to increase enrollments among specific target populations may influence parents' ability and willingness to steer their children into certain educational programs.[35]

Educational policies mediate resource allocation within families as well as individual educational outcomes through several key mechanisms. For example, policies aimed at expanding educational opportunities may help diminish some forms of stratification while institutionalizing others. At elementary and secondary levels, it appears that measures to expand access to education generally help decrease gender inequities in enrollment and grade completion. Research on industrialized countries indicates that this trend regarding gender differences in access to education even extends into the tertiary sector.

Declining gender differences (and in some cases reversals in gender differences) in access to elementary and secondary education are being observed in industrialized as well as industrializing countries around the world, including the Middle East and North Africa. Even in poor countries such as Vietnam or sub-Saharan Africa, traditional gender divisions appear to be narrowing. Finally, several Asian countries have also undergone similar transformations. Apparently, gender inequality in educational attainment decreased in Hong Kong when the government increased educational spending, so that changes in Hong Kong's educational policy mediated several family structure effects by decreasing the effects of sibship size, sex composition, and birth order on attainment. Relying on a classic resource allocation argument, sociologist Suet-Ling Pong argues that increased government spending on education benefits girls, because it decreases the impact of family-SES (income) on school attendance.[36]

By the same token, when state efforts to expand educational access fall short of demand for such opportunities – as has happened in Ghana and in Kenya – it results in high degrees of competitiveness, which may in fact exacerbate existing inequalities along gender, class, or ethnic lines. This is particularly the case for countries that also lack educational policies proactively seeking to incorporate women into the educational system. In fact, having younger siblings of either gender lessens the chance for older daughters in such diverse countries as Ghana, Taiwan, Hong Kong, and Malaysia regardless of the family's financial resources. While traditional gender roles appear especially oppressive for older daughters, sometimes situations work to the disadvantage of males. In the Philippines girls are more likely than boys to be enrolled in schools. Research by Deborah DeGraff and others suggest that paid employment lures boys away from schools, while girls are expected to stay in school since they are obligated to care for their parents in their senior years.[37]

However, at times gender dynamics recede into the background. In many countries educational policy is geared toward specific population groups, thus ultimately mediating family size effects on educational outcomes. For instance, government support for small-scale local peer support programs helps improve educational attainment among ethnic minorities in the Netherlands (in this case Turks and Moroccans) by providing extra-familial mentors. In Malaysia, two minority groups (those who are ethnically Chinese or Indian) are not subject to state affirmative action laws. Only among these groups does family size produce negative effects on educational attainment, especially among girls of the younger, post-independence generation. Ironically, the same polices designed to increase economic opportunities for ethnic Malaysian people may inadvertently reduce incentives for large families to enroll their children in secondary schools, thus widening ethnic disparities in educational attainment.[38]

At the same time, the overall impact of government spending on educational outcomes remains limited. Additional policy remedies known to minimize the effect of family-based resources also include making schooling compulsory and guaranteeing access on an open admissions basis. In Pakistan, where no compulsory education laws exist, gender and social class-specific differences in educational attainment persist even at basic levels – in part because single-sex schools (considered important by conservative Muslims) remain scarce in rural areas. And in Thailand, the diminishing gender gap in educational attainment is linked to a series of compulsory education laws.[39]

Moreover, practices such as school fees or state-sponsored two-tiered systems of public versus private (including parochial or religious) schools place additional resource-based constraints on access and may serve to institutionalize ethnic and gender segregation. In Hong Kong, the introduction of free schooling clearly benefited girls' access to elementary education. In contrast, public funding is limited in Ghana, and schools require tuition payments to meet costs. Consequently, parents are more likely to send sons than daughters to school. Thus the prevalence of tuition fees may also depend on the level of governmental subsidies for education. Moreover, in Israel, where the state maintains secular as well as religious high schools for Arabs as well as Jews, educational opportunities tend to be constrained by gender as well as ethnicity.[40]

Finally, institutional features of the educational system influence the ability of parents to become involved in schools, thus affecting student attainment and achievement. This includes factors such as whether parents have a choice in sending their children to different (public or private) schools and whether schools are comprehensive or differentiated (by means of tracking, ability grouping). Relatively few studies deal directly with the way in which organizational (school-level) processes influence individual educational outcomes, and it remains a noticeable blind spot in educational research on the United States and comparative-international research. Similarly, a series of studies outlines how "school choice" reforms popular in the 1980s and 1990s have shaped access to education around the world. While this debate has not yet been resolved, evidence indicates that school choice programs generally exacerbate existing inequalities (especially by class and ethnicity), unless governments stipulate that parents can choose public and private schools freely, without incurring additional expenses.[41]

Turning our attention to school-level factors, several researchers have noted that most comparative literature on schooling outcomes has underscored the tension between educational expansion and stratification and, in turn, has ignored classroom dynamics. Partly, this is a result of our tendency to focus on micro-level factors, which have a stronger impact on academic achievement in industrialized countries. But as much as twenty years ago, a classic study by Stephen Heyneman and William Loxley already showed that, in developing countries, school-level and related contextual factors play a bigger role than do micro-level (family) dynamics. In other words, the existing literature confirms that school context is a particularly strong determinant of academic achievement in countries where access to schooling and available resources (teachers, facilities, funding) are scarce.[42]

Regarding the impact of attending comprehensive as opposed to differentiated schools, Hans Oswald *et al.*'s study of Germany remains exemplary. It is one of the few studies that explicitly examine how school characteristics affect what we call resource allocation outside of the United States. The authors link institutional characteristics of individual schools to the way in which parents invest one particular type of resource – i.e. their own time – into their children's education. Specifically, they find that school charters, which delineate whether the school is comprehensive (similar to the United States) or offers instruction in one of the three traditional tracks (vocational, general, rigorous academic), influence parental involvement in their children's schools. By implication, this means that the organization of German schools not only affects resource allocation itself but most likely mediates the effects of resource allocation on student achievement/attainment. Tracking practices influence educational outcomes in other countries as well. For instance, a study on Israel finds that elementary school tracking has ethnically specific effects on achievement: Achievement gaps are largest between Sephardim and Ashkenazim if the students attend schools where ability grouping is practiced. And in South Africa, controlled access to science education at secondary and tertiary levels serves as a de facto tracking mechanism, leading to ethnically specific educational and occupational outcomes that have disproportionately benefited the white minority.[43]

To summarize, comparative-international research suggests that family size does not have a uniformly direct and negative effect on children's educational outcomes. Instead, educational policy can diminish or exacerbate the extent to which family structure mediates resource allocation as well as individual educational outcomes. Moreover, variations in the dominant gender ideology, which frames the value attributed to women's paid versus unpaid labor, demonstrably affect national social policy, including pension plans, minimum wage, and protective labor legislation, and in turn children's educational progress.

Summary

This review was motivated by a core question that sociologists and others interested in education have posed: How do families facilitate or impede children's educational prospects? Our focus here has been on one aspect of this question, namely, the micro link between sibship and, to a lesser degree, parental structure, and educational outcomes. While some aspects of this link are now resolved (e.g. that sibship size is negatively linked to educational attainment in the United States), others still need to be reconciled (e.g. the degree to which the sibship size link is artifactual or real), and others are just beginning to be rigorously explored (e.g. whether and, if so, how, parental age affects the allocation of resources to children).

To more fully appreciate the processes by which families shape children's educational chances, however, we argue that scholars must look beyond the micro level and toward the macro level. While many of the models and explanations presented earlier in this review are facile in predicting educational outcomes in the United States, they may have limited applicability to non-industrialized nations and even less applicability to other industrialized nations in which governments provide compensatory resources to children. New empirical patterns, such as those we report regarding parental age, need to be explored both in the United States and in other countries. The challenge for scholars, policy analysts, and members of the public-at-large who are looking for educational solutions outside of the school is to recognize not only the importance of families and communities, but also the instrumental role that social context plays in mediating the powerful influences that families play in their children's lives.

Notes

1 Direct all correspondence to Brian Powell, Department of Sociology, 744 Ballantine Hall, 1020 E. Kirkwood Ave., Indiana University, Bloomington, IN 47405; email: powell@indiana.edu. Authors' contributions to this chapter are equal. We are grateful to Simon Cheng, Robert Carini, Scott

Carter, Dalton Conley, Douglas B. Downey, Carl Ek, Christina Ek, Jeremy Freese, R. D. Fulk, Martin Groeger, and Joseph Steelman for their comments. This research was supported by NSF grants SBR-9810246 and SES-9912299 to Lala Carr Steelman, NSF grants SBR-9810246 and SES-9912667 to Brian Powell, and a NAE/Spencer grant and NSF grant SES-9986586 to Werum.

2 For a discussion of the community control movement see M. Gittell, "Urban school reform in the 1970s," *Education and Urban Society* 1, 1968, 9–20, or D. Ravitch, *The Great School Wars*, New York: Basic Books, 1974; on the spectrum of political commentary see S. Feldman, "Promises to keep: where we stand," http://www.aft.org/stand/previous/2001/0101.html, 2001 (January) or G. F. Will, "Broken families and school performance," *Washington Post*, p. B07, 2002 (January 6).

3 Also see D. Downey, B. Powell, L. C. Steelman, and S. Pribesh, "Much ado about siblings: change models, sibship size, and intellectual development," *American Sociological Review* 64, 1999, 193–198; B. Powell and L. C. Steelman, "The liability of having brothers: paying for college and the sex composition of the family," *Sociology of Education* 62, 1989, 134–147; B. Powell and L. C. Steelman, "Beyond sibship size: sibling density, sex composition, and educational outcomes," *Social Forces* 69, 1990, 181–206; B. Powell and L. C. Steelman, "The educational benefits of being spaced out: sibship density and educational progress," *American Sociological Review* 58, 1993, 367–381; B. Powell and L. C. Steelman, "Feeling the pinch: child-spacing and constraints on parental economic investments in children," *Social Forces* 73, 1995, 1465–1486; B. Powell, L. C. Steelman, and R. Carini, "Advancing age, advancing youth: parental age and the flow of resources to progeny," Nashville, TN: Annual Meetings of the Southern Sociological Society, 1999; L. C. Steelman, "A tale of two variables: a review of the intellectual consequences of sibship size and birth order," *Review of Educational Research* 55, 1985, 353–386; L. C. Steelman and B. Powell, "Acquiring capital for college: the constraints of family configuration,' *American Sociological Review* 54, 1989, 844–855; L. C. Steelman and B. Powell, "Sponsoring the next generation: parental willingness to pay for college," *American Journal of Sociology* 96, 1991, 1505–1529; L. C. Steelman and B. Powell, "The family devalued: the treatment of the family in the small groups literature," *Advances in Group Processes* 13, 1996, 211–236; L. C. Steelman, B. Powell, R. Werum, and S. Carter, "Reconsidering the effects of sibling configuration: recent advances and challenges," *Annual Review of Sociology* 28, 2002, 243–269 for a discussion of our general argument. Also see D. B. Downey and B. Powell, "Do children from single-parent families fare better living with same-sex parents?," *Journal of Marriage and the Family* 55, 1993, 55–71 or B. Powell and D. Downey, "Living in single-parent households: an investigation of the same-sex hypothesis," *American Sociological Review* 62, 1997, 521–539 for an analysis of parental structure.

4 See D. P. Baker, "In comparative isolation: why comparative research has so little influence on American sociology of education," *Research in Sociology of Education and Socialization* 10, 1994, 53–70 and J. Meyer and D. P. Baker, "Forming American educational policy with international data: lessons from the sociology of education," *Sociology of Education* 69, 1996, 123–130 for a discussion of myopia in U.S.-based research. See C. Buchmann and B. Dalton, "Interpersonal influences and educational aspirations in twelve countries: the importance of institutional context," *Sociology of Education* 75, 2002, 99–122; C. Buchmann and E. Hannum, "Education and stratification in developing countries: review of theories and research," *Annual Review of Sociology* 27, 2001, 77–102; Y. Shavit and W. Müeller, *From School to Work*, Oxford: Claren-

don Press, 1998 for empirical evidence concerning the impact of policy environments on educational outcomes.

5 For a comprehensive review of contemporary work regarding sibship effects see J. Blake, "Family size and the quality of children," *Demography* 18, 1981, 1096–1101; J. Blake, "Number of siblings, family background, and the process of educational attainment," *Social Biology* 33, 1986, 5–21; J. Blake, *Family Size and Achievement,* Berkeley, CA: University of California Press, 1989; D. B. Downey, "When bigger is not better: family size, parental resources, and children's educational performance," *American Sociological Review* 60, 1995, 746–761; D. B. Downey, "Number of siblings and intellectual development: the resource dilution explanation," *American Psychologist* 56, 2001, 497–504; D. Featherman and R. Hauser, *Opportunity and Change*, New York, NY: Academic Press, 1978; R. Hauser and W. Sewell, "Birth order and educational attainment in full sibships," *American Educational Research Journal* 22, 1985, 1–23; D. Heer, "Effects of sibling number on child outcomes," *Annual Review of Sociology* 11, 1985, 27–47; D. Heer, "Effect of number, order and spacing of siblings on child and adult outcomes," *Social Biology* 33, 1986, 1–4; L. C. Steelman and J. Mercy, "Unconfounding the confluence model: a test of sibship size and birth order effects on intelligence," *American Sociological Review* 45, 1980, 571–582; L. C. Steelman, "A tale of two variables: a review of the intellectual consequences of sibship size and birth order," *Review of Educational Research* 55, 1985, 353–386; Steelman and Powell 1989, op. cit.; P. Taubman and J. Behrman, "Effects of number and position of siblings and adult outcomes," *Social Biology* 33, 1986, 22–33; R. Zajonc and G. Markus, "Birth order and intellectual development," *Psychological Review* 82, 1975, 74–88.

6 For contradictory evidence on this pattern see D. F. Alwin and A. Thornton, "Family origins and the schooling process: early versus late influence of parental characteristics," *American Sociological Review* 49, 1984, 784–802; Blake 1981, op. cit.; Blake 1986, op. cit.; Blake 1989, op. cit.; P. M. Blau and O. D. Duncan, *The American Occupational Structure*, New York, NY: Wiley, 1967; Downey 1995, op. cit.; Downey 2001, op. cit.; Powell and Steelman 1993, op. cit.; Steelman, op. cit., Steelman and Powell 1989, op. cit.; Steelman and Powell 1991, op. cit.; Taubman and Behrman, op. cit.

7 The heritability and uterine fatigue arguments are discussed in S. H. Broman, P. L. Nichols, and W. A. Kennedy, *Preschool IQ: Prenatal and Early Developmental Correlates*, London: Earlbaum, 1975; H. Grotevant, S. Scarr, and H. Weinberg, "Intelligence and development in constellations with adopted and natural children: a test of Zajonc and Markus Model," *Child Development* 48, 1977, 1699–1703; for critiques of both arguments see J. V. Higgins, E. W. Reed, and S. C. Reed, "Intelligence and family size: a paradox resolved," *Eugenics Quarterly* 9, 1962, 84–90 and Powell and Steelman 1993, op. cit.

8 J. H. S. Bossard and E. S. Boll, *The Large Family System*, Philadelphia, PA: The University of Pennsylvania Press, 1956; G. H. Elder Jr. and C. Bowerman, "Family structure in childrearing patterns: the effect of family size and sex composition," *American Sociological Review* 28, 1963, 891–905; D. Heise and E. P. M. Roberts, "The development of role knowledge," *Genetic Psychology Monographs* 82, 1970, 83–115, provide insights into the way socialization strategies affect educational outcomes, while D. F. Alwin, "Trends in parental socialization values: Detroit, 1958–1983," *American Journal of Sociology* 90, 1984, 359–382 focuses on the role of parental values.

9 See G. Guo and L. Van Wey, "Sibship size and intellectual development: is the relationship causal?," *American Sociological Review* 64, 1999a, 169–187; G. Guo and L. Van Wey, "The effects of closely spaced and widely spaced sibship size on intellectual development," *American Sociological Review* 64, 1999b,

199–206, for details regarding the argument about spuriousness. For a critical assessment of their analysis see Downey, Powell, Steelman, and Pribesh, op. cit. or Downey 2001, op. cit.

10 For classic work using the confluence model see Zajonc and Markus, op. cit. or R. Zajonc, "Family configuration and intelligence," *Science* 192, 1976, 227–236. More recently, C. Ernst and J. Angst, *Birth Order: Its Influence on Personality*, Berlin, Germany: Springer–Verlag, 1983; Hauser and Sewell, op. cit.; E. Page and G. Grandon, "Family configuration and mental ability: two theories contrasted with U.S. data," *American Educational Research Journal* 16, 1979, 257–272; Powell and Steelman 1993, op. cit.; R. Retherford and W. Sewell, "Birth order and further tests of the confluence model," *American Sociological Review* 56, 1999, 141–158; Steelman, op. cit., and Steelman and Mercy, op. cit. have re-examined the issue.

11 A. Anastasi, "Intelligence and family size," *Psychological Bulletin* 53, 1956, 187–209; Blake 1981, op. cit.; Blake 1986, op. cit.; Blake 1989, op. cit. present the resource dilution hypothesis in detail. For empirical work on the resource dilution hypothesis see A. Adler, *The Individual Psychology of Alfred Adler: A Systematic Presentation in Selections From His Writings*, ed. and annotated by H. Ansbacher and R. Ansbacher, New York, NY: Basic Books, 1959; Blake 1989, op. cit.; G. S. Becker, *A Treatise on the Family*, Cambridge, MA: Harvard University Press, 1981; Downey 1995, op. cit.; Steelman and Powell 1989, op. cit.; Steelman, Powell, Werum, and Carter, op. cit.; Taubman and Behrman, op. cit.

12 For human, cultural, and social capital definitions see G. S. Becker, *Human Capital*, Cambridge, MA: Harvard University Press, 1964; Becker 1981, op. cit.; G. Becker and N. Tomes, "Child endowments and the quantity and quality of children," *Journal of Political Economy* 84, 1976, 143–162; P. Bourdieu, *Reproduction in Education, Society and Culture*, Beverly Hills, CA, 1977; J. S. Coleman, "Social capital in the creation of human capital," *American Journal of Sociology* 94, 1988, 95–120; N. Lin, "Social networks and status attainment," *Annual Review of Sociology* 25, 1999, 467–487; A. Portes, "Social capital: its origins and applications in modern sociology," *Annual Review of Sociology* 24, 1998, 1–24; J. Teachman, "Family background, educational resources and educational attainment," *American Sociological Review* 52, 1987, 548–557. See P. Bourdieu, "The forms of capital," in *Handbook of Theory and Research for the Sociology of Education*, ed. J. Richardson, New York, NY: Greenwood Press, 1986; J. S. Coleman 1988, op. cit.; J. S. Coleman, *Foundations of Social Theory*, Cambridge, MA: Harvard University Press, 1990; P. DiMaggio, "Cultural capital and school success: the impact of status cultures participation on the grades of U.S. high school students," *American Sociological Review* 47, 1982, 189–210; M. Lamont and A. Lareau, "Cultural capital: allusions, gaps, and glissandos in recent theoretical developments," *Sociological Theory* 6, 1988, 153–168; A. Lareau, *Home Advantage,* London/New York, NY: Falmer Press, 1989; V. Roscigno and J. Ainsworth-Darnell, "Race, cultural capital and educational resources: persistent inequalities and educational returns," *Sociology of Education* 72, 1999, 157–177; Teachman, op. cit. for detailed discussion of cultural and social capital. See Lareau, op. cit.; A. Lareau and E. Horvat, "Moments of social inclusion and exclusion: race, class and cultural capital in family-school relationships," *Sociology of Education* 72, 1999, 37–53; E. Useem, "Middle schools and math groups: parents' involvement in children's placement," *Sociology of Education* 65, 1992, 263–279 for discussion of "gatekeepers."

13 For a more detailed discussion of the link between parental investments and sibship size as well as other components of family structure, see Downey 1995, op. cit.; Downey 2001, op. cit.; Powell and Steelman 1989, op. cit.; Powell and Steelman 1990, op. cit.; Powell and Steelman 1993, op. cit.; Powell and Steel-

man 1995, op. cit.; Steelman and Powell 1989, op. cit.; Steelman and Powell 1991, op. cit.

14 On economic resources see T. Eppenshade, "Investing in children: new estimates of parental expenditures," Washington, DC: Urban Institute, 1984; D. Conley, "Capital for college: parental assets and postsecondary schooling," *Sociology of Education* 74, 2001, 59–72; Powell and Steelman 1989, op. cit.; Powell and Steelman 1991, op. cit. On parental participation in school see A. Valenzuela and S. Dornbusch, "Familism and social capital in the academic achievement of Mexican origin and Anglo adolescents," *Social Science Quarterly* 78, 1994, 713–719; on travel and dancing see Blake 1989, op. cit.; on other cultural activities and lessons see Downey 1995, op. cit.; on maternal reading to pre-school children see Powell and Steelman 1990, op. cit.; on the presence of educational resources see Downey 1995, op. cit. and Teachman, op. cit.; on financial inputs into post-secondary education Downey 1995, op. cit., Steelman and Powell 1989, op. cit., and Steelman and Powell 1991, op. cit.

15 Again, see Downey 1995, op. cit.; Steelman and Powell 1989, op. cit.; Portes, op. cit.

16 For discussion of parental structure and gender dynamics see Coleman 1988, op. cit.; F. Furstenberg Jr. and A. Cherlin, *Divided Families: What Happens to Children When Parents Part?* Cambridge, MA: Harvard University Press, 1991; E. M. Hetherington, "Coping with family transitions: winners, losers and survivors," *Child Development* 60, 1989, 1–14; S. McLanahan and G. Sandefur, *Growing Up with a Single Parent: What Hurts, What Helps*, Cambridge, MA: Harvard University Press, 1994; Powell and Downey, op. cit.; Steelman and Powell 1991, op. cit.

17 On age-spacing see Downey *et al.*, op. cit.; R. Gailbraith, "Sibling spacing and intellectual development: a closer look at the confluence model," *Developmental Psychology* 18, 1982, 151–174; Powell and Steelman 1990, op. cit.; Powell and Steelman 1993, op. cit.; Powell and Steelman 1995, op. cit.

18 On the sex composition debate see R. Hauser and D. Kuo, "Does the gender composition of sibships affect women's educational attainment?," *The Journal of Human Resources* 33, 1998, 644–657; D. Kuo and R. Hauser, "How does size of sibship matter? Family configuration and family effects on educational attainment," *Social Science Research* 26, 1997, 69–94; Powell and Steelman 1989, op. cit.; Powell and Steelman 1990, op. cit.; K. Butcher and A. Case, "The effect of sibling sex composition on women's education and earnings," *Quarterly Journal of Economics* 109, 1994, 531–563; Conley, op. cit.

19 For insight into the birth order debate see Zajonc and Markus, op. cit.; Zajonc, op. cit.; Blake 1989, op. cit.; Ernst and Angst, op. cit.; Hauser and Sewell, op. cit.; J. Mercy and L. C. Steelman, "Familial influence on the intellectual attainment of children," *American Sociological Review* 47, 1982, 532–543; Steelman and Mercy, op. cit.; Page and Grandon, op. cit.; Retherford and Sewell, op. cit.; A. Somit, A. Arwine, and S. Peterson, *Birth Order and Political Behavior*, Lanhan, MD: University Press of America, 1996. J. L. Rodgers, "What causes birth order-intelligence patterns," *American Psychologist* 56, 2002, 505–510 coined the term of the "birth order trap."

20 For examples of life course and parental age effects see Becker 1981, op. cit.; G. H. Elder Jr., *Life Course Dynamics*, Ithaca, NY: Cornell University Press, 1995; Eppenshade, op. cit.; D. L. Featherman and K. I. Spenner, "Class and the socialization of children: constance, change, or irrelevance?," in *Child Development in Life-Span Perspective*, ed. E. Hetherington, R. Lerner, and M. Perlmutter, Hillsdale, NJ: Lawrence Erlbaum Associates, 1988; A. Heuvel, "The Timing of parenthood and intergenerational relations," *Journal of Marriage & the Family* 50, 1988, 483–491; R. Mare and M. Tzeng, "Fathers' ages and the

social stratification of sons," *American Journal of Sociology* 95, 1989, 108–131; A. T. Geronimus, S. Korenman, and M. M. Hillemeier, "Does young maternal age adversely affect child development? Evidence from cousin comparisons in the United States," *Population and Development Review* 20, 1994, 585–609; J. Mirowsky, "Age and the sense of control," *Social Psychology Quarterly* 5, 1995, 31–43; E. Pavalko and J. Artis, "Women's caregiving and paid work: casual relationship in late midlife," *Journal of Gerontology: Social Sciences* 52B, 1997, S170–S179; Powell, Steelman, and Carini, op. cit.; R. A. Settersten Jr. and J. U. Mayer, "The measurement of age, age structure, and the life course," *Annual Review of Sociology* 23, 1997, 233–266; Steelman and Powell 1991, op. cit.

21 For more detail regarding this analysis, see Powell, Steelman, and Carini, op. cit.

22 See Blake 1989, op. cit.; Y. Shavit and J. Pierce, "Sibship size and educational attainment in nuclear and extended families: Arabs and Jews in Israel," *American Sociological Review* 56, 1991, 321–330; and D. B. Downey and S. Neubauer, "Is resource dilution inevitable? The association between number of siblings and educational outcomes across subgroups," paper presented at Annual Meetings of the American Sociological Association, San Francisco, CA, 1998.

23 For a detailed review of empirical literature on the relationship between family structure, resources, and educational attainment outside of the United States see Buchmann and Hannum, op. cit.; and D. Filmer and L. Pritchett, "The effect of household wealth on educational attainment: evidence from 35 countries," *Population and Development Review* 25, 1999, 85–120. For specific examples see S. Desai, "Children at risk: the role of family structure in Latin America and West Africa," *Population and Development Review* 18, 1992, 689–717; Shavit and Pierce, op. cit.; Downey 2001, op. cit.; Gailbraith, op. cit.; Downey and Neubauer, op. cit.; Blake 1989, op. cit.

24 On patterns in Germany see F. Büchel and G. Wagner, "Soziale Differenzen der Bildungschancen in Westdeutschland – unter besonderer Berücksichtigung von Zuwandererkindern," in *Lebenslagen in Wandel: Sozialberichterstattung im Längsschnitt*, ed. W. Zapf, J. Schupp, and R. Habich, Frankfurt: Campus, 1996; F. Büchel, K. Spiess, and G. Wagner, "Bildungseffekte vorschulischer Kinderbetreuung," *KölnerZeitschrift für Soziologie und Sozialpsychologie* 49, 1997, 528–539; R. Werum, "It's not what you know but whom you know: adult social capital and track placement of ethnic groups in Germany," paper presented at American Sociological Association Meeting, Washington, DC, 2000; R. Werum, "Does one shoe fit all? How parental social capital affects track placement of Caucasians and Latinos," paper presented at American Sociological Association Meeting, Anaheim, CA, 2001. On immigrants in Israel, see A. Leslau, E. Krausz, and S. Nussbaum, "The education of Iraqi and Romanian immigrants in Israel," *Comparative Education Review* 39, 1995, 178–194. See K. Marjoribanks, "Sibling correlates of young adults' status attainment: ethnic group differences," *The Journal of Psychology* 123, 1989, 507–516 on Australia; D. DeGraff, R. Bilsborrow, and A. Herrin, "Children's education in the Phillipines: does high fertility matter?," *Population Research and Political Review* 15, 1996, 219–247 on the Philippines; J. Knodel and M. Wongsith, "Family size and children's education in Thailand: Evidence from a National Sample," *Demography* 28, 1991, 119–131 on Thailand; T. S. Anh, J. Knodel, D. Lam, and J. Friedman, "Family size and children's education in Vietnam," *Demography* 35, 1998, 57–70 on Vietnam; N. Birdsall, "A cost of siblings: child schooling in urban Columbia," *Research in Population Economics* 2, 1980, 115–150 on Columbia; N. El-Sanabary, "Determinants of women's education in the Middle East and North Africa: illustrations from seven countries," PHTEE Background Paper Series, Washington, DC: World Bank, 1995 and A. Tomeh,

"Birth order and dependence patterns of college students in Lebanon," *Journal of Marriage and the Family* 34, 1972, 361–374 on the Middle East; C. Lloyd and A. Gage-Brandon, "Does sibsize matter? The implications of family size for children's education in Ghana," in *Fertility, Family Size and Structure*, ed. C. Lloyd, New York, NY: Population Council, 1993 on Ghana.

25 On the Netherlands see M. Crul, "Success factors in school careers of second-generation Turkish and Moroccan youth," *Tijdschrift voor Sociologie* 17, 1996, 403–420; M. Crul, "Turkish and Moroccan sibling support and school achievement levels: an optimistic view," *Netherlands Journal of Social Sciences* 35, 1999, 110–127; on Kenya see M. Gomes, "Family size and educational attainment in Kenya," *Population and Development Review* 10, 1984, 647–660 vs. C. Buchmann, "Family structure, parental perceptions and child labor in Kenya: what factors determine who is enrolled in school?," *Social Forces* 78, 2000, 1349–1379. See R. Rankin, A. Gaite, and T. Heiry, "Cultural modification of the effects of family size on intelligence," *Psychological Reports* 45, 1979, 391–397 for patterns on American Samoa.

26 On Taiwan see W. Parish and R. Willis, "Daughters, education, and family budgets: Taiwan experiences," *Journal of Human Resources* 28, 1993, 863–898; on Malaysia see L. Lillard and R. Willis, "Intergenerational educational mobility: effects of family and state in Malaysia," *Journal of Human Resources* 29, 1994, 1126–1166; on Columbia see Birdsall, op. cit.; on parental aspirations in the U.S. and Great Britain see M. A. Powell and T. Parcel, "Parental work, family size, and social capital effects on early educational outcomes: the United States and Great Britain," *Comparative Research in the Sociology of Work* 7, 1999, 1–30. See Crul 1996, op. cit. and Crul 1999, op. cit. on the Nethelands; F. Büchel and G. Duncan, "Do parents' social activities promote children's school attainments?," *Journal of Marriage and the Family* 60, 1998, 95–108 and Werum 2000, op. cit. on Germany; C. Lloyd and A. Blanc "Children's schooling in Sub-Saharan Africa: the role of fathers, mothers, and others," *Population and Development Review* 22, 1996, 265–298 on sub-Saharan Africa; Shavit and Pierce, op. cit. on Israel. J. Teachman, K. Paasch, and K. Carver, "Social capital and the generation of human capital," *Social Forces* 75, 1997, 1343–1359 pose the question concerning compensatory functions of different resources.

27 For comparative-international evidence see Buchmann and Hannum, op. cit.; for information on southern Africa see Lloyd and Blanc, op. cit., on Russia see T. Gerber, "Family structure and educational careers in Russia: the single/step model vs. evolutionary psychology," paper presented at the Semi-Annual Meetings of the Research Committee on Social Stratification (RC 28) of the International Sociological Association, Berkeley, CA, 2001; for Malaysia see S. Pong, "School participation of children from single-mother families in Malaysia," *Comparative Educational Review* 40, 1996, 231–249.

28 On the role of the demographic tradition see J. Caldwell, *A Theory of Fertility Decline*, New York, NY: Academic Press, 1982; Buchmann and Hannum, op. cit.; A. Hermalin, J. Seltzer, and C. Lin, "Transitions in the effect of family size on female educational attainment: the case of Taiwan," *Comparative Educational Review* 26, 1982, 254–270; Parish and Willis, op. cit.; J. Knodel, "Fertility decline and children's education in Thailand: some macro and micro effects," in *Fertility, Family Size and Structure*, ed. C. Lloyd, New York, NY: Population Council, 1993 describes a feedback loop between fertility trends and the expansion of pre-primary and secondary schooling in Thailand. He argues that the declining birth rate has led to smaller elementary classes, thus freeing up public resources (facilities, teachers, funding) for pre-school and high school programs.

29 Comparative information on economic policy effects are described in R. Arum, "Schools and communities: ecological and institutional dimensions," *Annual*

Review of Sociology 26, 2000, 395–418; K. Bradley and F. Ramirez, "World polity and gender parity: women's share of higher education: 1965–1985," *Research in the Sociology of Education and Socialization* 11, 1996, 63–91; N. Burbules and C. Torres (eds), *Globalization and Education: Critical Perspectives*, New York, NY: Routledge, 2000. Also see case studies of China (E. Hannum and Y. Xie, "Trends in educational gender inequality in China: 1949–1985," *Research in Social Stratification and Mobility* 13, 1994, 73–98), Germany (W. Müller and D. Haun, "Bildungsungleichheit im sozialen Wandel," *Kölner Zeitschrift fuer Soziologie und Sozialpsychologie* 46, 1994, 1–42), Malaysia (S. Pong, "Sibship size and educational attainment in Peninsular Malaysia: do policies matter?," *Sociological Perspectives* 40, 1997, 227–242; Shreeniwas, op. cit.), Vietnam (Anh *et al.*, op. cit.), and Thailand (Knodel, "The closing of the gender gap in schooling: the case of Thailand," *Comparative Education* 33, 1997, 61–86).

30 For case studies of China see S. Greenhalgh, Z. Chuzhu, and N. Lin, "Restraining population growth on three Chinese villages, 1988–93," *Population and Development Review* 20, 1994, 365–395 or Hannum and Xie, op. cit. For further studies of pro- and anti-natalist policies around the world see J. Gornick, M. Meyers, and K. Ross, "Supporting the employment of mothers: policy variation across fourteen welfare states," *Journal of European Social Policy* 7, 1997, 45–70; J. Misra, "Mothers of workers? the value of women's labor: women and the emergence of family allowance policy," *Gender and Society* 12, 1998, 376–399; Shreeniwas, op. cit.; M. Atoh, "Family change and education," *The Journal of Educational Sociology* 48, 1991, 21–41; H. Iwaki, "Educational and structural changes in demography as they relate to educational policy," *The Journal of Educational Sociology* 48, 1991, 78–101; N. Miyaji and M. Lock, "Monitoring motherhood: sociocultural and historical aspects of maternal and child health in Japan," *Daedalus* 123, 1993, 87–112; R. Smith, "Making village women into 'good wives and wise mothers' in Prewar Japan," *Journal of Family History* 8, 1983, 70–84.

31 For further examples of indirect policy effects in the U.S. see J. Gornick, M. Meyers, and K. Ross, "Public policies and the employment of mothers: a cross-national study," *Social Science Quarterly* 79, 1999, 35–54; L. Gordon (ed.), *Women, the State, and Welfare*, Madison, WI: Unversity of Wisconsin Press, 1990; H. McCammon, "The politics of protection: state minimum wage and maximum hours laws for women in the United States, 1870–1930," *Sociological Quarterly* 36, 1995, 217–249; S. Mettler, *Dividing Citizens: Gender and Federalism in New Deal Public Policy*, Cornell University Press, 1998; Misra, op. cit.; J. Quadagno, *The Color of Welfare*, New York, NY: Oxford University Press, 1994. For recent comparative international evidence on industrialized countries see S. Boocock, "Early childhood programs in other nations: goals and outcomes," *Future of Children* 5, 1995, 94–114 or T. Bielicki and A. Szklarska, "The stratifying force of family size: urbanization and parental education in socialist-era Poland," *Journal of Biosocial Science* 31, 1999, 525–536; for developing countries see J. Bruce and C. Lloyd, "Finding the ties that bind: beyond headship and household," in *Intrahousehold Resource Allocation in Developing Countries,* ed. L. Haddad, J. Hiddinott, and H. Alderman, Baltimore, MD: Johns Hopkins University, 1997; S. Desai, "When are children from large families disadvantaged? Evidence from cross-national analyses," *Population Studies* 49, 1995, 195–210.

32 On the Philippines see DeGraff, Bilsborrow, and Herrin, op. cit.; on East Asia see S. Greenhalgh, "Sexual stratification: the other side of 'growth with equity' in East Asia," *Population and Development Review* 11, 1985, 265–314.

33 Research has shown that educational policy has a direct effect on family struc-

ture by influencing overall fertility patterns. Unfortunately, a detailed review of this literature is beyond the scope of this chapter. For further information on the reciprocal nature of this relationship see e.g. Knodel 1993, op. cit.; L. Pritchett, "Desired fertility and the impact of population policies," *Population and Development Review* 20, 1994, 1–55. For details see B. Fuller and R. Rubinson (eds), *The Political Construction of Education: The State, School Expansion, and Economic Change*, New York, NY: Praeger, 1992; or Buchmann and Hannum, op. cit.; A. C. Kerckhoff, "Education and social stratification in comparative perspective," *Sociology of Education* 1, 2001, 3–18; and Powell and Parcel, op. cit.

34 Reviewing the substantial body of literature that examines the effects of educational policies on such educational trends at the aggregate level also is beyond the scope of this paper. For such institutionalist analyses see R. Arnove, P. Altbach, and G. Kelly (eds), *Emergent Issues in Education: Comparative Perspectives*, Albany, NY: State University of New York Press, 1992, Bradley and Ramirez, op. cit. or M. Shafer, "International nongovernmental organizations and Third World education in 1990: a cross-national study," *Sociology of Education* 72, 1999, 69–88 at a global scale; see D. Morales-Gómes and C. Torres (eds), *Education, Policy, and Social Change: Experiences from Latin America*, Westport, CT: Praeger, 1992; A. Szymanski, "International foundations in Latin America," *Revista Mexicana de Sociologia* 35, 1973, 801–817 and C. Torres, "The state, nonformal education, and socialism in Cuba, Nicaragua, and Grenada," *Comparative Education Review* 35, 1991, 110–130 on Latin America. See A. Benavot, Y. Cha, D. Kamens, J. Meyer, and S. Wong, "Knowledge for the masses: world models and national curricula, 1920–1986," *American Sociological Review* 56, 1991, 85–100 or D. Kamens, J. Meyer, and A. Benavot, "Worldwide patterns in academic secondary education curricula," *Comparative Education Review* 40, 1996, 116–138 for an analysis of international media discourse concerning curricular changes in the twentieth century. For a detailed discussion of how educational policy shapes alternative individual outcomes see, e.g. Buchman and Dalton (op. cit.) on aspirations.

35 For further examples of gendered educational policies in the U.S., see J. Powers, *The Girl Question in Education*, London: Falmer Press, 1992; J. Rury, *Education and Women's Work*, Albany, NY: State University of New York Press, 1991; D. Tyack and E. Hansot, *Learning Together: A History of Coeducation in American Schools*, New Haven, CT: Yale University Press, 1990; V. Sapiro, "The gender basis of American social policy," in *Women, the State, and Welfare*, ed. L. Gordon, Madison, WI: University of Wisconsin Press, 1990; R. Werum "Matching youth and jobs? Gender dynamics in new deal job training programs," *Social Forces* 81, 2002, 473–502; J. Wrigley (ed.), *Education and Gender Equality*, London: Falmer Press, 1992.

36 Lillard and Willis, op. cit.; Pong 1997, op. cit.; and Y. Shavit, "Expansion and inequality of opportunity in higher education," paper presented at the Annual Meetings of the American Sociological Association, Anaheim, CA, 2001 provide evidence regarding countervailing stratification trends. See Bradley and Ramirez, op. cit.; Müller and Haun, op. cit.; Shavit and Müller, op. cit. for evidence of gender-specific tertiary trends. Consult El-Sanabary, op. cit.; C. Griffiths, "Social development and women in Africa – the case of Morocco," *Journal of Gender Studies* 5, 1996, 630–679; Lloyd and Blanc, op. cit. on gender differences in the Middle East and several African regions/countries. For information on gender differences in Asian countries see Anh, *et. al.*, op. cit.; Hermalin, Seltzer, and Lin, op. cit. on Taiwan; Knodel 1997, op. cit. on Thailand; Lillard and Willis, op. cit. on Malaysia; DeGraff *et al.*, op. cit. on the Philippines. Similarly, see D. Post, "Educational stratification, school expan-

sion, and public policy in Hong Kong," *Sociology of Education* 67, 1994, 121–138 and D. Post and S. Pong, "The waning effect of sibship composition on school attainment in Hong Kong," *Comparative Education Review* 42, 1998, 99–117 on Hong Kong.

37 Continued gender inequalities are also documented in C. Buchmann, "The state and schooling in Kenya: historical developments and current challenges," *Africa Today* 46, 1999, 95–117; C. Lloyd (ed.) *Fertility, Family Size and Structure*, New York, NY: Population Council, 1993; T. Mwamwenda, "Women and education in Africa," *The South African Journal of Sociology* 25, 1994, 143–147; Parish and Willis, op. cit.; Post and Pong, op. cit.; and Shreeniwas, op. cit.

38 See Crul 1999, op. cit. on the Netherlands; Shreeniwas, op. cit., Pong 1997, op. cit. on Malaysia.

39 See the review piece by Buchmann and Hannum, op. cit.; and Z. Sathar and C. Lloyd, "Who gets primary schooling in Pakistan: inequalities among and within families?," *Pakistan Development Review* 33, 1994, 103–134 on Pakistan; Knodel 1997, op. cit. on Thailand.

40 See Post and Pong, op. cit.; Lloyd and Gage-Brandon, op. cit.; and H. Ayalon and A. Yogev, "The alternative worldview of state religious high schools in Israel," *Comparative Education Review* 40, 1996, 7–27, respectively.

41 For a detailed discussion of this blind spot in U.S. research see Arum, op. cit. or B. Fuller, "What school factors raise achievement in the Third World?," *Review of Educational Research* 57, 1987, 255–292 and D. P. Baker and G. LeTendre, "Comparative sociology of classroom processes, school organization, and achievement," in *Handbook of the Sociology of Education*, ed. M. Hallinan, New York, NY: Kluwer Academic/Plenum Publishers, 2000, p. 346 for an explicitly comparative perspective. On school choice reforms see F. Echols, A. McPherson, and D. Willms, "Parental choice in Scotland," *Journal of Education Policy* 5, 1990, 207–222 or D. Willms and F. Echols, "Alert and inert clients: the Scottish experience of parental choice of schools," *Economics of Education Review* 11, 1992, 399–450 on Scotland; L. Tikly and T. Mabogoane, "Marketisation as a strategy for desegregation and redress: the case of historically white schools in South Africa," *International Review of Education* 43, 1997, 159–178 on South Africa; A. Van Zanten, "Market Trends in the French school system: overt policy, hidden strategies, and actual changes," *Oxford Studies in Comparative Education* 6, 1996, 63–75 on France; or R. Shapira and P. Cookson (eds), *Autonomy and Choice in Context: An International Perspective*, New York, NY: Elsevier, 1997 comparing the United States, Great Britain, Canada, Israel, and the Netherlands.

42 For details see Baker and LeTendre, op. cit.; S. Heyneman and W. Loxley, "The effect of primary-school quality on academic achievement across twenty-nine high- and low-income countries," *American Journal of Sociology* 88, 1983, 1162–1194; Fuller, op. cit.

43 See H. Oswald, D. P. Baker, and D. L. Stevenson, "School charter and parental management in West Germany," *Sociology of Education* 61, 1988, 255–265 on Germany; M. Hallinan, "Equality of educational opportunity," *Annual Review of Sociology* 14, 1988, 249–268 on the United States; C. M. Broaded, "The limits and possibilities of tracking: some evidence from Japan," *Sociology of Education* 70, 1997, 36–53 on Taiwan; D. Willms and M. Chen, "The effects of ability grouping on the ethnic achievement gap in Israeli elementary schools," *American Journal of Education* 97, 1989, 237–257 on Israel; R. September, "How does it work, and who benefits: the distribution of scientific knowledge in South Africa," *International Review of Education* 36, 1990, 469–484 on South Africa.

5 Fathers

An overlooked resource for children's educational success

W. Jean Yeung[1]

> The President is determined to make committed, responsible fatherhood a national priority ... [T]he presence of two committed, involved parents contributes directly to better school performance, reduced substance abuse, less crime and delinquency, fewer emotional and other behavioral problems, less risk of abuse or neglect, and lower risk of teen suicide. The research is clear: fathers factor significantly in the lives of their children. There is simply no substitute for the love, involvement, and commitment of a responsible father.
>
> (*A Blueprint For New Beginnings: A Responsible Budget for America's Priorities,* released February 28, 2001)

As evidenced by official statements such as the above, as well as by federally funded programs such as Fatherhood Initiative and increasingly popular social organizations such as Promise Keepers, the family role of fathers has become a national concern in recent years. Some scholars and policy makers, from both conservative and liberal camps, have identified uninvolved fatherhood as the root of a myriad of contemporary social problems and called for strengthening fathers' roles in the family as a solution. Yet, the nature of fatherhood and how fathers matter for children's development are complex aspects of contemporary social life that have not been adequately understood even with the burgeoning literature on fatherhood in the last decade.[2]

A number of major socioeconomic changes in the past several decades have contributed to a heightened social expectation of men's family roles, particularly a dramatic increase in the labor force participation of married women with young children and the changing gender ideology. Previously expected to be primarily an economic provider and a moral teacher, the "new father" is now expected to also provide day-to-day physical and emotional care to children as an equal partner of the mother in order to compensate for the "lost time" when mothers are in the labor market. Despite findings of a considerably lower level of involvement by fathers in the child rearing activities than mothers,[3] recent studies have demonstrated that a father's involvement, both in absolute and relative quantitative terms, has increased.[4] How the nature of paternal involvement has changed and what the consequences of their involvement are to children's well-being, however, have not been well understood.

Much of the research on father involvement with children has focused on fathers' direct care of children and their financial provision for the family. A dearth of knowledge about fathers' contributions to other aspects of children's well-being has limited our understanding about the process of intergenerational transfer of resources and values as well as our ability to effectively identify family resources that are critical to promoting children's success and warrant policy attention. In the past few decades, social policies targeted at promoting responsible fatherhood have largely focused on child support reinforcement for nonresident fathers. This policy focus has been based on research findings that a father's financial support has a direct impact on children's welfare.[5] Though recent policies have started to place more emphasis on promoting the non-monetary aspects of paternal involvement, research has provided limited guidance to policy directions with solid empirical basis regarding which aspects of father's involvement are important and how they affect children's development.

Despite research that shows the critical role of families in promoting children's academic success,[6] families are generally left out of strategies proposed to strengthen America's human capital resources that are vital to our country's ability to succeed in a competitive global economy. The declining international standing of U.S. students' educational achievement, documented in the report *A Nation at Risk* two decades ago, raised concerns about American children's learning.[7] Despite a modest increase in students' test scores, a declining drop-out rate, and a substantial increase in the educational aspirations of high school seniors since the publication of that report,[8] American children's mathematics and science test scores remain below those of children in many industrialized countries. Studies report that as many as 30 to 40 percent of American children have either academic difficulties, socio-emotional difficulties, or both, and many students show a declining motivation to learn as they progress in school.[9]

Much of learning depends on both schools and families. Popular opinion, however, holds that schools are the key instruments for developing our young generation, as evidenced in debates about recent educational reforms that often focus on policy options such as reducing class size, lengthening school time, or raising the qualifications of teachers and the payment to them. Rarely, if ever, are government resources allocated to public schools invested in enhancing families' capacity to provide an environment that promotes their children's learning. Of all family resources, the father's contribution receives even less attention than that from the mothers. This failure to fully appreciate father's roles in shaping their children's education and career aspirations, and to mobilize these potent resources in our effort to improve children's educational success, can be very costly to our society.

The goal of this chapter is to demonstrate that fathers have a unique contribution to children's school success and to show the relative magnitude of various types of paternal resources. In addition, the mechanism through which paternal involvement affects children's human capital development is specified and examined. In the next section, I review literature on the conceptualization of fatherhood, why some fathers are more involved than others, and how different types of paternal resources affect children's school achievement.[10] Following the review, I propose a theoretical framework that allows examination of multiple types of fathers' contribution simultaneously and explores the mediating pathways through which paternal resources affect children's outcomes. Next, I discuss findings from my recent work which applies this framework to data collected in the Panel Study of Income Dynamics in order to shed light on father's role in children's human capital development. Finally, I discuss policy implications for mobilizing fathers' involvement as potential resources for enhancing children's school success.

Previous literature

Much of the research on the effect of family on children's schooling has examined the influence of parents as a family unit without separating effects of a mother's contribution from that of a father's. While mothers have always been perceived as playing a central role in the early cognitive and social development of young children, fathers' participation in child rearing has at times been regarded as of little importance and even as inappropriate.[11] The beneficial effects of fathers' involvement on children's well-being have only recently been supported in longitudinal studies.[12] In the past four decades, studies on fatherhood have made great strides both in theoretical conceptualization of fathers' involvement and in empirical inquiry. The cumulative result of this body of research has been a synthesis of work in many different disciplines such as psychology, sociology, economics, anthropology, family history, and education.

Conceptualization of father involvement

In the body of literature that examines the unique effect of a father's influence on children, different conceptualization models of paternal influences have evolved over time. Psychologists and family historians have made the most significant contribution to early literature of fatherhood by examining materials such as diaries, letters, literature, or art.

Michael Lamb's overview of the history of research of father involvement noted that "Fatherhood has always been a multifaceted concept, although over time the dominant or defining motif has shifted in turn from moral guidance to breadwinning to sex-role modeling, marital support, and finally nurturance."[13] Joseph Pleck identified four periods over the last two centuries of American history in which a different emphasis of fatherhood became dominant.[14] According to him, from Puritan times through the Colonial period into early Republican times, fathers' role was predominantly defined by responsibility for moral oversight and teaching. Family historian Steven Mintz also observed that fathers played a crucial role in the maintenance of social order in colonial times; that local government extended to them explicit responsibility

> to oversee all aspects of their dependents' lives (e.g. colonial law required fathers to lead their families in prayer, teach children and servants the catechism, report runaway servants, place children in a lawful calling or occupation, oversee children's choice of a spouse, and, above all, discipline wayward or disorderly household members).[15]

Pleck identified the time around the beginning of industrialization through the Great Depression as the second period when successful breadwinning became *the* criterion for a "good father." Breadwinning was the defining characteristic of men's familial role, providing their feelings of self-worth during that period. From the 1930s and early 1940s, the focus of fatherhood shifted to the father's function as a sex-role model, especially for his sons, as reflected by books and articles during this period of time. Finally, the mid-1970s marked the beginning of a fourth stage of fatherhood conceptualization, with the central emphasis being the nurturing and caring of children. A "good father" is defined in this period as one who is actively involved in the day-to-day care of his children and provides emotional support to his children. Although there may not be a consensus on the exact boundaries and the distinct emphasis on fatherhood in each stage, most scholars agree that fathers play diverse roles in children's lives.[16] Furthermore, Mintz pointed out that there has never been a single family role for men at any particular point in history, rather, profound variation has always existed along and across lines of race, ethnicity, class, and religion.[17]

Despite the multifaceted nature of fatherhood, as Michael Lamb noted, traditionally theorists and researchers have tended to restrict their focus to individual components of fatherhood, while paying little attention to other components of fatherhood and the interactions among multiple roles of fathers.[18]

Psychological literature in the early 1900s tends to focus on qualitative characteristics of fathers such as masculinity, dominance, and identity. After World War Two, emergent ideological concerns about sex roles, the effects of the absence of parents on children, and methodological advances fostered more quantitative approaches in research on fatherhood.[19] Empirical studies from the late 1960s to the early 1980s, mostly found in psychological literature, focus narrowly on describing the extent of fathers' direct interaction with children, most frequently with infants.[20] Later work concerning fathers' involvement has expanded beyond this limited focus to include two additional levels of involvement proposed by Lamb and his colleagues – "accessibility" and "responsibility."[21] Accessibility refers to the time when a father is available to children but not directly interacting with them, and responsibility represents the extent to which fathers take responsibility for organizing and planning children's lives as opposed to the care itself. Partly due to the availability of time use data, the first two levels of paternal involvement have been examined more frequently than the third level of involvement.[22] The application of this typology, however, assesses primarily the quantity of involvement, leaving many other aspects of paternal involvement unaccounted for.

Sociologists and economists have become increasingly active in fatherhood research during the last two decades. Concepts of "social capital", "financial capital", and "human capital" were introduced to study parents' resources to children's development in the framework of attainment/resources models. While also interested in the effect of fathers' human capital and income, sociologists focus more on fathers' social capital and how the social and cultural contexts shape fathers' behavior and identity.[23] These models, however, do not always separate mothers' resources from that of fathers'.

The study of parents' financial capital and human capital as important input to children's human capital development has a long history in economic theories and research.[24] Financial capital refers to the monetary resources such as income and wealth, and human capital refers to parents' skills and knowledge that are available for enhancing children's achievements. A voluminous body of literature has documented a positive association between family income and wealth and children's educational outcomes though scholars do not always agree on the magnitude, timing, and causality of the effect.[25] These resources can affect children's achievements through at least two mechanisms:

1 enabling children to have access to environment and opportunities that are conducive to children's learning,
2 reducing the psychological stress of the parents which tends to lower their capacity to provide supportive and firm parenting behavior.[26]

The bulk of the study on intergenerational transfer of the socioeconomic characteristics also shows that children who come from families with better-educated parents enjoy more years of schooling.[27] Parents' knowledge and skills can benefit children's school performance directly through parents helping with school work and daily learning, or indirectly through its effect on parents' attitudes regarding gender roles, parenthood ideology, parenting practices, or education expectation to children.

Despite the consistency and strength of the relationship between children's achievement and family finances and human capital, a large amount of variance remained unexplained in children's school success. James Coleman, among other scholars, introduced the concept of "social capital" as an additional type of parental resources that can benefit children's school achievements.[28] In fact, Coleman views the social capital crucial in the process of intergenerational transmission of resources. In his own words, "if human capital possessed by parents is not complemented by social capital embodied in family relations, it is irrelevant to the child's educational growth that the parent has a great deal, or a small amount, of human capital."[29] Existing empirical research has lent some support to this hypothesized mediating role of social capital.[30]

The notion of social capital, defined as resources that "inhere in family relations and in community organization and that are useful for the cognitive or social development of a child or young person,"[31] focuses on the process and structure of relationships. The relationship between parents and children, typically starting early in childhood, is especially crucial for the development of children and youth. To Coleman, family social capital includes both parents' nurturing activities and their efforts to constrain children's inappropriate behaviors. Parents who spend more time and effort in shared activities, who are more supportive of their children, and who are more attentive to children's whereabouts and activities are likely to build up social capital within the family.

Coleman argues that social capital outside the family is also beneficial to children's development. When the family is embedded in social relationships with other families and community institutions that adhere to common values, they command greater social capital and can transmit the benefits of those relationships to children. Research to date, however, has shown that family social capital tends to be more important resources for children than community social capital.[32]

There is considerable overlap between the resources framework in sociology and economics and literature found in Psychology. Theories in developmental psychology focus on individual-level interaction and view parenting orientation and style as key elements that influence children's mental health and developmental outcomes. Children of parents who are warm and supportive and spend time with children on educational and other developmentally appropriate activities tend to have higher levels of achievement and self-esteem and less behavior problems.[33] Although the emphasis on attention to developmental stages offers valuable insight to research on the impact of parental resources, these theories are in general agreement with the resources framework. The emotional support from parents and parenting styles correspond to the "process attribute" of relations at home outlined by the social capital theory, and parent–child time spent together on achievement-related activities corresponds to the emphasis on parental human capital investment in the resources framework. Some recent literature in child development has been calling for the need to go beyond this individual-level emphasis and to pay more attention to the "contexts" or the "ecological systems" in which a child is placed such as family, school, and neighborhood.[34] This attention to contexts corresponds, to a large extent, to the "structural attribute" of the social capital in sociological theory such as family types, racial/ethnicity subculture, and community that shape family processes and child development.

These models have not focused on the unique effect of fathers. Developmental psychology literature, influenced by Freud's psychoanalytic theory[35] and Bowlby's attachment theory,[36] has traditionally focused more on mothers' parenting behavior, especially during early stages of childhood. As to the resources/attainment models, although the formulations of the Wisconsin intergenerational model in the 1960s and 1970s included at least as many measures of fathers' characteristics (e.g. schooling and occupational prestige) as for mothers', more recent formulations of these intergenerational models had based more heavily on mothers' characteristics. Even literature that examines the influence of family social capital or family processes often uses a mother's attributes as proxies.[37] This emphasis on mothers' influence on children is partly due to an increasing cultural emphasis placed on the mother–child dyad, as noted by some family historians,[38] and the trend of an increasing number of children spending less time with fathers while growing up. Elsewhere, my colleagues and I had called research to "put fathers back in the picture."[39] We showed that fathers' characteristics and behavior add substantial predictive power to models that are primarily based on maternal characteristics. Another group of scholars examines the implications of the absence of fathers and child support payments for children's well-being.[40]

Research in the last decade has come to recognize the need to adopt a broader conceptualization of father involvement[41] and to go beyond the "deficit model" to investigate the impact of more active participation of fathers in children's lives. Palkovitz reconstructed earlier conceptualization of father involvement by Michael Lamb and his colleagues into a scheme that attempts to encompass the diverse and complex range of ways fathers can be involved with their children. He maintained that paternal involvement engages three overlapping domains of functioning that occur simultaneously – cognitive, affective, and behavioral. In every way that fathers are involved, their behavior is accompanied by a cognitive and an affective component. In his own words, numerous aspects of involvement "occupy the mind and require emotional or affective energy and investment."[42] He listed fifteen different ways that a father can be involved with the children, including direct care, indirect care, economic provisioning, teaching, monitoring, protection, communication, planning, affection, thought process, and so on. In addition, he proposed that paternal involvement should be understood as occurring on the following continua: time invested, degree of involvement, observability, salience, directness, proximity and appropriateness. This broader framework encompasses earlier conceptualization of fathers' involvement and represents a promising advancement for research in this field. It includes a father's financial and human capital contributions, as well as many relationship components articulated in the social capital and developmental psychology theories. It also takes into consideration all three levels of paternal involvement proposed by Lamb and his colleagues discussed earlier. However, critics on this framework have cited one of its limitations as being confounding many levels of concepts. For example, Ross Parke pointed out that the fifteen ways of paternal involvement confounded levels of involvement (e.g. availability) with context of involvement (e.g. teaching).[43] It is also difficult to measure the affection and cognitive domains that accompany every observed behavior of the fathers simultaneously, or all dimensions such as degree of involvement, observability, salience, directness, proximity, and appropriateness. Furthermore, the model does not specify how different ways of paternal involvement affect children's well-being. In sum, while Palkovitz's framework represents a significant progress in fatherhood literature, it falls short in providing a conceptually clear model to guide empirical research in this area.

Empirical research on paternal involvement and children's school performance

Among the research that does examine the unique effect of fathers' influence, more attention was paid to fathers' influence on children's behavior outcomes, such as self-regulation, self-esteem, life satisfaction, and behavior problems, than on their school outcomes.[44] A smaller body of literature examines the unique effect of fathers' involvement on children's school outcomes.

Among research that separated the effect of fathers' income from that of mothers, less consistency has been reported. One study found that fathers' earnings were positively associated with children's educational attainment,[45] another showed that fathers' earnings lowered the risk of children's dropping out of high school among white families but not black families.[46] Fathers' income effect is at times found to become non-significant when mothers' income was controlled for.[47] There is also some evidence that the effect of fathers' income may vary by the gender of a child. For example, my colleagues and I have shown that a father's income is a strong predictor of the son's years of schooling but not of the daughter's.[48] However, the overall pattern indicates a positive association between residential fathers' earnings and children's educational achievement. Research on child support payment from absent fathers generally found that child support payment is positively associated with children's reading and math scores,[49] and years of schooling.[50]

With regard to fathers' human capital, studies consistently show a positive association between residential fathers' education and children's school performance, such as grade point averages[51] and test scores,[52] even when mothers' education and other family characteristics such as income are held constant. Based on data that span over 28 years, my colleagues and I show that, for intact families, fathers' education is a significant predictor of children's educational attainment in young adulthood.[53] In studies on non-residential fathers, similar relationships were not found, suggesting that fathers' human capital may only be relevant when complimented by social capital.[54]

Among studies on fatherhood throughout the 1990s, those that contribute to knowledge about the consequences of fathers' social capital for children's school outcomes are most limited. Often, studies on social capital focus on mothers' relationship and network, with only an indicator of whether the father was present. For studies that do look at fathers' social capital, most examine its association with children's behavior and psychological well-being. Of a smaller number of studies that investigate children's school achievement, one found that fathers' monitoring of school progress is positively associated with high school students' grades, attendance, attitudes toward school and graduation, even after mothers' monitoring is controlled for.[55] A study on fathers' school involvement found that fathers' participation was positively associated with children's grades and reduced the likelihood of children repeating a grade, although the associations were weakened after controlling for the resident mothers' level of involvement in the children's schools.[56] Another study showed that how fathers spend time with their children in shared meals, leisure activities, home activities, reading, or helping with homework correlates positively with children's academic performance, measured by grades.[57] Elsewhere, my colleagues and I have demonstrated that activities of fathers that are not directly related to children's learning may also have an effect on children's academic outcome. For example, we found that father's church attendance had a positive effect on children's education, and that fathers' risk avoidance behavior such as wearing seatbelts, having savings, and having car insurance had a positive impact on sons', but not daughters', educational attainment in adulthood, perhaps suggesting that fathers act as a stronger role model for sons than for daughters.[58] Based on data from a German survey, researchers showed that fathers' social activities relate significantly to children's educational achievements. Children, especially boys, whose fathers frequently engaged in active sports and volunteer work were more successful in becoming enrolled in a university-track Gymnasium, suggesting the potential benefit of fathers' connection with the larger community to children's achievement. Regarding the gender differential of fathers' impact, further evidence was found that father's intellectual-academic support appeared to be important for boys, whereas fathers' physical-athletic encouragement was what seemed important for girls for predicting educational and wage outcomes.[59] These findings all point to a need to consider fathers' behavior beyond direct care of children.

Other studies measure a father's social capital with his relationship with the child and the mother. Father–child relationship was found to predict children's grade point average.[60] Another study reported that mothers' reports of fathers' support in childrearing activities is positively associated with children's academic competence while conflict between parents regarding parenting behavior (e.g. disagreements over how to raise the child) is negatively associated with children's school performance.[61]

Determinants of fathers' involvement and the mediating mechanism through which fathers affect children's well-being

To study how father's involvement influence children, it is critical to understand why some fathers are more involved than others and the process through which various types of fathers' involvement affect children's well-being. Joseph Pleck reviewed literature on the determinants of paternal involvement and noted that fathers' socioeconomic status, traditionally measured by fathers' education, income, and occupation, affects their level of involvement with children. In addition, characteristics of the mother such as age, education, and employment and child's attributes such as age, gender, and health also affect the nature and extent to which fathers are involved in children's lives.[62]

Besides these basic demographic characteristics of family members, Michael Lamb emphasized that fathers' influence cannot be adequately understood only in terms of father–child interaction but must be conceptualized in a broader family context since fathers are influenced by multiple factors outside of their relationship with their children. He proposed four factors that affect paternal involvement – motivation, skills, self-confidence, support, and institutional practices.[63] Fathers' motivation to be involved in their children's lives is seen as a necessary element; however, motivation alone cannot ensure high paternal involvement. Fathers' skills and confidence in their abilities to perform the fathering responsibilities are thought to increase the likelihood of participating in children's lives, as is support from other family members for fathers' involvement. The fourth factor considered as important in affecting fathers' involvement is practices in the workplace such as the level of flexibility of work schedules, provision of child care and paternity leave, all of which are thought to foster fathers' involvement in child-rearing. These various factors have not been empirically tested to date.

Several other researchers have suggested that the complex web of relationships between fathers, their children, and children's mothers often shape paternal involvement. Thus, it is essential to examine parent–child relationships as embedded in a social context that includes the marital relationship, social networks, and occupational experience of parents.[64]

Others stressed the importance of the mother's role in mediating the father–child relationship and noted that a satisfying marital relationship is the cornerstone of good family functioning which directly or indirectly facilitates effective parenting and the development of competent and adoptive children.[65] In this regard, Coleman also discussed the importance of *closure* to children, that is, a strong tie between a child and two (or more) adults, each having a positive relationship with the child.[66] When parents have a cooperative and harmonious relationship, and when they agree on rules and support each other's decision, children benefit from a consistent set of values and a united authority structure. Frank Furstenberg and Andrew Cherlin also noted the importance of the mother–father relationship and noted that fathers view their role as a "package deal", that is, as being connected to or contingent on their relationship with their children's mother.[67]

Another group of researchers has been interested in the social-psychological factors that may affect fathering behavior. They maintained that paternal behavior should be understood as an expression of paternal identity, defined as a father's self-perception of the meanings attached to the status and associated roles of fatherhood.[68] This self-perception stems from interaction and negotiations occurring within structured role relationship. Thus, it is important to consider the relationship between parents and the father–child relationship. A related concept is found in Erickson's generativity theory, which suggests that fatherhood has a profound psychological effect on men such that it stimulates them to develop a concern for the future generation and makes them more caring human beings. Thus, it is important to understand how these social-psychological factors affect men's fathering behavior.

In sum, research on father involvement has progressed from a narrow focus on direct interaction to a broader conceptualization of father involvement that encompasses major theoretical constructs from various disciplines to include financial, human, and social capital of the fathers, attitudes and ideology of the fathers, as well as various contexts that shape fathers' behavior and attitudes. The empirical research, however, remains patchy. Although existing literature provides some evidence of an independent effect of resources from fathers, a systematic examination of how multiple types of paternal resources affect children's educational performance is lacking. Studies tend to focus on either the socioeconomic characteristics of the father or the psychological resources of the fathers.[69] As a result, we know little about the relative magnitude of the effects from different paternal resources. Furthermore, most studies are limited in explaining the mediating process by which fathers' involvement affects children's outcomes. For example, whether and how family relations and attitudinal variables mediate the effect of financial and human capital from the fathers.

In light of literature reviewed above, fathers' involvement with children can be viewed as a function of a set of structural constraints and resources, relationship among family members (particularly between parents), fathers' gender orientation and fatherhood ideology, and children's characteristics. Resources refers to fathers' human capital and income, family assets, while constraints may include other demands on fathers, such as their jobs, how many other children there are in the family, or special demands of a child due to his/her physical or mental limitations. Relationship refers to fathers' parenting behavior, parent–child relationship and mother–father relationship. Previous literature rarely takes into account all these factors simultaneously, yielding incomplete pictures of paternal involvement and its impact on children's well-being.

A proposed conceptual framework

Figure 5.1 presents a conceptual framework for studying the mediating mechanism through which multiple types of paternal resources affect children's well-being based on previous literature. This model attempts to characterize factors that explain how fathers matter for children's well-being. A father's human capital is expected to have a positive effect on his earning capacity and employment hours. It is also expected to shape a set of attitudes about gender roles, fatherhood ideology, and both a mother's and his own perception of a father's role in children's development. Better-educated fathers are more likely to have a more egalitarian gender role orientation. They also tend to be more knowledgeable about child development, and more likely to think that fatherhood is an important social role and to feel more confident in men's parenting skills. Indirectly through these attitudes, a father's education can also affect the child's

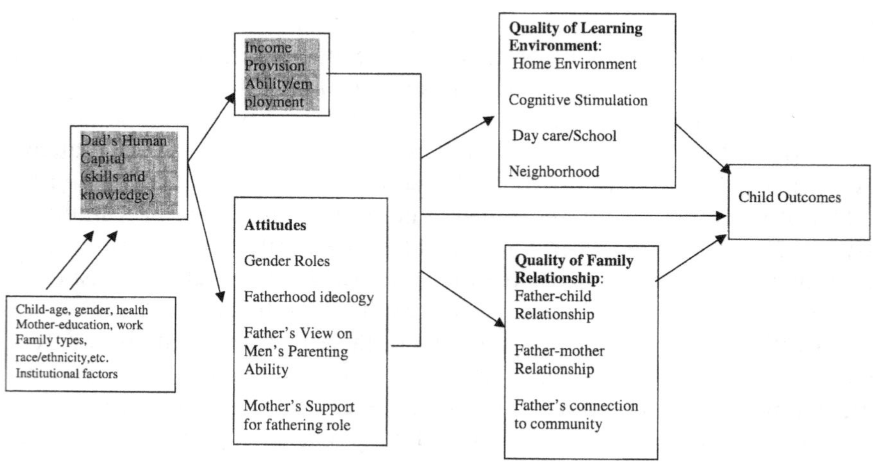

Figure 5.1 Conceptual framework for how multiple domains of paternal involvement affect children's well-being.

learning environment, father–mother relationship and the extent to which a father is involved with a child.

A father's earnings, work hours, and these attitudes in turn will affect the quality of a child's learning environment, relationship among family members, and the father's connection to the community. Indicators of the learning environment include the physical condition of the home, the cognitive stimulation, and the quality of school and neighborhood. Relationships include parent–child relationship, father–mother relationship, and father's connection to community. The quality of these relations in turn is expected to have a direct positive effect on children's school performance.

This framework also incorporates a set of mother's characteristics, including her education, earnings, attitudes, and her involvement with the child. For simplicity, only the constructs that are most relevant to theories discussed above are shown in the framework. A mother's support of paternal involvement is expected to be positively associated with her relationship with the father and to encourage father's participation in child-rearing. A child's gender, age, and health status are also seen as factors that may affect parents' attitudes, relationships, and involvement with the child. Another set of variables in the framework, capturing the structural or contextual attributes of the environment in which a family is situated (meso/macro level factors), includes race/ethnicity, family type, family size, urbanicity of the residence, and institutional factors such as public policy and work place institutional support.

An application of the model

In my recent work, I have attempted to apply such a model to data drawn from the 1997 Child Development Supplement to the Panel Study of Income Dynamics (PSID-CDS).[70] This supplement contains extensive information about family processes and measures of children's cognitive achievement.[71] Different survey instruments were used for the primary caregiver, in most cases, the mother, and another caregiver of the child (most frequently the father, if present). Many of the same questions appeared on both instruments. The extensive data on the socioeconomic characteristics of the family and a wide range of paternal involvement measures reported both by the fathers and the mothers provide a rare opportunity for researchers to examine the relative importance of multiple paternal resources while holding mother's characteristics and other family background constant.[72]

The sample used in that analysis consists of 713 children aged between six and twelve who lived with both their biological or adoptive parents in 1997.[73] Each child in the sample had his/her mother as the primary caregiver and father as the other caregiver. Structural equation modeling (SEM) was used for these analyses.[74] One of the limitations of the analyses is that contemporaneous measures of paternal involvement and children's school success were drawn from the 1997 survey. Thus, inferences based on these results about the causal relationship between fathers' involvement and children's well-being should be made with caution. Detailed description on the research methods for the analyses can be found in the paper itself. I will only summarize some of the critical variables here.

Children's school performance was assessed with the math and reading scores in the Woodcock-Johnson Revised Tests of Achievement (WJ-R).[75] Father's financial capital and human capital were assessed with his annual earnings and educational attainment respectively. The social capital of the father was assessed in many different ways, grouped to represent the relationship between father and the child, relationship between father and mother, and father's connection to community. Father–child relationship is measured by the mother's report of how close the child felt to his/her father and the father's own report of their communication about school activities.[76] In addition, I assessed the father's monitoring behavior with the father's own reports of how often he knew his children's whereabouts when they were not at home, and the number of his children's close friends that he knew by sight and by their first and last names.

Father–mother relationship was assessed in two ways, with:

1 father's co-parenting behavior assessed by his own report of the extent to which he agrees with the mother regarding child rearing practices and mother's behavior,[77]
2 how often family members have conflicts and how they usually resolve the conflict.

These measures capture a crucial aspect of the family social capital – the extent to which parents share the same norms, values, and models of disciplines such that they can reinforce each other. Father's connection to community was measured by his own report of whether or not he had participated in various community activities within the past month.[78] As indicated in the literature reviewed earlier, the extent to which a child resides in a family that is connected to a larger community network that reinforces values of the parents can be beneficial to children's well-being.

The quality of learning environment was also assessed in several ways. First, the cognitive stimulation at home was measured by many items modeled after The Home Observation for Measurement of the Environment (HOME),[79] which includes the frequency of children's activities such as reading, participating in a hobby, or going to a museum. The second indicator was the number of years the child attended private/religious school since kindergarten. This measure captures the quality of school and the extent to which the family and school share common values and reinforce each other, a form of family social capital. A third indicator was whether the family owns a home, which measures family wealth and, to some extent, of the stability of a child's life and connection to a neighborhood.

As for the mediating attitudinal variables, I included fathers' self-reports of their gender role orientation[80] and fatherhood ideology, or "motivation" in Michael Lamb's framework, to assess fathers' views on the significance of fathers' roles in their own and children's lives.[81] The skills/self-confidence of the fathers was assessed with items asking fathers how competent they feel about men's ability to parent.[82] I also included mothers' reports of their support to fathers' involvement, indicating how important they felt it was for fathers to be involved with children, and the extent to which they felt fathers were capable of caring for children. The analyses also included a battery of characteristics of the mother and the child as well as other family characteristics.[83]

Results from that analyses supported many of the hypothesized relationships. As expected, fathers' human capital affected children's cognitive achievement in multiple ways. It was positively associated with fathers' earnings, the level of cognitive stimulation in the learning environment outside of school, fathers' co-parenting behavior, and fatherhood ideology, all of which in turn were positively associated with a child's test scores. Better-educated fathers were also found to be closer to their children, more involved in community activities, and more likely to discuss school activities with the child. Fathers' income affected a child's test scores mainly through its impact on the quality of a child's learning environment in enabling a family to own a home and to send a child to a private/religious school. The number of years a child attended a private school since kindergarten was positively associated with his/her test scores and whether a family owns a home or not was marginally associated with a child's test scores.

Fathers' attitudes were found to have some impact on the level of involvement they had with a child. Those who had a less traditional gender orientation were more likely to know their children's whereabouts and their close friends. This monitoring behavior of the father, in turn, was positively associated with children's test scores (mothers' monitoring behavior is not statistically significant when both variables were included in the model). Furthermore, the more confident a father felt about men's ability to be a good parent, the closer his child felt to him.

As hypothesized, mothers' support for fathers' involvement with children was positively associated with fathers' monitoring behavior and how close a child felt to his/her father. Surprisingly, how close a child was to his/her father and how often the father discussed school activities with a child did not have a statistically significant effect on a child's test scores. Fathers' community involvement was found to be positively associated with a child's reading score though not the math score. How these results should be interpreted is unclear. It is likely that we do not have very good measures of fathers' connectivity to the child and to the community as measuring social capital remains a major challenge to scholars in this area. It can also be that fathers' actual behavior of supporting the mother and monitoring the child's activities are more important than how close a child feels to his/her father and the father's connection to the community.

In terms of the relative magnitude of various factors, the cognitive stimulation in the learning environment outside of school had the strongest direct effect on the test scores, followed by fathers' co-parenting behavior, fathers' human capital, monitoring behavior, and earnings. Contrary to Coleman's claim that without positive parent–child interaction, there is no mechanism to transmit available human and financial capital to children, fathers' earnings and education were both found to have a direct effect on a child's cognitive achievement in the analyses. However, it is possible that not all the mediating mechanisms have been captured with the variables included in the analysis. Further investigation is warranted to explore whether fathers' income and education have a direct net effect on children's human capital as it has important implications for the value of child support payment from absent fathers.

Among fathers' characteristics and behavior, fathers' human capital was found to have the strongest total effects, followed by his financial capital, and co-parenting behavior. In terms of the effect size, an increase of one year of fathers' schooling was associated with an average of 1.5 point increase in a child's test scores. Every $10,000 of fathers' income was associated with half a point increase. Fathers' co-parenting behavior had a nontrivial effect; one point of increase in this indicator was associated with an almost four-point increase in a child's test scores. The cognitive stimulation in a child's learning environment outside of school had the next largest total effect. Particularly noteworthy is the finding that all these factors had a stronger total and direct effect on a child's test scores than the number of years a child had attended a private school since kindergarten. Among fathers' social capital, fathers' monitoring behavior had the second largest impact, next to their co-parenting support to the mother.

To put the magnitude of fathers' influence in context of other family characteristics, mothers' education was the strongest predictor of all, stronger than fathers' human capital or financial capital. This may reflect findings from other studies that mothers tend to spend more time with children in achievement-oriented activities such as reading and homework, and be more involved in children's schools.[84] Mothers' education affected the cognitive stimulation outside of school and fathers' interaction with a child. Mothers' community involvement and monitoring behavior, when entered in the same model, were not significantly associated with the test scores of a child. Other factors that also affected children's test scores included children's age, gender, and ethnicity. Consistent with previous literature, on average girls received higher reading scores than boys and black children had significant lower test scores than white children. New in my analyses is the finding that black fathers were less likely to know their children's close friends and whereabouts when they are not home. Black fathers also tended to have fewer work hours, a lower income, and a higher level of disagreement with the mother regarding how to raise a child, and were less close to their children. Furthermore, the cognitive stimulation outside of school is also significantly lower for black children. All these factors contribute to black children's lower test scores.

Discussion

In my attempt to assess the potential contribution of the fathers to children's school success in this chapter, I have reviewed literature on how the conceptualization of father involvement has evolved over time, factors that affect fathers' involvement, and how different aspects of fathers' involvement affect children's well-being. I proposed a conceptual framework for examining the relative magnitude of various aspects of paternal involvement and the mediating pathways of how paternal involvement affects children's outcome. Finally, I presented results from my recent work to shed light on these issues.

My analyses underscore the importance of mobilizing fathers' potential resources to benefit children's human capital development. The findings show that fathers are as instrumental, if not more so, as mothers to children's human capital development. The systematic examination of multiple types of resources illustrates that many aspects of fathers' resources, net of mothers' behavior and other family characteristics, have significant independent effects on children's test scores. Fathers' education is crucial in this process as it affects both the material resources and their behaviors that are vital to children's cognitive development through its impact on family income and their own attitudes toward fatherhood and gender roles. That fathers' education has a larger direct and total effect than fathers' earnings and work hours may reflect genetic resemblance between the two generations. However, it may also suggest that policies that encourage young men to finish high school or to pursue higher education can have a long-lasting impact, and perhaps more cost effective than programs that provide assistance in job training and job search to fathers if the purpose is to increase fathers' capacity to enhance children's well-being. Long work hours may in fact have an unintended consequence in this regard as they may reduce fathers' social capital available to children. Tradeoff between fathers' income provisioning ability and his social capital and time available to the family need to be carefully evaluated when designing policies.

The extent to which a father supports a mother's parenting (specifically, sharing similar attitude toward childrearing practices and resolving family conflicts in a calm and compromising way), was found to be an especially important form of social capital that benefits children's cognitive achievement. Fathers' monitoring behavior also contributed to higher test scores of a child. There is some evidence of the beneficial effect of fathers' connection to the community. I also showed that the more supportive a mother was to the father, the more likely that the father would have a close relationship with the child and the more involved he would be. These findings underscore the importance of considering the complex web of relationship both at home and with the community when evaluating factors that affect a child's school performance.

Fathers' income, after controlling for mothers' and other family characteristics, has a significant impact on children's test scores. This lends support for the traditional public policy emphasis on securing financial support from the fathers. Nevertheless, particularly of significance is the finding that fathers' income has a smaller effect than his education and co-parenting behavior. This argues for more policies that encourage fathers' non-monetary involvement. Furthermore, all these factors have stronger impact on children's test scores than the number of years a child attended a private/religious school, an indicator of the quality of school. Although my analysis did not adequately assess many dimensions of school resources, these results nevertheless suggest that the impact of family resources on children's school performance may have been underestimated.

Overall, the results presented here provide further support for Coleman's argument that families play an important role in children's academic success. We as a nation pay a high price in continuing to ignore the call for acknowledging and mobilizing familial resources to improve school achievement. It is high time that this understanding be translated into more effective public policy efforts to incorporate measures that enhance families capacities to promote students' educational achievement into programs that aim at strengthening our nation's human capital. Cognitive stimulation at home is a highly important factor to children's school success. Fathers' potential contribution, in particular, has been a largely untapped resource in this regard. Regrettably, fathers' role as teacher and mentor to children which were greatly valued in early American history have eroded in contemporary society. An array of programs should be designed and delivered along side with effort of school reforms to help restore the vital role of fathers in enhancing children's human capital. Programs that encourage fathers to spend more time with children in reading, studying, general learning outside of school, and be more involved in school activities will certainly have a direct impact. Other options that go beyond paternal direct interaction, as demonstrated in this chapter, can also produce significant benefits. These options include programs that help cultivate a cooperative and supportive relationship between the parents, integrating individual fathers into the broader community networks, raising parents' education, facilitating a home environment in which members provide emotional support to each other, establishing open communication, and implementing effective conflict resolution strategies. Measures that encourage a mother's support of a father's involvement and those that enhance a father's skills and confidence in parenting are crucial in helping fathers become more active participants in children's development. These goals can be achieved with efforts in many different platforms through programs such as school-sponsored seminars or workshops for parents to discuss such topics and provide assistance, community programs that reach out to fathers or families, or large-scale media campaigns to raise awareness about a father's role in children's human capital development. The potential effect of programs that encourage joint custody of children warrants careful examination.[85]

The analyses I presented here have several limitations that hamper my ability to make policy recommendations. Most importantly, due to the cross-sectional nature of the data, causal inference about the relationship between fathers' resources and children's cognitive achievement is problematic. For example, problems in children's school performance may lead to more conflict between parents rather than the other way around. In future research, longitudinal analyses are needed to further investigate the relationship among constructs in the conceptual framework proposed in this chapter. My previous analysis also falls short in shedding light on the contributions from non-residential fathers and stepfathers due to our focus on intact families. However, results do indicate that a father's relationship with the mother as a co-parent and the extent to which a father monitors a child's behavior benefit a child above and beyond what his income can provide. This suggests that these relationships could also be pivotal resources from non-residential fathers and other father figures in a child's life. Clearly, however, detailed examination of the relative importance of different aspects of involvement with non-residential fathers and other father figures is needed. Furthermore, the necessarily limited scope of my analysis cannot do justice to cultural variations and structural constraints in various contexts such as work place and the public policy domains. These are important topics that await future investigation. Despite these limitations, the results presented here strongly support the need for policy makers to heed more attention to the school–family link, in particular the largely missing link between fathers and schools, in considering policy options for improving children's human capital development.

Notes

1 Direct correspondence to Jean Yeung at jean.yeung@nyu.edu or Room 445, 269 Mercer Street, New York University, New York, NY 10003. Funding for this research is provided by a grant from the National Institute of Child Health and Human Development (R03 HD38860–02).

2 See J. H. Pleck, "Paternal involvement: levels, sources, and consequences," in *The Role of the Father in Child Development*, New York, NY: John Wiley & Sons, 1997 for a review of work on fatherhood.

3 See A. C. Acock and D. H. Demo, *Family Diversity and Well-Being*, Thousand Oaks, CA: Sage, 1994; H. B. Biller, *Fathers and Families: Paternal Factors in Child Development*, Westport, CT: Auburn, 1993; K. M. Harris and S. P. Morgan, "Fathers, sons, and daughters: differential paternal involvement in parenting," *Journal of Marriage and the Family* 53, 1991, 531–544; and

R. LaRossa, "Fatherhood and social change," *Family Relations* 37, 1988, 451–458 for evidence of lower involvement of fathers.

4 See S. Bianchi, "Maternal employment and time with children: dramatic change or surprising continuity?," *Demography* 37, 2000, 401–414; M. E. Lamb, J. H. Pleck, E. L. Charnov, and J. A. Levine, "Paternal behavior in humans," *American Zoologist* 25, 1985, 883–894; J. H. Pleck, *Working Wives, Working Husbands*, Beverly Hills, CA: Sage, 1985; Pleck, op. cit.; W. J. Yeung, J. F. Sandberg, P. E. Davis-Kean, and S. L. Hofferth, "Children's time with fathers in intact families," *Journal of Marriage and Family Review* 63, 2001, 136–154 for evidence of increase in paternal involvement over the past few decades.

5 Examples of such studies include V. W. Knox and M. Bane, "Child support and schooling," in *Child Support and Child Well-Being*, edited by I. Garfinkel, S. S. McLanahan, and P. K. Robins, Washington, DC: Urban Institute, 1994, 285–316; V. King, "Nonresident father involvement and child well-being: can dads make a difference?," *Journal of Family Issues* 15, 1994, 78–96; and S. S. McLanahan, J. A. Seltzer, T. L. Hanson, and E. Thomson, "Child support enforcement and child well-being," in *Child Support and Child Well-Being*, edited by I. Garfinkel, S. S. McLanahan, and P. K. Robins, Washington, DC: Urban Institute, 1994, 239–256.

6 J. S. Coleman, E. Campbell, C. Hobson, J. McPartland, A. Mood, F. D. Weinfeld, and R. York, *Equality of Educational Opportunity*, Washington DC: Department of Health, Education and Welfare, 1966; C. S. Jencks, M. Smith, M. Bane, D. Cohen, H. Gintis, B. Heyns, and S. Michelson, *Inequality: A Reassessment of the Effect of Family and Schooling in America*, New York, NY: Basic Books, 1972; C. S. Jencks, S. Bartlett, M. Corcoran, J. Crouse, D. Eaglesfield, G. Jackson, K. McClelland, P. Mueser, M. Olneck, J. Schwartz, S. Ward, and J. Williams, *Who Gets Ahead? The Determinants of Economic Success in America,* New York, NY: Basic Books, 1979.

7 U.S. Department of Education, "A Nation At Risk: The Imperative for Educational Reform," http://www.ed.gov/pubs/NatAtRisk/index.html, 1983.

8 P. D. Forgione, "Third international mathematics and science study," National Center for Educational Statistics, U.S. Department of Education, Washington, DC, 1999.

9 J. S. Eccles, A. Wigfield, and U. Schiefele, "Motivation," in *Handbook of Child Psychology*, vol. 3, edited by N. Eisenberg, New York, NY: Wiley, 1997, 1017–1095.

10 I rely on previous reviews by Pleck 1997, op. cit.; P. Amato, "More than money? Men's contribution to their children's lives," in *Men in Families: When Do They Get Involved? What Difference Does It Make?*, edited by A. Booth and A. C. Crouter, London: Lawrence Erlbaum Associates, 1998, 241–278; and M. E. Lamb, "The history of research on father involvement: an overview," *Marriage and the Family Review* 29, 2000, 23–42.

11 See discussions in I. M. Josselyn, "Cultural forces, motherliness and fatherliness," *American Journal of Orthopsychiatry* 26, 1956, 264–271 and J. Nash, "The father in contemporary culture and current psychological literature," *Child Development* 36, 1965, 262–297.

12 A. D. Green and K. A. Moore, "Predictors of father involvement and the consequences for children," in *Father Involvement*, Washington, DC, 1996; K. M. Harris and J. K. Marmer, "Poverty, paternal involvement, and adolescent well-being," *Journal of Family Issues* 17, 1996, 614–640; D. Popenoe, *Life Without Father*, New York, NY: The Free Press, 1996; J. Snarey, *How Fathers Care for the Next Generation*, Cambridge, MA: Harvard University Press, 1993; W. J. Yeung, G. J. Duncan, and M. S. Hill, "Putting fathers back in the picture," *Journal of Marriage and Family Review* 4, 2000, 97–114.

13 Lamb, op. cit., p. 23.
14 J. H. Pleck, "Changing fatherhood," unpublished manuscript Wellesley, MA, 1984.
15 S. Mintz "From patriarchy to androgyny and other myths: placing men's family roles in historical perspective," in *Men in Families: When Do They Get Involved? What Difference Does It Make?*, edited by A. Booth and A. C. Crouter, London: Lawrence Erlbaum Associates, 1998, p. 6. Also see S. Mintz, "Children, families, and the state: American family law in historical perspective," *Denver University Law Review* 69, 1992, 639–640.
16 See LaRossa, op. cit.; S. Coltrane and K. Allan, "New fathers and old stereotypes: representations of masculinity in 1980s television advertising," *Masculinities* 2, 1994, 1–25; and Mintz 1998, op. cit. for literature that analyze changes in cultural images of fathers.
17 Mintz 1998, op. cit.
18 Lamb, op. cit.
19 Ibid.
20 For example, S. S. Feldman and S. C. Nash, "Interest in babies during young adulthood," *Child Development* 49, 1978, 617–622; M. Frodi and M. E. Lamb, "Sex differences in responsiveness to infants: a developmental study of psychophysiological and behavioral responses," *Child Development,* 49, 1978, 1182–1188; M. Frodi, A.D. Murray, M. Lamb, and J. Steinberg, "Biological and social determinants of responsiveness to infants in 10- to 15-year-old girls," *Sex Roles* 10, 1984, 639–649. See Pleck 1997, op. cit. for a review.
21 Lamb *et al.*, op. cit.
22 See Pleck 1997, op. cit. for an overview of studies on early paternal time use with children. See also Yeung *et al.* 2000, op. cit.; Bianchi, op. cit.; and S. L. Hofferth and J. F. Sandberg, "Changes in American children's time, 1981–1997," in *Children at the Millennium: Where Have We Come From, Where Are We Going? Advances in Life Course Research*, vol. 6, edited by T. J. Owens and S. L. Hofferth, New York, NY: Elsevier Science, 2001, 193–229 for recent work in this area.
23 See F. F. Furstenberg Jr., "Good dads-bad dads: two faces of fatherhood," in *The Changing American Family and Public Policy*, edited by A. J. Cherlin, Washington, DC: Urban Institute, 1988; K. Gerson, *No Man's Land: Men's Changing Commitments toFamily and Work,* New York, NY: Basic Books, 1993; R. L. Griswold, *Fatherhood in America: A History*: New York, NY: Basic Book, 1993.
24 G. Becker, *A Treatise on the Family*, Cambridge, MA: Harvard University Press, 1981; F. T. Juster and F. P. Stafford, "Time, goods, and well-being," Institute for Social Research, University of Michigan, 1985.
25 D. Conley, *Being Black, Living in the Red: Race, Wealth, and Social Policy in America*, Los Angeles, CA: University of California Press, 1999; G. J. Duncan and J. Brooks-Gunn, *Consequences of Growing Up Poor*, New York, NY: Russell Sage Foundation Press, 1997; G. J. Duncan, W. J. Yeung, J. Brooks-Gunn, and J. Smith, "How much does childhood poverty affect the life chances of children?," *American Sociological Review* 63, 1998, 406–423; S. E. Mayer, *What Money Can't Buy: Family Income and Children's Life Chances,* Cambridge, MA: Harvard University Press, 1997.
26 G. Guo and K. M. Harris, "The mechanisms mediating the effects of poverty on children's intellectual development," *Demography* 37, 2000, 431–448; W. J. Yeung, M. Linver, and J. Brooks-Gunn, "How money matters for young children's development: parental investment and family processes," *Child Developmen* 73, 2002, 1861–1879.
27 P. M. Blau and O. D. Duncan, *The American Occupational Structure*, New

York, NY: Wiley, 1967; D. Featherman and R. Hauser, *Opportunity and Change*, New York, NY: Academic Press, 1978; R. H. Haveman, B. S. Wolfe, and J. Spaulding, "Childhood events and circumstances influencing high school completion," *Demography* 28, 1991, 133–157.

28 P. Bourdieu, "Le capital social: notes provisoires," *Actes Research Science Social* 31, 1980, 2–3; J. S. Coleman, "Social capital in the creation of human capital," *American Journal of Sociology* 94, 1988, 95–120; N. Lin, W. Ensel, and J. C. Vaughn, "Social resources and strength of ties: structural factors in occupational attainment," *American Sociological Review* 46, 1981, 393–405; R. D. Putnam, "The prosperous community: social capital and public life," *American Prospect*, 1993, 35–42.

29 Coleman 1988, op. cit., p. 110.

30 Drawing on data from the National Educational Longitudinal Survey, Teachman and his colleagues found support for the hypothesis that family social capital mediates the effect of parental financial and human capital on the likelihood of children dropping out of high school. (J. Teachman, K. Paasch, and K. Carver, "Social capital and the generation of human capital," *Social Forces* 75, 1997, 1343–1359.)

31 J. S. Coleman, *Equality and Achievement in Education*, Boulder, CO: Westview, 1990, p. 300.

32 F. F. Furstenberg, Jr. and M. E. Hughes, "Social capital and successful development among at-risk youth," *Journal of Marriage and the Family* 57, 1995, 580–593; G. D. Israel, L. L. Beaulieu, and G. Hartless, "The influence of family and community social capital on educational achievement," *Rural Sociology* 66, 2001, 43–68.

33 Eccles *et al.*, op. cit.; S. G. Timmer, J. S. Eccles, and K. O'Brien, "How children use time," in *Time, Goods, and Wellbeing*, edited by T. F. Juster and F. P. Stafford, Ann Arbor, MI: Institute for Social Research, The University of Michigan, 1985.

34 See for example, U. Bronfenbrenner, "Contexts of child rearing: problems and prospects," *American Psychologist,* 35, 1979a; U. Bronfenbrenner, *The Ecology of Human Development: Experiments by Nature and Design*, Cambridge, MA: Harvard University Press, 1979b; Eccles *et al.*, op. cit.; P. E. Davis-Kean and J. S. Eccles, "It takes a village to raise a child: an executive function and community management perspective," 2002; J. Brooks-Gunn, G. J. Duncan, and Lawrence Aber, *Neighborhood Poverty: Contexts and Consequences for Children*, New York, NY: Russell Sage Foundation, 1997.

35 S. Freud, "Analysis of a phobia in a five-year-old boy," in *The Sexual Enlightenment of Children*, New York, NY: Collier, 1909; S. Freud, "The passing of the Oedipus complex," in *Collected Papers*, vol. 2, London: Hogarth, 1924.

36 J. Bowlby, "The nature of the child's ties to his mother," *International Journal of Psychoanalysis* 39, 1958, 350–373; J. Bowlby, *Attachment and Loss*, vol. 1, New York, NY: Basic Books, 1969.

37 One example of this emphasis on mothers' characteristics is the body of literature on the popular "family process/stress model" such as V. C. McLoyd, "The impact of economic hardship on Black families and children: psychological distress, parenting, and socioemotional development," *Child Development* 61, 1990, 311–346. Main constructs in these models are mother's parenting practice and mother's depressive affect. Few studies took fathers' attributes into account; R. D. Conger, K. J. Vonger, G. H. Elder, F. O. Lorenz, R. L. Simons, and L. B. Whitebeck, "A family process model of economic hardship and adjustment of early adolescent boys," *Child Development* 63, 1992, 526–541 is an exception that took father's presence into account.

38 For example, Mintz 1998, op. cit.

39 Yeung, Duncan, and Hill, op. cit.
40 Examples of recent work include K. Edin, "Single mothers and absent fathers: the possibilities and limits of child support policy," Center for Urban Policy Research Report, New Brunswick, NJ: Rutgers University, 1994; S. S. McLanahan and G. Sanddefur, *Growing Up with a Single Parent,* Cambridge, MA: Harvard University Press, 1995; McLanahan *et al.*, op. cit.
41 See A. J. Hawkins, S. L. Christiansen, K. P. Sargent, and E. J. Hill, "Rethinking fathers' involvement in child care: a developmental perspective," in *Fatherhood: Contemporary Theory, Research, and Social Policy*, edited by W. Marsiglio, Thousand Oaks, CA: Sage, 1995, 41–56; R. Palkovitz, "Reconstructing 'involvement,' expanding conceptualizations of men's caring in contemporary families," in *Generative Fathering: Beyond Deficit Perspectives*, edited by A. J. Hawkins a. D. C. Dollahite, Thousand Oaks, CA: Sage, 1997; A. J. Hawkins and R. Palkovitz, "Beyond the ticks and clicks: the need for more diverse and broader conceptualizations and measures of father involvement," *Journal of Men's Studies* 8, 1999, 11–32.
42 Hawkins and Palkovitz, op. cit., p. 208.
43 R. D. Parke, "Father Involvement: a developmental psychological perspective," *Marriage and Family Review* 29, 2000, 43–58.
44 For example, Harris and Marmer, op. cit.; Pleck 1997, op. cit.; Amato, op. cit.
45 M. S. Hill and G. J. Duncan, "Parental family income and the socioeconomic attainment of children," *Social Science Research* 16, 1987, 39–73.
46 R. W. Rumberger, "Dropping out of high school: the influence of race, sex, and family background," *American Educational Research Journal* 20, 1983, 199–220.
47 F. D. Blau and A. J. Grossberg, "Maternal labor supply and children's cognitive development," *Review of Economics and Statistics* 74, 1992, 474–481.
48 Yeung, Duncan, and Hill, op. cit.
49 King, op. cit.
50 Knox and Bane, op. cit.; J. W. Graham, A. H. Beller, and P. M. Hernandez, "The effects of child support on educational attainment," in *Child Support and Child Well-Being*, edited by I. Garfinkel, S. S. McLanahan, and P. K. Robins, Washington, DC: Urban Institute, 1994, 317–354; McLanahan *et al.*, op. cit.
51 D. F. Alwin and A. Thornton, "Family origins and the schooling process: early versus late influence of parental characteristics," *American Sociological Review* 49, 1984, 784–802; Yeung, Duncan, and Hill, op. cit.
52 For example, Blau and Grossberg, op. cit.; and T. L. Parcel and E. G. Menaghan, *Parental Jobs and Children's Lives*, New York, NY: de Gruyter, 1994.
53 Yeung, Duncan, and Hill, op. cit.
54 Knox and Bane, op. cit.
55 N. Astone and S. McLanahan, "Family structure, parental practices and high school completion," *American Sociological Review* 56, 1991, 309–320.
56 C. W. Nord, D. Brinhall, and J. West, "Fathers' involvement in their children's schools," National Center for Education Statistics, U.S. Department of Education, Office of Educational Research and Improvement, 1997.
57 E. C. Cooksey and M. M. Fondel, "Spending time with his kids: effects of family structure on fathers' and children's lives," *Journal of Marriage and the Family* 58, 1996, 693–707.
58 Yeung, Duncan, and Hill, op. cit.
59 Snarey, op. cit.
60 R. Forehand, N. Long, G. H. Brody, and R. Fauber, "Home predictors of young adolescents' school behavior and academic performance," *Child Development* 57, 1986, 1528–1533.
61 G. Brody, Z. Stoneman, D. Flor, C. McCrary, L. Hastings, and O. Conyers, "Financial resources, parental psychological functioning, parent co-caregiving,

and early adolescent competence in rural two-parent African-American families," *Child Development* 65, 1994, 590–605.

62 Pleck 1997, op. cit.

63 M. E. Lamb, *The Role of the Father in Child Development*, New York, NY: Wiley, 1976; M. E. Lamb, "The changing roles of fathers," in *The Fathers' Role: Applied Perspectives*, edited by M. E. Lamb, New York, NY: Wiley, 1986, 3–27; M. E. Lamb, J. H. Pleck, and J. A. Levine, "A biosocial perspective on paternal behavior and involvement," in *Advances in Clinical Child Psychology*, vol. 8, edited by B. Lahey and A. Kazdin, New York, NY: Plenum, 1987, 229–266.

64 J. Belsky, "The determinants of parenting: a process model," *Child Development* 55, 1984, 83–96; B. L. Volling and J. Belsky, "Multiple determinants of father involvement during infancy in dual-earner and single earner families," *Journal of Marriage and the Family* 53, 1991, 461–474.

65 See P. T. Davis and E. M. Cummings, "Marital conflict and child adjustment: an emotional security hypothesis," *Psychological Bulletin* 116, 1994, 387–411 for a review.

66 Coleman 1990, op. cit.

67 F. F. Furstenberg Jr. and A. J. Cherlin, *Divided Families: What Happens to Children When Parents Part*, New York, NY: Cambridge University Press, 1991.

68 M. Ihinger-Tallman, K. Pasley, and C. Buehler, "Developing a middle-range theory of father involvement postdivorce," *Journal of Family Issues* 14, 1993, 550–571; Hawkins *et al.*, op. cit.; Snarey, op. cit.

69 See Hawkins *et al.*, op. cit.; and Palkovitz, op. cit. for calls for a broader conceptualization of fatherhood.

70 W. J. Yeung, "How multiple domains of paternal involvement affect children's well-being," paper presented American Sociological Association Annual Meeting, Chicago, 2001.

71 See S. L. Hofferth, W. J. Yeung, and F. P. Stafford, "Panel study of income dynamics," *Inter-University Consortium for Political and Social Research Bulletin* 15, 1996, 6–22 on details about the PSID core survey. See S. L. Hofferth, P. Davis-Kean, J. Davis, and J. Finkelstein, "User guide for the child development supplement of the panel study of income dynamics," 1998 on details about the PSID Child Development Supplement.

72 See discussion in Amato, op. cit. about problems related to relying solely on mother's reports of father's behavior.

73 The sample is limited to children in intact families because many of the measures of interest are not available for absent fathers and other father figures.

74 See R. E. Schumacker and R. G. Lomax, *A Beginner's Guide to Structural Equation Modeling*, Mahwah, NJ: Lawrence Erlbaum Associates, 1996; SEM allows for simultaneous tests of all the associations between constructs – the direct and indirect associations of all predictors can be assessed while taking into account a variety of control variables.

75 Broad math scores are combined scores from the Calculation test and the Applied Problem subscales, and broad reading scores are combined scores from the Passage Comprehension and the Letter-Word subscales. These scores are standardized to children's age. See Hofferth, Davis-Kean, Davis and Finklestein, op. cit. for details about these measures.

76 This measure assesses how frequently the father discussed the following with the child:

1 school activities or event of particular interest to the child
2 things the child has studied in class
3 the child's experience in school.

77 Father's co-parenting behavior was assessed with his self reports of the extent to which he agreed with the mother about how to raise children, disciplining children, how and how much money to spend on children, mother's completion of household chores, friends the mother spends time with, leisure activities they do together, and mother's use of alcohol or drugs.

78 These activities include neighborhood meetings, church or other religious clubs or activities (not religious service), parenting classes or parent support groups, athletic teams, visiting a friend or neighbor's house, going to an institution like a YMCA, scouting (boy scouts, girl scouts), and neighborhood watch.

79 See B. M. Caldwell, and R. H. Bradley, *Home Observation for Measurement of the Environment*, Little Rock, AR: University of Arkansas at Little Rock, 1984 for description of these measures. These measures include how often the child reads for enjoyment, whether parents encourage child start and keep doing hobbies, whether the child has any musical instruments, whether the child participates in extra curricular activities, how often the child goes to museums, musicals or theatrical performances, and whether parents discuss TV programs with the child when they watch TV together.

80 Father's gender ideology is assessed with six items that measures the extent to which the father agreed to statements such as, "It is much better for everyone if the man earns the main living and woman takes care of the home and family," "Most of important decisions in life should be made by the man of the house," and "If a husband and a wife both work full-time, they should share the household tasks equally." An index, formed by taking the average scores of these items, is coded so that 4 indicates a more egalitarian gender role and 1 indicates a traditional gender orientation.

81 These items include "Being a father and raising children is one of the most fulfilling experiences a man can have," "It is essential for the child's well-being that fathers spend time interacting and playing with their children," and "A father should be as heavily involved in the care of his child as the mother." An index was created by taking the average of scores in these items.

82 Assessed by father's self report about the extent to which he agreed with statements such as "In general, fathers and mothers are equally good at meeting their children's needs," and "It is difficult for men to express tender and affectionate feelings toward children." An index, ranging from 1 to 4, indicates low to high skills/confidence levels.

83 Children's characteristics included age, gender, and health of the child. Mother's characteristics include education, earnings, work hours, her emotional support to the child, her involvement in school, and her community involvement. Two other family characteristics are also included as control variables – the number of children under 18 in the family and the ethnicity of the family head.

84 J. F. Sandberg and S. L. Hofferth, "Changes in children's time with parents, U.S. 1981–1997," *Demography* 38, 2001, 423–436; Yeung, Sandberg, Davis-Kean, and Hofferth, op. cit. found a low level of paternal engagement in educational-related activities such as reading, studying, and doing homework with a child, averaging about five minutes per day.

85 See J. A. Seltzer, "Father by law: effects of joint legal custody on nonresident fathers' involvement with children," *Demography* 35, 1998, 135–146; R. Bauserman, "Child adjustment in joint custody versus sole-custody arrangements: a meta-analytic review," *Journal of Family Psychology* 16, 2002, 91; and J. Henderson, "Two are better than one: the fact that a husband and wife break up doesn't make either of them less a parent," in *Global and Mail*, 1988.

6 Intergenerational assets and the black/white test score gap

Ariel Kalil, Mary Pattillo, and Monique R. Payne[1]

In 1999, The College Board released "Reaching the Top: A Report of the National Task Force on Minority High Achievement."[2] While the title suggests an analysis of the positive achievement of students of color, the content is less sanguine, reporting in detail the deep racial gap in test scores. One finding is particularly startling and motivates the research in this chapter: black students with college educated parents score lower on standardized tests than white youth whose parents did not graduate from high school. While it is well-documented that controls for family characteristics do not fully account for the racial test score gap, the chasm represented by this stark finding demands a deeper interrogation of the meaning of family background for blacks and whites and its influence on academic outcomes.

To address this issue, we use survey data on nearly 600 black and white public school students and their families in Prince George's County, MD (the Maryland Adolescent Development in Context [MADIC] Study).[3] Prince George's County, a suburb of Washington, DC, is one of few locales in the U.S. where the income and occupational range among blacks is nearly comparable to that of neighboring whites. Median household income in 1990 for white and black households in Prince George's County was $46,822 and $41,265, respectively. The fact that this income difference by race *is* significantly different is a topic to which we will return. For now, we focus on the facts that these figures far exceed median household income nationally – with white households earning $31,231 compared to $18,676 for black households – and the racial gap is significantly less pronounced – black income is 88 percent of white income in Prince George's County versus 60 percent of white income nationally. To be sure, this suburb is not affluent. The families in Prince George's County generally represent the middle of the income distribution for whites across the country and the upper-middle segment of the income distribution for blacks. Moreover, despite having a relatively advantaged black population, there is notable variation across its 172 Census tracts, with median tract income ranging from $12,000 to $75,500 in 1990. As a shorthand and on average, both blacks and whites in this study can be called *middle class*, albeit differently positioned vis-à-vis others in their racial group, and with varying experiences of that socioeconomic reality. Even though it falls well short of equality, Prince George's County is perhaps the closest approximation of socioeconomic parity between blacks and whites among locales in the United States.

Yet, among adolescents in the study families, we nonetheless find significant racial differences in standardized test scores. We do not intend to duplicate The College Board study, but instead we investigate the correlates of academic achievement for white and black youth focusing on intergenerational assets. In addition to parents' human and financial capital (i.e. education and income), we also include information on grandparents' education and their social contact with their grandchildren. Including grandparents in the analysis embeds children within a broader set of progenitors, and provides a richer understanding of the family background of parents and thus the stock of resources that they can impart to their children. Including grandparents also allows us to inquire about the lasting effects of racial inequalities in previous generations. Before presenting the empirical analysis, we discuss three literatures that inform our theoretical approach. First, we review the literature on the black/white test score gap to illustrate its persistence in the face of myriad controls. Second, drawing on the sociological tradition of mobility studies, we present a framework for studying outcomes within a three-generational family context and argue that including grandparents improves our understanding of racial stratification. Finally, we review the small but growing literature on grandparenting, elaborate our theory of the transference of capital across generations, and state our hypotheses about the effect of grandparents on children's test scores.

Black/white achievement

There has been longstanding concern over the racial gap in test scores, which appears at very early ages and endures into adulthood. Indeed, the original report by James Coleman was borne of such concern, responding to Section 402 of the Civil Rights Act of 1964, which called for a survey to study "the lack of availability of equal educational opportunities for individuals by reason of race, color, religion, or national origin in public educational institutions."[4] James Coleman's findings on the severity of the achievement gap between black and white students between and within regions, and between and within schools, pointed to the greater importance of families over schools for determining educational outcomes. Coleman concluded the following in a later summary essay:

> Altogether, the sources of inequality of educational opportunity appear to lie first in the home itself and the cultural influences immediately surrounding the home; then they lie in the schools' ineffectiveness

> to free achievement from the impact of the home, and in the schools' cultural homogeneity which perpetuates the social influences of the home and its environs.[5]

Not surprisingly, there was considerable controversy following these proclamations because they undermined common liberal notions that achievement differences between blacks and whites were the result of the unequal distribution of resources, measured by such things as per pupil expenditures, textbook holdings, overcrowded classrooms, or the rigor of the curriculum. Such controversies over the relative weight of home versus outside forces on children's achievement continue to guide contemporary research. For example, a volume devoted to the black/white test score gap edited by Christopher Jencks and Meredith Phillips included chapters on the influence of families and home environments, teachers, school resources, and student body compositions, revisiting the same domains investigated by James Coleman over thirty years prior. Nonetheless, there have been some new interests raised by current research.

In general, there are five areas frequently investigated when building a causal argument for racial differences in achievement: student characteristics and attitudes, family/home characteristics, peers, schools and teachers, and neighborhoods. Student-level variables include attributes such as age and sex, attitudinal measures of the student's commitment to school, aspirations and goals, and behavioral indicators like time spent on homework, delinquency, or extracurricular involvement. Family characteristics include relatively straightforward observations of family structure, income, or number of siblings, as well as contextual information such as the presence of learning materials in the home, extent and quality of parent/child interaction, or parental expectations. The interest in peers arises because youth are affected by the company they keep, and thus measures of school composition, and peer attitudes, behaviors, expectations, and performance are often included. Next, studies include possible correlates of test scores that are within the school itself, represented by variables such as per pupil expenditures, and teacher qualifications and expectations. Finally, and perhaps newest in this line of research, all of these arenas are embedded within a larger neighborhood context, important aspects of which may include the predominance or absence of different kinds of families and people (e.g. married couples, professionals), or levels of violence and disorder.

There is a voluminous literature on each of these milieus, studied separately as well as in various combinations with each other, and with some relatively well-established findings and other that remain under debate. For example, it is perhaps not surprising that parents' socioeconomic status (income, education, or occupation) should positively affect children's test scores, and this is almost always confirmed.[6] A more contested variable is family structure. While most studies find that growing up in a single parent family is correlated with lower grades and test scores, many studies find this effect to be small, non-existent or variable by group, or in the opposite direction.[7]

For our discussion of the black/white test score gap, the relevant story is that the test score gap almost always persists despite extensive controls in the areas discussed above, including socioeconomic status, youth attitudes toward school, family structure and background, school variables, and neighborhood indicators.[8] One study provides a rare example of a model that reduces the gap between white and black test scores to non-significance. Jeanne Brooks-Gunn, Paula Klebanov, and Greg Duncan include child, family, and neighborhood characteristics to study the gap in IQ scores among five–year-olds. They find that the "home learning environment" (e.g. learning materials, parent/child interaction, cognitive stimulation) has a strong and significant independent effect on children's test scores, mediates the effects of family income, and fully accounts for the influence of mother's aptitude and race on children's achievement.[9] These conclusions are not too unlike James's Coleman's findings and bring us back to the centrality of families for children's outcomes.

Our research does not attempt to duplicate these findings, and in light of the extensive literature that rarely fully accounts for the race gap in test scores and educational outcomes, we do not aim or expect to fully model the process of academic achievement in black and white youth. Instead, we hope to add to the list of variables considered relevant to youth's outcomes, particularly in the realm of the family, which has proven so central. Parents matter for children's test scores because of the stock of capital that they represent, but their attributes are partially a product of their own family background and parental characteristics. Thus, examining the characteristics of the prior generation – that is, children's grandparents – may better account for resources available to families.

Intergenerational mobility and racial stratification

By focusing on parents and grandparents we are following in a long tradition of research on stratification and mobility across generations.[10] In efforts to gauge the amount of mobility in a society, this literature generally assesses the relative importance of family background factors versus individual characteristics in determining a particular outcome (e.g. educational attainment, wages, etc.).[11] For example, current consensus regarding earnings in the United States is that family background accounts for roughly 40 percent of the overall variation in earnings among men.[12] This illustrates the ability of individuals to rise above (or fall below) the station of their parents, but it also shows that a substantial portion of individual achievement is attributable to the family in which they were reared. In another area, sociologist Dalton Conley finds that the observed black/white wealth gap can be explained by differences in parental wealth;

and parental wealth also has significant effects on outcomes such as going to college, graduating from college, premarital births and welfare receipt.[13]

It is clear from this literature that parents matter. For example, sociological studies have repeatedly found that parental education and occupational status are associated with children's educational and occupational aspirations.[14] Starting with Peter Blau and Otis Dudley Duncan's classic model of inheritance, the status attainment literature has focused on the route between parental occupation and child occupation. Their simple five-variable model, in which son's occupation is predicted by father's education and occupation through the mediators of son's education and first job, is one of the first and most basic regression-based treatments of the relationship between parental and child occupation. Several generations of scholars have elaborated on the model, paying more attention to mediators between parent and child job[15] and looking to effects in the third generation.[16] Yet, while the literature has established substantial intergenerational correlations in parent and child educational and occupational attainment, it has not fully investigated the more micro-level, within-family mechanisms behind this transmission.[17] Our study addresses this issue by including an examination of the role of social interactions between grandparents and their grandchildren.

Social psychologist Melvin Kohn and his colleagues' research also provides us with a framework for understanding how intra-familial social interactions might play a role in intergenerational mobility processes.[18] This research suggests that much of children's access to information and opportunities regarding future career choices flows through their parents and through interactions and observations that occur within the home. These researchers hypothesized that parents' job characteristics influence behaviors that are valued and encouraged in children, thus providing the link to children's developmental outcomes. Parents are expected to value behaviors and attitudes that are adaptive in their own employment setting and subsequently express these values in their parenting practices. Thus, for example, when parents' jobs involve greater self-direction, parents more often tend to use reason (as opposed to power assertion) when disciplining their children and tend to expect their children to internalize adult norms. These child-rearing practices are expected to foster children's own values of, for example, the importance of self-direction, and to shape their occupational aspirations accordingly. This model has been termed the "occupational linkage hypothesis."[19] Although our study is not designed to examine the role of grandparents' occupational status in shaping grandchildren's occupational aspirations, the model's emphasis on the importance of parent–child social interactions helps to guide our suggestion that social interactions between grandparents and grandchildren might play a role in intergenerational mobility patterns.

Family background factors may be especially important for understanding racial stratification. In the case of adolescents' test scores, controlling for parents' characteristics essentially attempts to compare children from similar kinds of families, with the assumption that under analogous conditions, children should have similar outcomes. But what this logic does not address is that measures of current status do not account for the stock of resources that parents were exposed to (or not exposed to) when they themselves were growing up. That is, a black and white adult may now share similar attributes, for example, a college education, a home, a middle class income. However, their childhood experiences and exposures may differ significantly. Comparing a black adult who was reared in a poor family and has only recently achieved middle class status to a white adult who was reared in a middle class family misses the package of skills and styles that these two individuals possess as created by their own upbringing, and thus what they are able to impart to their children. This example characterizes the recent history of African Americans and is important to a story of outcomes for contemporary black youth.

African Americans have made impressive socioeconomic gains in this country, especially since World War Two. Educational attainment has increased and performance has improved. The poverty rate for blacks, while still alarmingly high, is well below the 80 percent black poverty rate in 1950.[20] Blacks have a visible presence in politics, business, and entertainment. And the black middle class has grown in terms of both absolute numbers and its proportion in the black community overall. The status of the black middle class represented by many of the families in our study area of Prince George's County should be of paramount importance to those interested in the future of African Americans as a group. These are families and individuals who have invested in education and hard work in order to climb the occupational hierarchy into white-collar professional, sales, clerical, managerial, and entrepreneurial occupations. Yet despite these upward strides, the experience of middle–class status is not uniform across groups. Instead, it is colored by the crosscutting reality and history of race. In our own data, while median black family income nears that of neighboring whites, it is still significantly lower, illustrating the paucity of black families at the higher end of the income distribution and their relative inability to establish communities in which they are clustered. Other examples of enduring racial inequities between even "middle class" blacks and whites include gross differences in wealth holdings, disparities in neighborhood quality, and the occupational segregation of blacks into public sector employment.[21] A central racial difference that we study here is the first generation middle class status of blacks as compared to whites.

The emergence of a sizeable black middle class is a very recent phenomenon, beginning after World War Two and continuing to the present, although growth slowed in the 1970s. It is important to recognize that the young people who are the subjects of the contemporary studies of the black/white test score gap are only one and at most two generations removed from the segregated conditions in both the north and the south.

This segregation existed in schooling and most other arenas of life and, after some progress in the 1970s, such segregation in schools is on the rise again.[22] Second to the importance of families in determining children's outcomes in the Coleman report was the fact that schools were racially homogeneous, segregating students and teachers with poorer preparation for school success.

The recency of the black middle class suggests its upward mobility from poverty or working class backgrounds to middle class status Indeed, national data show that middle class blacks are significantly more likely than middle class whites to have been poor as adolescents, and their parents have lower educational attainment than the parents of middle class whites.[23] Thus, this chapter addresses the general question: Does the more disadvantaged family background of African American parents as compared to white parents negatively affect black youths' educational performance relative to their white peers? To the numerous studies that have investigated this question using parental data, we add information on grandparents.

How should grandparents matter?

A relatively large body of work suggests that non-nuclear families have historically been more prevalent, and contribute more to household well-being and children's development, in black (and Hispanic) families than in non-Hispanic white families.[24] Longstanding dominant cultural norms (as well as socioeconomic needs) support the black extended family, and research shows that black two-parent families participate in extended-family activities significantly more than do their non-Hispanic white counterparts.[25] Some suggest that black grandparents perceive themselves as more involved than white grandparents in teaching their grandchildren (and that they rate teaching as their greatest strength) and perceive themselves as more effective in the grandparent role more generally.[26] Overall, however, research on the effects of grandparent involvement on family life among two-parent, middle class black families is sparse compared to studies of extended family activities among groups such as teenage mothers, unemployed men, and the elderly.[27] We therefore rely on theory to guide our hypotheses about how grandparent involvement should matter for children in mostly middle class families.

Once again building on the monumental work of James Coleman, we begin with the notion that human capital – skills, educational qualifications, and aptitudes – can be transferred across generations through social connections and interactions, or social capital.[28] The obverse is also true: the lack of human capital in families of origin can translate into less human capital in later generations, even when social networks are dense and strong. We study connections to and characteristics of parents and grandparents as indicators of the educationally relevant social capital available to youth. The social capital literature is vast and growing. Sociologist Alejandro Portes, in his review essay on social capital, references French sociologist Pierre Bourdieu as having the first and clearest exposition of the concept, which "focus[ed] on the benefits accruing to individuals by virtue of participation in groups."[29] These groups can be families, neighborhoods, co-workers, racial groups, friendship networks, or school peers, and the benefits that result from such connections can be as varied as lower neighborhood crime rates, better mental health, employment (versus unemployment), fuller democracy, or, most relevant to us, improved educational outcomes, such as high school graduation, better grades, or college attendance.

To be quite specific about our operationalization of this concept, there are two important components of social capital. First, it inheres in the structure of relations between actors and among actors.[30] Thus social capital can be partially measured by the presence/absence and strength/weakness of a certain social tie. In our data, we assess the level of involvement of grandparents with their adolescent grandchildren. This information can indicate the existence (or lack thereof) of a source of social capital. Because social networks are sources of information, the tie with a grandparent can *in theory* be a source of learning opportunities. For example, contact with a grandparent can represent another source of adult socialization in a manner relevant for school success, such as someone with whom the child can read, or practice language skills, or do math drills.

However, these theoretical potentialities may not in fact characterize the capacity that the tie with a grandparent represents. Grandparents' socialization strategies and behaviors depend on their own experiences, education, occupation, and attitudes. Sociologists Valerie King and Glen Elder report that better-educated grandparents are more likely than less educated grandparents to participate in activities with and teach skills to their grandchildren, while less educated grandparents report a greater likelihood of being their grandchild's friend.[31] Thus, the second quality of social capital is that it is "productive, making possible the achievement of certain ends that in its absence would not be possible."[32] That is, these networks are only useful if they provide information or provisions that can promote a certain desired outcome in a particular domain. For our purposes, the social ties between grandparents and grandchildren generate positive educational achievement outcomes only if the grandparent possesses sufficient and relevant education and skills (i.e. human capital) that they can impart to their grandchildren. In sum, human capital can only be imparted when a social tie exists, and social capital is only productive when the social tie is imbued with useful information for the particular domain. Mechanisms linking parents' human capital to children's outcomes operate according to the same principles.

Empirically, this hypothesis will be tested by examining statistical interactions between grandparents' education and the extent of the cross-generational social tie. Based on Coleman's theory, we expect to find the strongest positive effects on youth academic achievement when high levels of grandparent education are combined with high levels of grandparent–youth social interaction. Even at similar levels of involvement with their grandchildren, black grandparents' lower educational attainment (or conversely, white grandparents' more favorable characteristics) may contribute to the gap between white and black children's achievement because of differences in the amount and nature of the human capital being imparted across the generations. If white children get a boost to, or at the very least a reinforcement of, what they learn in school on their visits and interactions with their grandparents while black children do not have this extra (or reinforcing) endowment, this may contribute to the black/white test score gap.

Another important issue in this literature relates to the relative contribution of grandparent versus parent capital. While it is well-established that children's outcomes (educational and otherwise) depend significantly on parental characteristics, the small literature on the importance of grandparents has yielded two competing findings:

1 Grandparents only matter indirectly through the effects their characteristics have on the parental generation;
2 grandparents matter even after controlling for a wide range of parental characteristics.[33]

Because of the distance between grandparents and grandchildren in terms of age and, often, geography, most researchers assume the former hypothesis: grandparents' characteristics work through their effect on parents. Yet, Meredith Phillips and colleagues argued convincingly for the latter by demonstrating that maternal grandparents' education affects grandchildren's test scores even after controlling for key variables such as parents' educational attainment, family income and wealth, and parent psychological characteristics.[34] Empirically, we test these effects by examining the extent to which parent education mediates the effects of grandparent education on youth test scores in multivariate regression analyses.

Because we are particularly interested in explaining the racial gap in test scores and grades within a mostly middle class sample, our theory depends on disparities not only in parental characteristics and resources, but also in grandparents' resources. Hence, the significance of our study rests on the fact of the recency of the black middle class. Parents of middle class black adults (i.e. the grandparents of children like those in our sample) have less education, were less likely to be employed in white-collar jobs, and were more likely to be poor while the parent was growing up. These factors affect the endowment and socialization from grandparents to parents (e.g. being a model for leisure reading, the use of specific vocabularies, being able to help with homework, maintaining a link with the school) which may have an effect on the stock of human capital that parents can impart to their children. Indeed, Phillips and colleagues find that a significant proportion of the effect of grandparents' characteristics on the test score gap among preschoolers is mediated by the home environment that parents create. Based on these findings, we hypothesize that grandparents' effects on the test score gap will most likely operate indirectly.

The hypotheses and interests presented above are summarized in the following research questions:

1 Do grandparents' characteristics have a direct effect on children's test scores, or do they operate only through their effect on parents' attainment?
2 Does the association between grandparental involvement with the child and children's test scores depend on the grandparents' education?
3 Are there race differences in the effects of grandparents' education and involvement on children's test scores?
4 What does a three-generational model contribute to our understanding of the black/white test score gap?

Description of data and analytic sample

The MADIC Study examines the influences of the home, school, neighborhood, and peer group on adolescents' academic, emotional, and social development. While a broad range of the socioeconomic spectrum is represented, this sample is unique in that it contains a significant proportion of middle class families, especially among blacks, which allows us to focus on the particular quandary of black middle class underachievement relative to whites. Face-to-face interviews and self-administered questionnaires were collected from adolescents and their primary caregivers (for the most part, mothers) in the family's home. Achievement and attendance measures were collected from school records. The study was begun in 1991 (the start of the adolescents' seventh grade school year), with several successive waves of data collected approximately every one to two years.

Approximately 1,356 black and white families were interviewed in the first wave (61 percent black and 35 percent white). We impose several restrictions on our analytic sample. First, we include only students whose parent(s) reported being of the same race as their child ($n = 1{,}311$), thus excluding the small number of mixed-race families. We also exclude students who had grandparents as primary caregivers (and who therefore lack parent data; $n = 1{,}281$ with this exclusion criterion). Most variables for our analysis come from the first wave of the study. However, several variables were not available until later waves of the survey (e.g. grandparents' education was not asked until the third wave of the study, the youth's eleventh grade school year); therefore, attrition from the longitudinal sample affects our final sample size. The available sample drops to 760 once we include only those families who were in the necessary follow-up waves. Finally, only about 85 percent of students had information on standardized test scores, which were collected from the schools. After pairwise deletion of missing data in the regression analyses, our sample is 587.

The standardized test scores were based on the youth's fifth grade California Achievement Test. This widely-used test is a standardized achievement test designed to provide valid measurements of basic academic skills. It consists of seven sub-parts: reading vocabulary, reading comprehension, language mechanics, language expression, mathematics computation, mathematics concepts and application, and spelling.

As mentioned above, the baseline survey was in the youth's seventh grade school year and most of the demographic information we use draws from this wave of the study. However, grandparents' involvement in the child's life was assessed when the youth was in the eighth grade, and standardized test scores (collected from school records) are from the youth's fifth grade in school. Ideally, our measures of grandparent involvement and children's test scores would be simultaneously measured. Unfortunately, we do not have CAT scores taken after the fifth grade. Thus, our use of these measures requires making several assumptions. First, because we are interested in predicting test scores from the grandparents' involvement with the child, we must assume that grandparent involvement has been stable between the youth's eighth grade (when the measure was collected) and fifth grade (when the test was administered). We must also assume that the nature or type of involvement has not changed during this time. These may not be appropriate assumptions; therefore, we present these results with these caveats in mind.

Table 6.A.1 provides a description of the variables used in this study and Table 6.A.2 presents a description of race differences in these variables in our sample. Black grandparents have lower levels of education than do white grandparents. As in other studies on grandparenting, black grandparents are significantly more involved than white grandparents with their grandchildren.[35] There is a significant difference in educational attainment among the parent generation, although the magnitude of this difference is not quite as large as among grandparents. Black families in our sample have significantly lower incomes than do whites in this sample, have fewer educational materials in the house, and are less likely to be two-parent families. Despite these race differences, it is important to note that the black families represented here are nonetheless quite advantaged on these dimensions relative to national data for blacks. We control for parent's communication with the child in order to include an intervening generation measure of "involvement." There are no significant race differences in this measure. Black youth have fewer siblings than do their white counterparts, but there are no other differences in the sample in children's characteristics. Finally, black students have significantly lower CAT test scores than do white students.

Figures 6.1 and 6.2 provide more detailed information on one of the key variables of interest: grandparents' education. As can be seen, white

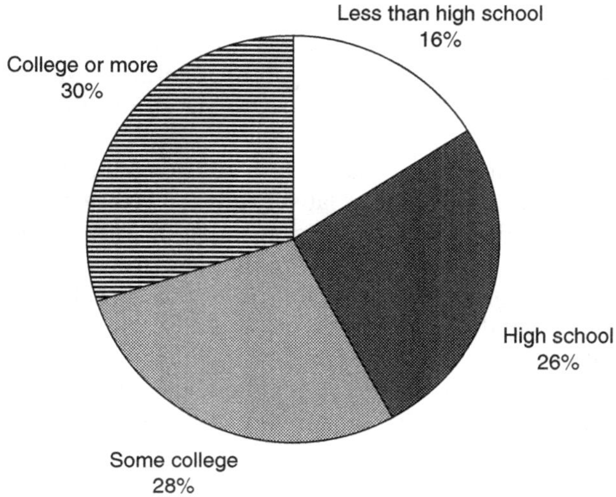

Figure 6.1 Highest grandparent education for white students.

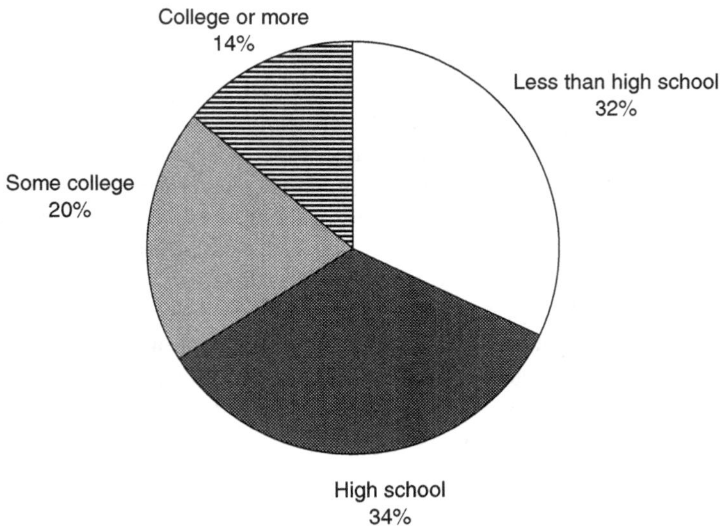

Figure 6.2 Highest grandparent education for black students.[a]

Note

a Chi square = 40.643 with 8 degrees of freedom and $p = 0.000$.

grandparents are much less likely than their black counterparts to have very low levels of education (less than high school); conversely, white grandparents are more likely to have college-level or higher education level. For comparison, we also examined detailed information on parental education. Here, the racial disparities in education are not as striking as were those in the grandparent generation. Many more black parents have achieved higher levels of education than did their own parents. Indeed, the rate of four-year college completion (14 percent) is nearly twice as high in the parent generation compared to the grandparent generation and is substantially higher than current national rates of attainment of a bachelor's degree (six percent) for blacks.[36]

Thus, the education and income levels of the black parents indicate the prevalence of middle class status in this relatively advantaged sample. But, as we have shown, racial disparities in socioeconomic characteristics are much more pronounced in the previous generation. Table 6.A.3 elaborates on this issue. Black grandmothers and grandfathers worked in substantially less prestigious occupations than did their white counterparts during their working lives (racial disparities in occupational prestige and in educational attainment are more pronounced among grandfathers than grandmothers). Black parents are significantly more likely to report that they were worse off economically as children than they are now. They are also much less likely to currently own their own home than are whites. Together, these characteristics illustrate the socioeconomic disadvantages of the families of origin among this current generation of black middle class families.

Results

Regression analyses predicting the standardized fifth-grade CAT score revealed three main points.[37] First, the effect of grandparent education operates via parents' education; once parent education is added to the model, grandparent education is not significant. This is similar to findings of Warren and Hauser and suggests an indirect effect of grandparent education on grandchildren's test scores.[38] The second point is that demographic variables behave as expected – parent education and family income are associated with test scores in the expected direction. The third point is that, taken together, all of these variables explain relatively little of the test score gap. As seen in Figure 6.3, adding the grandparent variables (education and involvement) reduces the gap by 8.7 percent; adding the parent variables in the parent and interaction models reduces the gap by an additional 8.7 percent. Although statistically significant, these effect sizes are modest. The interaction between grandparent involvement and grandparent education is not significant.

When only the white subsample is examined, grandparent education again is significant until parent education is added to the model and higher levels of income are also associated with higher test scores. In addition, the

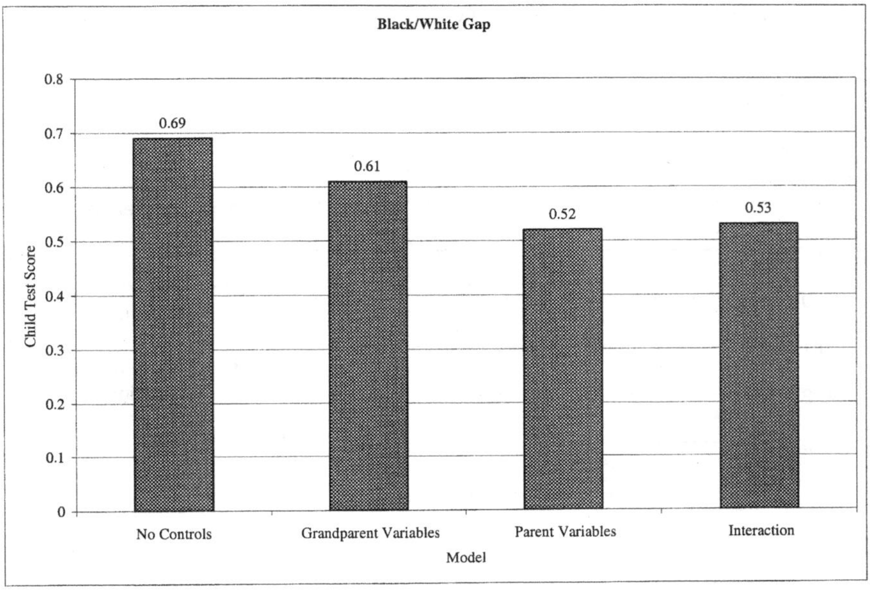

Figure 6.3 Size of black/white test score gap in regression analyses.[39]

greater the number of siblings a white child has, the lower is his or her CAT score, consistent with theories of resource dilution. The interaction between grandparent involvement and grandparent education is not significant. Age is also significant and probably reflects the negative effects of being overage for grade. The interaction term for whites is not significant.

When we examine the results for black youth we find that the effect of grandparent education appears to operate through parents' education. Both parental education and income are associated with higher CAT scores, while the educational materials in the household are weakly associated with test scores. In contrast to the white subsample analysis, the interaction term for grandparent involvement and grandparent education is significant in the black subsample. This interaction is depicted in Figure 6.4. The results suggest that higher levels of involvement by highly-educated grandparents are associated with modestly higher test scores, but high levels of involvement with a poorly-educated grandparent are more strongly associated with lower test scores. This finding is significantly different from the one we reported for whites.

These analyses of the fifth grade CAT scores suggests the following two conclusions: first that for both blacks and whites, grandparents affect children's test scores indirectly through parent's education; and second that the combination of grandparental capital with the amount of time they

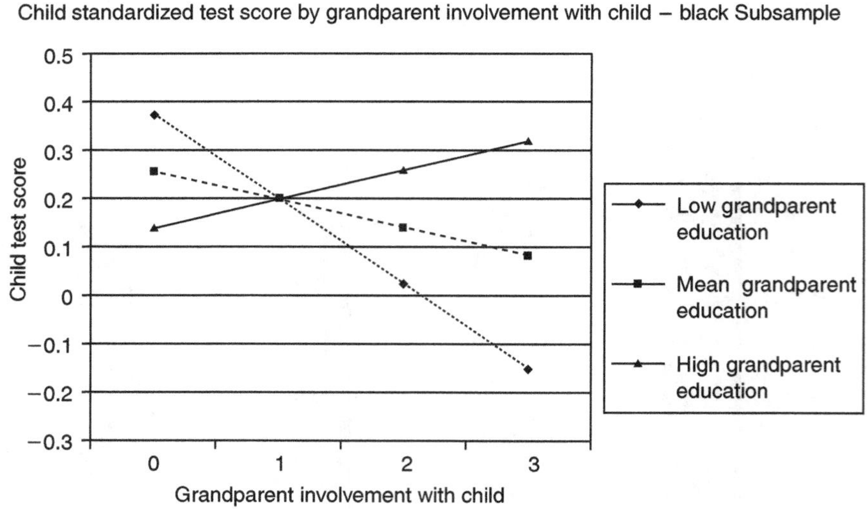

Figure 6.4 Graph of interaction terms for black students from Table 6.A.5 by child's standardized fifth grade test score.[a]

Note

a Using female students from intact families, with at least one grandparent living, and with all other values held at their means. Low and High PCG Parent Education equal one standard deviation below and above the mean. The respective figures for black students are 9.13, 12.05, and 14.97 years.

spend with their grandchildren matters only for black students' test scores, and is most important through the possible presence of "negative" capital for grandchildren, a finding we did not expect, but which we discuss below.

Conclusions

This chapter examined the influence of grandparents' education and involvement with grandchildren on the standardized test scores of black and white middle class adolescents. We posed the following four questions:

1 Do grandparents' characteristics have a direct effect on children's test scores, or do they operate only through their effect on parents' attainment? We found that the influence of grandparents' education operated through the educational attainment of the parent generation;
2 Does the association between grandparental involvement with the child and children's test scores depend on the grandparents' education? Despite no residual direct effect of grandparents on grandchildren, we have some suggestive evidence that for blacks, grandparents' education may be associated with youth's test scores through its inter-

action with the level of grandparental involvement. This finding supports the general hypothesis that "human capital" is transferred across generations through "social capital," or the social ties between individuals;

3 Are there race differences in the effects of grandparents' education and involvement on children's test scores? For the black youth in our study, low levels of grandparent education when combined with high levels of grandparent–grandchild interaction are associated with lower test scores. We did not find this association for whites;

4 What does a three-generational model contribute to our understanding of the black/white test score gap? While including grandparents' characteristics did not account for the difference in black and white youth's test scores, we did uncover an unexpected relationship for black families. We expected to find that high levels of grandparent education benefited children through high levels of grandparent–grandchild interaction. However, the stronger relationship appears to be between low levels of grandparent education combined with high involvement, which is associated with lower youth test scores for black families.

We can only speculate on the meaning of these findings. First, why are there race differences in the transmission of grandparental capital through social ties? It is possible that the measure of grandparent involvement carries different meanings in black and white families. Although there are no race differences in our sample in grandparent co-residence, we know that in national samples, black grandparents are more likely to be primary caregivers or co-resident than white grandparents.[40] If the black respondents in our study were comparing their parents' involvement with their understanding of the average level of involvement for their racial group, then black parents' reports of grandparental involvement could in fact represent *less* involvement than white parents' report. That is, an objectively similar level of involvement by a grandparent could be rated as "not so involved" by a black parent who is comparing that involvement with other blacks, but "somewhat involved" by a white parent whose reference group is other whites. Thus, the possibility that black grandparent/grandchild involvement is more intense than our measure indicates could account for the racial difference in effects.

The level of involvement as we assess it also does not address the quality or nature of that involvement. As King and Elder report, grandparents with some college education are significantly more likely to teach the grandchild skills and are more likely to discuss the grandchild's plans for the future than they are to play the role of "friend."[41] This suggests that involvement with middle class grandparents might help in the transference of class status in ways that involvement with a less-educated grandparent does not.

Again, our simple level of involvement may not capture important differences in the intensity or quality of involvement, which may differentially affect the transference of human capital through the social bond. We also do not know if this measure is capturing other disadvantages that grandparents represent in black families, such as poor-quality neighborhoods, so that perhaps "involvement" between them and their grandchild increases grandchildren's exposure to negative influences in the neighborhood that are associated with test scores. Unfortunately, we do not have any information about the grandparents' environment or the specific nature of their involvement with their grandchildren. Nevertheless, these findings suggest that characteristics of the families' of origin of the black middle class, which we and others have demonstrated differ substantially from those of their white counterparts, have a continuing influence on the performance and behaviors of the third generation.

The second question raised by these findings is the following: For blacks, why is there "negative" social capital, but not as strong "positive" social capital? That is, why is it that highly educated black grandparents who are highly involved with their grandchildren boost children's test scores as strongly as less educated grandparents depress test scores? One hypothesis is that low performing students are actually *selected into* grandparental involvement. This causal story would suggest that parents of adolescents who are having problems in school enlist the help of their parent for either additional monitoring, help with homework, etc. Because black children have lower test scores, they are perhaps more likely to be in families where grandparents are enlisted for such help. And since black grandparents have lower education, we might find the strong relationship between low test scores and low grandparental education in situations of high involvement. However, we have already tested and rejected this possibility by examining a regression that predicts grandparent involvement using parent and child characteristics that might show possible selection bias. We used variables that are likely to be related to children's test scores, but not test scores specifically because that would simply show the same correlation found earlier. Specifically, we posited that parental employment, poor parental mental health, child's involvement in negative activities, and child class failure and school suspension are all likely to predict grandparent involvement. In this scenario, grandparents might be called in to assist in difficult child rearing or if parents have less time due to employment. However, results show no correlation of any of these variables with grandparents' involvement. The only significant result from this analysis indicates that white families with higher incomes are less likely to have involved grandparents. Unfortunately, we do not have a measure of grandparent proximity, which we expect to be the most highly correlated variable with grandparent involvement.

Another possible explanation for this finding of "negative" social capital is that the educational experiences of black and white grandparents are not comparable across levels of educational attainment. That is, it is conceivable that black grandparents received poorer quality education at every level than did their white counterparts. Thus, higher education when many of these grandparents generally lived under the constraints of de facto and de jure racial segregation still did not equip them with sufficient skills to endow the third generation in this domain. On the other hand, low education was likely accompanied by an even more oppressive segregationist regime, perhaps in rural areas. Generally, this finding illustrates the need to specify the conditions under which "social capital" generates positive and negative effects.[42] Despite these findings, we are not arguing that low educated black grandparents be discouraged from interacting with their grandchildren. Educational achievement is just one domain of child development. We imagine that high levels of grandparent involvement are likely to be beneficial in other domains, such as feelings of love and security or measures of kin connectedness.[43] These results also underscore the importance of studying intergenerational capital as domain specific.

The findings of this research have important policy implications. We know that grandparents generally matter most for children's test scores through their impact on the parent generation. This leads us back to Coleman's central argument of the primacy of home experiences and directs policy attention toward opportunities for parents' continuing education to enhance their children's performance in school. However, for black families, grandparents may also have some direct influence on grandchildren's test scores that seems unlikely to be addressed with contemporary policies. This calls our attention yet again to the endurance of discrimination against and unequal treatment of blacks across generations, particularly in the field of educational attainment and achievement. As in many other studies, the test score gap persists in our study even in the face of information from three generations. More work remains to be done to identify the sources of this gap and develop interventions to close it.

Appendix

Table 6.A.1 Variable definitions[a]

Variable	*Definition*
GP highest education	Education level of most highly educated grandparent. Categorical variable from eighth grade or less to graduate/ professional degree recoded as continuous assigning years to each category. (Question: What was the highest year in school that your mother/father completed?)
GP/ highest child involvement	Involvement level of most highly involved grandparent. Continuous variable from 0 (deceased/not at all involved) to 3 (very involved) for both grandmother and grandfather. (Question: How involved is your mother/father with child now?)
Both GP dead	Dummy variable, 1 = Both grandparents dead, 0 = at least one grandparent living. (Question: How involved is your mother/father with child now? 1 mother/father dead, 0 not at all involved, etc.)
Parent education	Continuous variable of self-reported educational attainment. (Question: What is the highest grade of school you have completed?)
Family income (in $10,000)	Categorical variable of income ranges (e.g. between $10,000 and $14,999) recoded as continuous variable, assigning each category the midpoint for each range. In regression analyses, natural log of income is used. (Question: From all sources of income you mentioned, tell me your total family income before taxes in 1990.)
Intact family	Dummy variable indicating parent married to other parent of the child. (Question: What is the secondary caregiver's relationship to child? 1 = mother, father, or parent).
Educational materials	Continuous variable summing categorical responses, where 1 = yes if the household contained: dictionary, encyclopedia, musical instruments, instructional books, fiction books, educational books/magazines, newspapers, athletic equipment, computer, video games, and religious books. Range = 0 to 11.
Child number of siblings	Family size minus parent and other adults.
Parent communicates with child	Continuous variable that averages responses to how often parent talks with child about the following issues: his/her life, his/her friends, his/her future plans, his/her problems in school, his/her future jobs, courses to take for future employment. Range = 1 to 6.
Child black	1 = black, 0 = white, all other races excluded.
Child female	0 = Male, 1 = Female.
Child age	Continuous measure of child's age in seventh grade.

Note

a All information on "Parent" is for the Primary Caregiver to whom the survey was administered. Grandparents are parents of this primary caregiver, who is most often, but not always, the mother.

Table 6.A.2 Descriptive statistics for all study variables

Variable	*Total*	*Whites*	*Blacks*	
Grandparent generation				
GP highest education	12.58 (3.09)	13.36 (3.18)	12.05 (2.92)	***
GP/highest child involvement	1.47 (1.13)	1.31 (1.07)	1.56 (1.16)	**
Both GP Dead	0.13 (0.34)	0.12 (0.32)	0.14 (0.35)	
Parent generation				
Parent education	14.11 (2.47)	14.48 (2.66)	13.87 (2.30)	**
Family income (in $10,000)	5.05 (1.95)	5.48 (1.76)	4.76 (2.02)	***
Intact family	0.72 (0.45)	0.82 (0.39)	0.65 (0.48)	***
Educational materials	8.95 (2.01)	9.44 (1.61)	8.63 (2.18)	***
Child generation				
Child number of siblings	2.01 (1.20)	2.33 (1.20)	1.81 (1.15)	***
Parent communicates with child	3.92 (0.95)	3.90 (0.83)	3.93 (1.02)	
Child black	0.60 (0.49)	–	–	
Child female	0.51 (0.50)	0.53 (0.50)	0.49 (0.50)	
Child age	12.21 (0.49)	12.19 (0.42)	12.22 (0.53)	
Dependent variable				
California Achievement Test (5th Grade)	497.08 (52.71)	518.76 (54.03)	482.78 (46.66)	***

Notes
** $p<0.01$; *** $p<0.001$.
Standard deviations in parentheses.

Table 6.A.3 Descriptive statistics of additional grandparent and parent characteristics

Variable	*Total*	*Whites*	*Blacks*	
Grandparent Generation				
Highest grandparent occupational prestige score	49.03 (11.94)	52.09 (11.48)	47.01 (11.83)	***
Grandmother's occupational prestige score	43.41 (11.31)	45.06 (9.26)	42.33 (12.37)	**
Grandfather's occupational prestige score	43.38 (13.83)	47.42 (14.01)	40.40 (12.92)	***
Highest grandparent education	12.58 (3.09)	13.36 (3.18)	12.05 (2.92)	***
Grandmother's education	11.74 (2.77)	12.32 (2.70)	11.35 (2.75)	***
Grandfather's education	11.53 (3.51)	12.55 (3.68)	10.80 (3.19)	***
Parent generation				
Number of Siblings with college education[a]	0.99 (1.35)	1.01 (1.46)	0.97 (1.27)	
Parent worse off economically as child than at present	0.56 (0.50)	0.49 (0.50)	0.60 (0.49)	**
Parent owns home	0.68 (0.47)	0.80 (0.40)	0.60 (0.49)	***

Notes
** $p<0.01$; *** $p<0.001$.
a Wave 4 variable.

Table 6.A.4 Regression of standardized fifth grade test scores on grandparent and parent characteristics, whites only

Variable	*Model 1*	*Model 2*	*Model 3*
GP highest education	0.05* (0.02)	0.00 (0.02)	0.04 (0.03)
GP/child involvement	0.00 (0.07)	0.02 (0.06)	0.35 (0.24)
Both GP dead	0.04 (0.22)	0.02 (0.21)	−0.02 (0.21)
Parent education	–	0.09*** (0.03)	0.09*** (0.03)
Natural log of family income	–	0.38** (0.13)	0.37** (0.13)
Intact family	–	0.11 (0.18)	0.11 (0.18)
Educational materials	–	0.04 (0.04)	0.04 (0.04)
Child number of siblings	–	−0.16** (0.05)	−0.16** (0.05)
Parent communicates with child	–	−0.05 (0.07)	−0.05(0.07)
Child female	–	0.07 (0.12)	0.07 (0.12)
Child age	–	−0.28* (0.13)	−0.29* (0.13)
GP/child involvement × GP education	–	–	−0.03 (0.02)
Constant	−0.72* (0.30)	−1.95 (2.19)	−2.25 (2.19)
Adjusted R^2	0.016	0.188	0.192
R^2 change (based on unadjusted R^2)	0.029$^+$	0.197***	0.007
N	237	237	237

Notes
Pairwise deletion used. + $p<0.1$; * $p<0.05$; ** $p<0.01$; *** $p<0.001$.

Table 6.A.5 Regression of standardized fifth grade test scores on grandparent and parent characteristics, blacks only

Variable	*Model 1*	*Model 2*	*Model 3*
GP highest education	0.05** (0.02)	0.02 (0.02)	−0.04 (0.03)
GP/child involvement	−0.14 (0.06)	−0.10$^+$ (0.05)	−0.54** (0.19)
Both GP dead	−0.07 (0.19)	−0.03 (0.17)	−0.07 (0.17)
Parent education	–	0.08** (0.03)	0.08** (0.03)
Natural log of family income	–	0.26* (0.10)	0.24* (0.10)
Intact family	–	−0.03 (0.13)	−0.04 (0.13)
Educational materials	–	0.04$^+$ (0.03)	0.04 (0.03)
Child number of siblings	–	0.05 (0.04)	0.06 (0.04)
Parent communicates with child	–	0.01 (0.05)	0.00 (0.05)
Child female	–	0.16 (0.10)	0.16 (0.10)
Child age	–	−0.32*** (0.09)	−0.32*** (0.09)
GP/child involvement × GP education	–	–	0.04* (0.02)
Constant	−0.42$^+$ (0.24)	−0.63 (1.55)	0.38 (1.60)
Adjusted R^2	0.025	0.175	0.187
R^2 change (based on unadjusted R^2)	0.034**	0.168***	0.013*
N	349	349	349

Notes
Pairwise deletion used. + $p<0.1$; * $p<0.05$; ** $p<0.01$; *** $p<0.001$.

Notes

1 Support for this research was provided by the Office of the Vice-President for Research at Northwestern University and by the Spencer Foundation. We thank Greg Duncan, Tom Cook, Robert Hauser, Jennifer Romich, David Harris, Jeff Morenoff, Tom DeLeire, and participants at the Institute for Policy Research Seminar at Northwestern University for helpful comments.

2 College Board, *Reaching the Top: A Report of the National Task Force on Minority High Achievement*, 1999, http://www.collegeboard.org/press/html9900/html/ReachingTheTop.pdf.

3 J. S. Eccles, D. Early, K. Fraser, E. Belansky, and K. McCarthy, "The relation of connection, regulation, and support for autonomy to adolescents' functioning," *Journal of Adolescent Research* 12, 1997, 263–286.

4 J. S. Coleman, E. Q. Campbell, C. J. Hobson, J. McPartland, A. M. Mood, F. D. Weinfeld, and R. L. York, *Equality of Educational Opportunity,* Washington, DC: U.S. Government Printing Office, 1966, p. iii.

5 J. Coleman, *Equality and Achievement in Education*, Boulder, CO: Westview Press, 1990.

6 G. Farkas, *Human Capital or Cultural Capital: Ethnicity and Poverty Groups in an Urban School District*, New York, NY, Aldine de Gruyter, 1996; M. Phillips, J. Brooks-Gunn, G. J. Duncan, P. Klevanov, and J. Crane, "Family background, parenting practices and the black-white test score gap," in *The Black-White Test Score Gap*, eds. C. Jencks and M. Phillips, Washington DC: Brookings Institution Press, 1998.

7 On the negative effects of single parents see V. Roscigno, "Race and the reproduction of educational disadvantage," *Social Forces* 76, 1998, 1033–1060; M. Thompson, K. L. Alexander, and D. R. Entwisle, "Household composition, parental expectations, and school achievement," *Social Forces* 67, 1988, 424–451. On small effects, see J. Heiss, "Effects of African American family structure on school attitudes and performance," *Social Problems* 43, 1996, 246–267; L. Mulkey, R. Crain, and A. Harrington, "One-parent households and achievement: economic and behavioral explanation of a small effect," *Sociology of Education* 65, 1992, 48–65. On non-existent or variable findings by group, see A. M. Milne, D. E. Myers, A. S. Rosenthal, and A. Ginsburg, "Single parents, working mothers, and the educational achievement of school children," *Sociology of Education* 59, 1986, 125–139. On results pointing to the positive effects of single mothers, see J. Battle, "What beats having two parents: educational outcomes for African American students in single- versus dual-parent families," *Journal of Black Studies* 28, 1998, 783–801.

8 C. Bankston III, "Family structure, schoolmates, and racial inequalities in school achievement," *Journal of Marriage and the Family* 60, 1998, 715–723; D. R. Entwisle and K. L. Alexander, "Summer setback: race, poverty, school composition, and mathematics achievement in the first two years of school," *American Sociological Review* 57, 1992, 72–84; M. A. Hill and J. O'Neill, "Family endowments and the achievement of young children with special reference to the underclass," *Journal of Human Resources* 29, 1994, 1064–1100; C. Jencks and M. Phillips, *The Black-White Test Score Gap*, Washington DC: Brookings Institution Press, 1998; Roscigno, op. cit.; V. Roscigno, "The black-white achievement gap, family-school links, and the importance of place," *Sociological Inquiry* 69, 1999, 159–186; V. Roscigno and J. Ainsworth-Darnell, "Race, cultural capital, and educational resources: persistent inequalities and achievement returns," *Sociology of Education* 72, 1999, 158–178.

9 J. Brooks-Gunn, P. K. Klebanov, and G. J. Duncan, "Ethnic differences in

children's intelligence test scores: role of economic deprivation, home environment, and maternal characteristics," *Child Development* 67, 1996, 396–408. Also see J. Ainsworth-Darnell and D. B. Downey, "Assessing the oppositional culture explanation for racial/ethnic differences in school performance," *American Sociological Review* 63, 1998, 536–553.

10 See P. Blau and O. D. Duncan, *The American Occupational Structure*, New York, NY: Wiley, 1967; O. D. Duncan, "Inheritance of poverty or inheritance of race," in *On Understanding Poverty*, ed. Daniel Moynihan, New York: Basic Books, 1969; M. Corcoran, R. Gordon, D. Laren, and G. Solon, "The Association between men's economic status and their family and community origins," *Journal of Human Resources* 27, 1992, 575–601.

11 O. Ashenfelter and D. J. Zimmerman, "Estimates of the returns to schooling from sibling data: fathers, sons and brothers," *The Review of Economics and Statistics* 79, 1997, 1–9; H. D. Kuo and R. Hauser, "Trends in family effects on the education of black and white brothers," *Sociology of Education* 68, 1995, 136–160; G. Solon, M. Corcoran, R. Gordon, and D. Laren, "A longitudinal analysis of sibling correlations in economic status," *Journal of Human Resources* 26, 1991, 509–534.

12 G. Solon, "Intergenerational mobility in the labor market," in *Handbook of Labor Economics*, eds. O. Ashenfelter and D. Card, Amsterdam: North Holland, forthcoming.

13 D. Conley, *Being Black, Living in the Red: Race, Wealth, and Social Policy in America*, Berkeley, CA: University of California Press, 1999; D. Conley, "Capital for college: parental assets and postsecondary schooling," *Sociology of Education* 74, 2001, 59–72; M. Oliver and T. Shapiro, *Black Wealth/White Wealth: A New Perspective on Racial Inequality*, New York, NY: Routledge, 1995.

14 Blau and Duncan, op. cit.; W. H. Sewell and R. M. Hauser, *Education, Occupation, and Earnings: Achievement in the Early Career*, New York, NY: Academic Press, 1975.

15 R. Hauser and D. Featherman, "Trends in the occupational mobility of U.S. men, 1962–1970," *American Sociological Review* 38, 1973, 302–310.

16 J. Warren and R. M. Hauser, "Social stratification across three generations: new evidence from the Wisconsin longitudinal study," *American Sociological Review* 62, 1997, 561–572.

17 With the very notable exceptions of a body of sociological literature that has examined the role of parents' connections to other adults and cultural capital and institutions outside of the family (see P. Bourdieu, "The forms of capital," pp. 241–260 in J. Richardson (ed.), *Handbook of Theory and Research for the Sociology of Education*, New York, NY: Greenwood Press, 1986; A. Lareau, *Home Advantage: Social Class and Parental Intervention in Elementary Education*, London: Falmer Press, 1989; B. Schneider and J. Coleman, *Parents, Their Children, and Schools*, Boulder, CO: Westview Press, 1993).

18 M. Kohn and C. Schooler, "Job conditions and personality: a longitudinal assessment of their reciprocal effects," *American Journal of Sociology* 87, 1982, 1257–86; J. Miller, C. Schooler, M. Kohn, and K. Miller, "Women and work: The psychological effects of occupational conditions," *American Journal of Sociology* 85, 1979, 66–94.

19 S. Bowles and H. Gintis, *Schooling in Capitalist America: Educational Reform and the Contradictions of Economic Life*, New York, NY: Basic Books, 1976.

20 G. Jaynes and R. Williams, *A Common Destiny: Blacks and American Society*, Washington, DC: National Research Council, 1989.

21 Oliver and Shapiro, op. cit.; R. D. Alba, J. Logan, and B. Stults, "How segregated are middle-class African Americans?," *Social Problems* 47, 2000, 543–558;

M. Pattillo-McCoy, *Black Picket Fences: Privilege and Peril among the Black Middle Class*, Chicago, IL: University of Chicago Press, 1999; S. Collins, "The Making of the Black Middle Class," *Social Problems* 30, 1983, 369–382.

22 G. Orfield, *Schools More Separate: Consequences of a Decade of Resegregation*, Cambridge, MA: The Civil Rights Project, 2001.

23 M. Pattillo-McCoy and C. M. Heflin, "Poverty in the family: siblings of the black and white middle class," paper presented at the Annual Meeting of the American Sociological Association, Chicago, IL, 1999. For more discussion of the recency of the black middle class, see A. Billingsley, *Climbing Jacobs Ladder: The Enduring Legacy of African American Families*, New York, NY: Simon and Schuster, 1992; and Pattillo-McCoy, op. cit.

24 For a classic treatise on this issue, see C. Stack, *All Our Kin: Strategies for Survival in a Black Community*, New York, NY: Harper and Row, 1974.

25 M. N. Wilson, "Child development in the context of the Black extended family," *American Psychologist* 44, 1989, 380–385; J. Watson and S. Koblinksy, "Strengths and needs of working class African-American and Anglo-American grandparents," *International Journal of Aging and Human Development* 44, 1997, 149–165.

26 Watson and Koblinksy, op. cit.; R. Strom, P. Collingsworth, S. Strom, and D. Griswold, "Strengths and needs of black grandparents," *International Journal of Aging and Human Development* 36, 1993, 255–268.

27 Wilson, op. cit.

28 J. Coleman, "Social capital in the creation of human capital," *American Journal of Sociology* 94, 1988, S95–S120.

29 A. Portes, "Social capital: its origins and applications in modern sociology," *Annual Review of Sociology* 24, 1998, 1–24.

30 Coleman 1988, op. cit., p. S98.

31 V. King and G. Elder, "Education and grandparenting roles," *Research on Aging* 20, 1998, 450–474.

32 Coleman 1988, op. cit., p. S98.

33 On grandparents' indirect effects see Warren and Hauser, op. cit. On grandparents' direct effects, see Hill and O'Neill, op. cit. and Phillips *et al.*, op. cit.

34 Phillips *et al.*, op. cit.

35 A. Cherlin and F. Furstenberg Jr., *The New American Grandparent: A Place in the Family, A Life Apart*, New York, NY: Basic Books, 1986.

36 L. Keister, "Family structure, race, and wealth ownership: A longitudinal exploration of wealth accumulation processes," The Ohio State University: Department of Sociology, 2000, working paper No. 304.

37 The fifth-grade CAT score includes math, reading and spelling. Separate analyses using just the math sub-tests yielded similar results and are available upon request. We present regression results for whites and blacks separately in Tables 6.A.4 and 6.A.5, respectively.

38 Warren and Hauser, op. cit.

39 In the No Controls Model only youth's race was considered; in the Grandparent Model, highest grandparent education, involvement, and whether or not both grandparents are dead was also considered; in the Parent Model, parent income, education and marital status, along with communication with youth, educational materials in the home, number of siblings, and youth's gender and race was also considered; and in the Interaction Model, grandparent education multiplied by grandparent involvement was considered.

40 K. Bryson and L. Kasper, "Coresident grandparent and grandchildren," *Current Population Reports*, 1999, 23–198.

41 King and Elder, op. cit.

42 For a discussion of the various kinds of social capital, see Portes, op. cit.

43 As an illustration of the domain-specific nature of these findings, we examined regressions on child mental health using grandparent education and involvement and the other control variables. In these analyses grandparent education and grandparent involvement were not significant predictors of child mental health in any of the models for blacks or whites, and the interaction coefficient was also insignificant.

Part III

Family backgrounds, schooling, and the labor market

7 Teenage employment and high school completion

John Robert Warren, Jennifer C. Lee, and Emily Forrest Cataldi[1]

Many parents and educators worry that high school students spend too much time working at paid jobs during the school year. They fear that working long hours – especially on school nights – hurts students' performance in the classroom. Many teachers report that their students who work long hours come to class unprepared and less well rested. At the same time, advocates of teenage employment assert that holding a job plays an important role in preparing young people for the adult labor force. It teaches some specific job skills, but more importantly it teaches responsibility, time management, the "value of a dollar," and other valuable life skills.[2] However one views teenage employment, it is clearly commonplace: a recent report from the Bureau of Labor Statistics shows that about two in three 16 year olds and about three in four 17 year olds held paid jobs at some point during the 1998–1999 school year.[3]

It is equally clear that high school students who work many hours per week at paid jobs are substantially less likely to graduate from high school than their peers who do not work or who work less intensively.[4] As we will show later in this chapter, students who work intensively – that is, more than 15 or 20 hours per week – leave high school without a diploma much more frequently than their peers. Why are high school students who work intensively at paid jobs so much less likely to graduate from high school? From one point of view, it may be that intensive employment has the direct effect of pushing students out of high school by interfering with their performance in the classroom. This perspective is fundamentally premised on the assumption that dropouts would have remained in school until graduation had they been less intensively involved in the paid labor market. From another point of view, it may be that some students perceive – correctly or not – that paid employment is a better long-term strategy than obtaining a high school diploma. From the latter perspective, intensive employment does not directly cause students to leave high school before graduating; it is an alternative activity pursued by students who see themselves as unlikely to be academically successful and who perceive that investments in their jobs will pay off more in the long run than investments in their educations. Other industrialized nations have more formal systems of sorting some students into early vocational training and labor market entry and other students into advanced secondary and post-secondary schooling. Perhaps American students effectively sort themselves into these paths, and this is what gives rise to lower rates of high school completion among intensively employed students.

Adjudicating between these competing points of view is more than an academic issue. If intensive employment is directly causing students to leave high school who would otherwise have graduated and perhaps gone on for post-secondary schooling, then we might reasonably act to restrict teenagers' employment behaviors, to amend or better enforce child labor laws, or to more forcefully warn students and their parents of the potentially serious consequences of working long hours. However, if some students are turning to intensive employment as an activity that offers greater perceived prospects for future success, our recommendations for policy action will need to be different. In that case we might act to make school more relevant or attractive to students, to convince them of the relative long-term benefits of high school graduation, or perhaps to provide more formal linkages between schools and employers in order to more efficiently and effectively facilitate the transition from school to work for teenagers who do not complete secondary schooling – as many European and Asian countries do.

Regardless of why intensively employed students are less likely to graduate from high school, it is clear that teenage employment is an important issue if we wish to understand how family socioeconomic background affects high school completion. As documented by sociologist James Coleman in his 1966 report *Equality of Educational Opportunity* and by innumerable observers subsequently, educational achievements are heavily influenced by the social and economic circumstances of students' families of origin; this is represented as path ❶ in Figure 7.1. As we document below, teenagers' paid employment behaviors – including how intensively they work – also vary in important ways by family socioeconomic origins (represented by path ❷), and so it makes sense to think of teenage employment as an important link in the overall association between family socioeconomic origins and high school completion. In this sense, our work speaks to the issues at the core of this volume. Rates of high school completion vary markedly by family socioeconomic background. If high school students' employment behaviors are also stratified by family socioeconomic background, and if those employment behaviors have a direct bearing on students' chances of completing high school, then employment behaviors are an important out-of-school factor that stratifies students' educational achievements.

The extent to which teenage employment mediates the association between family socioeconomic origins and high school completion is a function of the magnitude of path ❸ in Figure 7.1, and so that path is the focus of most of our attention in this chapter. The way we have drawn

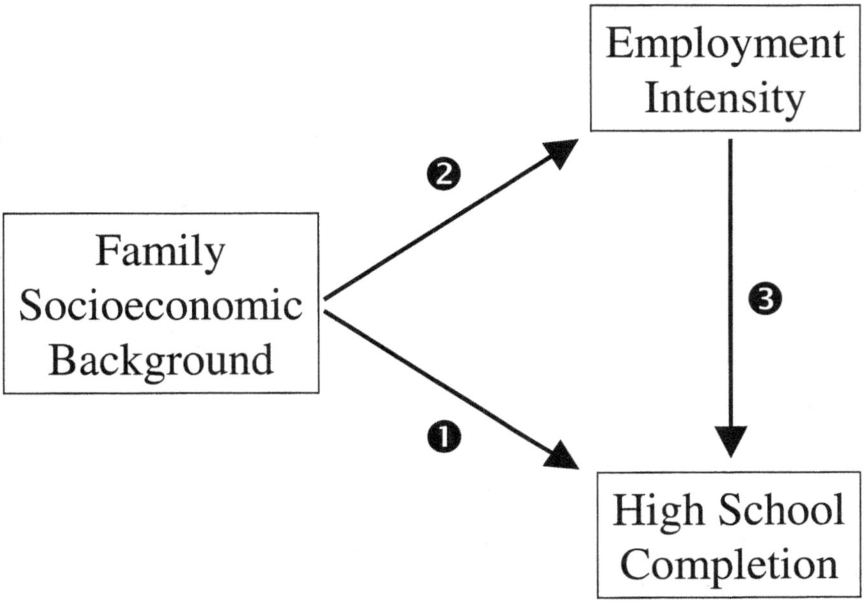

Figure 7.1 Conceptual model of the connections between family socioeconomic background, employment intensity, and high school completion.

path ❸ should not be interpreted as endorsing the conclusion that employment intensity directly impedes high school completion; as we describe below, we perform our analyses while taking an agnostic view of the source of the association between employment intensity and high school completion. The mission of our empirical analyses is to carefully document the extent to which that association varies over time and across different groups of students, and in so doing to understand how teenagers' employment plays into patterns of socioeconomic inequalities in rates of high school completion.

The goal of this chapter is to understand the contours of the relationships between family socioeconomic origins, student employment, and high school completion. In Part I we take a historical perspective on teenage employment behaviors. We examine changes over time in the employment behaviors of students from different socioeconomic, demographic, and academic backgrounds (that is, changes over time in path ❷ above), and we estimate changes over time in the relationship between teenage employment and high school completion (that is, changes over time in path ❸ above). In Part I we show that – in sharp contrast to most parents' and educators' perceptions – student employment behaviors have not changed much in the past 30 or 40 years; that social, economic, and demographic inequalities in student employment behaviors have largely remained stable over time; and that the relationship between intensive employment and high school completion has also remained stable over time.

In Part II we focus on the extent to which the connection between intensive employment and high school completion varies by teenagers' personal characteristics and the characteristics of the labor markets in which they live. That is, we ask whether the magnitude of path ❸ in Figure 7.1 is the same for different types of students and for students in different labor market contexts. We show that the connection between intensive employment and high school completion is more or less the same for students from all sorts of social, economic, and educational backgrounds, and that it is more or less the same for students under different labor market circumstances. Taken together, our results show that family socioeconomic background affects how intensively high school students work at paid jobs, and that intensive employment is strongly associated with high school completion – regardless of the mechanism that gives rise to that association. That these patterns hold over time, across labor markets, and for students with divergent backgrounds suggests that teenage employment is an important and long-standing mediator of the impact of social and economic conditions on high school completion.

Part I: teenage employment and high school completion over time

Is it true that more high school students are working – and working a lot – these days, as many concerned educators and parents perceive? Have changes in paid employment behaviors occurred evenly among all segments of the student population, or have documented patterns of socioeconomic, race/ethnic, and sex inequalities in student employment behaviors[5] been alleviated – or exacerbated – over time? If changes over time in employment behaviors have been uneven across students from different socioeconomic and/or demographic groups, how has this altered the association between employment behaviors and high school students' chances of completing high school? In Part I of this chapter we address three specific questions. First, how have rates of employment and employment intensity among high school sophomores and seniors changed in recent decades? Second, have the socioeconomic, demographic, and/or academic characteristics of employed and intensively employed sophomores and seniors changed since the mid-1960s? That is, have patterns of selection into employment and intensive employment changed over that period? Third, how has the relationship between sophomore-year employment and high school completion (net of changes in socioeconomic background and academic factors) changed since the mid-1960s?

The first question addresses the common perception among educators and parents that more high school students are working these days, and that they are working longer hours than ever before. Whether rates and intensity of employment have changed or not, the second question explores changes in the composition of the populations of employed and intensively employed students. Even if rates of employment and intensive employment have remained steady, it may still be the case that the socioeconomic, demographic, and/or academic characteristics of intensively employed students have changed. We might imagine, for instance, that as rates of high school completion have increased over time the population of intensively employed students has come to include greater shares of lower-achieving and less socio-economically advantaged students and race/ethnic minorities. On the other hand, if rates of intensive employment have increased, it may be that the population of intensively employed students has come to include students from a wider variety of social and economic backgrounds.

The third question assesses trends in the relationship between employment behaviors and high school completion. If we find that there have been changes in the composition of the populations of employed and intensively employed students, then we might reasonably expect the relationship between employment behaviors and high school completion to have changed as well. If, for example, the population of intensively employed students has come to include more and more students who are from advantaged socioeconomic backgrounds and who do well in school, then we might sensibly expect the link between employment intensity and early school-leaving to have weakened over time.

Long-term trends in teenage employment behaviors

Although our focus in Part I will mainly be on trends in teenage employment since the late 1960s, it is useful to look at longer-term trends to gain a better sense of historical context. At the onset of the twentieth century, very few teenagers were enrolled in school. Most were principally occupied with maintaining farms or working for pay. At the onset of the twenty-first century, high school completion is nearly universal – teenagers are now primarily busy obtaining a diploma. The latter fact does not mean that high school age adolescents are no longer active in the paid labor force – as we described at the outset, the vast majority of high school students hold paid jobs during the school year.

Using data from the U.S. Bureau of the Census,[6] Figure 7.2 presents trends between 1940 and 2000 in the percentage of enrolled 16 and 17 year olds who worked for pay in the week preceding their survey;[7] the top panel reports these trends separately for male and female students, and the bottom panel reports these trends separately for white and black students. Both panels show that few 16- and 17-year-old students were employed in 1940; that rates of employment increased steadily until about 1980; and that these rates have remained relatively stable since then. The top panel reveals

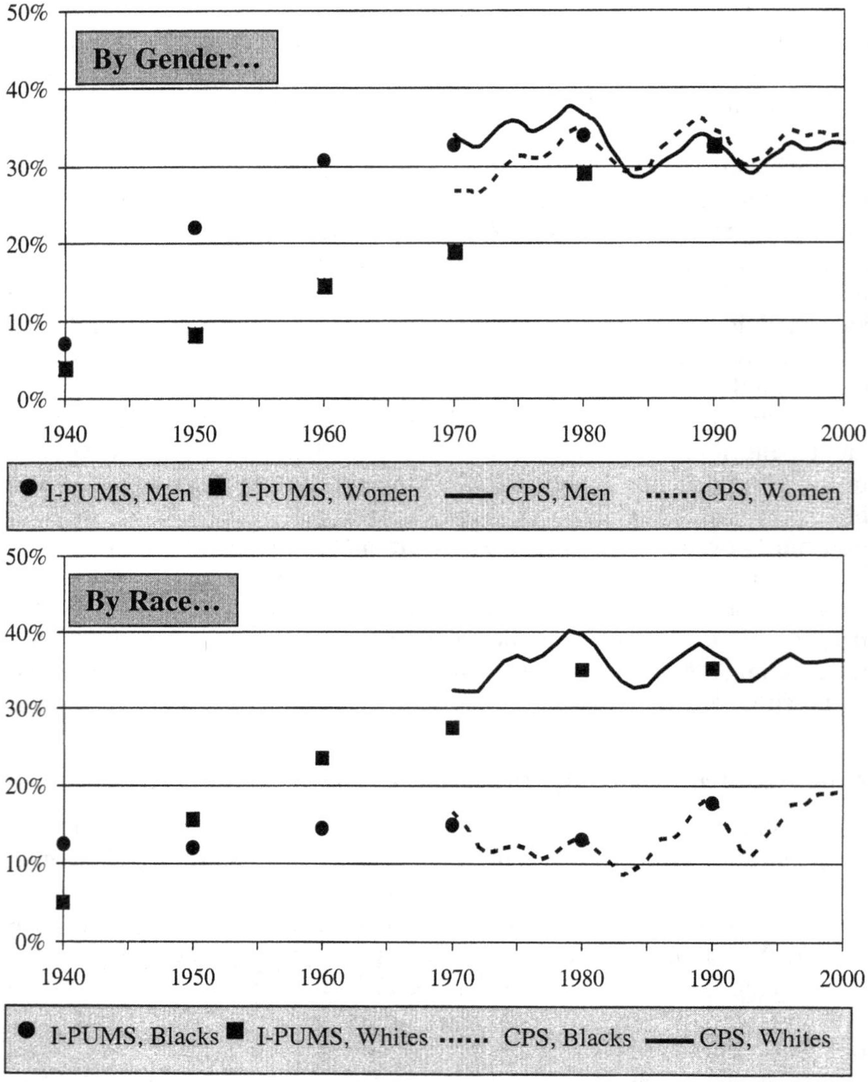

Figure 7.2 Percent employed among 16–17-year-old enrolled students, 1940–2000, by gender and race.

Source: 1940 through 1990 Integrated Public Use Microdata Samples (IPUMS; see Ruggles and Sobek 1997) and 1968 through 2000 Uniform October Current Population Survey file (CPS; see Hauser 1993). Note that CPS figures are three year moving averages that there were substantial sex differences in student employment rates until the mid-1970s, such that male students were far more likely than female students to work for pay; these differences essentially disappeared after about 1980. The bottom panel shows that the long-term increase in employment rates among 16- and 17-year-olds took place primarily among white students; employment rates for black students have remained more or less stable since at least 1940. Consequently, large black-white differences in student employment rates emerged between about 1950 and about 1980.

Putting aside these race/ethnic differences, which are interesting in their own right and deserving of further attention, Figure 7.2 makes an important point and raises an interesting question. The point is that 16- and 17-year-old students were not much more likely to have paid jobs in 2000 than they were in 1970 – roughly a generation earlier. The question concerns the increase in rates of paid employment among 16- and 17-year-old students between 1940 and 1980 or so. This trend could have come about through one or both of two processes. First, it could be – as many people believe – that during this period greater and greater numbers of 16- and 17-year old students chose to enter the paid labor market in addition to attending school. Second, it could be that during this period greater and greater numbers of employed 16 and 17 year-old adolescents chose to attend (or remain in) school in addition to holding paid jobs.

Figure 7.3 is designed to shed light on these two possible explanations for the increase in rates of employment among 16- and 17-year-old students between 1940 and 1980. The figure classifies all 16- and 17-year-olds in each decennial census year into one of four categories: just working for pay, just enrolled in school, both, or neither. The top panel pertains to men, and demonstrates that the increase in rates of student employment appears to have largely come at the expense of the "just employed" category. That is, for 16- and 17-year-old boys the increasing share of enrolled students who also hold paid jobs should be viewed as a movement by employed boys into school at least as much as a movement by enrolled boys into the labor force. The bottom panel pertains to women, and confirms that the proportion of 16- to 17-year-old women who both worked for pay and were enrolled in school increased sharply between 1940 and 1980. It appears that until 1970 the increasing share of enrolled women who also worked for pay came at the expense of the "neither employed nor enrolled" category, which likely consists of homemakers. Between 1970 and 1980 it appears that many enrolled 16- to 17-year-old women moved into the labor force. Overall, then, increases between 1940 and 1970 in the proportion of enrolled 16- and 17-year-old boys and girls who held paid jobs were largely due to increases in the proportion of male workers and female homemakers who also attended (or remained in) school. The broad trend in the second half of the twentieth century was not toward paid employment in addition to schooling, it was toward schooling in addition to homemaking or paid employment.

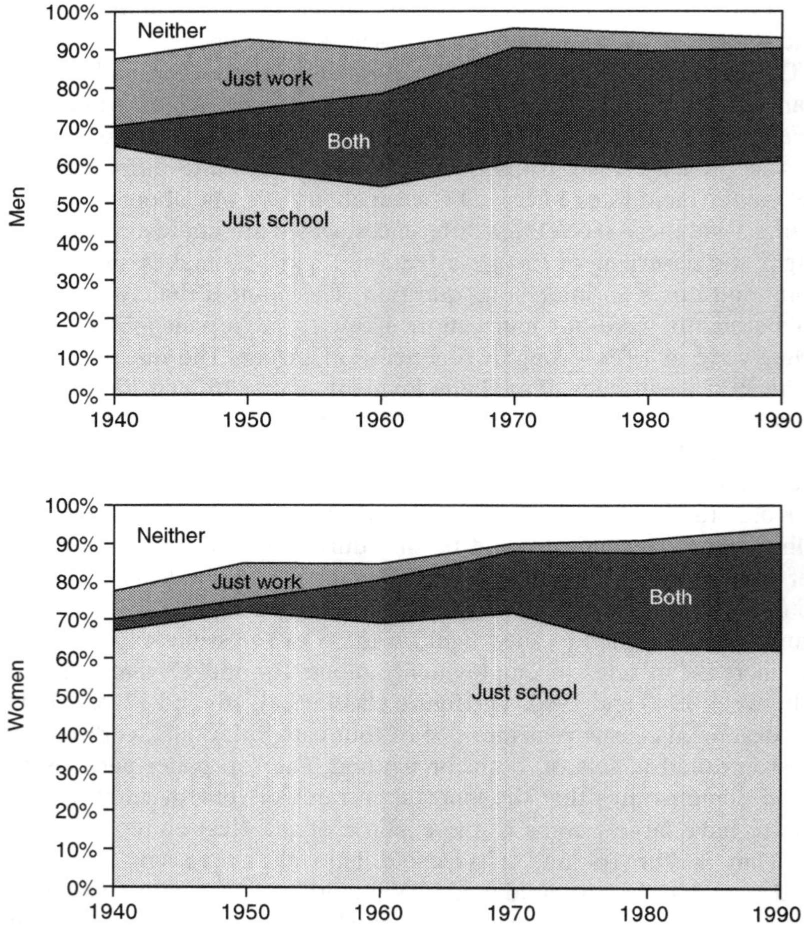

Figure 7.3 Employment and schooling among 16–17-year-olds, 1940–1990, by gender.

Source: 1940 through 1990 Integrated Public Use Microdata Samples (IPUMS; see Ruggles and Sobek 1997).

Finally, Figure 7.4 reports trends in mean hours worked per week among employed 16- and 17-year-old students, separately by sex (in the top panel) and race (in the bottom panel). Since about 1940 employed 16- and 17-year-old students have typically worked between 15 and 20 hours per week. There is little evidence of any trend in the number of hours worked per week by employed high school students. Boys tend to work a few more hours per week than girls, and there is some evidence that blacks work a few more hours per week than whites; neither of these differences has grown substantially larger or smaller since at least 1940.

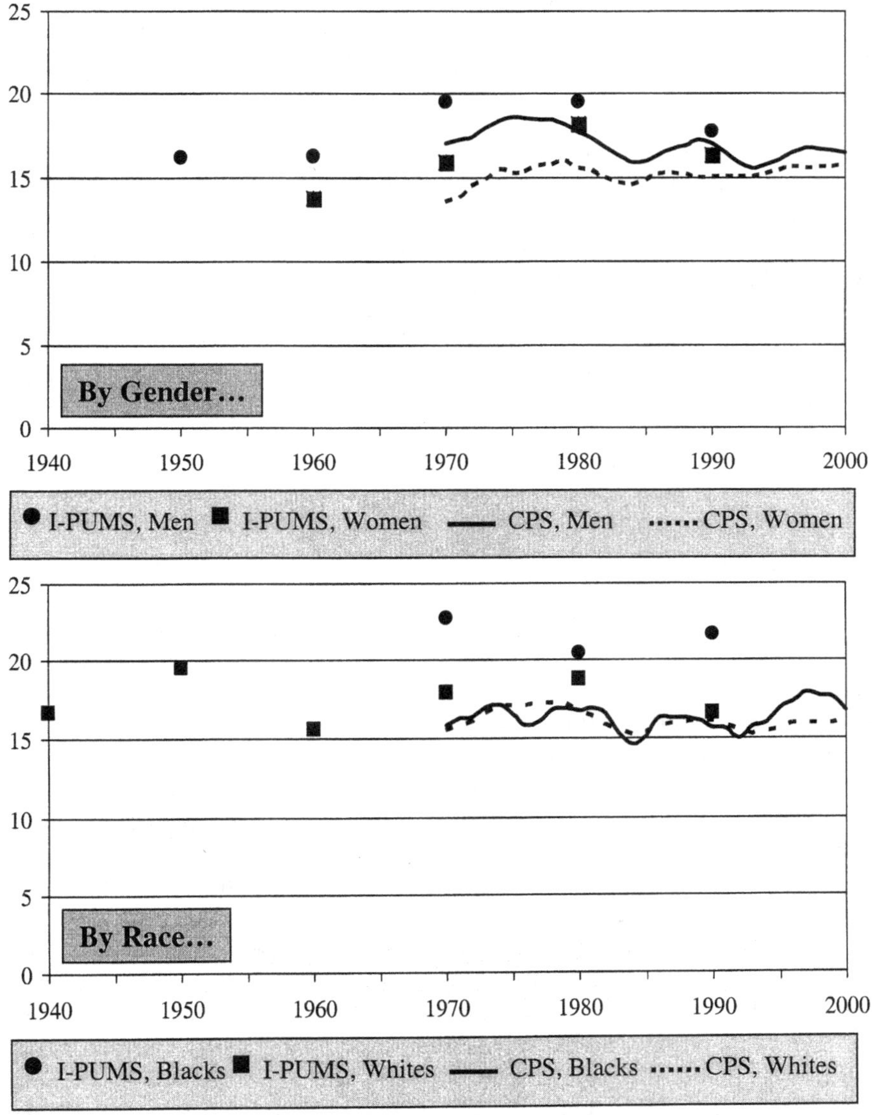

Figure 7.4 Hours worked per week among employed 16–17 year-old students, 1940–2000, by gender and race.

Source: 1940 through 1990 Integrated Public Use Microdata Samples (IPUMS; see Ruggles and Sobek 1997) and 1968 through 2000 Uniform October Current Population Survey file (CPS; see Hauser 1993). Note that CPS figures are three year moving averages.

Data and measures

To analyze trends in the composition of the populations of employed and intensively employed students and the connection between those behaviors and high school completion, we use five nationally representative data sets that contain samples of high school sophomores and/or seniors; together, these surveys span the years 1966 to 1997.[8] The National Longitudinal Surveys of Young Men and Young Women (NLS) include samples of sophomore and senior men in 1966 and women in 1968, respectively.[9] The 1979 National Longitudinal Survey of Youth (NLSY-79) and the 1980 wave of High School and Beyond (HS&B) each include samples of both sophomores and seniors.[10] The 1990 wave of the National Educational Longitudinal Study of 1988 (NELS:88) consists of a sample of sophomores, and the 1992 wave of NELS:88 consists of a sample of seniors.[11] Finally, the 1997 National Longitudinal Survey of Youth (NLSY-97) includes a sample of sophomores.[12] In all five samples of sophomores we also observe enrollment/graduation status two years later. From each data set we have extracted records for all enrolled sophomores and seniors (except from NLSY-97, from which we have only extracted records for sophomores). This yields five nationally representative samples of sophomores spanning the years 1966 to 1997 and four nationally representative samples of seniors spanning the years 1966 to 1992. As described below, we can identify whites and blacks in each survey, but we cannot consistently identify members of other race/ethnic groups; consequently, each sample is restricted to whites and blacks.

Within each of the data sets we have constructed nine measures: employment status, hours worked per week, race/ethnicity, sex, parents' education, family structure, age/grade delay, college aspirations/expectations, and senior-year enrollment/graduation status. Given differences across surveys in question wording and response options, a key challenge in this part of our research has been to construct these measures in such a way as to make them comparable across surveys. The source variables we use from each survey, as well as question wording and response options, are available in the appendix; descriptive statistics for each variable, by sample, are available in Table 7.A.1. From all samples we exclude cases with missing data on any variable. The resulting samples include the vast majority (at least 70 percent, but usually about 90 percent) of all possible white and black respondents to these surveys.

The questions measuring employment status and hours worked per week are reasonably consistent across surveys, both conceptually and technically.[13] Because we are interested in the effects of intensive employment – that is, the effect of working "a lot" – we have divided students into three groups: those who are not employed, those who are employed but who work 20 or fewer hours per week, and those who work more than 20 hours per week.[14]

The measures of sex in each of our surveys are straightforward, although the source of the information varies. The race/ethnicity variables are very different between surveys, but we can consistently identify whites and blacks.[15] In any case, the sex and race/ethnic compositions of our samples are reasonably consistent across surveys.

We express socioeconomic origins in terms of parental education and family structure.[16] All surveys except NELS:88 measure mother's and father's highest level of education completed (as opposed to attended), although they differ considerably in whether education is expressed as years of schooling or as highest credential attained. In practice we use a variable that indicates whether or not the respondent's head of household[17] attended at least some college. The family structure measure indicates whether respondents lived with both their own (implicitly biological) mother and father; unfortunately, the time referent for this concept varies across surveys. Despite all of these differences, the distributions of the parental education and family structure variables are impressively consistent across surveys; as expected, there are trends toward greater educational attainment and fewer intact families over time.

Having been made to repeat a grade in school – sometimes referred to as age/grade delay – is an important predictor of whether students complete high school. Direct measures of whether a student has ever been held back appear only in NELS:88 and NLSY-97. Consequently, in all surveys we classified respondents as age/grade delayed if they are above each of the ages that are modal for their grade (e.g. if they are 19 or older as seniors, or 17 or older as sophomores). Rates of age/grade delay vary between 3 percent and 7 percent across surveys.

Each survey measures students' college aspirations and/or expectations, where the former refers to how far students would like to go in school and the latter refers to how far they expect to go. Although the distinction between aspirations and expectations is an important one, our surveys are inconsistent in their choice of concept. We have simply taken the measure that we can get in each survey. This conceptual blurring of expectations and aspirations is unfortunate, but it is the best we can do with these data. In four of the five surveys, about 75 percent of sophomores and about 80 percent of seniors aspire/expect to go on to at least some college. Rates of college expectations are much lower in NLSY-79, however, because of the unfortunate way in which the concept was measured.[18]

Finally, we have measures of whether students in each survey dropped out in the two years after they were interviewed as sophomores. In NLS, NLSY-79, and NLSY-97 this is determined by students' enrollment status and highest grade completed two years after their sophomore year interviews. In HS&B and NELS:88, this measure was ascertained from administrative records. Also, only in NELS:88 can we identify students who left school and then returned at some later date; we do not classify these students as dropouts in our analyses. As expected, we observe a modest decline in dropout rates across these surveys.

Analytical approach

To analyze trends in the composition of the populations of employed and intensively employed students and the connection between those behaviors and high school completion, we begin by performing separate analyses of each data set. That is, within each of the five samples we model the predictors of employment status and intensity separately for sophomores and seniors using multinomial regression models; we then model the association between sophomore year employment status and intensity and high school completion using logistic regression models.[19]

After performing these separate analyses of each data set, we take the coefficient estimates and their variances/covariances from these analyses and carry out a form of meta-analysis that can be viewed as a special case of two level hierarchical modeling.[20] After estimating our "within study" models for each sample, we estimate a "between study" model that attempts to explain the variability across studies in important parameter estimates. This model recognizes that differences across studies in substantively important parameter estimates reflect both random sampling variability and systematic differences across studies – and thus over time. In other words, our estimates of the effects of race/ethnicity on employment intensity (for example) might differ somewhat across studies, and we can think of these differences as being due both to random sampling variability and to actual changes across studies in these effects. Our real interest lies in assessing the extent to which variability across studies in parameter estimates can be attributed to the calendar year in which the studies were administered. In other words, our meta-analysis assesses the extent to which changes across studies in parameter estimates are reflective of changes over time in the determinants of teenagers' employment behaviors and in the association between teenagers' employment and high school completion;[21] we describe our analytic procedures in more detail elsewhere.[22]

Trends in the predictors of teenage employment

We begin by estimating the effects of race/ethnicity, gender, parents' education,[23] family structure, grade retention, and educational aspirations/expectations on students' employment behaviors, separately by study. Table 7.A.2 presents detailed results for sophomores, and Appendix Table 7.A.3 presents detailed results for seniors. We estimate the effects of these variables on the odds of not working relative to working one to 20 hours per week while simultaneously estimating the effects of these variables on the odds of working 21 or more hours per week relative to working one to 20 hours per week. We chose one to 20 hours per week as our reference category because this allows us to make inferences about the factors that lead some students to remain out of the labor force and also about the factors that lead other students to work intensively. Furthermore, there is evidence that students who work – but who only work a modest number of hours per week – do best on a wide variety of educational and other outcomes.[24] By setting up our analyses in this way, we are able to compare not employed and intensively employed students to the group of students that is least at risk of dropping out.

In general, black high school sophomores and seniors are substantially less likely than their white counterparts to be employed; when employed, they work intensively about as often as whites. There are interesting relationships between gender and employment behaviors; as we describe below, these relationships vary substantially over time. Our results also show that students from advantaged family socioeconomic backgrounds – that is, those whose head of household has completed at least some college or who live with both parents – are likely to work less intensively. The same is true of students who have not been held back and who aspire or expect to complete at least some college. In other words, students who are advantaged with respect to family socioeconomic background and academic characteristics tend to be concentrated in the "working one to 20 hours per week" category; as described above, students in this category are least likely to drop out.

The results of our meta-analyses suggest that most parameter estimates vary significantly across studies for sophomores and/or seniors – which is not to say that they necessarily vary in any systematic fashion.[25] Among sophomores, none of the parameter estimates vary as a function of calendar year. This result suggests that although parameter estimates vary from year to year because of sampling variability, there is no evidence that the effects of these predictors on employment behaviors among sophomores have changed systematically over time. Among seniors, our results show that women and students who aspire or expect to complete at least some college are increasingly likely to be employed, whereas blacks are decreasingly likely to be employed.[26] In general, the results of our meta-analyses (described in detail in Tables 7.A.2 and 7.A.3) suggest that the most important changes over time in the determinants of teenagers' employment behaviors have to do with race/ethnicity and gender – but only among seniors. Family socioeconomic background and academic background certainly affect employment behaviors in important ways, but these effects have not changed systematically over time. On the other hand, female seniors are increasingly likely to be employed and black seniors are decreasingly likely to be employed. These findings reflect the broader societal trend toward greater labor force involvement among women in recent decades, but also reflect what we showed in Figure 7.2 – that black/white differences in high school students' paid employment behaviors are striking and are increasing over time.

Trends in the association between teenage employment and high school completion

We next estimate models in which high school completion is expressed as a function of employment status and intensity, race/ethnicity, gender, parents' education, family structure, age/grade delay, and college aspirations/expectations; detailed results are presented in Table 7.A.4. Compared to sophomores who work between one and 20 hours per week, students who are not employed are more likely to drop out in each of our five studies; however, these differences are never statistically significant. On the other hand, employed sophomores who work more than 20 hours per week are consistently more likely than students who work between one and 20 hours per week to drop out; these coefficients are statistically significant in two of the five studies. That is, our results generally confirm prior evidence that intensively employed sophomores are more likely to drop out. Coefficients pertaining to other variables reproduce a great deal of what we already know about the determinants of high school completion. All else constant, women are generally more likely than men to drop out, and there are no race/ethnic differences in high school completion. There are strong relationships between family socioeconomic background and high school completion. As expected, students who are age/grade delayed are between two and a half and five and a half times as likely to leave school without graduating, whereas students who aspire/expect to go on to college are substantially less likely to do so.

Although it was an open empirical question, we might be surprised to find that the associations between sophomores' employment behaviors and high school completion have changed over time. We found no evidence that the demographic, socioeconomic, or academic predictors of employment and intensive employment among sophomores changed systematically between 1966 and 1997.[27] Figure 7.5 plots the estimated change in the odds of dropping out associated with working more than 20 hours per week (relative to working between one and 20 hours per week). In the figure, we have plotted point estimates (with dots) and 95 percent confidence intervals (with dashes) for the estimates in each of the five studies. The solid line represents the estimate from the meta-analyses, and the dashed lines represent a 95 percent confidence interval around that line. Because this estimate is constant across years, this line has a slope of zero. To summarize, Figure 7.5 depicts what our meta-analyses confirm more formally: differences across surveys in estimates of the association between intensive employment and high school completion can be attributed to sampling variability. After adjusting for a series of demographic, socioeconomic, and academic factors, students who work more than 20 hours per week are about twice as likely as students who work less intensively to drop out of high school. This is a large, statistically significant, and substantively important association, but it has not changed significantly in the last 30 years or so.

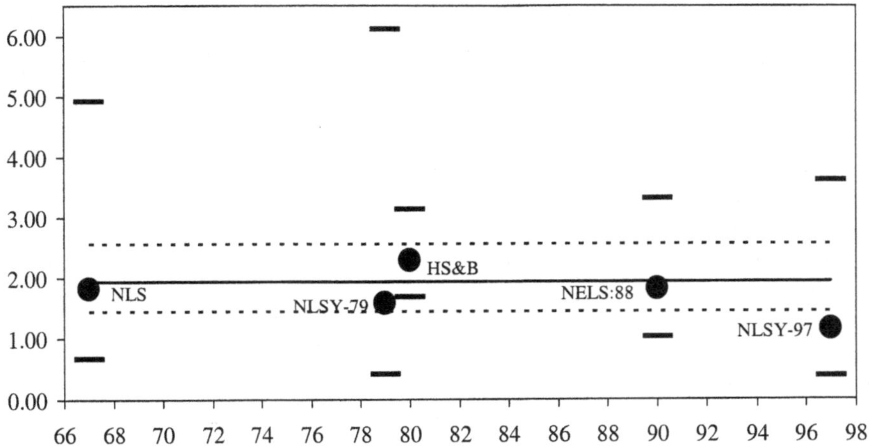

Figure 7.5 Estimated effects on the odds of dropping out of high school of working more than 20 hours per week (relative to working 1–20 hours).

Source: Data from the National Longitudinal Studies (NLS) of Young Men and Young Women, the National Longitudinal Study of Youth – 1979 (NLSY-79), High School & Beyond (HS&B), and the National Educatinal Longitudinal Study of 1988 (NELS:88). For each data source, a dot represents the point estimae and dashes represent a 95% confidence interval for that estimate. The solid line represents point estimates from our meta-analysis, and the dashed lines represent 95% confidence intervals around those point estimates. See text for details regarding modeling strategy.

Returning to the central theme of this volume, the results of Part I provide evidence that employment behaviors play a role in stratifying educational attainment by family socioeconomic origins. The socioeconomic predictors of intensive employment have not changed in recent decades, but family socioeconomic background is an important determinant of which students work intensively. The strong association between intensive employment and high school completion has also not changed in recent decades. Combined, these two points make clear that employment behaviors are – and long have been – an important out-of-school factor that stratifies adolescents' educational outcomes along family socioeconomic dimensions.

Part II: teenage employment and high school completion: Differences by individual and labor market characteristics

Is the association between teenage employment and high school completion the same for all groups of students and for students in different labor market contexts? While Part I focused on variations over time in the relationship between teenage employment and high school completion, in Part II we focus on variations in this relationship across social groups and across labor market contexts. We begin by considering how the relationship between teenage employment and high school completion – as observed in the early 1990s – varies by student characteristics like family socioeconomic background, race/ethnicity, sex, and academic plans and experiences. We pay special attention to family socioeconomic background and race/ethnic differences in this relationship, since – as noted in Part I – there are pronounced socioeconomic and race/ethnic differentials in teenage employment behaviors.

Next, and somewhat parenthetically, we ask whether local labor market circumstances influence high school completion. If employment opportunities influence the decision to leave school before graduation, we should observe that – all else constant – dropout rates vary by the quantity and nature of local economic opportunities for young people. Finally, we ask whether the association between employment behaviors and high school completion varies by local labor market circumstances. Beyond shedding light on the ways in which the relationship between employment behaviors and high school completion varies across labor markets, these latter questions also concern the mechanisms that are responsible for giving rise to this relationship: if it is true that employment pulls students out of high school, then we should expect to see more early school-leaving – especially among intensively employed students – in areas with greater employment opportunities for young people. In any case, as we describe below there are good reasons to suppose that the relationship between teenage employment and high school completion varies by both individual-level and labor market-level factors.

Individual-level variation in the relationship between teenage employment and high school completion

Research on the relationship between teenage employment and schooling outcomes – including high school completion – has typically begun from a zero-sum perspective: an hour spent at work is seen as an hour not spent doing homework, studying, or resting for school, and commitment to the workplace is seen as antithetical to commitment to school. From this perspective, there is reason to expect that the association between teenage employment and high school completion might vary by some individual-level variables. For example, students who are doing poorly in school can presumably least afford to have time taken away from studying or doing homework, and so intensive employment may be more closely linked to early school-leaving for this group of students. More recently, research on the educational consequences of teenage employment has moved away from the zero-sum perspective and has focused on the implications of the selective nature of that activity. As we demonstrated above, employment behaviors vary by students' socio-demographic and academic characteristics[28] and they also vary by students' perceptions of the relative role and future importance of schooling and paid employment in their lives.[29] From this perspective, there is also reason to suspect that the association between teenage employment and high school completion might vary by any number of individual-level student attributes. Whether employment – and particularly intensive employment – is related to high school completion may depend on students' prior educational achievements as well as their aspirations and expectations for life after high school. Intensively employed students who see themselves as bound for college may be less likely to drop out than other students with the same employment behaviors who do not see college attendance – or even success in high school – in their futures. Given socioeconomic, gender, and race/ethnic differentials in school performance and educational aspirations, we might expect the association between teenage employment and high school completion to vary by such characteristics as race/ethnicity, sex, socioeconomic origins, prior school performance, and/or future educational plans and aspirations.

Labor market-level variation in the relationship between teenage employment and high school completion

There is also good reason to suspect that local labor market characteristics condition the association between teenage employment and high school completion. Prior work has established an empirical link between labor market factors and school-leaving decisions.[30] For example, educational researchers Robert Bickel and George Papagiannis found greater high school completion rates in districts with higher wages and lower unemployment rates for high school graduates. In a replicate study, Robert Bickel found that projected per capita income and projected job expansion were positively related to high school completion rates.[31] Taken at face value, these findings call into question the notion that as the opportunity to work grows, students are increasingly "pulled out" of high school. However, it is important to recognize that socioeconomic factors bias our observations about the association between labor market opportunities and high school completion; a key question in our analyses is whether labor market factors affect high school completion net of the effects of socioeconomic and demographic characteristics. There is evidence that students engage in some form of rational calculus, weighing the costs and benefits of leaving high school without a diploma in order to take on full time employment.[32] As opportunities increase, the calculus may lean more in favor of dropping out, since the perceived costs of dropping out may be diminished.

Taking this logic one step further, we might expect that as labor market opportunities for young people change, the association between student employment and high school completion changes as well. We begin with the presumption that employed high school students represent a selective cross-section of all high school students. Prior work – including evidence presented in Part I – has demonstrated that intensively employed students tend to be less academically successful, less engaged in school, and more likely to drop out.[33] Conversely, less intensively employed students tend to be more academically successful than students who either do not work or who work intensively, and are least likely to drop out.[34] When there are relatively few job opportunities for high school students in a labor market, only a selective group of students will have jobs. When there are relatively many job opportunities, the population of employed students will be more diverse.

The socioeconomic, demographic, and academic background composition of the population of students who work will have consequences for the association between employment behaviors and high school completion. It is not clear at the outset what those consequences might be. If, in a labor market with few job opportunities, only bright, academically successful, highly motivated students – those least likely to drop out – can find work, then the association between employment and high school completion will be weaker than in an "average" labor market. On the other hand, if a labor market with few opportunities means that only those students who are willing to work long and/or inconvenient hours (traditionally those students more likely to drop out) can find work, then this association might be stronger than in an average labor market.

Differences in local labor market circumstances may produce socioeconomic and race/ethnic differences in the association between employment behaviors and high school completion. As we saw in Part I, White high school students are more likely than others to be employed,[35] and students from less advantaged family backgrounds are more likely to work intensively. These race/ethnic differences are true throughout high school, but become more pronounced in each successive year.[36] It makes sense to us that pervasive patterns of residential segregation by socioeconomic background and especially by race/ethnicity[37] may produce very different employment opportunities for students in different labor markets. For example, in his 1989 book *Getting Paid* anthropologist Mercer Sullivan finds that the students he observed usually sought and found their first jobs within their local neighborhood. He also showed that young people who lived in neighborhoods that were isolated from centers of employment had more limited work opportunities. Whether these patterns translate into socioeconomic and/or race/ethnic differences in the association between teenage employment and high school completion are interesting empirical questions that we address below.

Data and measures

To understand whether the association between teenage employment and high school completion varies by student or labor market characteristics, we analyze data from the National Educational Longitudinal Study of 1988 (NELS:88), a longitudinal survey of the eight-grade student cohort of 1988. In the base year, the sample included more than 25,000 randomly selected students in 1,000 randomly selected U.S. schools. The initial student cohort has been re-interviewed in 1990, 1992, 1994, and 2000. We use data from the 1990 and 1992 follow-ups, when the bulk of students were in grades 10 and 12, respectively. Information about local labor markets was obtained by matching students' tenth grade high schools to ZIP code data available from the 1990 U.S. Census.[38] After constructing all labor market variables (described below) for all ZIP codes in the United States, we collapsed across the first three digits of ZIP codes; this resulted in a set of 881 "labor markets" that typically contained about 180,000 people. For each tenth grade high school, we used the characteristics of the surrounding labor market in 1990 – as defined by aggregated ZIP code characteristics – as proxies for the labor market in which students reside. A key assumption, of course, is that the labor market conditions that prevail in the region around a students' school accurately reflect the pool of jobs available to students who go to that school. Our measures mischaracterize students' actual labor markets to the extent that students live in far outlying areas that have substantially different labor markets and to the extent that labor market characteristics vary geographically within aggregate ZIP code areas.

In tenth grade, students were asked about their employment activities; we use these measures to determine students' employment status at the time of their interview and how many hours they typically work per week.[39] As in Part I, we classify employed students as working either a "moderate" number of hours per week – between one and 20 – or an "intensive" number of hours per week – more than 20. The key independent variable in our regression analyses – student employment in tenth grade – is specified in terms of two measures. The first indicates whether students were working a moderate number of hours per week at the time of the tenth grade survey; the second indicates whether students were working an intensive number of hours per week. In our multivariate analyses in Part II, students without jobs are the omitted category.

Our analyses begin with the 18,479 students who participated in the 1990 NELS:88 in-school follow-up survey and are subsequently restricted to cases in which:

1. respondents were in school (regardless of whether they were in tenth grade);[40]
2. respondents reported their race/ethnicity and sex;
3. respondents were either Black, Hispanic, or non-Hispanic White;[41]
4. ZIP code data could be obtained.[42]

This leaves us with 14,787 students in 499 labor markets.[43]

The individual-level variables that we use in our analyses are described in detail in Table 7.A.5. These include employment intensity, enrollment status, sex, race/ethnicity, a composite measure of family socioeconomic background, curriculum track, mathematics achievement test scores, college plans, mathematics coursework in high school, and grade retention. The dropout indicator is derived from the second follow-up variable that indicates students' enrollment status as of the 1992 survey wave; students who left school but then returned to school by the 1992 follow-up are not classified as dropouts for our purposes. Consistent with results presented in Part I, students who were employed but who worked a moderate number of hours per week in 1990 were least likely to have dropped out by 1992. Those who worked more than 20 hours per week were especially likely to have dropped out.

The characteristics of the labor markets in which students' tenth grade schools are located are described in detail in Table 7.A.6. Students who did not drop out and students who work – but only a moderate number of hours per week – tend to live in areas with fewer African Americans, fewer Hispanics, fewer adult high school dropouts, and less poverty. For each labor market area we computed the percentage of 16- to 19-year-old students and high school dropouts who were in the labor force, and then we computed the percentage of those in the labor force who were currently employed, all using data from the 1990 U.S. Census. Students in our sample tend to live in areas in which about 45 percent of students and 60 percent of high school dropouts are in the labor force; about 85 percent of students in the labor market actually have jobs, compared to only about 70 percent of dropouts in the labor market. Our results reveal modest but consistent differences between dropouts and non-dropouts in the local availability of jobs for students and dropouts; non-dropouts tend to live in areas with relatively greater employment opportunities. In general the relationships between students' own employment behaviors and the local availability of jobs are also modest, but suggest that moderately employed students live in areas with greater opportunities.

In our analyses we also consider the labor market proportion of adults' jobs that are in service, sales, and blue-collar occupations, where occupations are coded to the standards of the 1990 U.S. Census Occupational Classification. The "service" category includes occupations like waiters and waitresses, cooks, barbers, and amusement and recreation facility attendants; the "sales" category includes occupations like sales counter clerks, cashiers, and real estate agents; and the "blue-collar" category includes a wide range of occupations like motion picture projectionists, lathe operators, truck drivers, stock handlers and baggers, and construction laborers. These categorizations are not ideal for characterizing the types of jobs available to high school students because they each contain specific occupations that are very typical for high school students and others that are more typical for adults; they are, however, the best we can do with these data. Our results indicate that the types of jobs available to unemployed, moderately employed, and intensively employed students and to dropouts and non-dropouts are roughly similar, although intensively employed students and students who dropped out tend to live in areas with relatively more blue-collar occupations.

Analytical approach

Our research questions involve estimating effects at two levels of analysis.[44] First, we are interested in the relationships between student attributes – including employment behaviors – and high school completion within labor markets. Second, we are interested in the relationship between labor market attributes and high school completion (net of individual-level characteristics) and in the way in which labor market attributes condition the association between employment behaviors and high school completion. Hierarchical modeling allows us to model individual-level outcomes within labor markets – referred to as *within-labor market models* – and then to model between labor market differences in parameters – referred to as *between-labor market models*; elsewhere we provide full details regarding our analysis strategy.[45] A between-labor market model uses estimated parameters from within-labor market models as its dependent variable. For example, we might estimate the association between employment status and high school completion within each labor market; the between-labor market model then uses these estimates as its dependent variable. Continuing with this example, we are thus able to: estimate the "typical" or average association between employment and high school completion across labor markets; estimate the variability across labor markets in this association; attempt to explain that variability using labor market-level predictors.

Modeling high school completion

We begin by estimating a series of models that assess the association between teenage employment and high school completion – net of socioeconomic, demographic, and academic performance measures – and by considering how that association varies by race/ethnicity, sex, socioeconomic status, and academic plans and experiences; detailed results of these models appear in Table 7.A.7.

Our baseline model – that is, our model that simply expresses dropout status as a function of employment behaviors – demonstrates that the overall dropout rate is about 4.8 percent; relevant statistics indicate that the dropout rate does vary significantly across labor markets. The next model adds a series of predictors to the within-labor market model, including measures of sex, race/ethnicity, family socioeconomic background, college track, mathematics IRT test score, perceived chances of going to college, mathematics coursework, grade retention, and measures of employment status and intensity. After controlling for these individual-level variables, there is relatively little residual variation in dropout rates across labor markets. That is, after controlling for individual-level differences in socioeconomic background, demographic characteristics, and academic factors, we observe no significant differences across labor markets in high school dropout rates.

The results of this model again reproduce a great deal of prior research on high school completion. All else constant, boys are slightly less likely than girls to drop out, and there are no significant differences in high school completion rates between race/ethnic groups. Students from more advantaged family socioeconomic backgrounds, students in the college track, students with higher mathematics test scores, students who say they are very likely to go on to college, and students who have never been held back a grade in school are all less likely to drop out. Holding these factors constant, students who work a moderate number of hours per week are no more or less likely to drop out, while students who work intensively are consistently more likely to drop out. Based on the results of this model, high school students who have paid jobs are about as likely as their unemployed peers to drop out, as long as they work fewer than about 20 hours per week; beyond that point, employment is associated with increased risk of early school-leaving.

Next we supplement this model by adding interaction terms between employment behaviors and a number of other individual-level variables to the within-labor market model.[46] These models test hypotheses about whether the association between employment intensity and high school completion varies by sex, race/ethnicity, and so forth. We find very little evidence that the associations between employment behaviors and high school completion vary by sex, race/ethnicity, family socioeconomic background, curriculum track, or grade retention. By and large, the connection between teenage employment intensity and high school completion is about the same for all students, regardless of these demographic, socioeconomic, and academic factors.

We end our empirical analyses with two final questions. First, do local labor market circumstances influence high school completion? Second, does the association between teenage employment intensity and high school completion vary by local labor market circumstances? We begin with a within-labor market equation that is the same as described above, and then add between-labor market equations for the coefficient for moderate employment and the coefficient for intensive employment. This model allows the conditional associations between moderate employment and high school completion and between intensive employment and high school completion to vary across labor markets, but fixes the intercept and the effects of all other individual-level variables to be the same across labor markets. Detailed results of this model are presented in Table 7.A.8.

In order to assess whether local labor market circumstances influence high school completion we add labor market-level predictors to the between-labor market model for the intercept; this tells us whether the adjusted dropout rate for a labor market depends on the numbers and types of jobs available to students in that labor market and/or the socioeconomic characteristics of that labor market. The only significant coefficient is for the percentage of African Americans in labor markets; labor markets with higher percentages of African Americans tend to have lower rates of high school completion, even after accounting for student-level characteristics like family socioeconomic background.

Finally, to assess whether the associations between moderate employment and high school completion and between intensive employment and high school completion vary by local labor market circumstances, we add labor market-level predictors to the between-labor market models for those parameters; these models tell us whether the conditional associations between moderate and/or intensive employment and high school completion vary by the numbers and types of jobs available to students. We begin by adding measures of the number and types of jobs that typify labor markets in the between-labor market models for the moderate and intensive employment coefficients; we then include measures of the socioeconomic circumstances of labor markets. With only very few exceptions, we find no significant effects of labor market-level factors on the coefficients for moderate or intensive employment. The several models described above show two things. First, these labor market-level variables have no impact on rates of high school completion; indeed our results indicate that dropout rates are about the same across labor markets once individual student-level factors are accounted for. Second, the association between teenage employment intensity and high school completion does not vary significantly across local labor markets.

Discussion

In this chapter we have documented the extent to which high school students' paid employment behaviors are associated with high school completion, and we have described the ways in which this association has varied over time, across social groups, and between labor markets. We conclude by summarizing our results and by further considering the mechanisms that link teenage employment to high school completion. We also return to our discussion of the role of adolescent employment in reproducing socioeconomic inequalities in rates of high school completion.

In Part I we asked three questions. First, we asked how rates of employment and employment intensity among high school students changed between 1966 and 1997. The short answer: not much. Our analyses suggest that rates of employment among high school students have not changed substantially since about 1980, especially for boys. There were large increases between 1940 and 1980 in the proportions of enrolled 16- to 17-year-old students who also held paid jobs, but these increases appear to be due to the increasing tendency for employed boys to remain enrolled in school and to the increasing tendency for girls – and women more broadly – to be involved in the paid labor force. As we noted above, in general the broad trend in the late twentieth century was not toward employment in addition to schooling, it was toward schooling in addition to employment or homemaking.

Second, we asked how the socioeconomic and academic characteristics of the employed student population changed between 1966 and 1997. That is, did changes in rates and intensity of student employment take place primarily among students from particular socioeconomic or demographic groups? The short answer: yes, but mostly with respect to gender and race/ethnic differences in employment behaviors in twelfth grade. The gap in employment rates between senior males and females has diminished over time, whereas the gap between senior blacks and whites has increased over time.

Third, we asked how the relationship between sophomore-year employment and high school completion (net of socioeconomic background and academic factors) changed between 1966 and 1992. The short answer: not at all. We find that associations between employment behaviors and high school completion have remained stable over this time period. All else constant, sophomores who work more than 20 hours per week are about twice as likely to drop out of high school as students who work fewer hours per week. This is a large and important association, but it has not changed over time. Along the way we also observed one other noteworthy pattern that has remained constant in recent decades: relative to white teenagers, black teenagers are substantially less likely to hold paid jobs. The source of this racial difference is unclear to us, especially since – as shown in other work that we have done[47] – it seems to persist even after adjusting for differences in the socioeconomic composition of labor markets and the number and types of jobs available to young people in them.

In Part II we posed three questions that were designed to assess whether the association between employment intensity and high school completion varies across groups of students and to understand the role of labor market characteristics in high school completion decisions and in the relationship between teenage employment and high school completion. First, we asked whether the relationship between teenage employment and high school completion varies by students' socio-demographic and/or academic characteristics. Our results suggest that they do not; that is, the relationship between employment intensity and high school completion is quite similar for boys and girls; blacks, whites, and Hispanics; students from varying family socioeconomic backgrounds; and students with different academic backgrounds.

Second, we asked about the impact of local labor market characteristics on the odds that students dropped out of high school. After controlling for individual-level socio-demographic and academic variables, we found that dropout rates do not vary significantly across labor markets; consequently, we were not surprised to find few significant effects of labor market characteristics on dropout rates, net of student-level characteristics.

Dropout rates are no higher in areas with relatively few or relatively many job opportunities for adolescents, and the types of jobs that typify labor markets have little bearing on students' chances of dropping out.

Third, we asked whether the association between teenage employment and high school completion depends on the number and/or types of jobs available to students. We hypothesized that the opportunities available in a labor market would affect the composition of the populations of employed and intensively employed students; for example, in areas with many employment opportunities, the population of employed students might be less selective than in other areas with fewer opportunities. As a result, we supposed that the association between teenage employment and high school completion would vary by labor market characteristics. However, after controlling for individual-level covariates, we concluded that the relationships between employment status and intensity and high school completion do not vary significantly across labor markets.

Teenage employment is significantly related to high school completion. Intensively employed tenth graders are more likely to drop out of high school, even after adjusting for a host of individual- and labor market-level factors. Students from a variety of backgrounds are more likely to drop out when they work intensively, and this is also true for students who face differing labor market circumstances. Although the association between teenage employment and high school completion is not particular to any group of students, it is still clear to us that teenage employment is one mechanism through which socioeconomic inequalities are reproduced. Intensively employed tenth grade students are disproportionately from less advantaged family socioeconomic backgrounds and have been less academically successful in earlier grades (as evidenced by lower test scores and high rates of grade retention). Because teenage employment behaviors are stratified by family socioeconomic background, race/ethnicity, sex, and prior academic achievement, and because high school completion varies by employment behaviors, we view teenage employment as one potentially important mechanism in the process of stratifying educational outcomes like high school completion.

Although we have concluded that the relationship between intensive employment and high school completion does not vary by individual- or labor market-level variables and cannot be explained by differences in local labor market opportunities, we have still not said much about the mechanisms that link intense employment and early school-leaving. As described in the beginning of this chapter, there are at least two ways to interpret the fact that high school students who work intensively are more likely to leave school before graduating. First, we might imagine that employment directly detracts from schooling or otherwise pulls students away from academic pursuits. If this were true, we should probably also observe in Part II that dropout rates and/or the association between teenage employment and dropout rates are higher in areas with relatively more job opportunities for young people. We did not. Second, we might imagine that students who are already more likely to drop out select themselves into intensive employment. In this chapter we were unable to directly adjudicate between these competing perspectives, but our analyses have helped to more clearly define the problem: why are teenage employment and high school completion associated with one another, and why does this association seem to hold for diverse groups of students in disparate labor market contexts?

Most research on teenage employment has operated under the assumption that teenage employment matters for schooling outcomes because of issues of time and energy allocation. According to this zero-sum perspective, an hour spent on the job is an hour not spent doing homework or studying, and the physical, mental, and emotional energy spent on the job is energy not available for school. How, then, might intensive employment influence the decision to drop out of high school? From this perspective, intensive employment affects specific schooling outcomes such as grades, test scores, and engagement in schooling; when grades, test scores, and academic engagement wane, dropping out becomes more likely. The problem with this account is that there is growing evidence that teenage employment has no direct consequences for specific educational outcomes – with the possible exception of high school completion. For example, the association between employment intensity and grades may be spurious owing to pre-existing background differences between students.[48]

Moving beyond the zero sum perspective, it is plausible to think that the association between teenage employment and schooling outcomes – including high school completion decisions – has to do with students' social psychological orientations toward work and school. If students view schooling as centrally important to their lives and employment as a secondary activity, then intensive employment and early school-leaving are each less likely to occur – regardless of labor market context or students' other characteristics. On the other hand, if paid work is of central importance to students and schooling is less important then we can imagine that intensive employment and a partial or complete withdrawal from the educational enterprise might each follow – again, regardless of labor market context or students' other characteristics. From this perspective, intensive employment does not directly interfere with schooling success; it is an activity pursued by students who are already less likely to achieve academic success or to complete their high school degree. All of this implies that the association between intensive employment and high school completion might be more carefully understood by considering students' social psychological orientations toward paid work and schooling, and by viewing intensive employment as a strategy taken by some students – rightly or wrongly – as a way of maximizing post-school labor market outcomes.

However, to speculate that intensive employment has no causal impact on high school completion is not to say that intensive employment plays no important role in stratifying educational outcomes by family socioeconomic origins or other ascribed characteristics. What emerges from our work and from the efforts of other researchers in this area is an understanding that over time students from disadvantaged socioeconomic origins tend to become less engaged in school, to do poorly in the classroom, and to lower their expectations and aspirations for future educational attainment. At the same time, these same students tend to turn to paid employment more intensively, sometimes out of financial need but more often out the desire to engage in an activity in which they might succeed both in the short and the long term. The result is a student body in which students from advantaged socioeconomic origins tend to work at paid jobs a few hours per week and go on to graduate, while students from disadvantaged socioeconomic origins tend to work more intensively and are less likely to graduate. Even if intensive employment has no direct, independent effect on high school completion, analyses like those presented above shed light on a process that stratifies students' educational and employment trajectories along socioeconomic lines.

Appendix

This appendix describes the measures used to construct comparable variables across surveys for the analyses presented in Part I.

Sampling weight

NLS – Young Men
REF #2 – "SAMPLING_WEIGHT_1966"

NLS – Young Women
REF #2 – "SAMPLING_WEIGHT, 68"

NLSY – 79
R2161 – "SAMPLING WEIGHT"

HS&B (1980 Sophomores)
BYWT – "WEIGHT FOR BASE YEAR PARTICIPANTS"

HS&B (1980 Seniors)
BYWT – "WEIGHT FOR BASE YEAR PARTICIPANTS"

NELS:88
F2F1PNWT – "PANEL WEIGHT FOR F1 – F2 COMPLETERS"

NLSY – 97
R12362 – "Round 1 Cross-Sectional Sampling Weight"

Age

NLS – Young Men
REF #22 – "AGE, 1966"
- Respondent's Age in Years from Cover Page of 1966 Questionnaire
- Response Options: Open-ended

NLS – Young Women
REF #31 – "AGE, 1968"
- Respondent's Age in Years from Cover Page of 1968 Questionnaire
- Response Options: Open-ended

NLSY – 79
R6 – "AGE OF R 79 INT"
- Question 1a and 1b from Section 1 of 1979 questionnaire: "(A) First, when were you born? (B) And that makes you . . ."
- Variable expresses age, in years.
- Response Options: Open-ended

HS&B (1980 Sophomores)
BB085 – "AGE"
- Question 85 from base-year sophomore questionnaire: "Age: (Mark One)"
- Response Options: 13 or younger, 14, . . . 20, 21, or older

HS&B (1980 Seniors)
BB084 – "AGE"
- Question 84 from base-year senior questionnaire: "Age: (Mark One)"
- Response Options: 13 or younger, 14, . . . 20, 21, or older

NELS:88
BIRTHMO – "MONTH OF BIRTH"
- Question 11 from base-year student questionnaire
- Response Options: 1–12

BIRTHYR – "YEAR OF BIRTH"
- Question 11 from base-year student questionnaire.
- Response Options: 72 = 1972 or before, 73 = 1973, 74 = 1974, 75 = 1975, or after

NLSY – 97
KEY!AGE – "Youth's current age"
- Constructed variable computed by comparing the day, month, and year of the respondent's birth to the day, month, and year in which the youth's personal interview was administered; expressed in years.
- Response Options: Open-ended

Sex

NLS – Young Men
Not Applicable – Sample Consists Only of Men

NLS – Young Women
Not Applicable – Sample Consists Only of Women

NLSY – 79
R2148 – "SEX OF R 79 INT"

- Constructed variable in 1979 data.
- Response Options: Male, Female

HS&B (1980 Sophomores)
BB084 – "SEX"

- Question 84 from base-year sophomore questionnaire: "SEX: (Mark One)"
- Response Options: Male, Female

HS&B (1980 Seniors)
BB083 – "SEX"

- Question 83 from base-year senior questionnaire: "SEX: (Mark One)"
- Response Options: Male, Female

NELS:88
F1SEX – "COMPOSITE SEX"

- F1SEX is a composite variable based primarily on base-year Question 12: "What is your sex?" Information for freshened students and base-year non-respondents was collected in the first follow-up new student supplement, and supplemented when necessary by school records, by guesses based on students' names, and – if all else failed – by random assignment.
- Response Options: Male, Female

NLSY – 97
KEY!SEX – "Gender of Youth"

- Constructed variable derived from household roster data
- Response Options: Male, Female

Race

NLS – Young Men
REF #23 – "RACE"

- Respondent's Race from Cover Page of 1966 Questionnaire
- Response Options: White, Negro, Other

NLS – Young Women
REF #32 – "RACE"

- Respondent's Race from Cover Page of 1968 Questionnaire
- Response Options: White, Negro, Other

NLSY – 79

R96 – "1st OR ONLY RACE/ETHNIC ORIGIN 79 INT"

- Question 30 from Section 1 of 1979 questionnaire: "What is your origin or descent?"
- Response Options: Black, Afro-American or Negro, Chinese, English, Filipino or Philipino, French, German, Greek, Hawaiian or Pacific Islander, Indian-American or Native American, Indian-Asian, Irish, Italian, Japanese, Korean, Latino or Spanish Descent – Cuban or Cubano, Latino or Spanish Descent – Chicano, Latino or Spanish Descent – Mexican or Mexicano, Latino or Spanish Descent – Mexican-American, Latino or Spanish Descent – Puerto Rican, Latino or Spanish Descent – Other Latino, Latino or Spanish Descent – Other Spanish Descent, Polish, Portuguese, Russian, Scottish, Vietnamese, Welsh, Other (SPECIFY), American (IF VOLUNTEERED), NONE

HS&B (1980 Sophomores)

BB089 – "RACE"

- Question 90 from base-year sophomore questionnaire: "What is your race? (Mark One)"
- Response Options: Black, White, American Indian or Alaskan Native, Asian or Pacific Islander, Other

HS&B (1980 Seniors)

BB089 – "RACE"

- Question 89 from base-year senior questionnaire: "What is your race? (Mark One)"
- Response Options: Black, White, American Indian or Alaskan Native, Asian or Pacific Islander, Other

NELS:88

F1RACE – "COMPOSITE RACE"

- F1RACE is a composite variable that indicates students' race/ethnicity. It was constructed using the base-year composite variable RACE (which is created using base year Question 31A: "Which best describes you?" and a series of follow-up questions), the first follow-up new student supplement Question 8a, the base year parent survey Question 10, and school reported data
- Response Options: Asian, Pacifc Islander, Hispanic, Black, Not Hispanic, White, Not Hispanic, American Indian

NLSY – 97

KEY!RACE

- Constructed variable derived from the Screen, Household Roster, and Non-Resident Roster Questionnaire. A household informant identifies the race of each household member.
- Response Options: White, Black or African American, American Indian, Eskimo, or Aleut, Asian or Pacific Islander, Something Else?

Enrollment status and grade level

NLS – Young Men

REF #43 – "ENROLLMENT_STATUS, 1966 – IS RESPONDENT CURRENTLY ENROLLED?"

- Question #1 from 1966 Questionnaire: "Are you attending or enrolled in regular school?"
- Response Options: Yes, No

REF #44 – "GRADE_ATTENDING, 1966"

- Question #2 from 1966 Questionnaire: "What grade are you attending?" (Asked only if response to Question #1 is "Yes")
- Response Options: Elem. 1 2 3 4 5 6 7 8, High 1 2 3 4, College 1 2 3 4 5 6+

NLS – Young Women

REF #50 – "ENROLLMENT_STATUS, 68 – IS RESPONDENT CURRENTLY ENROLLED?"

- Question #1 from 1968 Questionnaire: "Are you attending or enrolled in regular school?"
- Response Options: Yes, No

REF #53 – "GRADE_ATTENDING, 68"

- Question #2a from 1968 Questionnaire: "What grade are you attending?" (Asked only if response to Question #1 is "Yes")
- Response Options: Elem. 1 2 3 4 5 6 7 8, High 1 2 3 4, College 1 2 3 4 5 6+

NLSY – 79

R156 – "CURRENTLY ATTENDING OR ENROLLED IN SCHOOL?"

- Question 1a from Section 4 of 1979 questionnaire: "Are you currently attending or enrolled in regular school, that is, in an elementary school, a middle school, a high school, a college, or a graduate school?"
- Response Options: Yes, No

R157 – "GRADE ATTENDING"

- Question 2a from Section 4 of 1979 questionnaire: "What grade or year of school is that?"
- Response Options: 1st grade, 2nd grade, . . . , 12th grade, 1st year of college, . . . , 8th year of college

HS&B (1980 Sophomores)

Not Applicable – Sample Consists Only of High School Sophomores

HS&B (1980 Seniors)

Not Applicable – Sample Consists Only of High School Seniors

NELS:88

F1SEQFLG – "ENROLLED 10TH GR. WHEN QUEX ADMINISTERED"

- F1SEQFLG is a composite variable that indicates whether or not students were enrolled in 10th grade or some other grade when surveyed in the Spring of 1990.
- Response Options: ENROLLED IN 10TH GRD, ENROLLED IN OTHR GRD, NOT APPLICABLE

NLSY – 97

R00305 – "CURRENTLY ATTENDING OR ENROLLED IN SCHOOL?"

- Question 305 from youth's personal interview: "Are you currently attending or enrolled in regular school, that is in an elementary school, a middle school, a high school, a college, or a graduate school?"
- Response Options: Yes, No

R00330 – "GRADE CURRENTLY ATTEND"

- Question 330 from youth's personal interview: "What grade of school [are you currently attending/did you last attend]?"
- Response Options: 6th, 7th . . . , 12th

Employment status and hours worked per week

NLS – Young Men

REF #168 – "ACTIVITY MOST OF SURVEY_WEEK_1966"

- Question 37 from 1966 Questionnaire: "What were you doing most of LAST WEEK . . .?"
- Response Options: WK – Working, J – With a job but not at work, LK – Looking for work, S – Going to school, U – Unable to work, OT – Other

REF #169 – "DID RESPONDENT WORK AT ALL SURVEY_WEEK_1966?"

- Question 38a from 1966 Questionnaire: "Did you do any work at all LAST WEEK, not counting work around the house?" (Asked only if response to Question 37 is "With a job but not at work," "Looking for work," "Going to school," or "Other.")
- Response Options: Yes, No

REF #170 – "NUMBER OF HOURS_WORKED SURVEY_WEEK_1966 (ACTUAL)"

- Question 38b from 1966 Questionnaire: "How many hours did you work LAST WEEK at all jobs?"
- Response Options: Open-ended

NLS – Young Women

REF #158 – "ACTIVITY MOST OF SURVEY_WEEK_68"

- Question 34a from 1968 Questionnaire: "What were you doing most of LAST WEEK . . .?"
- Response Options: WK – Working, J – With a job but not at work, LK – Looking for work, S – Going to school, KH – Keeping house, U – Unable to work, OT – Other

REF #159 – "DID RESPONDENT WORK AT ALL SURVEY_WEEK_1968?"

- Question 35a from 1968 Questionnaire: "Did you do any work at all LAST WEEK, not counting work around the house?" (Asked only if response to Question 37 is "With a job but not at work," "Looking for work," "Going to school," or "Other.")
- Response Options: Yes, No

REF #160 – "NUMBER OF HOURS_WORKED SURVEY_WEEK_68"

- Question 35b from 1968 Questionnaire: "How many hours did you work LAST WEEK at all jobs?"
- Response Options: Open-ended

NLSY – 79

R2149 – "EMPLOYMENT STATUS RECODE"

- Question 1 from Section 8 of 1979 questionnaire: "Now I'd like some information on what you were doing last week. What were you doing most of last week – working, going to school, or something else?"
- Response Options: Working, With a job but not at work, Looking for work, Keeping house, Going to school, Unable to work, Other

R436 – "HOURS WORKED DURING SURVEY WEEK CPS ITEM"

- Question 3 from Section 8 of 1979 questionnaire: "How many hours did you work last week at all jobs?"
- Response Options: Open-ended

HS&B (1980 Sophomores)

BB019 – "WORKED FOR PAY LAST WEEK"

- Question 22 from base-year sophomore questionnaire: "Did you do any work for pay last week, not counting work around the house?"
- Response Options: Yes, No

BB022 – "HOURS WORKED PER WEEK"

- Question 25 from base-year sophomore questionnaire: "How many hours do/did you work a week on your current or most recent job?"
- Response Options: 1–4 hours per week, 5–14 hours per week, 15–21 hours per week, 22–29 hours per week, 30–34 hours per week, 35 hours or more per week

HS&B (1980 Seniors)

BB019 – "WORKED FOR PAY LAST WEEK"

- Question 22 from base-year senior questionnaire: "Did you do any work for pay last week, not counting work around the house?"
- Response Options: Yes, No

BB022 – "HOURS WORKED PER WEEK"

- Question 25 from base-year senior questionnaire: "How many hours do/did you work a week on your current or most recent job?"
- Response Options: 1–4 hours per week, 5–14 hours per week, 15–21 hours per week, 22–29 hours per week, 30–34 hours per week, 35 hours or more per week

NELS:88

F1S84 – "R CURRENTLY EMPLOYD OR EVER BEEN EMPLOYD"

- Question 84 from first follow-up questionnaire: "Are you currently employed or have you ever been employed?"
- Response Options: Never Employed, Not Employed Now, Not Employed This Yr, Employd Prior Summer, Currently Employed

F1S85 – "HOW MANY HRS DOES R USUALLY WORK A WEEK"

- Question 85 from first follow-up questionnaire: "How many hours do/did you usually work a week on your current or most recent job?" (Asked only if response to Question 84 is not "Never Employed.")
- Response Options: 0–10 hours a week, 11–20 hours a week, 21–30 hours a week, 31–40 hours a week, Over 40 hours a week

NLSY – 97

R00029 – "R DO ANY WORK FOR PAY LAST WEEK"

- Question 28 from youth's personal interview: "LAST WEEK, did you do ANY work for pay?" (Only asked of respondents who were at least 15 years of age and who did not own their own business or farm)
- Response Options: Yes, No, Retired, Disabled, Unable to Work

R00096 – "USUAL HOURS PER WEEK WORKED AT JOB CPS01"

- Question 96 from youth's personal interview: "How many hours per week do you USUALLY work at your job?"
- Response Options: Open-Ended

Mother's educational attainment

NLS – Young Men

REF #413 – "HIGHEST GRADE_ATTENDED BY MOTHER, 1966"

- Question 105a from 1966 Questionnaire: "What was the highest grade (or year) of regular school your mother ever attended?"
- Response Options: Elem. 1 2 3 4 5 6 7 8, High 1 2 3 4, College 1 2 3 4 5 6+

REF #414 – "DID MOTHER COMPLETE HIGHEST GRADE_ ATTENDED?"

- Question 105b from 1966 Questionnaire: "Did she finish this grade (or year)?"
- Response Options: Yes, No

NLS – Young Women

REF #409 – "HIGHEST GRADE_ATTENDED BY RESPONDENT'S MOTHER, 68"

- Question 106a from 1968 Questionnaire: "What was the highest grade (or year) of regular school your mother ever attended?"
- Response Options: Elem. 1 2 3 4 5 6 7 8, High 1 2 3 4, College 1 2 3 4 5 6+

REF #410 – "DID MOTHER COMPLETE HIGHEST GRADE_ ATTENDED? – 68"

- Question 106b from 1968 Questionnaire: "Did she finish this grade (or year)?"
- Response Options: Yes, No

NLSY – 79

R65 – "HIGHEST GRADE COMPLETED BY R's MOTHER – 79INT"

- Question 16 from Section 1 of 1979 questionnaire: "What was the highest grade or year of regular school that your mother ever completed?"
- Response Options: 1st grade, 2nd grade, . . . , 12th grade, 1st year of college, . . . , 8th year of college

HS&B (1980 Sophomores)

BB42 – "MOTHER'S EDUCATION"

- Question 42 from base-year sophomore questionnaire: "What was the highest level of education your mother (stepmother or female guardian) completed?"
- Response Options: Do not live with mother (stepmother or female guardian), Less than high school graduation, High school graduation only, Vocational, trade or business school after high school – Less than two years, Vocational, trade or business school after high school – Two years or more, College Program – Less than two years of college, College Program – Two or more years of college (including two-year degree), College Program – Finished college (four- or five-year degree), College Program – Master's degree or equivalent, College Program – Ph.D., M.D., or other advanced professional degree

HS&B (1980 Seniors)

BB42 – "MOTHER'S EDUCATION"

- Question 42 from base-year senior questionnaire: "What was the highest level of education your mother (stepmother or female guardian) completed?"
- Response Options: Do not live with mother (stepmother or female guardian), Less than high school graduation, High school graduation only, Vocational, trade or business school after high school – Less than two years, Vocational, trade or business school after high school – Two years or more, College Program – Less than two years of college, College Program – Two or more years of college (including two-year degree), College Program – Finished college (four- or five-year degree), College Program – Master's degree or equivalent, College Program – Ph.D., M.D., or other advanced professional degree

NELS:88

BYS34B – "MOTHER'S HIGHEST LEVEL OF EDUCATION"

- Question 34b from base-year student questionnaire: "How far in school did your parents go? . . . Mother (or female guardian)"
- Response Options: Not finish H.S., Graduated H.S., Junior College, College LT 4 YRS, Graduates College, Master's Degree, Ph.D., M.D., Etc.

BYP30 – "HIGHEST LEVEL OF EDUCATION R COMPLETED"

- Question 30 from base-year parent questionnaire: "What is the HIGHEST LEVEL of education you have completed?"
- Response Options: EIGHTH GRADE OR LESS, NOT H.S GRADUATION, GED, H.S GRADUATION, VOC, TRADE, BUS < 1 YR, VOC, TRADE, BUS 1–2 YRS, VOC, TRADE 2 YRS OR >, LESS THAN 2 YRS COLL, 2 OR MORE YRS COLL, FINISHED 2 YR PROGRAM, FINISHED 4–5 YR PROG, MASTER'S DEGREE, PH.D., M.D., OTHR PRO

F1N20B – "HOW FAR IN SCHOOL DID R'S MOTHER GO"

- Question 20b from first follow-up new student supplement: "How far in school did your parents go? . . . Mother (or female guardian)"
- Response Options: Did not finish H.S., H.S. Diploma, GED, Voc/Jr Coll/2 YR SCH, Some College, No Deg, College Graduate, Masters Degree/Equiv, MD/PHD/LB/OTH, Don't Know

NLSY – 97

R08714 through R08729 – "HIGHEST GRADE COMPLETED BY HH 1 [–16]"

- Questions R08714 through R08729 from the Screen, Household Roster, and Non-Resident Roster Questionnaire: "What is the highest grade of school that [you have/this person has] completed?" This question is asked with reference to each person in the household.
- Response Options: 0 = Did Not Attend, 1–20 = Years of School Attended (12 = 12th Grade, 20 = 8 Years of College)

R10007 through R10063 – "WHAT IS HIGHEST GRADE COMPLETED BY NHH?"

- Questions R10007 through R10063 from the Screen, Household Roster, and Non-Resident Roster Questionnaire: "What is the highest grade of school completed by [this nonresident person]?" This question is asked with reference to each nonresident person.
- Response Options: 0 = Did Not Attend, 1–20 = Years of School Attended (12 = 12th Grade, 20 = 8 Years of College)

Father's educational attainment

NLS – Young Men

REF #406 – "HIGHEST GRADE_ATTENDED BY FATHER, 1966"

- Question 103a from 1966 Questionnaire: "What was the highest grade (or year) of regular school your father ever attended?"
- Response Options: Elem. 1 2 3 4 5 6 7 8, High 1 2 3 4, College 1 2 3 4 5 6+

REF #407 – "DID FATHER COMPLETE HIGHEST GRADE_ ATTENDED?"

- Question 103b from 1966 Questionnaire: "Did he finish this grade (or year)?"
- Response Options: Yes, No

NLS – Young Women

REF #403 – "HIGHEST GRADE_ATTENDED BY RESPONDENT'S FATHER, 68"

- Question 104a from 1968 Questionnaire: "What was the highest grade (or year) of regular school your father ever attended?"
- Response Options: Elem. 1 2 3 4 5 6 7 8, High 1 2 3 4, College 1 2 3 4 5 6+

REF #404 – "DID FATHER COMPLETE HIGHEST GRADE_ ATTENDED? – 68"

- Question 104b from 1968 Questionnaire: "Did he finish this grade (or year)?"
- Response Options: Yes, No

NLSY – 79

R79 – "HIGHEST GRADE COMPLETED BY R's FATHER – 79INT"

- Question 23 from Section 1 of 1979 questionnaire: "Let's go back to your father now. What was the highest grade or year of regular school that your mother ever completed?"
- Response Options: 1st grade, 2nd grade, . . . , 12th grade, 1st year of college, . . . , 8th year of college

HS&B (1980 Sophomores)

BB39 – "FATHER'S EDUCATION"

- Question 39 from base-year sophomore questionnaire: "What was the highest level of education your father (stepfather or male guardian) completed?"
- Response Options: Do not live with mother (stepfather or male guardian), Less than high school graduation, High school graduation only, Vocational, trade or business school after high school – Less than two years, Vocational, trade or business school after high school – Two years or more, College Program – Less than two years of college, College Program – Two or more years of college (including two-year degree), College Program – Finished college (four- or five-year

degree), College Program – Master's degree or equivalent, College Program – Ph.D., M.D., or other advanced professional degree

HS&B (1980 Seniors)

BB39 – "FATHER'S EDUCATION"

- Question 39 from base-year senior questionnaire: "What was the highest level of education your father (stepfather or male guardian) completed?"
- Response Options: Do not live with mother (stepfather or male guardian), Less than high school graduation, High school graduation only, Vocational, trade or business school after high school – Less than two years, Vocational, trade or business school after high school – Two years or more, College Program – Less than two years of college, College Program – Two or more years of college (including two-year degree), College Program – Finished college (four- or five-year degree), College Program – Master's degree or equivalent, College Program – Ph.D., M.D., or other advanced professional degree

NELS:88

BYS34A – "FATHER'S HIGHEST LEVEL OF EDUCATION"

- Question 34a from base-year student questionnaire: "How far in school did your parents go? . . . Father (or male guardian)"
- Response Options: Not finish H.S., Graduated H.S., Junior College, College LT 4 YRS, Graduates College, Master's Degree, Ph.D., M.D., Etc.

BYP31 – "SPOUSE'S HIGHEST LEVEL OF EDUC COMPLETED"

- Question 31 from base-year parent questionnaire: "What is the HIGHEST level of education your spouse/partner has completed?"
- Response Options: EIGHTH GRADE OR LESS, NOT H.S GRADUATION, GED, H.S GRADUATION, VOC, TRADE, BUS < 1 YR, VOC, TRADE, BUS 1–2 YRS, VOC, TRADE 2 YRS OR >, LESS THAN 2 YRS COLL, 2 OR MORE YRS COLL, FINISHED 2 YR PROGRAM, FINISHED 4–5 YR PROG, MASTER'S DEGREE, PH.D., M.D., OTHR PRO

F1N20A – "HOW FAR IN SCHOOL DID R'S FATHER GO"

- Question 20a from first follow-up new student supplement: "How far in school did your parents go? . . . Father (or male guardian)"
- Response Options: Did not finish H.S., H.S. Diploma, GED, Voc/Jr Coll/2 YR SCH, Some College, No Deg, College Graduate, Masters Degree/Equiv, MD/PHD/LB/OTH, Don't Know

NLSY – 97

R08714 through R08729 – "HIGHEST GRADE COMPLETED BY HH 1 [–16]"

- Questions R08714 through R08729 from the Screen, Household Roster, and Non-Resident Roster Questionnaire: "What is the highest

grade of school that [you have/this person has] completed?" This question is asked with reference to each person in the household.
- Response Options: 0 = Did Not Attend, 1–20 = Years of School Attended (12 = 12th Grade, 20 = 8 Years of College)

R10007 through R10063 – "WHAT IS HIGHEST GRADE COMPLETED BY NHH?"
- Questions R10007 through R10063 from the Screen, Household Roster, and Non-Resident Roster Questionnaire: "What is the highest grade of school completed by [this nonresident person]?" This question is asked with reference to each nonresident person.
- Response Options: 0 = Did Not Attend, 1–20 = Years of School Attended (12 = 12th Grade, 20 = 8 Years of College)

Family structure

NLS – Young Men
REF #397 – "PERSON RESPONDENT LIVED WITH AT AGE_14"
- Question 99 from 1966 Questionnaire: "With whom were you living when you were 14 years old?"
- Response Options: Father and mother, Father and step-mother, Mother and step-father, Father, Mother, Some other adult MALE relative, Some other adult FEMALE relative, Some other arrangement, On my own

NLS – Young Women
REF #391 – "PERSON RESPONDENT WAS LIVING WITH AT AGE_14"
- Question 100 from 1968 Questionnaire: "With whom were you living when you were 14 years old?"
- Response Options: Father and mother, Father and step-mother, Mother and step-father, Father, Mother, Some other adult MALE relative, Some other adults FEMALE relative, Some other arrangement, On my own

NLSY – 79
R88 – "DO R'S MOTHER AND FATHER LIVE IN SAME HOUSEHOLD?"
- Question 28c from Section 1 of 1979 questionnaire: "Do your mother and father live in the same household?"
- Response Options: Yes, No

HS&B (1980 Sophomores)
BB036A through BB036K
- Question 36 from base-year sophomore questionnaire: "Which of the following people live in the same household with you? (MARK ALL THAT APPLY)"

- Response Options: I live alone, Father, Other male guardian, Mother, Other female guardian, Brother(s) and/or Sister(s) (including step- or half-), Grandparent(s), My husband/wife, My child or children, Other relative(s) (children or adults), Non-relative(s) (children or adults)

HS&B (1980 Seniors)
BB036A through BB036K

- Question 36 from base-year senior questionnaire: "Which of the following people live in the same household with you? (MARK ALL THAT APPLY)"
- Response Options: I live alone, Father, Other male guardian, Mother, Other female guardian, Brother(s) and/or Sister(s) (including step- or half-), Grandparent(s), My husband/wife, My child or children, Other relative(s) (children or adults), Non-relative(s) (children or adults)

NELS:88
F1S92A – "FATHER LIVES IN SAME HOUSEHOLD AS R"

- Question 92a from first follow-up student questionnaire: "Which of the following people live in the same household with you? . . . Father"
- Response Options: Applies, Does Not Apply

F1S92D – "MOTHER LIVES IN SAME HOUSEHOLD AS R"

- Question 92d from first follow-up student questionnaire: "Which of the following people live in the same household with you? . . . Mother"
- Response Options: Applies, Does Not Apply

NLSY – 97
R12053 – "RS RELATIONSHIP TO HOUSEHOLD PARENT FIGURE"

- Constructed variable indicating the relationship of the parent figure(s) in the household to the youth as of the survey date.
- Response Options: Both biological parents, Two parents, biological mother, Two parents, biological father, Biological mother only, Biological father only, Adoptive parent(s), Foster parent(s), No parents, grandparents, No parents, other relatives, Anything else

Age/grade delay

NLS – Young Men
Not available

NLS – Young Women
Not available

NLSY – 79
Not available

HS&B (1980 Sophomores)
Not Available

HS&B (1980 Seniors)
Not Available

NELS:88
F1N22 – "HAS R EVER BEEN HELD BACK A GRADE IN SCH"

- Question 22 from the first follow-up new student supplement questionnaire: "Were you ever held back (made to repeat) a grade in school?" (Supplemented with data from base year)
- Response Options: No, Yes, I repeated

NLSY – 97
R06742 – "R EVER REPEATED ANY GRADE"

- Question 6742 from parent's personal interview: "Now I have some general questions about this youth's schooling. Please think about this youth's entire school history, not just what [he/she] did at one particular school. Has this youth ever repeated any grade?"
- Response Options: Yes, No

College aspirations/expectations

NLS – Young Men
REF #154 – "EDUCATIONAL GOAL, 1966"

- Question 34a from 1966 Questionnaire: "How much more education would you like to get? (If "None," mark current grade and follow appropriate skip pattern)"
- Response Options: Less than high school, High School: 1 year, 2 years, 3 years, 4 years, College: 2 years (complete junior college or equivalent), 4 years (graduate from 4-year college), 6 years (obtain Master's degree or equivalent), 7+ years (obtain Ph.D. or professional degree)

NLS – Young Women
REF #142 – "EDUCATIONAL GOAL OF THOSE ENROLLED, 68"

- Question 29a from 1968 Questionnaire: "How much more education would you like to get? (If "None," mark current grade and follow appropriate skip pattern)"
- Response Options: Less than high school, High School: 1 year, 2 years, 3 years, 4 years, College: 2 years (complete junior college or equivalent), 4 years (graduate from 4-year college), 6 years (obtain Master's degree or equivalent), 7+ years (obtain Ph.D. or professional degree)

NLSY – 79
R1718 – "EDUCATIONAL EXPECTATIONS – IN SCHOOL OR NOT IN 5 YEARS"

- Question 9 from Section 22 of 1979 questionnaire: "Do you expect to be in school 5 years from now?"
- Response Options: Yes, No

HS&B (1980 Sophomores)

BB065 – "SCHOOLING YOU THINK YOU WILL GET"

- Question 69 from base-year sophomore questionnaire: "As things stand now, how far in school do you think you will get?"
- Response Options: Less than high school graduation, High school graduation only, Vocational, trade or business school after high school – Less than two years, Vocational, trade or business school after high school – Two years or more, College Program – Less than two years of college, College Program – Two or more years of college (including two-year degree), College Program – Finished college (four- or five-year degree), College Program – Master's degree or equivalent, College Program – Ph.D., M.D., or other advanced professional degree

HS&B (1980 Seniors)

BB065 – "SCHOOLING YOU THINK YOU WILL GET"

- Question 65 from base-year sophomore questionnaire: "As things stand now, how far in school do you think you will get?"
- Response Options: Less than high school graduation, High school graduation only, Vocational, trade or business school after high school – Less than two years, Vocational, trade or business school after high school – Two years or more, College Program – Less than two years of college, College Program – Two or more years of college (including two-year degree), College Program – Finished college (four- or five-year degree), College Program – Master's degree or equivalent, College Program – Ph.D., M.D., or other advanced professional degree

NELS:88

F1S64B – "CHANCES THAT R WILL GO TO COLLEGE"

- Question 64b from first follow-up student questionnaire: "Think about how you see the future. What are the chances that . . . You will go to college?"
- Response Options: Very Low, Low, About Fifty-Fifty. High, Very High

NLSY – 97

R05151 – "PERCENT CHANCE R HAS COLLEGE DEGREE BY 30 YEARS OLD"

- Question 5151 from the youth's personal interview: "What is the percent chance that you will have a four-year college degree by the time you turn 30?"
- Response Options: Open-ended (0%–100%)

High school dropout

NLS – Young Men

REF #1170 – "ENROLLMENT_STATUS, 1968 – IS RESPONDENT CURRENTLY ENROLLED?"

- Question 1 from 1968 Questionnaire: "Are you currently enrolled in regular school?"
- Response Options: Yes, No

REF #1638 – "HIGHEST GRADE_COMPLETED AS OF 1968 (REVISED)"

- Constructed variable indicating highest year of schooling completed

NLS – Young Women

REF #1475 – "ENROLLMENT_STATUS, 70 – IS RESPONDENT CURRENTLY ENROLLED?"

- Question 1 from 1970 Questionnaire: "Are you attending or enrolled in regular school?"
- Response Options: Yes, No

REF #2114 – "HIGHEST GRADE_COMPLETED, 70 (REVISED)"

- Constructed variable indicating highest year of schooling completed

NLSY – 79

R4168 – "CURRENTLY ATTENDING OR ENROLLED IN SCHOOL?"

- Question 1b from Section 4 of 1981 questionnaire: "Are you currently attending or enrolled in regular school?"
- Response Options: Yes, No

R4169 – "GRADE ATTENDING"

- Question 1c from Section 4 of 1981 questionnaire: "What grade or year of regular school are you attending or enrolled in?"
- Response Options: 1st grade, 2nd grade, . . . , 12th grade, 1st year of college, . . . , 8th year of college, Ungraded

HS&B (1980 Sophomores)

F1STUTYP – "FU1 STUDENT TYPE"

- Constructed variable indicating students' status in school in 1982, at the time of the first follow-up.
- Response Options: In school, Dropout, Transfer, Early graduate

HS&B (1980 Seniors)

Not Applicable – Sample Consists Only of High School Seniors

NELS:88

F2DOSTAT – "DROPOUT STATUS"

- Variable constructed from various sources.
- Response Options: DID NOT DROP OUT, NOT DETERMINED, DROPOUT, RETURNED, ALTRNATIVE STDNT, SCHL RPTD DRPOUT, DROPOUT, NO RETRN

NLSY – 97
R3881500 – "Enrollment Status 1999"

- Composite variable constructed from various sources
- Response Options: Not enrolled, no high school degree, no GED; Not enrolled, GED; Not enrolled, high school degree; Not enrolled, some college; Not enrolled, 2-year college graduate; Not enrolled, 4-year college graduate; Not enrolled, graduate degree; Enrolled in grades 1–12, not a high school graduate; Enrolled in a 2-year college; Enrolled in a 4-year college; Enrolled in a graduate program

Table 7.A.1 Descriptive statistics for employment, demographic, family background, and schooling variables, by data source and grade

	Tenth-grade students					*Twelth-grade students*			
Study	*NLS*	*NLSY-79*	*HS&B*	*NELS:88*	*NLSY-97*	*NLS*	*NLSY-79*	*HS&B*	*NELS:88*
Year(s)	*1966/68*	*1979*	*1980*	*1990*	*1997*	*1966/68*	*1979*	*1980*	*1992*
Not employed	70%	70%	64%	72%	66%	52%	43%	44%	49%
Employed, 1–20 hours/week	27%	26%	30%	20%	29%	33%	33%	35%	35%
Employed, >20 hours/week	3%	4%	6%	8%	6%	15%	23%	21%	17%
Mean hours/week (if employed)	10.6	12.2	12.1	16.3	11.8	17.6	19.7	19.5	17.7
Black	12%	16%	16%	13%	17%	11%	16%	13%	13%
Female	48%	50%	52%	50%	53%	42%	49%	52%	50%
Head of HH: HS graduate or less	80%	67%	56%	46%	54%	79%	63%	54%	45%
Head of HH: at least some college	20%	33%	44%	54%	46%	21%	37%	46%	55%
Living with both parents	85%	77%	71%	62%	56%	84%	78%	72%	65%
Ever held back in school	3%	4%	5%	3%	6%	4%	5%	3%	3%
Asp./exp.: HS graduate or less	26%	42%	25%	26%	26%	24%	72%	20%	18%
Asp./exp.: at least some college	74%	58%	75%	74%	74%	76%	28%	80%	82%
Dropped out of high school	12%	6%	8%	5%	8%	n/a	n/a	n/a	n/a
Full sample	1,140	1,041	26,512	13,267	1,036	928	893	25,066	12,616
Analysis sample	1,075	922	23,859	13,082	931	928	893	25,008	12,081
Attrition	6%	11%	10%	1%	10%	0%	0%	0%	4%

Notes

NLS = National Longitudinal Surveys of Young Men and Young Women; NLSY-79 = National Longitudinal Survey of Youth – 1979; HS&B = High School and Beyond; NELS:88 = National Educational Longitudinal Study of 1988; NLSY-97 = National Longitudinal Survey of Youth – 1997.

Full sample restricted to enrolled tenth- and twelth-grade students who reported their race/ethnicity as (non–Hispanic) White or Black. Analysis sample restricted to cases with no missing data on employment or dropout variables. See text for variable definitions. Data from each sample were weighted in such a way as to make each sample representative of the national population of tenth- and/or twelth-graders in that year. NELS:88 and HS&B data are further weighted in such a way as to adjust for design effects. Again, see text for details.

Table 7.A.2 Multinomial logistic regressions of employment intensity on sophomores' demographic, family background, and schooling variables, by data source

	Relative odds of not working versus working 1 to 20 hours/week							*Relative odds of working >20 hours/week versus working 1 to 20 hours/week*						
Study	*NLS*	*NLSY-79*	*HS&B*	*NELS:88*	*NLSY-97*	*Parameter homo-*	*Annual change in*	*NLS*	*NLSY-79*	*HS&B*	*NELS:88*	*NLSY-97*	*Parameter homo-*	*Annual change in*
Year(s)	*1966/68*	*1979*	*1980*	*1990*	*1997*	*geneity*	*parameter*	*1966/68*	*1979*	*1980*	*1990*	*1997*	*geneity*	*parameter*
	e^b (|b/s.e.|)	e^b (|b/s.e.|)	e^b (|b/s.e.|)	e^b (|b/s.e.|)	e^b (|b/s.e.|)	p-value	*b* (|b/s.e.|)	e^b (|b/s.e.|)	e^b (|b/s.e.|)	e^b (|b/s.e.|)	e^b (|b/s.e.|)	e^b (|b/s.e.|)	p-value	*b* (|b/s.e.|)
White	–	–	–	–	–	–	–	–	–	–	–	–	–	–
Black	**1.67** **(2.07)**	**3.97** **(4.53)**	**2.59** **(11.31)**	**1.94** **(4.32)**	**2.16** **(3.23)**	0.069	−0.001 (0.052)	1.04 (0.06)	2.12 (1.30)	1.12 (0.66)	1.14 (0.55)	1.42 (0.74)	0.000	0.00 (0.006)
Male	–	–	–	–	–	–	–	–	–	–	–	–	–	–
Female	**1.36** **(2.18)**	1.23 (1.34)	0.91 (1.77)	1.01 (0.13)	1.24 (1.41)	0.002	−0.005 (0.520)	**0.22** **(2.98)**	0.94 (0.16)	**0.42** **(7.71)**	**0.58** **(3.75)**	**0.38** **(2.80)**	0.000	0.002 (0.124)
Parent: HS graduate or less	–	–	–	–	–	–	–	–	–	–	–	–	–	–
Parent: at least some college	1.04 (0.19)	0.81 (1.25)	**0.87** **(2.50)**	1.01 (0.07)	0.95 (0.35)	> 0.500	–	0.27 (1.55)	**0.34** **(2.32)**	0.88 (1.14)	**0.66** **(2.49)**	**0.49** **(2.00)**	0.000	0.007 (0.256)
Not living with both parents	–	–	–	–	–	–	–	–	–	–	–	–	–	–
Living with both parents	1.03 (0.15)	1.16 (0.78)	0.94 (1.01)	0.90 (1.09)	0.99 (0.06)	> 0.500	–	1.01 (0.02)	1.20 (0.40)	0.84 (1.50)	0.80 (1.51)	1.46 (1.12)	0.000	0.006 (0.326)

Never held back in school	–	–	–	–	–	–	–	–	–	–	–	–	–	–
Ever held back in school	1.67	1.76	1.03	1.29	0.80	> 0.500	–	**11.85**	**4.65**	**1.87**	**2.56**	1.25	0.031	−0.057
	(1.00)	(1.07)	(0.23)	(0.83)	(0.72)			**(3.51)**	**(2.04)**	**(3.08)**	**(2.46)**	(0.39)		(1.767)
Asp./exp.: HS graduate or less	–	–	–	–	–	–	–	–	–	–	–	–	–	–
Asp./exp.: At least some college	1.03	0.89	**0.87**	0.88	0.95	> 0.500	–	0.73	1.14	**0.66**	**0.56**	0.78	0.000	−0.010
	(0.19)	(0.71)	**(2.33)**	(1.22)	(0.27)			(0.79)	(0.35)	**(3.47)**	**(3.56)**	(0.70)		(0.594)
Constant	**1.98**	**2.09**	**2.33**	**3.84**	**1.88**	–	–	**0.21**	**0.16**	**0.41**	0.94	**0.30**	–	–
	(2.89)	**(3.37)**	**(11.11)**	**(11.05)**	**(3.35)**			**(2.72)**	**(3.73)**	**(6.24)**	(0.34)	**(3.42)**		
N	1,075	922	23,859	13,082	931			1,075	922	23,859	13,082	931		

Notes
NLS = National Longitudinal Surveys of Young Men and Young Women; NLSY-79 = National Longitudinal Survey of Youth – 1979; HS&B = High School and Beyond; NELS:88 = National Educational Longitudinal Study of 1988; NLSY-97 = National Longitudinal Survey of Youth – 1997. Full sample restricted to enrolled tenth- and twelth-grade students who reported their race/ethnicity as (non-Hispanic) White or Black. Analysis sample restricted to cases with no missing data on employment or dropout variables. See text for variable definitions. Data from each sample were weighted in such a way as to make each sample representative of the national population of tenth- and/or twelth-graders in that year. NELS:88 and HS&B data are further weighted in such a way as to adjust for design effects. Columns labeled "Parameter homogeneity" report *p*-values for the null hypothesis that parameter estimates are equivalent across samples. Columns labeled "Annual change in parameter" report estimates derived from meta-analyses of the annual change in that parameter. See text for details. Bolded entries represent coefficients that are twice their standard errors.

Table 7.A.3 Multinomial logistic regressions of employment intensity on seniors' demographic, family background, and schooling variables, by data source

	Relative odds of not working versus working 1 to 20 hours/week						Relative odds of working >20 hours/week versus working 1 to 20 hours/week					
Study	*NLS*	*NLSY-79*	*HS&B*	*NELS:88*	*Parameter homo-geneity*	*Annual change in parameter*	*NLS*	*NLSY-79*	*HS&B*	*NELS:88*	*Parameter homo-geneity*	*Annual change in parameter*
Year(s)	*1966/68*	*1979*	*1980*	*1992*			*1966/68*	*1979*	*1980*	*1992*		
	e^b (|b/s.e.|)	e^b (|b/s.e.|)	e^b (|b/s.e.|)	e^b (|b/s.e.|)	p-value	*b* (|b/s.e.|)	e^b (|b/s.e.|)	e^b (|b/s.e.|)	e^b (|b/s.e.|)	e^b (|b/s.e.|)	p-value	*b* (|b/s.e.|)
White	–	–	–	–	–	–	–	–	–	–	–	–
Black	1.37 (1.25)	**1.91 (2.81)**	**2.18 (9.81)**	**2.63 (7.24)**	0.044	**0.026 (2.380)**	1.16 (0.41)	**0.66 (1.37)**	**0.65 (3.57)**	1.07 (0.37)	0.042	0.000 (0.007)
Male	–	–	–	–	–	–	–	–	–	–	–	–
Female	**1.58 (3.02)**	0.81 (1.33)	0.93 (1.47)	**0.69 (4.60)**	0.000	**−0.032 (3.363)**	**0.38 (3.86)**	**0.61 (2.69)**	**0.51 (10.76)**	**0.61 (4.66)**	0.242	–
Parent: HS graduate or less	–	–	–	–	–	–	–	–	–	–	–	–
Parent: at least some college	1.35 (1.54)	1.14 (0.77)	0.90 (1.91)	0.98 (0.26)	0.014	−0.012 (1.128)	1.11 (0.35)	**0.64 (2.20)**	**0.76 (4.29)**	**0.67 (3.45)**	0.321	–
Not living with both parents	–	–	–	–	–	–	–	–	–	–	–	–
Living with both parents	1.23 (0.96)	**0.60 (2.45)**	0.95 (0.99)	0.88 (1.42)	0.082	−0.011 (0.616)	1.14 (0.42)	0.67 (1.67)	0.90 (1.52)	0.80 (1.89)	> 0.500	–

Never held back in school	–	–	–	–	–	–	–	–	–	–	–	–
Ever held back in school	**3.73**	2.24	**1.49**	1.12	0.061	−0.048	**5.77**	2.19	1.32	1.49	0.076	−0.052
	(2.17)	(1.89)	**(2.66)**	(0.37)		(1.895)	**(2.57)**	(1.67)	(1.52)	(1.13)		(1.389)
Asp./exp.: HS graduate or less	–	–	–	–	–	–	–	–	–	–	–	–
Asp./exp.: at least some college	**1.64**	1.22	**0.76**	**0.66**	0.000	**−0.037**	**0.58**	0.74	**0.79**	**0.52**	0.023	−0.006
	(2.72)	(1.12)	**(4.17)**	**(3.52)**		**(2.441)**	**(2.37)**	(1.35)	**(2.92)**	**(4.51)**		(0.349)
Constant	0.63	**1.67**	**1.55**	**2.31**	–	–	0.65	1.55	1.20	**1.38**	–	–
	(1.72)	**(2.34)**	**(5.51)**	**(6.31)**			(1.23)	(1.79)	(1.90)	**(2.01)**		
N	928	893	25,008	12,081			928	893	25,008	12,081		

Notes
NLS = National Longitudinal Surveys of Young Men and Young Women; NLSY-79 = National Longitudinal Survey of Youth – 1979; HS&B = High School and Beyond; NELS:88 = National Educational Longitudinal Study of 1988; NLSY-97 = National Longitudinal Survey of Youth – 1997. Full sample restricted to enrolled tenth- and twelfth-grade students who reported their race/ethnicity as (non-Hispanic) White or Black. Analysis Sample restricted to cases with no missing data on employment or dropout variables. See text for variable definitions. Data from each sample were weighted in such a way as to make each sample representative of the national population of tenth- and/or twelth-graders in that year. NELS:88 and HS&B data are further weighted in such a way as to adjust for design effects. Columns labeled "Parameter homogeneity" report *p*-values for the null hypothesis that parameter estimates are equivalent across samples. Columns labeled "Annual change in parameter" report estimates derived from meta-analyses of the annual change in that parameter. See text for details. Bolded entries represent coefficients that are twice their standard errors.

Table 7.A.4 Logistic regressions of dropout on employment, demographic, family background, and schooling variables, by data source

Study	*NLS*		*NLSY-79*		*HS&B*		*NELS:88*		*NLSY-97*		*Parameter homogeneity*	*Estimated annual change in parameter*	
Year(s)	*1966/68*		*1979*		*1980*		*1990*		*1997*				
	e^b	(|b/s.e.|)	e^b	(|b/s.e.|)	e^b	(|b/s.e.|)	e^b	(|b/s.e.|)	e^b	(|b/s.e.|)	p-*value*	*b*	(|b/s.e.|)
Not employed	1.10	(0.39)	1.18	(0.46)	1.08	(0.78)	1.18	(0.73)	1.18	(0.55)	>0.500		–
Employed, 1–20 hours/week	–		–		–		–		–		–		–
Employed, >20 hours/week	1.82	(1.17)	1.59	(0.67)	**2.29**	**(5.18)**	**1.83**	**(1.99)**	1.16	(0.25)	>0.500		–
White	–		–		–		–		–		–		–
Black	1.09	(0.28)	0.54	(1.34)	0.91	(0.81)	1.08	(0.35)	0.75	(0.86)	–		–
Male	–		–		–		–		–		–		–
Female	**1.72**	**(2.64)**	1.14	(0.45)	1.10	(1.02)	**1.54**	**(2.60)**	1.61	(1.73)	–		–
Parent: HS graduate or less	–		–		–		–		–		–		–
Parent: at least some college	**0.35**	**(2.57)**	0.51	(1.56)	**0.68**	**(3.53)**	**0.36**	**(4.59)**	**0.41**	**(2.65)**	–		–
Not living with both parents	–		–		–		–		–		–		–
Living with both parents	0.93	(0.27)	0.54	(1.86)	**0.43**	**(9.50)**	**0.55**	**(3.60)**	**0.40**	**(3.17)**	–		–
Never held back in school	–		–		–		–		–		–		–
Ever held back in school	**3.36**	**(3.08)**	2.55	(1.80)	**5.38**	**(13.46)**	**2.44**	**(3.01)**	**4.57**	**(4.26)**	–		–
Asp./exp.: HS graduate or less	–		–		–		–		–		–		–
Asp./exp.: at least some college	**0.30**	**(5.95)**	**0.31**	**(3.46)**	**0.31**	**(12.82)**	**0.24**	**(8.15)**	**0.22**	**(5.23)**	–		–
Constant	**0.21**	**(4.56)**	**0.14**	**(4.55)**	**0.24**	**(11.10)**	**0.13**	**(7.84)**	**0.22**	**(4.61)**	–		–
N	1,075		922		23,859		13,082		931				

Notes
NLS = National Longitudinal Surveys of Young Men and Young Women; NLSY-79 = National Longitudinal Survey of Youth – 1979; HS&B = High School and Beyond; NELS:88 = National Educational Longitudinal Study of 1988; NLSY-97 = National Longitudinal Survey of Youth – 1997. Full Sample restricted to enrolled tenth- and twelfth-grade students who reported their race/ethnicity as (non-Hispanic) White or Black. Analysis sample restricted to cases with no missing data on employment or dropout variables. See text for variable definitions. Data from each sample were weighted in such a way as to make each sample representative of the national population of tenth- and/or twelth-graders in that year. NELS:88 and HS&B data are further weighted in such a way as to adjust for design effects. Columns labeled "Parameter homogeneity" report *p*-values for the null hypothesis that parameter estimates are equivalent across samples. Columns labeled "Annual change in parameter" report estimates derived from meta-analyses of the annual change in that parameter. See text for details. Bolded entries represent coefficients that are twice their standard errors.

Table 7.A.5 Description of individual-level variables by employment status and intensity and dropout status

	Analysis sample (N = *14,787*)		*Not employed* (N = *11,197*)		*Employed, 1–20 hrs/wk* (N = *2,516*)		*Employed, 21+ hrs/wk* (N = *1,074*)		*Did not drop out* (N = *13,857*)		*Dropped out* (*N = 930*)	
	Mean	*(S.D.)*	*Mean*	*(S.D.)*	*Mean*	*(S.D.)*	*Mean*	*(S.D.)*	*Mean*	*(S.D.)*	*Mean*	*(S.D.)*
Proportion who dropped out by grade 12 (F2DOSTAT)	0.06	(0.24)	0.06	(0.24)	0.04	(0.20)	0.12	(0.33)	–		–	
Proportion currently employed, grade 10 (F1S84)	0.24	(0.43)	–		–		–		0.24	(0.43)	0.26	(0.44)
Proportion working 1–20 hours/week, grade 10 (F1S85)	0.17	(0.38)	–		–		–		0.17	(0.38)	0.11	(0.32)
Proportion working 21+ hours/week, grade 10 (F1S85)	0.07	(0.26)	–		–		–		0.07	(0.25)	0.14	(0.35)
Proportion male (F1SEX)	0.49	(0.50)	0.47	(0.50)	0.51	(0.50)	0.64	(0.48)	0.49	(0.50)	0.48	(0.50)
Proportion non-Hispanic White (F1RACE)	0.78	(0.41)	0.76	(0.43)	0.86	(0.35)	0.82	(0.39)	0.79	(0.41)	0.67	(0.47)
Proportion Black (F1RACE)	0.12	(0.33)	0.13	(0.34)	0.08	(0.27)	0.11	(0.31)	0.12	(0.32)	0.17	(0.37)
Proportion Hispanic (F1RACE)	0.10	(0.30)	0.11	(0.31)	0.07	(0.25)	0.07	(0.26)	0.09	(0.29)	0.16	(0.37)
Socioeconomic status composite, grade 10 (F1SES)	−0.01	(0.77)	−0.01	(0.78)	0.06	(0.72)	−0.17	(0.66)	0.03	(0.76)	−0.58	(0.66)
Proportion in the college track, grade 10 (F1HSPROG)	0.37	(0.48)	0.37	(0.48)	0.39	(0.49)	0.25	(0.43)	0.38	(0.49)	0.10	(0.29)
Mathematics IRT-est. number right, grade 10 (F12XMIRR)	43.49	(13.73)	43.45	(13.81)	45.45	(13.20)	39.03	(13.11)	44.25	(13.55)	31.20	(10.41)
Proportion very likely to go to college, grade 10 (F1S64B)	0.50	(0.50)	0.50	(0.50)	0.52	(0.50)	0.37	(0.48)	0.52	(0.50)	0.14	(0.35)
Mathematics coursework in high school (F1S22A-J)	4.67	(2.46)	4.66	(2.42)	4.71	(2.58)	4.69	(2.59)	4.68	(2.41)	4.57	(3.19)
Proportion ever held back, grade 10 (F1N22)	0.14	(0.35)	0.13	(0.34)	0.15	(0.36)	0.27	(0.44)	0.13	(0.34)	0.38	(0.49)

Notes
Sample restricted to cases in which the respondents were in school during the 1990 follow-up, reported their sex, were non-Hispanic White, Black, or Hispanic, and in which ZIP-code-based data could be obtained. Data are weighted using F2F1PNWT after dividing the weight for each case by the mean of F2F1PNWT across cases in the analysis sample. See text for details of variable construction. Terms in parentheses are NELS:88 variable names used to construct each measure.

Table 7.A.6 Description of labor market-level variables by employment status and intensity and dropout status

	Analysis sample (N = *14,787*)		*Not employed* (N = *11,197*)		*Employed, 1–20 hrs/wk* (N = *2,516*)		*Employed, 21+ hrs/wk* (N = *1,074*)		*Did not drop out* (N = *13,857*)		*Dropped out* (*N* = *930*)	
	Mean	*(S.D.)*	*Mean*	*(S.D.)*	*Mean*	*(S.D.)*	*Mean*	*(S.D.)*	*Mean*	*(S.D.)*	*Mean*	*(S.D.)*
% African American in area	10.66	(12.74)	11.06	(13.01)	8.78	(11.30)	10.92	(12.73)	10.53	(12.70)	12.58	(13.27)
% Hispanic in area	7.73	(13.18)	8.24	(13.99)	6.03	(9.86)	6.40	(10.54)	7.59	(13.03)	9.81	(15.12)
% of adults w/o high school diploma	26.88	(8.30)	27.33	(8.51)	25.00	(7.23)	26.61	(7.79)	26.73	(8.29)	29.07	(8.11)
% below the poverty line	13.33	(6.47)	13.72	(6.70)	11.78	(5.31)	12.89	(5.93)	13.22	(6.47)	14.97	(6.26)
% in central city area	54.08	(49.84)	53.62	(49.87)	55.83	(49.67)	54.67	(49.80)	54.33	(49.81)	50.37	(50.03)
% of students (age 16 to 19) in labor force	44.66	(8.05)	44.03	(8.14)	46.92	(7.42)	45.87	(7.46)	44.72	(8.10)	43.71	(7.36)
% of students (age 16 to 19) in labor force w/jobs	84.18	(5.17)	83.86	(5.33)	85.44	(4.34)	84.62	(4.73)	84.26	(5.17)	83.11	(4.97)
% of dropouts (age 16 to 19) in labor force	58.14	(7.91)	57.76	(8.02)	59.43	(7.32)	59.09	(7.72)	58.18	(7.96)	57.65	(7.20)
% of dropouts (age 16 to 19) in labor force w/jobs	69.51	(8.74)	69.17	(8.87)	70.68	(8.21)	70.40	(8.25)	69.58	(8.78)	68.50	(8.03)
% of jobs that are in service	11.26	(2.16)	11.25	(2.14)	11.25	(2.23)	11.33	(2.20)	11.25	(2.17)	11.43	(2.03)
% of jobs that are in sales	11.61	(1.66)	11.61	(1.65)	11.65	(1.68)	11.56	(1.68)	11.63	(1.67)	11.37	(1.52)
% of jobs that are blue collar	15.82	(5.31)	15.89	(5.34)	15.46	(5.17)	15.95	(5.39)	15.77	(5.31)	16.57	(5.29)

Notes
Sample restricted to cases in which the respondents were in school during the 1990 follow-up, reported their sex, were either non-Hispanic White, Black, or Hispanic, and in which ZIP-code-based data could be obtained. Data are weighted using F2F1PNWT after dividing the weight for each case by the mean of F2F1PNWT across cases in the analysis sample. See text for details of variable construction.

Table 7.A.7 Regressions of dropout status on sex, race, family background, school performance, and employment status and intensity

	Model 1		*Model 2*		*Model 3*		*Model 4*		*Model 5*		*Model 6*		*Model 7*		*Model 8*	
Level-1 N = *14,787 Level-2* N = *499*	*exp(b)*	*(b/s.e.)*	*exp(b)*	*(b/s.e.)*	*exp(b)*	*(b/s.e.)*	*exp(b)*	*(b/s.e.)*	*exp(b)*	*(b/s.e.)*	*exp(b)*	*(b/s.e.)*	*exp(b)*	*(b/s.e.)*	*exp(b)*	*(b/s.e.)*
Student-level equation																
Male	–		**0.86**	**(−1.96)**	0.86	(−1.90)	0.89	(−1.34)	0.86	(−1.91)	0.86	(−1.89)	0.86	(−1.89)	0.86	(−1.90)
Black	–		0.90	(−0.78)	0.93	(−0.57)	0.93	(−0.57)	0.92	(−0.61)	0.93	(−0.56)	0.93	(−0.57)	0.93	(−0.56)
Hispanic	–		1.07	(0.67)	1.06	(0.51)	1.05	(0.49)	1.04	(0.30)	1.06	(0.52)	1.05	(0.51)	1.06	(0.52)
SES composite, grade 10	–		**0.62**	**(−8.25)**	**0.62**	**(−8.09)**	**0.62**	**(−8.10)**	**0.62**	**(−8.10)**	**0.63**	**(−7.23)**	**0.62**	**(−8.05)**	**0.62**	**(−8.09)**
College track, grade 10	–		**0.61**	**(−4.01)**	**0.62**	**(−3.88)**	**0.62**	**(−3.87)**	**0.62**	**(−3.89)**	**0.62**	**(−3.87)**	**0.54**	**(−4.29)**	**0.62**	**(−3.87)**
Math IRT, grade 10	–		**0.95**	**(−11.96)**	**0.95**	**(−11.68)**	**0.95**	**(−11.69)**	**0.95**	**(−11.68)**	**0.95**	**(−11.59)**	**0.95**	**(−11.68)**	**0.95**	**(−11.67)**
Very likely to go to college, grade 10	–		**0.34**	**(−9.23)**	**0.33**	**(−9.03)**	**0.33**	**(−9.02)**	**0.33**	**(−9.01)**	**0.34**	**(−9.02)**	**0.33**	**(−9.02)**	**0.33**	**(−9.02)**
Math coursework in high school	–		0.99	(−0.95)	0.99	(−1.00)	0.99	(−1.02)	0.99	(−0.98)	0.99	(−1.01)	0.99	(−0.99)	0.99	(−1.01)
Ever held back, grade 10	–		**1.93**	**(7.87)**	**1.92**	**(7.70)**	**1.91**	**(7.69)**	**1.92**	**(7.68)**	**1.92**	**(7.70)**	**1.92**	**(7.70)**	**1.88**	**(6.52)**
Working 1–20 hours/week, grade 10	–		0.80	(−1.89)	0.81	(−1.82)	0.83	(−1.13)	0.83	(−1.41)	**0.72**	**(−2.26)**	**0.70**	**(−2.82)**	0.79	(−1.53)
Working 21+ hours/week, grade 10	–		**1.40**	**(2.85)**	**1.43**	**(3.04)**	**1.65**	**(2.78)**	**1.34**	**(2.02)**	**1.57**	**(3.24)**	**1.40**	**(2.59)**	**1.38**	**(2.04)**
Working 1–20 hours/week × male	–		–		–		0.95	(−0.22)	–		–		–		–	
Working 21+ hours/week × male	–		–		–		0.79	(−1.03)	–		–		–		–	
Working 1–20 hours/week × Black	–		–		–		–		0.71	(−0.88)	–		–		–	
Working 21+ hours/week × Black	–		–		–		–		1.37	(0.97)	–		–		–	
Working 1–20 hours/week × Hispanic	–		–		–		–		1.01	(0.04)	–		–		–	
Working 21+ hours/week × Hispanic	–		–		–		–		1.16	(0.43)	–		–		–	
Working 1–20 hours/week × SES	–		–		–		–		–		0.76	(−1.45)	–		–	
Working 21+ hours/week × SES	–		–		–		–		–		1.22	(1.12)	–		–	
Working 1–20 hours/week × college track	–		–		–		–		–		–		**2.10**	**(2.63)**	–	
Working 21+ hours/week × college track	–		–		–		–		–		–		1.14	(0.29)	–	
Working 1–20 hours/week × held back	–		–		–		–		–		–		–		1.06	(0.21)
Working 21+ hours/week × held back	–		–		–		–		–		–		–		1.09	(0.37)
Residual variance in Level-1 intercept	0.245		0.086		–		–		–		–		–		–	
Degrees of freedom	498	498			–		–		–		–		–		–	
χ^2	654.0***		490.7		–		–		–		–		–		–	
% of variance in Level-1 intercept explained	–		64.9%		–		–		–		–		–		–	
Adjusted mean of Level-1 intercept	**0.05**	**(−67.78)**	**0.02**	**(−58.14)**	**0.02**	**(−55.17)**	**0.02**	**(−55.20)**	**0.02**	**(−55.13)**	**0.02**	**(−55.83)**	**0.02**	**(−55.28)**	**0.02**	**(−55.41)**

Notes

All results are from population-average models with robust standard errors. See text for sample restrictions and variable definitions. Bold entries represent coefficients that are twice their standard errors.

* $p<0.05$; ** $p<0.01$; *** $p<0.001$.

Table 7.A.8 Regressions of dropout status on labor market characteristics, sex, race, family background, school performance, and employment status and intensity

	Model 1		*Model 2*		*Model 3*		*Model 4*		*Model 5*	
Level-1 N = *14,787 Level-2* N = *499*	*exp(b)*	*(b/s.e.)*	*exp(b)*	*(b/s.e.)*	*exp(b)*	*(b/s.e.)*	*exp(b)*	*(b/s.e.)*	*exp(b)*	*(b/s.e.)*
Labor market-level equations for intercept										
% of students (16–19) in LF (×10)	–		0.99	(−0.12)	0.96	(−0.43)	0.96	(−0.40)	0.96	(−0.42)
% of students (16–19) in LF w/jobs (×10)	–		0.92	(−0.53)	1.14	(0.75)	1.14	(0.71)	1.14	(0.72)
% of dropouts (16–19) in LF (×10)	–		1.10	(1.12)	1.13	(1.40)	1.13	(1.45)	1.13	(1.37)
% of dropouts (16–19) in LF w/jobs (×10)	–		0.99	(−0.15)	0.98	(−0.27)	0.97	(−0.45)	0.97	(−0.46)
% of jobs that are in service (×10)	–		1.12	(0.30)	1.20	(0.39)	1.09	(0.20)	1.07	(0.16)
% of jobs that are in sales (×10)	–		1.35	(0.72)	1.31	(0.66)	1.26	(0.57)	1.25	(0.55)
% of jobs that are blue collar (×10)	–		1.07	(0.56)	1.22	(1.24)	1.22	(1.23)	1.25	(1.36)
Area is 25% + African American	–		–	–	**1.16**	**(3.31)**	**1.16**	**(3.25)**	**1.15**	**(3.08)**
Area is 25% + Hispanic	–		–	–	1.00	(0.02)	1.00	(0.05)	1.01	(0.18)
% of adults w/o high school diploma	–		–	–	0.87	(−1.04)	0.86	(−1.17)	0.84	(−1.34)
% below the poverty line	–		–	–	1.14	(0.69)	1.16	(0.79)	1.18	(0.89)
Central city	–		–	–	1.09	(0.68)	1.08	(0.67)	1.08	(0.64)
Labor market-level equations for "working 1–20 hours/week, grade 10" coefficient										
% of students (16–19) in LF (×10)	–		–		–		1.14	(0.59)	1.20	(0.73)
% of students (16–19) in LF w/jobs (×10)	–		–		–		0.78	(−0.75)	0.65	(−0.89)
% of dropouts (16–19) in LF (×10)	–		–		–		1.20	(0.88)	1.16	(0.73)
% of dropouts (16–19) in LF w/jobs (×10)	–		–		–		**0.68**	**(−2.15)**	**0.69**	**(−2.03)**
% of jobs that are in service (×10)	–		–		–		0.25	(−1.65)	0.21	(−1.60)
% of jobs that are in sales (×10)	–		–		–		1.80	(0.60)	1.88	(0.60)
% of jobs that are blue collar (×10)	–		–		–		1.07	(0.20)	1.00	(0.00)
Area is 25% + African American	–		–		–		–		0.89	(−0.98)
Area is 25% + Hispanic	–		–		–		–		1.01	(0.08)
% of adults w/o high school diploma	–		–		–		–		1.03	(0.08)
% below the poverty line	–		–		–		–		1.04	(0.07)
Central city	–		–		–		–		0.88	(−0.37)

Labor market-level equations for "working 21+ hours/week, grade 10" coefficient										
% of students (16–19) in LF (×10)	–		–		–		0.99	(−0.04)	1.18	(0.62)
% of students (16–19) in LF w/jobs (×10)	–		–		–		1.09	(0.27)	0.93	(−0.18)
% of dropouts (16–19) in LF (×10)	–		–		–		1.01	(0.06)	1.05	(0.23)
% of dropouts (16–19) in LF w/jobs (×10)	–		–		–		0.83	(−0.90)	0.86	(−0.70)
% of jobs that are in service (×10)	–		–		–		1.21	(0.33)	1.01	(0.02)
% of jobs that are in sales (×10)	–		–		–		3.47	(1.18)	2.69	(0.94)
% of jobs that are blue collar (×10)	–		–		–		1.32	(0.86)	0.71	(−0.74)
Area is 25%+ African American	–		–		–		–		0.96	(−0.31)
Area is 25%+ Hispanic	–		–		–		–		0.86	(−1.01)
% of adults w/o high school diploma	–		–		–		–		1.73	(1.67)
% below the poverty line	–		–		–		–		0.89	(−0.29)
Central city	–		–		–		–		0.94	(−0.17)
Adjusted mean of level-1 intercept	**0.02**	**(−55.29)**	**0.02**	**(−55.97)**	**0.02**	**(−57.01)**	**0.02**	**(−57.15)**	**0.02**	**(−57.11)**
Adjusted mean of level-1 coefficient for "Working 1–20 hours/week"	0.81	(−1.83)	0.81	(−1.81)	0.80	(−1.90)	**0.75**	**(−2.33)**	**0.76**	**(−2.22)**
Adjusted mean of level-1 coefficient for "Working 21+ hours/week"	**1.43**	**(3.04)**	**1.43**	**(3.03)**	**1.41**	**(2.89)**	**1.38**	**(2.63)**	**1.38**	**(2.59)**
Residual variance in level-1 intercept	–		–		–		–		–	
Degrees of freedom	–		–		–		–		–	
χ^2	–		–		–		–		–	
Residual variance in "Working 1–20 hours/week" coefficient	0.006		–		–		–		–	
Degrees of freedom	452		–		–		–		–	
χ^2	344.0		–		–		–		–	
Residual variance in "Working 21+ hours/week" coefficient	0.015		–		–		–		–	
Degrees of freedom	452		–		–		–		–	
χ^2	398.8		–		–		–		–	

Notes

For Model 1, the χ^2 statistic is based on only 453 of 492 Level-2 units with sufficient information for computation. The coefficients for labor market-level variables pertaining to employment rates and types of jobs express the impact of a ten percentage point increase in those variables. All results are from population-average models with robust standard errors. All models include sex, race/ethnicity, socioeconomic status, track location, mathematics test scores, perceived chances of going to college, mathematics coursework, and grade retention history as covariates in the student-level equation; estimates of these effects are not shown, but are substantively the same as those presented in Table 7.A.7. See text for sample restrictions and variable definitions. Bold entries represent coefficients that are twice their standard errors.

* $p<0.05$; ** $p<0.01$; *** $p<0.001$

Notes

1 Part I of this research was supported by a graduate student research fellowship from the Center for Studies in Demography and Ecology at the University of Washington and by a grant from the American Educational Research Association which receives funds for its "AERA Grants Program" from the National Science Foundation and the U.S. Department of Education's National Center for Education Statistics and the Office of Educational Research and Improvement under NSF Grant #RED-9980573. Support for Part II of this research was provided by the National Academy of Education/Spencer Foundation Postdoctoral Fellowship Program and by the Royalty Research Fund of the University of Washington. We also thank Eric Grodsky, Adam Gamoran, Kevin Quinn, Jerry Herting, Paul LePore, Ralph McNeal, and Christopher Jencks for valuable advice and suggestions on various aspects of our work. However, opinions reflect those of the authors and do not necessarily reflect those of the granting agencies or our advisors. Please direct correspondence to John Robert Warren, University of Minnesota, Department of Sociology, 909 Social Sciences, 267 ~ 19th Ave S., Minneapolis, MN, 55455 or email warre046@tc.umn.edu.

2 E. Greenberger and L. D. Steinberg, *When Teenagers Work: The Psychological and Social Costs of Adolescent Employment*, New York, NY: Basic Books, 1986; J. T. Mortimer and M. D. Finch, "The effects of part-time work on adolescent self-concept and achievement," Pp. 66–89 in *Becoming a Worker*, edited by Reisman, Norwood, NJ: Ablex Publishing Corp, 1986; J. T. Mortimer, J. Staff, and S. Oesterle, "Adolescent work and the early socioeconomic career," in *Handbook of the Life Course*, edited by J. T. Mortimer and M. Shanahan, NY: Kluwer Academic/Plenum Publishers, 2003, 437–459.

3 U.S. Department of Labor, *Employment Experience of Youths: Results From a Longitudinal Survey*, USDL 00–353, Washington, DC: U.S. Department of Labor, Bureau of Labor Statistics, 2000a.

4 R. D'Amico, "Does employment during high school impair academic progress?," *Sociology of Education* 57, 1984, 152–164; H. W. Marsh, "Employment during high school: character building or a subversion of academic goals?," *Sociology of Education* 64, 1991, 172–189; R. B. McNeal, Jr., "Are students being pulled out of high school? The effect of adolescent employment on dropping out," *Sociology of Education* 70, 1997, 206–220; M. Schoenhals, M. Tienda, and B. Schneider, "The educational and personal consequences of adolescent employment," *Social Forces* 77, 1998, 723–762; J. R. Warren, P. C. LePore, and R. D. Mare, "Employment during high school: consequences for students' grades in academic courses," *American Educational Research Journal* 37, 2000, 943–969; J. R. Warren and J. C. Lee, "The impact of adolescent employment on high school dropout: differences by individual and labor market characteristics," *Social Science Research* 32, 2003, 98–128.

5 Warren and Lee, op. cit.; Schoenhals *et al.*, op. cit.

6 S. Ruggles and M. Sobek, "Integrated public use microdata series: version 2.0," Minneapolis, MN: Historical Census Projects, University of Minnesota, 1997; R. M. Hauser, "Current population surveys: uniform October files, 1968–1990," Washington, DC: U.S. Dept. of Commerce, Bureau of the Census [producer], 1990: Ann Arbor, MI: Inter-university Consortium for Political and Social Research [distributor], 1993.

7 Data for these and subsequent figures come from the 1940 through 1990 Integrated Public Use Microdata Samples or IPUMS and the 1968 through 2000 Uniform October Current Population Survey file or CPS, and are restricted to White and Black 16 and 17 year olds who were enrolled at the time of their interview. Analyses of the IPUMS data use the "small samples" which contain

approximately 21,000 randomly selected households in each decennial Census year. Statistics derived from CPS data are three year moving averages.

8 The validity of our results depends on the assumption that each sample represents an independent random draw from the populations of American high school sophomores and/or seniors. Each of the five projects used stratified, multiple-stage probability sampling designs; consequently, analyses of all five data sets require adjustments for unequal probabilities of selection, stratification, and clustering. The sampling weights used for all surveys are described in more detail in the appendix. These weights are designed to produce unbiased results by accounting for over-sampling, attrition in panel surveys, and so forth. In our analyses we divide the weights by study-specific mean weights so that standard errors reflect the size of samples and not of the populations from which they were drawn. Also, to adjust for design effects in HS&B and NELS:88, we further divide weights in these samples by study-specific values of DEFF. (National Center for Education Statistics, *High School and Beyond, 1980: Sophomore Cohort and Second Follow-Up (1984)*, Washington, DC: U.S. Department of Education, 1986; National Center for Education Statistics, *National Educational Longitudinal Study of 1988: Second Follow-Up, Student Component, Data File Users Manual*, Washington, DC: U.S. Department of Education, 1994.)

9 Center for Human Resource Research, *NLS Users' Guide: 1995*, Columbus, OH: Center for Human Resource Research, The Ohio State University, 1995.

10 National Center for Education Statistics 1986, op. cit.; U.S. Department of Labor 2000b, op. cit.

11 National Center for Education Statistics 1994, op. cit.

12 Center for Human Resource Research, *NLSY97 Users' Guide*, Columbus, OH: Center for Human Resource Research, The Ohio State University, 1998.

13 We can assess whether NLS and NLSY-79 respondents were "working" or "with a job but not at work" last week. Similarly, we can assess whether HS&B respondents did "any work for pay last week, not counting work around the house" and whether NLSY-97 respondents did "any work for pay" last week. The definition of employment in NELS:88 (currently employed or ever been employed) is somewhat different, but we are able to identify "currently employed" students. Consequently, in all surveys we will classify students as employed if they worked "recently" – that is, within the last week or so. Finally, we can ascertain hours worked per week in all surveys, although the responses are reported in terms of grouped categories in the NCES surveys; in these cases we have assigned the midpoints of categories.

14 Most prior research operationalizes employment intensity as hours worked per week (and sometimes also as hours worked per week squared). The difference between working 4 and 9 hours per week is likely trivial, as is the distinction between working 34 and 39 hours per week. A great deal of prior research in the literature on high school employment suggests or demonstrates that there is a threshold – somewhere between 10 and 20 hours per week – beyond which the costs of employment outweigh potential benefits. We contend that our operationalization better reflects the notion that it is working "a lot" that matters.

15 Unfortunately, in NELS:88 we are forced to label non-Hispanic Whites and Blacks simply as "Whites" and "Blacks," respectively, and in NLSY-79 we created the "White" category by combining all non-Latino, non-Asian, non-Black and non-Native American categories.

16 One problem we encounter is that surveys define "parents" differently. Looking just at "mothers," NLS-YM, NLS-YW, and NLSY-79 refer to "mother," NELS:88 refers to "mother or female guardian," HS&B refers to

"mother (stepmother or female guardian)," and NLSY-97 provides information about all members of the respondent's household (including mothers and stepmothers). The situation is the same with reference to fathers. Consequently, even though we will use education variables for "mothers" and "fathers," these variables will actually express the educations of the people who serve as respondents' primary male and female parent-figures; when given the option, we have used information about biological parents instead of step-parents.

17 The head of household is taken to be the father, but we use mother's education if information about father's education is missing. We use head of household's education – instead of separate measures of mother's education and father's education – to limit the number of cases dropped from our analyses because of missing data.

18 In surveys other than NLSY-79, students were asked how far in school they expect or would like to go; response categories included options like "high school graduate," "two-year college degree," "four-year college degree," and so forth. In NLSY-79, students were asked how likely it was that they would be in school five years from the date of their survey. A 12th grade respondent who answered that it was unlikely that they would be in school in five years may have either been indicating that they did not expect to go to college, or that they expected to finish college after two or four years.

19 As described above, we utilize the relevant sampling weights in each study in order to adjust for over-sampling, differential participation rates, and panel attrition; the weights for HS&B and NELS:88 are further adjusted to account for design effects.

20 A. Bryk and S. Raudenbush, *Hierarchical Linear Models*, Newbury Park, CA: Sage, 1992; A. Bryk, S. Raudenbush, Y. F. Cheong, and R. Congdon, *HLM 5: Hierarchical Linear and Nonlinear Modeling*, Lincolnwood, IL: Scientific Software International, Inc., 2000; J. J. Hox, *Applied Multilevel Analysis*. Amsterdam: TT-Publikaties, 1995.

21 Our meta-analyses are performed using the "V Known" or "variance known" procedures in HLM 5. (Bryk *et al.*, op. cit.) These routines can be used for applications where the level-1 (in this case, study level) variances and covariances are known (or, in our case, estimated separately).

22 J. R. Warren and E. F. Cataldi, "Trends in the selectivity and consequences of adolescent employment, 1966–1997," unpublished manuscript, Department of Sociology, University of Minnesota, 2003.

23 Because missing data was most prevalent in the measures of mother's education and father's education, we have combined those two measures into one. The new measure represents father's education when that information is available, or mother's education when information about father's education is unavailable. Also, we have collapsed the four parental education categories into two for ease of model estimation.

24 D'Amico op. cit; Warren *et al.*, op. cit.; Warren and Cataldi, op. cit.; J. C. Lee, "Cash for hash? Explaining the relationship between adolescent employment and substance abuse," unpublished manuscript, Department of Sociology, University of Minnesota, 2001.

25 These results are derived from our meta-analyses, in which we formally test hypotheses about the homogeneity of parameters across surveys. See Tables 7.A.2 and 7.A.3 for details.

26 Again, these results are derived from our meta-analyses. For parameters that vary significantly across studies, we estimated the annual change in that parameter.

27 Indeed the final columns of Table 7.A.4 indicate that we cannot reject hypotheses that the conditional associations between employment behaviors and dropout are homogeneous across studies, and thus over time.

28 Marsh op. cit; Warren *et al.*, op. cit.; J. R. Warren, "Reconsidering the relationship between student employment and academic outcomes: A new theory and better data," *Youth & Society* 33, 2002b, 366–393.
29 Warren, op. cit.
30 McNeal, op. cit.; G. J. Papagiannis, R. N. Bickel, and R. H. Fuller, "The social creation of school dropouts," *Youth & Society* 14, 1983, 363–392; R. Bickel, "Post high school opportunities and high school completion rates in an Appalachian state: a near-replication of Florida research," *Youth & Society* 21, 1989, 61–84; R. Bickel and G. J. Papagiannis, "Post high school prospects and district-level dropout rates," *Youth & Society* 20, 1988, 123–147.
31 Bickel and Papagiannis, op. cit.; Bickel, op. cit.
32 R. V. Carr, J. D. Wright, and C. J. Brody, "Effects of high school work experience a decade later: evidence from the National Longitudinal Survey," *Sociology of Education* 69, 1996, 66–81; M. Fine and P. Rosenberg, "Dropping out of high school: the ideology of school and work," *Journal of Education* 165, 1983, 257–272.
33 L. D. Steinberg, and S. M. Dornbusch, "Negative correlates of part-time employment during adolescence: replication and elaboration," *Developmental Psychology* 27, 1991, 304–313; L. D. Steinberg, S. Fegley, and S.M. Dornbusch, "Negative impact of part-time work on adolescent adjustment: evidence from a longitudinal study," *Developmental Psychology* 29, 1993, 171–180; D'Amico, op. cit.; Warren *et al.*, op. cit.; Warren and Cataldi, op. cit.
34 Sociologist Ronald D'Amico, for example, concluded in a 1984 paper that all females and White males are less likely to drop out as they work more weeks at modest levels of intensity in grade 11. (D'Amico, op. cit.)
35 Warren and Cataldi, op. cit.; Schoenhals *et al.*, op. cit.; B. N. Kablaoui and A. J. Paulter, "The effects of part-time work experience on high school students," *Journal of Career Development* 17, 1991, 195–211.; R. T. Michael and N. B. Tuma, "Youth employment: does life begin at 16?," *Journal of Labor Economics* 2, 1984, 464–476.; A. Ahituv, M. Tienda, L. Xu, and V. J. Hotz, "Initial labor market experiences of Black, Hispanic and White men," in *Population Research Center Discussion Paper Series, Working Paper* 94–5, Chicago: University of Chicago, 1994.
36 Warren, *et al.*, op. cit.
37 D. A. Massey and N. A. Denton, *American Apartheid: Segregation and the Making of the Underclass*, Cambridge, MA: Harvard University Press, 1996.
38 To make this match, we used the five measures available in the private-release version of the first follow-up NELS:88 data that characterize the ZIP codes in which students' tenth grade high schools are located. These variables were originally derived by the National Center for Education Statistics (NCES) from the STF3B Census file. We then made an extract from the STF3B Census file that contained these five measures and the measures that we desired for every ZIP code in the country. Finally, we matched the Census data to NELS:88 records using the five measures that both files had in common as key variables.
39 Specifically, students were asked, "Are you currently employed or have you ever been employed?" Response options to this question allow us to determine whether students were employed at the time of their survey. Subsequently, students who had ever been employed were asked, "How many hours do/did you usually work a week on your current or most recent job?" The available response options included 0–10 hours, 11–20 hours, 21–30 hours, 31–40 hours, and over 40 hours per week.
40 We recognize the potential bias introduced by omitting from our analyses those students who dropped out before the date of their 10th grade interview.

41 There were too few American Indians or Asian Americans to sustain separate analyses for these groups.

42 Cases were dropped if the five ZIP code-level measures available on the private release version of the NELS:88 data were missing. This typically occurred when the school administrator failed to return or completely fill out the school questionnaire.

43 Throughout our descriptive analyses, cases are weighted by F2F1PNWT, the NCES-provided weight to be used for producing student panel statistics when both first follow-up and second follow-up data are employed in the analyses. We do not employ sample weights in our multivariate analyses, in part because we include many of the stratifying variables in our analyses (e.g. race/ethnicity and urbanicity) and in part because we estimate our models using version 5.04 of the software package HLM, which does not allow weighting in non-linear hierarchical models. As described below, we are able to estimate some of our models both with and without weighting; we find that not being able to use sampling weights in our hierarchical generalized linear models has little bearing on substantive results. Finally, to handle missing data on individual-level variables in our multivariate analyses, we employ group mean substitution (where groups are defined by sex, race/ethnicity, and employment status and intensity) and include dummy variables in our individual-level models to indicate that such an imputation took place; since the coefficients for these dummy variables are rarely significant, we say nothing more about them.

44 Because the central outcome variable – whether or not a student dropped out of school by grade 12 – is dichotomous, and because we employ variables at both the individual and labor market levels, our analyses consist of a series of hierarchical generalized linear models using the logit link function.

45 Warren and Lee, op. cit.

46 Based on the results of the previous model pertaining to the residual variation in intercepts, in these subsequent models we fix the intercept to be equal across labor markets. By fixing the intercepts to be equal across labor markets, these models become fixed effects models; none of the parameters of the within-labor market models vary across labor markets. Since it is also possible to estimate these models in SPSS or any other standard statistical software package, we were able to estimate these models both with and without employing sampling weights. The results of the two sets of models are virtually identical, suggesting that our inability to employ sampling weights in our HLM analyses does not substantially affect our results.

47 Warren and Lee, op. cit.

48 Warren *et al.*, op. cit.; Schoenhals *et al.*, op. cit.

8 School–community relationships and the early labor market outcomes of sub-baccalaureate students

Richard Arum and Sandra Way[1]

The fact that children from families with low socioeconomic status perform on average educationally below their middle and upper class peers is well established. Partially as a result of low academic achievement, such children are also more likely to be unemployed or employed in low wage, low prestige occupations as adults. Although schools are often implicated in discussions of this phenomenon, less clear are the specific mechanisms by which this social class reproduction occurs. While there is some indication that schools at times help reduce inequality, more frequently social scientists have emphasized the degree to which schools serve to perpetuate social class disadvantage, or as in the wake of the Coleman report, have claimed that schools are largely irrelevant in shaping student outcomes.[2]

Curricular tracking of students is a frequent target of criticism for those who argue that schools magnify and reproduce academic difficulties among lower class students. Most secondary school systems in the United States historically have tracked some students into vocational or occupational coursework to prepare them for direct entry into the labor market. Some opponents of these programs have claimed that vocational education reproduces class and race inequalities by placing poor and minority youth into educational experience where they are taught only the skills and dispositions needed to occupy low-pay, low-prestige occupations.[3] Several studies show that vocational courses do enroll students with disadvantaged backgrounds at higher rates than other students, reducing the odds that these individuals will attend university and enter higher paid professional occupations.[4]

While such criticisms bring attention to real limitations inherent in vocational education, this perspective also tends to ignore the complexity of how socioeconomic background influences educational achievement and the realities of current United States post-secondary, as well as labor market, opportunity structures. Differential vocational participation rates are in large part due to the weaker academic position disadvantaged students occupy at the time they reach high school. Since achievement trajectories are shaped early in life, by the time students reach high school the accrued advantages or disadvantages of social class origins have already been translated into significant differences in academic achievement.

The proliferation of open-enrollment practices and a recent emphasis on encouraging all students to attend college has expanded the likelihood of post-secondary attainment. Although college aspirations and enrollment among youths of all social backgrounds have dramatically increased within the last few years, many of these youth, particularly low achievers, have been unable to translate their aspirations into college degrees.[5] Rosenbaum and colleagues found that among high school seniors with college plans and low high school grades (C or lower), only 68 percent received any college credit and only 13 percent completed an associate degree or higher.[6] Unable to fulfill their college aspirations, many of these youth are left without back-up plans and are unprepared to enter the job market possessing neither a post-secondary degree nor any secondary occupational training. In light of these facts, evaluating vocational education only through the examination of its effect on post-secondary outcomes or standardized test performance is inadequate. An alternative approach assesses vocational education's effectiveness at facilitating school-to-work transitions for labor market bound youth.

School-to-work transitions for young adults without four year college degrees in the United States are comparatively difficult. While most public high schools and many post-secondary institutions in this country offer occupational coursework to train students for entry into the workforce, U.S. schools are often still criticized for failing to provide adequate assistance to young adults entering the labor market.[7] Relative to countries, such as Japan and Germany, U.S. schools have limited institutional ties to employers, which increases uncertainty in school-to-work transitions.

While school-business institutional relationships can be structured in myriad ways – including supplementary resource support for schools, greater curriculum articulation with the needs of industry, and provision of firm-based training sites and other learning opportunities for students[8] – one direct and concrete way that students can benefit from institutional relationships between schools and employers is schools' facilitating student job placement. Employers, however, are only likely to utilize school assisted job placement when it serves their interests – for example, when school personnel are clearly in a position to sort and screen job candidates on the basis of job relevant skills. Government organizations such as the Secretary's Commission on Achieving Necessary Skills have blamed youth labor market problems on the inability of U.S. schools to provide students with academic skills assumed generally in demand by employers.[9] Empirical investigation of employer hiring decisions, however, indicates significant variation in the demand for academic skills by occupation and gender.[10] Given a labor market characterized by profound occupational sex segregation, women are more dependent on the mastery of academic skills for low wage work in clerical and sales occupations than men are for the attainment of blue-collar work. Occupational sex segregation of low wage work thus is likely to produce significant differences in employer reliance on school information and school assisted job placement by gender. Little research focusing on either this practice or gender differences in its utilization, however, exists.

When testing for gender differences in the use of school assisted job placement, several interrelated questions arise: How common a practice is school assisted job placement for the most economically vulnerable of students, those who generally do not continue on to receive baccalaureate college education? Is school assisted job placement associated with secondary and post-secondary vocational education, the other programmatic effort by schools to improve student school-to-work transitions? Finally, what effect do these job placements have on young adult early labor market outcomes?

Given the occupational vulnerability of sub-baccalaureate youth, we believe that focusing on the school-to-work transition can lead to insights on how to improve labor market outcomes for the approximately 75 percent of students who do not obtain a bachelor's degree. Schools are typically evaluated for their ability to teach students academic subjects such as reading, science and math. Researchers of vocational education redirect the focus of analysis to how schools can provide students with information and skills corresponding to certain segments of the labor market. We shift the focus in yet another direction by concentrating on how "after the bell" school-business relationships can structure student outcomes. Through examining school assisted job placement, we seek to explore a non-curricular mechanism that can work to facilitate better occupational outcomes for students who are most vulnerable to labor market failure.

Human capital and institutional components of vocational education

Despite past social scientific critiques of tracking in general, recent research has identified positive effects of vocational secondary and post-secondary programs on the labor market outcomes of young adults, particularly women. These studies have found that enrollment in vocational coursework reduces the likelihood and duration of unemployment, increases the likelihood that an individual will attain a routine non-manual or skilled manual job, and raises initial wages for women.[11] Post-secondary vocational education, although often maligned for its shortcomings and limitations, also generates largely positive economic returns relative to the simple attainment of high school degrees, particularly for women.[12] Supporters of vocational education and training often attribute these positive effects to the improvement of student occupational skills and workplace dispositions: individuals with greater human capital investment reduce related skill deficiencies and thus lessen the likelihood of subsequent labor market failure.

Difficulties in student transitions to the labor market, however, are also likely related to the institutional environment surrounding schools. For example, in their examination of 13 countries, Walter Mueller and Yossi Shavit demonstrated that vocational education has greater benefits in countries with certain institutional characteristics.[13] School systems with greater stratification, standardization, post-secondary educational opportunities and vocational specificity provide more effective vocational programs (with the latter two factors arguably particularly salient). In Germany and Japan researchers have identified an additional institutional mechanism producing positive associations between student enrollment in vocational education and subsequent success in the labor market: school assisted job placement.[14] In the United States, schools seldom provide occupational placement assistance for students. Vocational programs, however, have recently worked to create greater linkages with local industry. The latest version of institutional relationships fostered by vocational education programs has been school-business partnerships sponsored by federal, state, and local grants. These partnerships have encouraged vocational student placement in the workplace.[15] Research has generally ignored, however, the extent to which secondary and post-secondary vocational education previously utilized school assisted job placement as a mechanism to facilitate student school-to-work transitions.

Institutionalists, like Mueller and Shavit, argue that organizational linkages, not simply investment in education, are responsible for variation in the effects of schooling on labor market outcomes.[16] Vocational education is more effective in Germany than in the United States not simply due to higher levels of resource investment there, but because of the close relationship between schools and industry in that country.[17] German schools also rely largely on an apprenticeship system to place students in jobs with particular employers.

School assisted job placement is a clear manifestation of closer school-industry linkages. School assisted job placement can be the result of either formal or informal relationships. Schools can provide: formal placement offices for students looking for employment; vocational programs which connect students with local business apprenticeships; and more informal connections to firms based on teacher's personal networks that are often embedded in local industry. In different ways, each of these school job placement resources rely on relationships with employers that are dependent on both institutional and network connections.

Employers will develop and utilize these types of institutional ties with schools more frequently when such relationships provide solutions to specific problems faced by firms. Organizational research indicates that while organizational behavior is not solely motivated by rational economizing, firms will seek to lower transaction costs and reduce risks of uncertainty when making hiring decisions.[18] Network relationships, such as those implicit in most school assisted job placements, "are particularly apt for circumstances in which there is a need for efficient reliable information."[19] Research on job finding largely confirms employer use of formal and informal network relationships to fill vacancies in this manner. Mark Granovetter's study of professional, managerial and technical job changers, for example, demonstrates the usefulness of informal, weak interpersonal ties in locating a job.[20] More recent studies of job search strategies have identified how interpersonal ties provide information to individuals about job openings and help employers screen for desirable candidates.[21] Employers can rely both on informal relationships between individuals or more formal relationships with schools to lower risks of hiring unreliable or incompetent workers.

James Rosenbaum and Amy Binder's description of high school assisted job placement also fits sociological conceptions of the organizational use of network relationships. Rosenbaum and Binder note that employers use high school linkages to screen applicants who otherwise are likely to present limited reliable information. These researchers also demonstrate that employers have an interest in the information that school personnel possess. Specifically, 69 percent of managers of businesses in the primary labor market consider basic academic skills necessary for entry-level jobs, with 34 percent of these businesses actually having established close relationships with schools.[22] These school-business relationships were long-term and utilized school assisted job placement: "When these employers have job openings, they ask school staff to nominate students. Employers see these long-term linkages as a way to get the straight scoop on young graduates' skills."[23] Rosenbaum and Binder's limited sample size (N = 51), however, prevented adequate exploration of variation along either the dimension of gender or occupation.

School-business ties are also useful for individuals. For some job seekers, relying on formal relationships with schools may provide more benefit than relying on informal relationships that often are solely comprised of personal family and friendship ties. Personal contacts are one of the most frequently used methods to obtain employment. While common, obtaining employment through interpersonal ties has varying returns that are dependent on education, socioeconomic status, race, and gender. Job seekers do not have equally useful personal contacts and thus vary in terms of relative advantages when searching for employment.[24] Because networks for lower socioeconomic families tend to be more kin oriented and less cosmopolitan, the higher status weak ties that are important for the attainment of better jobs may be absent for disadvantaged individuals. For these students, schools can provide a valuable connection to businesses that otherwise would not be established. Many teachers, vocational teachers in particular, are adeptly situated to broker employment opportunities for disadvantaged youth.[25]

In contrast to the system of high school assisted job placement described by Rosenbaum and Binder, the effectiveness of post-secondary school assisted job placement is more questionable. While community college vocational instructors can provide useful assistance in job placement, Norton Grubb and colleagues suggest that "the majority of instructors seem to do little placement" and placement offices at community colleges "concentrate not on employment of students leaving the institution but on part-time work for students to support themselves during their education."[26]

School assisted job placement might have a different character at the secondary and post-secondary levels due to the process of credentialing. One mechanism whereby schools produce desirable labor market outcomes is through providing students with recognizable credentials.[27] In the U.S., high school degrees have only a limited ability to signal employee competencies; given these limits, additional ties between schools and employers would be particularly helpful. Post-secondary degrees and certificates likely have clearer meanings attached to them and thus would be somewhat less dependent on school-employer direct relationships.

Gender variation in early labor market outcomes and incentives for formal job placement

While research on the organizational use of network relationships highlights the need for greater attention to the actual mechanisms and processes whereby students obtain their initial jobs after high school, this research tradition also suggests that formal, institutional support for initial job placement could be particularly important for women. This is true for two reasons. First, while jobs found through informal networks lead to better jobs than those found through formal channels for men, women are significantly less likely than men to use informal channels. This gender difference is related to the fact that women have fewer occupationally associated individuals in their personal networks than do men.[28]

In an occupationally segregated labor market, such as in the United States, employers have more incentive to rely on school information about women than about men when filling jobs requiring less educated workers. Research based on employer hiring preferences and decisions in the Multi-City Study of Urban Inequality demonstrate this tendency at least for firms located in Atlanta, Boston, Detroit, and Los Angeles.[29] Close to 50 percent of new positions for non-college educated women in these cities are located in clerical occupations, compared to less than 15 percent for men. Non-college educated men continue to rely on blue-collar jobs where women still are greatly under-represented.[30] Because of these differences, new hires for non-college jobs rely more heavily on the use of academic skills for women than men. Employers report the assessment of English and verbal skills of applicants as "important interview factors" twice as often when job vacancies are in clerical as opposed to laboring occupations (82 percent compared to 40 percent). In addition, 65 percent of jobs requiring the use of computers were filled by women, while 64 percent of jobs not requiring this proficiency were filled by men. Women were hired to fill 59 percent of jobs requiring an ability to communicate with customers compared to 32 percent of jobs not requiring this facility. Because school personnel are in a position to assess individual competencies in these areas, employers are more likely to rely on school assisted job placements for women.

Assessment of the role of school assisted job placement in facilitating school-to-work transitions requires sensitivity to certain general characteristics of male and female early labor market experiences. Both men and women face particularly high rates of job turnover and unemployment spells during this period. In the first eight years out of school, the average individual holds eight jobs with related risk of unemployment between these positions.[31] Annual earnings for young adults are largely, and increasingly, determined by the ability to find stable employment and to accumulate significant amounts of hours worked.[32] Youth unemployment reached post-World War Two highs during the economic recession in the early 1980s and remained relatively elevated through the mid-1980s.[33] In 1987, unemployment for those between ages 16 and 25 was 12.6 percent for men, and 11.7 percent for women. Unemployment rates vary, however, among different types of occupations with individuals working in clerical jobs experiencing lower associated unemployment risks than workers in sales, skilled manual and unskilled manual occupations.[34] Variation in unemployment rates by occupation have a differential effect on men and women given the high levels of occupational and vocational-course sex segregation.

Research on how school assisted job placement affects early labor market outcomes thus requires careful attention to gender, the high risk of unemployment, and the specific type of occupation students attain as some occupations provide greater protection from labor market uncertainty and failure. While previous research has identified the benefits of vocational education for non-baccalaureate students, the mechanisms producing these positive occupational outcomes have not been adequately explored. Our research identifies one possible mechanism: school assisted job placement.

Our findings suggest that while school assisted job placement is rarely used in the U.S., when schools do facilitate employment through relationships with employers, labor market benefits occur – particularly for women. These institutional connections between schools and employers also account for some of the gains women receive from taking high school vocational business coursework. Men use school assistance for finding employment even less than women, and receive fewer benefits from these relationships.

Descriptive analysis

Table 8.1 identifies the percentage of students with school assisted job placement by business and trade-technical curriculum concentration as well as by gender. Gender and curriculum are the primary determinants of school assisted job placement.[35] The top half of the table provides statistics based on the high school sample where curriculum is measured by high school course concentration and school assisted job placement is measured solely for first job after high school; the bottom half of the table is based on data from the post-secondary sample where curriculum is measured as attainment of post-secondary degree and school assisted job placement is measured less precisely as school assisted job placement for any job (not necessarily the first position after completion of schooling). Business and trade-technical programs are the largest occupational programs within secondary vocational education. For this table, linear measures of occupational coursework are collapsed and recoded into categorical variables with the following values: 0 percent occupational coursework; 1–9 percent occupational coursework; 10–19 percent occupational coursework; and more than 20 percent occupational coursework.

School assisted job placement is a rare occurrence for both men and women who complete their education in high school. Women, however, are significantly more likely than men to have received school assistance in

Table 8.1 Percentage of students with school assisted job placement by business and trade-technical course concentration or degree, and gender

High school sample				
	Women		*Men*	
Course concentration	*Business*	*Trade-tech.*	*Business*	*Trade-tech.*
0	3.6% (120)	8.7% (1,079)	3.6% (769)	4.4% (532)
0.01–0.09	4.4% (470)	7.6% (373)	6.1% (1,091)	4.7% (884)
0.10–0.19	9.5% (617)	0.0% (22)	3.1% (211)	6.3% (510)
0.20+	14.5% (268)	0.0% (1)	3.9% (28)	2.9% (172)
Total	8.3% (1,473)		4.9% (2,098)	

Post-secondary sample				
	Women		*Men*	
Post-secondary degree	*Business*	*Trade-tech.*	*Business*	*Trade-tech.*
No	18.9% (1,170)	21.6% (1,296)	11.5% (989)	10.7% (913)
Yes	47.2% (129)	51.0% (3)	12.0% (18)	18.9% (93)
Total	21.7% (1,299)		11.5% (1,006)	

Note
Percent with school assisted job placement.
N in cell.

finding a job.[36] 8.3 percent of female students who completed their education in high school received school assisted job placement compared to 4.9 percent of men. This gender difference is largely due to the different effects of business coursework on the probability that a female student will receive school assistance in locating initial employment. Women with more than 10 percent business coursework on their high school transcripts are significantly more likely than women with no business coursework to receive school assistance in finding a job: only 3.6 percent of women with no business coursework received school assisted job placement compared to 9.5 percent of women with 10–19 percent business coursework and 14.5 percent of women with more than 20 percent business coursework. Women with more than 10 percent business coursework are also significantly more likely than men with similar coursework to receive school assisted job placement. Only 3.1 percent of men with 10–19 percent business coursework and 3.9 percent of men with more than 20 percent business coursework receive school assisted job placement. This finding supports our expectation that sex-segregation in occupations and coursework, due to corresponding differences in the centrality of academic skills in these areas, leads to pronounced differences in the utilization of this institutional practice.

In additional analysis we also explored whether school assisted job placement was more likely in vocational high schools and the extent to which this relationship varied by gender (results not shown in tables). Women in specialized vocational high schools were less likely than either women in regular high schools or men in specialized vocational high schools to receive school assisted job placement. Only 2.5 percent of women in vocational high schools received school assistance finding employment compared to 8.5 percent of women in regular high schools and 12.8 percent of men in vocational high schools. In high schools specializing in vocational training, school personnel concentrate on placing male students, the opposite of the pattern for regular high schools. Employers might recognize that: school personnel from vocational high schools are in a better position to assess the occupational competencies of male students specializing in narrowly focused trade-technical subjects than the general academic competencies of individuals preparing for clerical occupations; and school personnel from vocational high schools likely have more knowledge about trade-technical vocational students' occupational competencies than would corresponding staff members at comprehensive high schools.

In the post-secondary sample, slightly more individuals have received school assisted placement than in the high school sample, but this is primarily because of our alternative measurement technique which relies on measurement of multiple placement opportunities. Again, however, a similar pattern emerges with respect to gender and curricular content. Women again have nearly twice the rate of school assisted job placement compared to men: 21.7 percent of women with post-secondary experience have received placement assistance compared to 11.5 percent of men. As is the case at the secondary-level, women who have focused on business curriculum are particularly likely to utilize school assisted job placement. Nearly half of women who have earned post-secondary business degrees have received school assisted job placement: more than twice the rate of women who have not received such training and more than four times the rate of men in the post-secondary sample. Similar to the pattern in vocational secondary schools, vocational trade-technical post-secondary degrees for men are also related to an increased likelihood of school assisted job placement compared to other men (18.9 percent); however, the probability of school assistance is still no greater even than the average woman in the sample with no vocational training.

Table 8.1 also indicates the number of cases in each occupational curricular category by gender. Differences in number of cases in each cell demonstrate the well-known dissimilarity in male and female occupational course enrollment patterns.[37] Sex-segregation is pronounced in both high school and post-secondary programs. In high school trade-technical programs, only 1.6 percent of women have taken more than 10 percent coursework compared to 32.5 percent of men; in high school business programs, 60.1 percent of women have taken more than 10 percent coursework compared to 11.4 percent of men. In the post-secondary sample, 9.9 percent of women earned a business certificate compared to 1.8 percent of men, while only 0.3 percent of women earned a certificate in a trade-technical specialty compared to 9.2 percent of men.

Table 8.2 presents descriptive statistics on the percentage of students who found jobs in clerical occupations by school assisted job placement and vocational business curricular concentration. The top panel presents data on the high school sample and identifies the percentage of individuals who were in first jobs with clerical occupations; the bottom panel provides data from the post-secondary sample on the percentage of individuals whose most recent current job (as of four years out of high school) was in a clerical occupation. The results suggest that the labor market experiences of a recent cohort of students remain characterized by a pattern of occupational sex segregation with women greatly over-represented in clerical occupations. 31.5 percent of women who have no post-secondary educational experience compared to 5.3 percent of men find first jobs in clerical situations. In the post-secondary sample, 42.3 percent of women had jobs in clerical occupations four years after high school compared to only 10.3 percent of the men.

Women are significantly more likely to find first jobs after high school in clerical occupations if they take more business coursework or receive school assistance in finding employment. In the high school sample, 37.8 percent of women with 10 or more percent of business coursework in high school find first jobs after high school in clerical occupations compared to

Table 8.2 Percentage of students with jobs in clerical occupation by school assisted job placement, business course concentration or degree, and gender

High school sample	*Women*		*Men*	
Course concentration	*With school placement*	*Total. sample*	*With school placement*	*Total sample*
0–0.09	21.2% (25)	22.0% (589)	11.3% (94)	4.9% (1,859)
0.10+	66.5% (97)	37.8% (884)	7.2% (8)	8.5% (239)
Total	57.2% (122)	31.5% (1,473)	11.0% (102)	5.3% (2,098)

Post-secondary sample	*Women*		*Men*	
Post-secondary business degree	*With school placement*	*Total sample*	*With school placement*	*Total sample*
No	39.1% (221)	39.9% (1,170)	14.5% (113)	10.2% (989)
Yes	67.2%(61)	64.5% (129)	19.8% (2)	13.9% (18)
Total	45.1% (282)	42.3% (1,299)	14.6% (115)	10.3% (1,006)

Note
Percent current job clerical.
N in cell.

22.0 percent of women who take less than 10 percent occupational coursework. 57.2 percent of women who receive school assistance in placement for their initial jobs find employment in clerical occupations compared to 31.5 percent for the entire sample. The percentage of men who find first jobs in clerical occupations is not significantly affected by business coursework nor school assisted job placement.[38] Again, these findings suggest that school assisted job placement is structured by occupational and course sex-segregation.

A significantly different pattern emerges in the association between business curricular specialization, school assisted job placement and clerical employment in the post-secondary sample. While women who attain post-secondary business degrees are more likely to have received school assistance in locating a job, they are not dependent on that assistance for locating a job in a clerical field. Simply having earned a business degree is sufficient to produce a high likelihood of working in a clerical occupation.

The different role of school assisted job placement in facilitating the process of obtaining clerical employment for high school and sub-baccalaureate post-secondary students is worth emphasizing. For women who finish their education in high school, business coursework likely provides the skills necessary to increase the likelihood of clerical employment, but without the additional assistance of school services or personnel, clerical employment is still unlikely. In contrast, women with post-secondary business degrees have obtained both additional skills and a *credential* which is not dependent on further school assistance to signal workplace competencies.

Multivariate analysis

Multivariate analysis is used to identify the effects of school assisted job placement on individual-level labor market outcomes and the extent to which vocational education relies on this process to improve student labor market results. The appendix provides detailed results of Tobit regressions predicting the likelihood and duration of unemployment, as well as ordinary least square regression analysis of annual income, for individuals in their early years of labor market experience. 32.4 percent of women and 30.3 percent of men who had no post-secondary education reported being unemployed at one point during this time period, compared to 28.9 percent of women and 25.1 percent of men in the post-secondary sample.

Discussing first the results for the high school sample – the group most at risk for labor market failure – women taking greater amounts of business coursework during high school significantly reduce their unemployment. A 10 percent increase in business coursework reduces a woman's probability of unemployment during their early labor market experiences by 3.9 percent. A 10 percent increase in business coursework is also associated with a high school educated woman being unemployed approximately one half week less per year assuming she has ever experienced an unemployment spell. The magnitude of these effects can be assessed relative to the effects of high school graduation on male and female unemployment. A woman who completes high school reduces the probability of unemployment by 12 percent and the duration of unemployment by 1.7 weeks per year if ever unemployed; a male high school graduate reduces the probability of unemployment by 6 percent and the duration by 1.1 weeks per year if ever unemployed.[39]

A partial explanation for the effects of business coursework on reducing the likelihood of unemployment for women is due to the greater likelihood that women in these courses will receive assistance in locating their first jobs. Women who received a school assisted job placement after high school had a 15 percent lower probability of unemployment and were unemployed for 2.1 fewer weeks per year if ever unemployed.[40] While women who were employed in clerical first jobs have slightly lower rates of subsequent unemployment experiences, this factor is largely not responsible for the benefits of school assisted job placement. While high school work experience is not associated with lower risks of unemployment for women, post-high school work experience is an effective deterrent for this hazard. Women with an additional year of work experience in their first two years after high school, reduce their risk of subsequent unemployment by 6 percent and the duration of unemployment by 0.9 weeks per year if

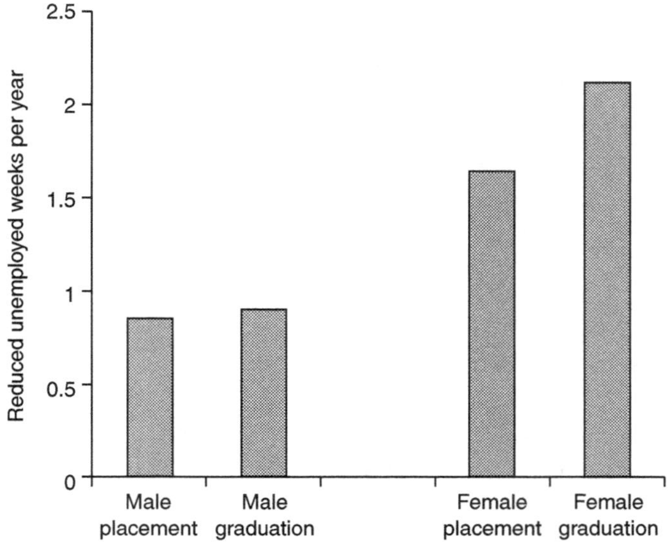

Figure 8.1 Effects of high school placement and graduation on unemployment.

Note
Results based on high school sample, Table 8.A.2, model 2.

ever unemployed. Post-high school work experience is also partially responsible for the benefits of both school assisted job placement and business coursework. The association of business coursework with job placement, clerical first job and the acquisition of early work experience, accounts for 30 percent of the initial positive effect of business coursework on female unemployment. For men, both high school and post-high school work experience reduce subsequent unemployment. Men with a year of high school work experience have a 14 percent lower probability of experiencing an unemployment spell and 1.4 fewer weeks per year unemployed if ever experiencing this state. Men with an additional year of post-high school work experience also reduce their risk of subsequent unemployment, but to a lesser degree.[41]

In the supplementary post-secondary analysis, less evidence exists of school effects on unemployment likelihood and duration. While prior work experience discourages unemployment for both men and women, only a few educational measures explain the variation in this limited sample. Women in the post-secondary sample have less unemployment if they were part of a rare group that experienced vocational trade-technical education or if they received a post-secondary certificate in health, cosmetology, or another occupational specialty other than that provided in traditional business and trade-technical vocational programs. Men in the

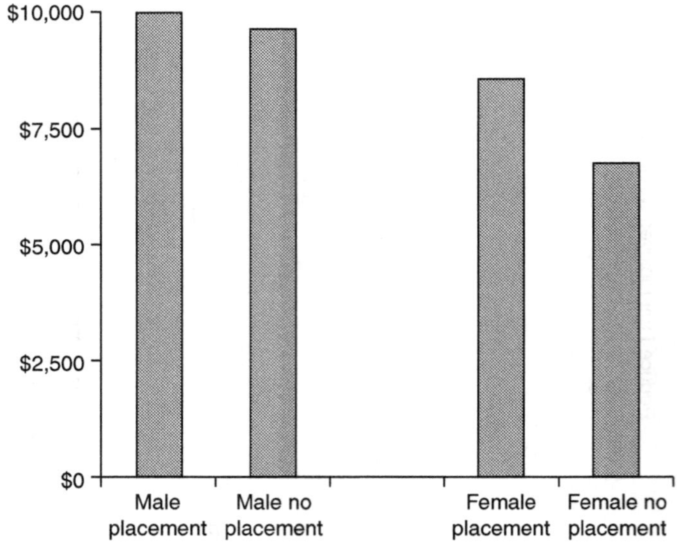

Figure 8.2 Earnings three years after high school (1985).

Note
Results based on high school sample, Table 8.A.3, model 2.

post-secondary sample had a reduced unemployment likelihood only if they had earned a junior college non-vocational degree in the two years immediately following high school. School assisted job placement is only marginally related to unemployment in this post-secondary sample.[42]

In terms of expected income for individuals who are in the most precarious position vis-à-vis the labor market, men in the high school sample who took vocational trade and technical coursework earned significantly higher incomes than their peers who neither continued on to college nor had this type of occupational training. Men with 20 percent trade and technical coursework made $10,700 in 1985 compared to $8,940 if they had taken no trade and technical coursework. Male and female high school graduates had significantly higher earnings than dropouts. Female high school graduates earned 20.3 percent more ($7,120 compared to $5,670); male high school graduates made 13.5 percent more ($9,920 compared to $8,580).[43]

Women in the high school sample who received their first job after high school with the use of school assisted job placement had significantly higher wages than otherwise ($8,560 compared to $6,760) – a 21.1 percent difference, roughly equivalent to the gap between female high school graduates and female high school dropouts. School assisted job placement, however, does not significantly affect male earnings. Women who find clerical employment in their first job after high school made considerably more than other women ($7,860 compared to $6,490). 19 percent of the effects of school assisted job placement are accounted for considering effects of a clerical first job. Men, however, do not gain relative to other men by being employed initially after high school in clerical occupations. Work experience during high school is related to increased annual earnings for men, but not women. Men who had a year of work experience while in high school increase their earnings three years out of high school from $8,940 to $9,840 (approximately 9 percent). Men are thus able to use high school work experience as a path to increased early labor market earnings. This mechanism is not available to women, who instead rely on school assisted job placement to support transition into the labor market.

Work experience after high school is clearly related to earnings for both men and women. A woman who has two years, instead of one year, work experience after high school increases her earnings from $6,430 to $7,890 (a man's earnings would increase from $8,580 to $10,060). This increase in work experience is largely responsible for the positive effects of school assisted job placement on women's earnings.[44] Women who receive school assisted job placement for their first post high school job end up with more post high school work experience, which employers in turn reward with higher wages and salaries. This finding is consistent with the results of the earlier Tobit regressions on unemployment: school assisted job placement reduces unemployment and thus contributes to labor market success.[45]

Gender differences in the effects of school assisted job placement on earnings are related to the association between high school assisted job placement and clerical first job. In unreported analysis, we explored this possibility by interacting clerical first job with school assisted job placement.[46] While the earlier presented descriptive statistics suggest that school assisted job placement is associated with roughly double the odds of attaining a clerical first job for both men and women (Table 8.2), school assisted job placement in clerical occupations has significantly different effects on male and female labor market outcomes. Given the structure of occupational sex segregation, the attainment of clerical jobs for women who do not pursue any post-secondary education is associated with higher earnings relative to other women; but such is not the case for men. In the context of these different relative rewards for the attainment of a clerical position, school assisted job placement of a male student in a clerical occupation is associated with significantly lower annual earnings compared to the earnings of other men.

Turning to the results for the post-secondary sample, a similar but slightly different pattern emerges. Women in the post-secondary sample receive higher earnings if they have received a post-secondary vocational business degree. Assuming mean values on other variables, a woman in the post-secondary sample without a vocational business degree will have earned $7,170 three years out of high school compared to $9,460 if she had earned such a degree. Adding school assisted job placement to the model accounts for approximately 20 percent of the original effect. School assisted job placement significantly improves the earnings of young women: a woman in the post-secondary sample earns approximately 20 percent more if she has received a school assisted job placement. Given the association among business certificates, school assisted job placement and clerical occupations (see Table 8.2), it is not surprising that adding clerical occupation to the model accounts for a portion of the positive effects of business coursework, but has no appreciable role in explaining the advantages school assisted job placement provide. While work experience does improve individual earnings, the effects of school assisted job placement, clerical occupation, and business degree are not accounted for by this inclusion.

Men in the post-secondary sample receive unclear rewards from school assisted job placement, but significant benefits from vocational curriculum. Men in the post-secondary sample have higher annual earnings from having taken vocational coursework in high school, suggesting the benefit of secondary vocational education articulation with further education at the post-secondary level. Men also receive significant benefit from earning a post-secondary trade-technical degree: earning approximately 22 percent more than otherwise. The benefits of secondary and post-secondary vocational curricular exposure in this sample are independent of either school assisted job placement or work experience.

Conclusions

Although school assisted job placements in the United States are utilized by only a small portion of students, it is a significant factor in structuring young adult labor market outcomes. School assisted job placement provides female high school graduates who immediately enter the workforce with higher initial earnings and reduced unemployment than women who did not take advantage of these services. In addition, school assisted job placement is associated with higher earnings for women with sub-baccalaureate post-secondary educations. While male students receive modest labor market benefits from high school trade-technical vocational coursework as well as post-secondary trade-technical certificates, these effects are largely unrelated to school assisted job placement.

We believe that men are largely not affected by school assisted job placement because of the different skill demands employers make of men and women in an occupational structure characterized by profound sex segregation.[47] We speculate that entry-level jobs for male high school graduates are usually concentrated in occupations that require less mastery of basic academic skills, such as English and mathematics, and instead demand more job-specific occupational proficiencies. Female high school graduates, however, face an occupational structure which demands and rewards greater competency in general academic skills (e.g. requirements of English mastery for clerical occupations and mathematics for retail occupations). It is probable that there are corresponding differences in coursework: closer pedagogical links likely exist between academic subject matter and business coursework than between academic subject matter and trade and technical coursework. As James Rosenbaum and Amy Binder's research on employers' relationship with high school students suggests: firms that do not need employees with academic skills seldom develop close linkages with schools. Thus for women who have taken business coursework in high school, school assisted job placement becomes particularly important. For men, school assisted job placement is less useful or possibly even detrimental when male students receive assistance in finding employment in clerical occupations where women are concentrated.

Theoretically, the work suggests the importance of recent theorizing about the significance of school-employer institutional relationships. This earlier work, however, gave little attention to the possibility that the importance of institutional relationships might vary by gender. Since women have fewer occupationally related network connections and more often rely on formal channels to obtain employment, institutional assistance in obtaining employment for female students is particularly useful and important. Employers again also have greater interest in school assessment of candidates' academic abilities for clerical jobs.

The results demonstrate the important role school assisted job placement can have in the success of vocational business programs, but also suggests possible limitations to reliance on these practices. Recent efforts to revitalize vocational education have emphasized the significance of institutional relationships by advocating formation of school-employer partnerships.[48] If one seeks to emulate the success of vocational education in Germany and elsewhere, strengthening school-employer institutional relationships with greater use of school assisted job placement can, under certain limited conditions, improve student labor market transitions.

While our analysis does not directly address issues of race and class, the results of this study and others suggest that school-business ties may be particularly advantageous for minority groups that have historically been disadvantaged in the labor force. Several factors lead to this conclusion. First, although our findings only show school-business linkages to have benefits for women, there is evidence of more far reaching effects. A recent qualitative study by James Rosenbaum and colleagues demonstrates that trade and technical employers also use and benefit from business-school ties.[49] Second, when these linkages are present, employers may be more willing to hire individuals who do not fit their preconceived notions of good employees. Rosenbaum's study also found that employers hesitant to hire female and minority students are more likely to do so when they are recommended by trusted vocational teachers. Third, research suggests that members of these groups have fewer network-based resources to utilize when searching for a job. In addition to less valuable personal contacts, female and minority students have fewer work related ties. White and male high school students are more likely to work during high school, building up both experience and future contacts. Given the amount of time students spend in school, school personnel are in a good position both to supply employers with information and to supplement or provide students with these valuable network connections.

Because of their educational attainment level, most of the students who are the focus of this study are economically vulnerable. This is particularly true for the high school only sub-sample. While certain groups of students may benefit more or less from school-business ties, school assisted job placement has the potential to assist all of these work-bound youth. In our sample, school assisted job placement is associated with business coursework and clerical occupations. Productive school-business ties could also be encouraged in trade-technical occupations as well, particularly if schools were able to demonstrate credible assessment of student competencies in these areas. Regardless of this possibility, our results clearly indicate that non-curricular factors are implicated in school-to-work outcomes. Students from economically disadvantaged backgrounds, who historically have frequently been exposed to vocational coursework, are dependent to a large degree on factors such as who their teachers know and what businesses their schools have relationships with, when attempting to make successful school-to-work transitions. This recognition highlights the extent to which family and institutional mechanisms – that operate "after the bell" and outside of a student's direct control – structure the effects of schooling.

Appendix

Our analysis of the role of school assisted job placement in determining subsequent occupational outcomes utilizes data from the High School and Beyond (HSB) survey, a national longitudinal study of high school seniors and sophomores. The HSB is a two-stage stratified probability sample, with 1,122 high schools selected to include an oversampling of various racial categories and school types. The original survey contains educational and occupational data, including transcript records and school level information, on a subsample of 14,825 students who were sophomores in 1980. We focus our analysis on the school-to-work transitions of the most vulnerable young adults: individuals who either completed their education in high school or have only limited sub-baccalaureate post-secondary education beyond high school. It is these individuals who are at the highest risk for early labor market failure.

We divide the sub-baccalaureate population into two separate analyses for both conceptual and methodological reasons. Theoretically, we focus attention specifically on those who end their education with high school, because they have the fewest resources to draw on when making school-to-work transitions. Methodologically, we analyze those who have completed their education in high school separately, since they make only one clearly defined school-to-work transition – i.e. they make a distinct transition from school to first job after high school. For those individuals who have post-secondary educational experience, there are often multiple school-to-work transitions. An analysis of a similar cohort in the National Longitudinal Study of Youth found that almost half of individuals who had completed two years of post-secondary education had made two or more school-to-work transitions.[50] In addition, once individuals attend post-secondary institutions they have the ability to rely on more than one school for assistance in finding employment. For the post-secondary sample, HSB does not allow accurate identification of which school has actually assisted a student with finding employment.

We analyze data in a high school sample of only those individuals with a high school diploma or less, who report no post-secondary schooling in the four years immediately following high school. There are 3,571 cases that meet these criteria and, because of their limited educational attainment, face the greatest challenge in successfully making school-to-work transitions. For this high school sample, we are able to identify precisely whether school assistance was utilized by students when locating their first job after high school. In addition, we are also able to identify the occupational characteristics of the first job they have attained after school. HSB is the only nationally representative dataset that provides detailed records of high school coursework, early labor market experience, and job search method. We provide a supplementary analysis of an additional 2,303 individuals who have enrolled in post-secondary education between June 1982 and August 1984 (slightly two years after on-time completion of high school), but who are not enrolled in school between September 1984 and March 1986. This supplementary analysis, because of the methodological reasons specified above, relies on a broader operationalization of school assisted job placement. For the post-secondary sample where individuals have often made more than one school-to-work transition: we operationalize school assisted job placement not solely for initial job, but at any time during respondent's early labor market experience; and we examine the occupational characteristics of jobs roughly four years after high school. Our two samples combine to include 5,874 individuals, slightly less than half of the original HSB cohort. Weights are included to account for oversampling in the HSB dataset. Table 8.A.1 provides descriptive statistics on all variables used in the analyses. To identify gender differences in the effects of school assisted job placement on occupational outcomes, separate analysis is conducted for men and women.

Our analysis proceeds in three steps. First, to establish the utilization of school assisted job placement in vocational programs, we present in the text of the chapter descriptive statistics identifying: the relationship between occupational coursework and the likelihood that an individual received school assisted job placement; and the association between business coursework, school assisted job placement, and obtaining clerical employment. Second, we present in Table 8.A.2 and discuss in the text of the chapter, results from Tobit regressions on percent of time unemployed. The Tobit regression provides estimates of effects, which simultaneously account for both the likelihood of an unemployment spell during this period and the duration of unemployment for those ever experiencing this state. We analyze Tobit results based on methodology suggested by McDonald and Moffit (1980) and Roncek (1992). We measure unemployment from March 1984 to March 1986 for the high school sample, roughly between two to four years after typical high school graduation; for the post-secondary sample, we measure unemployment from September 1984 to March 1986 to allow individuals two full years and a summer to complete their post-secondary education. Based on the number of observations of unemployment which are non-zero, the Tobit model calculates estimates based on the assumption that for the high school sample 73 percent of the effect of variables for women and 80 percent for men is associated with the likelihood of experiencing any unemployment spell; while in the post-secondary sample, the Tobit model assumes that 75 percent of the effect of variables for women and 77 percent for men operates on the likelihood of unemployment spell (see Roncek 1992 for description of the methodology used in this calculation). Third, we show in Table 8.A.3 and discuss in the text of the chapter results from O.L.S. regressions on self-reported 1985 annual earnings (logged). Individuals who report positive earnings and are not self-employed are included in our analysis. We examine 1985 earnings, rather than wages of initial job, because the former is a better indicator of significant and lasting variation in labor market experiences.

Regressions on unemployment and earnings are each run four ways. All models control for the effects of individual background, school characteristics, social context, family status at time of outcome measure, cognitive ability and educational experience (due to space limitations, we only report and discuss the set of variables on educational experience).[51] Analysis of the high school sample measures educational experience as high school graduation and the percentage of business and trade-technical coursework taken in high school;[52] in the post-secondary sample, we examine educational experience by incorporating measures of the highest level of post-secondary educational enrollment (junior college or four year college) and specific degree or certificate earned (business, trade-technical, other vocational, and junior college non vocational). Model 1 thus gives a baseline indication of the effects of the main types of occupational coursework on labor market outcomes. Model 2 then adds to Model 1 a variable measuring school assisted job placement. This second model thus identifies both the effects of school assisted job placement on early labor market outcomes and the extent to which the effects of occupational coursework are attributable to the school's assisting a student in finding employment. Model 3 adds to Model 2 a variable measuring whether the individual obtained a clerical occupation (again for the high school sample this is measured for first job after high school; in the supplementary post-secondary analysis, it is measured to coincide with the labor market outcomes analyzed). As noted above, clerical occupations have significantly lower unemployment rates than many other occupations. Model 3 thus indicates whether positive effects of school assisted job placement are simply the result of respondent's finding employment in a clerical occupation – i.e. a job with more employment stability. Lastly, Model 4 adds to Model 3 measures of work experience, thus identifying the degree to which the effects of school assisted job placement on labor market outcomes is related to an increase in the overall amount of an individual's work experience. Control variables with missing values are assigned mean values with additional dummy variables included in the model when a substitution was made.

Independent variables

School assisted job placement is measured by self-reports of whether respondents report "school employment or placement service" used as a method to find their first job after high school (or any job for the supplementary analysis of the post-secondary sample). While a few respondents who reported finding a job through school assisted job placement may have been informally referred by a teacher or school counselor, the use of "service" in the wording of the response choice suggests the use of more formal avenues such as a placement office. Other possible responses were public employment service, private employment agency, newspaper advertisement, checked with employer directly, through a relative, through a friend, civil service application, and other.

We refer in the text to school *assisted* job placement because specific details on the actual system of placement are unavailable in the dataset. At times, school assistance might be as limited as simply providing students with the names of potential employers. It is likely, however, that if the data provided greater specification of placement type, more formal and elaborated systems of placement would produce even larger effects than those identified in our research. Ambiguities in the definition of school assisted job placement in this study thus likely yield an under-estimation of the effects of placement systems which actually rely on more formalized school-employer institutional ties.

Two variables for high school occupational coursework are included in the analysis. Each variable refers to classes taken in one of the two most common areas of vocational training, business or trade-technical, and is measured as a ratio of coursework in that area to total high school coursework. Business and trade-technical vocational coursework are the two vocational program areas where previous research has identified positive occupational outcomes associated with student enrollment.[53] The student's coursework profile was obtained from high school transcript records: HSB course codes 6.0000–8.9999 were coded as *business coursework*; HSB course codes 46.0000–49.9999 were considered *trade-technical coursework*. Post-secondary occupational coursework was measured as the attainment of a vocational degree or certificate in similarly defined curricular areas (transcript data was used if available, otherwise we relied on respondent self-reports). In addition, high school graduation is measured for the high school sample; for the post-secondary sample, we measure enrollment in the higher of junior or four year college.

The variable *clerical first job* indicates whether the first job out of high school was in a clerical position; for the post-secondary analysis, the variable *clerical occupation* was measured simultaneously to the other labor market outcomes. Self-reported occupations for first job were coded according to 1970 U.S. census occupation codes.

Work experience is measured both as high school work experience and, work experience after high school but prior to the measure of unemployment and earnings. *High school work experience* is a measure of the years that a respondent worked 30 hours or more a week while attending high school. Previous research demonstrates that high school work experience is associated with higher earnings and lower unemployment in early labor market outcomes.[54] *Work experience to 1984* is based on self reports of years of work experience after high school until the start of our measurement of the possibility of unemployment spell. *Work experience to 1985* is based on years of work after high school through the end of 1984 and is used in regressions on 1985 annual earnings.

Table 8.A.1 Descriptive statistics on variables by gender for high school and post-secondary samples

	Women				*Men*			
	High school		*Post-secondary*		*High school*		*Post-secondary*	
	Mean	*S.D.*	*Mean*	*S.D.*	*Mean*	*S.D.*	*Mean*	*S.D.*
Educational experiences								
Trade-tech. coursework in high school	0.009	0.023	0.008	0.019	0.083	0.085	0.065	0.073
Business coursework in high school	0.123	0.087	0.113	0.078	0.042	0.049	0.053	0.052
High school graduate	0.857	0.352			0.798	0.418		
Junior college enrollment			0.399	0.490			0.411	0.493
Four year college enrollment			0.258	0.438			0.242	0.429
Junior college non-vocational degree			0.042	0.200			0.037	0.190
Other post-sec. vocational degree or certificate			0.145	0.353			0.061	0.239
Trade-tech. post-sec. vocational degree/certificate			0.002	0.049			0.092	0.290
Business post-sec. vocational degree/certificate			0.099	0.299			0.018	0.132
Intervening mechanisms								
School assisted job placement first job	0.083	0.277			0.049	0.224		
School assisted job placement any job			0.217	0.412			0.115	0.319
Clerical first job	0.315	0.467			0.053	0.233		
Clerical occupation (current)			0.424	0.495			0.103	0.304
High school work experience	0.275	0.372	0.185	0.337	0.430	0.479	0.313	0.452
Work experience after high school (prior to 1985)	1.338	0.864	1.057	0.716	1.726	1.139	1.232	0.852
Work experience after high school (prior to 1984)	0.861	0.855	0.575	0.716	1.232	1.135	0.740	0.849
Dependent variables								
Annual earnings (logged)[a]	8.838	0.807	8.905	0.880	9.173	0.812	9.160	0.900
Percent of months unemployed	0.075	0.163	0.055	0.134	0.062	0.137	0.056	0.136
	N = 1,473		N = 1,298		N = 2,098		N = 1,005	

Note

a Percent missing on variable: 39.2, high school women; 19.8, post-secondary women; 24.3, high school men; 12.1, post-secondary men.

Table 8.A.2 Tobit regression of school assisted job placement and other variables on percent of months unemployed by gender

High school sample	*Women (N = 1,473)*				*Men* (N = *2,098)*			
	(1)	*(2)*	*(3)*	*(4)*	*(1)*	*(2)*	*(3)*	*(4)*
Sigma	0.340**	0.339**	0.339**	0.335**	0.313**	0.312**	0.312**	0.308**
	(0.013)	(0.013)	(0.013)	(0.012)	(0.010)	(0.010)	(0.010)	(0.009)
High school graduate	−0.114**	−0.108**	−0.108**	−0.130**	−0.071**	−0.069**	−0.069**	−0.075**
	(0.036)	(0.036)	(0.036)	(0.036)	(0.023)	(0.023)	(0.023)	(0.023)
Trade coursework	0.343	0.271	0.273	0.254	−0.001	−0.002	−0.002	0.022
	(0.486)	(0.485)	(0.486)	(0.482)	(0.104)	(0.104)	(0.104)	(0.103)
Business coursework	−0.371**	−0.327*	−0.294*	−0.258	−0.071	−0.069	−0.068	−0.058
	(0.137)	(0.138)	(0.139)	(0.138)	(0.186)	(0.186)	(0.186)	(0.185)
School assisted job placement		**−0.140****	**−0.129****	**−0.105***		**−0.065**	**−0.064**	**−0.048**
		(0.047)	**(0.048)**	**(0.047)**		**(0.042)**	**(0.042)**	**(0.042)**
Clerical first job			−0.043	−0.047			−0.001	−0.017
			(0.026)	(0.025)			(0.038)	(0.038)
Work experience to 1984				−0.060**				−0.018*
				(0.016)				(0.009)
High school work experience				−0.019				−0.125**
				(0.033)				(0.021)

Post-secondary sample

	Women (N = 1,298)				*Men (N = 1,005)*			
	(1)	*(2)*	*(3)*	*(4)*	*(1)*	*(2)*	*(3)*	*(4)*
Sigma	0.315**	0.314**	0.314**	0.313**	0.329**	0.329**	0.328**	0.324**
	(0.013)	(0.013)	(0.013)	(0.013)	(0.017)	(0.017)	(0.017)	(0.017)
Trade-tech. coursework in	−1.385*	−1.351*	−1.353*	−1.279	−0.253	−0.248	−0.248	−0.197
high school	(0.668)	(0.666)	(0.664)	(0.662)	(0.215)	(0.215)	(0.214)	(0.213)
Business coursework in	−0.114	−0.102	−0.089	−0.077	0.010	0.044	0.003	0.026
high school	(0.152)	(0.153)	(0.153)	(0.153)	(0.282)	(0.284)	(0.285)	(0.285)
Junior college enrollment	−0.011	−0.012	−0.010	−0.014	0.064	0.061	0.056	0.058
	(0.029)	(0.029)	(0.029)	(0.029)	(0.036)	(0.036)	(0.036)	(0.036)
Four year college enrollment	−0.021	−0.019	−0.017	−0.026	0.017	0.015	0.010	0.001
	(0.033)	(0.033)	(0.033)	(0.033)	(0.042)	(0.042)	(0.042)	(0.042)
Other post-sec. vocational	−0.110**	−0.107**	−0.111**	−0.116**	−0.028	−0.016	−0.015	−0.009
degree/certificate	(0.040)	(0.040)	(0.040)	(0.040)	(0.070)	(0.071)	(0.070)	(0.070)
Junior college non-vocational	−0.102	−0.099	−0.099	−0.109	−0.260**	−0.262**	−0.257**	−0.275**
degree	(0.068)	(0.068)	(0.068)	(0.067)	(0.098)	(0.098)	(0.098)	(0.098)
Trade-tech. post-sec.	0.423	−0.420	−0.426	−0.433	−0.004	−0.001	0.008	−0.001
vocational degree/certificate	(0.405)	(0.410)	(0.407)	(0.397)	(0.053)	(0.053)	(0.053)	(0.052)
Business post-sec. vocational	−0.006	0.002	0.008	−0.009	0.054	0.055	0.060	0.059
degree/certificate	(0.040)	(0.040)	(0.041)	(0.041)	(0.093)	(0.094)	(0.093)	(0.092)
School assisted job placement		**−0.028**	**−0.029**	**−0.032**		**−0.052**	**−0.055**	**−0.058**
		(0.029)	**(0.029)**	**(0.029)**		**(0.048)**	**(0.048)**	**(0.048)**
Clerical occupation			−0.025	−0.025			0.080	0.058
			(0.024)	(0.024)			(0.046)	(0.046)
High school work experience				0.014				−0.038
				(0.037)				(0.037)
Work experience after				−0.044*				−0.042*
high school (prior to 1984)				(0.019)				(0.019)

Notes

All models include controls for individual characteristics, family status and school/social context.

* $p < 0.05$; ** $p < 0.01$.

Table 8.A.3 O.L.S. regression of school assisted job placement and other variables on 1985 annual earnings by gender

High school sample	*Women (N=1,473)*				*Men (N=2,098)*			
	(1)	*(2)*	*(3)*	*(4)*	*(1)*	*(2)*	*(3)*	*(4)*
High school graduate	0.227*	0.221*	0.202*	0.279**	0.145**	0.144**	0.144**	0.211**
	(0.096)	(0.096)	(0.096)	(0.096)	(0.053)	(0.053)	(0.053)	(0.053)
Trade coursework	−0.001	0.127	0.112	0.040	0.895**	0.895**	0.886**	0.858**
	(1.152)	(1.149)	(1.142)	(1.113)	(0.241)	(0.241)	(0.241)	(0.235)
Business coursework	0.088	0.010	−0.168	−0.220	0.489	0.491	0.505	0.307
	(0.317)	(0.318)	(0.320)	(0.312)	(0.406)	(0.407)	(0.407)	(0.398)
School assisted job placement		**0.237***	**0.192***	**0.087**		**0.036**	**0.040**	**−0.029**
		(0.095)	**(0.096)**	**(0.094)**		**(0.090)**	**(0.090)**	**(0.088)**
Clerical first job			0.192**	0.217**			−0.054	0.020
			(0.057)	(0.056)			(0.083)	(0.081)
High school work experience				0.179*				0.144**
				(0.078)				(0.042)
Work experience after high school (prior to 1985)				0.169**				0.146**
				(0.034)				(0.020)
R^2	0.142	0.149	0.160	0.204	0.125	0.125	0.125	0.172

Post-secondary sample

	Women (N = 1,041)				*Men (N = 882)*			
	(1)	*(2)*	*(3)*	*(4)*	*(1)*	*(2)*	*(3)*	*(4)*
Trade-tech. coursework in high school	1.810 (1.580)	1.601 (1.575)	1.830 (1.564)	1.806 (1.550)	1.525** (0.431)	1.516** (0.431)	1.513** (0.431)	1.329** (0.427)
Business coursework in high school	0.349 (0.355)	0.288 (0.354)	0.176 (0.353)	0.123 (0.350)	1.419* (0.603)	1.313* (0.607)	1.278* (0.609)	1.337* (0.601)
Junior college enrollment	−0.026 (0.069)	−0.017 (0.069)	−0.040 (0.068)	−0.040 (0.068)	0.133 (0.075)	0.147 (0.075)	0.142 (0.075)	0.145 (0.075)
Four year college enrollment	0.062 (0.077)	0.058 (0.077)	0.037 (0.076)	0.065 (0.076)	0.128 (0.087)	0.134 (0.087)	0.131 (0.087)	0.168 (0.086)
Junior college non-vocational degree	0.102 (0.134)	0.071 (0.134)	0.088 (0.133)	0.146 (0.132)	0.088 (0.163)	0.075 (0.163)	0.081 (0.163)	0.143 (0.161)
Other post-sec. vocational degree/certificate	0.052 (0.084)	0.045 (0.083)	0.083 (0.083)	0.101 (0.082)	−0.042 (0.131)	−0.075 (0.133)	−0.075 (0.133)	−0.087 (0.132)
Trade-tech. vocational post-sec. degree/certificate	0.546 (0.594)	0.389 (0.594)	0.490 (0.590)	0.653 (0.585)	0.219* (0.111)	0.206 (0.111)	0.213 (0.112)	0.258* (0.111)
Business vocational post-sec. degree/certificate	0.277** (0.090)	0.222* (0.092)	0.172 (0.092)	0.188* (0.091)	0.230 (0.218)	0.230 (0.217)	0.232 (0.218)	0.246 (0.214)
School assisted job placement		**0.202**** **(0.066)**	**0.200**** **(0.065)**	**0.221**** **(0.065)**		**0.136** **(0.094)**	**0.132** **(0.094)**	**0.138** **(0.094)**
Clerical occupation			0.224** (0.054)	0.229** (0.054)			0.073 (0.099)	0.129 (0.098)
High school work experience				0.144 (0.088)				0.155* (0.072)
Work experience after high school (prior to 1985)				0.144** (0.042)				0.143** (0.040)
R^2	0.133	0.141	0.156	0.174	0.107	0.109	0.109	0.137

Notes
All models include controls for individual characteristics, family status and school/social context.
* $p < 0.05$; ** $p < 0.01$.

Notes

1 Earlier versions of this manuscript were presented at the After the Bell Education Solutions Outside the School Conference, Jerome Levy Institute, Bard College (June 2001); the School-to-Work Conference, University of Washington (July 2000); and the International Sociology Association's Meeting of the Research Committee on Social Stratification, Montreal, Canada (July 1998). During the time of research financial support for the first and second authors was provided by the National Academy of Education Spencer Postdoctoral and Dissertation Fellowship programs (respectively). Address correspondence to Richard Arum, Department of Sociology, New York University, 269 Mercer – 4th Floor, New York, NY 10003–6687 (e-mail: richard.arum@nyu.edu).

2 For example, Alexander and Entwisle find that during the summer when children are not in school lower socioeconomic children academically fall behind their higher socioeconomic peers. During the school year, schools help to reduce this inequality. (K. Alexander and D. Entwisle, *Family-School Links: How Do They Affect Educational Outcomes*, Mahwah, NJ: Lawrence Erlbaum Associates, 1996, 67–88.) In contrast, Bourdieu and Lareau discuss how schools reinforce inequalities by rewarding middle class values, culture and knowledge. (P. Bourdieu, *Reproduction in Education, Society and Culture*, Beverly Hills, CA: Sage, 1977). Finally, the Coleman report's finding that much variation in student achievement is attributable to family background and student composition of the school led many researchers to conclude that school curriculum and resources did not have much effect on student achievement. (J. Coleman, E. Campbell, C. Hobson, J. McPartland, A. Mood, F. Weinfeld, and R. York, *Equality of Educational Opportunity*, Washington DC: U.S. Government Printing Office, 1966.)

3 One of the most well known critiques of high school tracking is Jeannie Oakes examination of 300 high school English and mathematics classes. (J. Oakes, *Keeping Track: How Schools Structure Inequality*, New Haven, CT: Yale University Press, 1985.) See Bowles and Gintis for a theoretical argument for how schools prepare youth from low socioeconomic circumstance for lower level work. Also see Gamoran and Berends for general review of tracking literature. (S. Bowles and H. Gintis, *Schooling in Capitalist America*, New York, NY: Basic Books, 1976; Gamoran, A. and Berends, M. "The effects of stratification in secondary schools: synthesis of survey and ethnographic research," *Review of Educational Research* 57, 1987, 415–435.)

4 A. Gamoran and R. Mare, "Secondary school tracking and educational inequality: reinforcement, compensation, or neutrality?," *American Journal of Sociology* 94, 1989, 1146–1183; J. Oakes, A. Gamoran, and R. Page, *Handbook of Research on Curriculum*, New York, NY: Macmillan, 1992, 570 –608.

5 See Schneider and Stevenson for evidence and discussion regarding the mismatch between adolescents' rising educational and occupational ambitions and the odds of success. (B. Schneider and D. Stevenson, *The Ambitious Generation*, New Haven, CT: Yale University Press, 1999.)

6 This finding was based on an analysis of 14,700 high school students surveyed for High School and Beyond, a longitudinal study conducted by the National Center for Education Statistics. (J. Rosenbaum, *Beyond College for All: Career Paths for the Forgotton Half*, New York, NY: Russell Sage Foundation, 2001.)

7 For examples of critiques see F. Frazier, *Transition from School to Work: Linking Education and WorksiteTraining,* Washington, DC: General Accounting Office; GAO/HRD, 1991, 91–105; William T. Grant Foundation (1988); and J. Grasso and J. Shea, *Vocational Education and Training: Impact on Youth*, Berkeley, CA: The Carnegie Foundation for the Advancement of Teaching,

1979. Paradoxically, U.S. schools are also criticized by social reproduction theorists for their effectiveness at channeling working class students into working class jobs (see e.g. S. Bowles and H. Gintis, *Schooling in Capitalist America*, New York, NY: Basic Books, 1976.)

8 For discussion of these types of institutional relationships see Olson, and Stern, Raby and Dayton (L. Olson, *The School-to-Work Revolution: How Employers and Educators are Joining Forces to Prepare Tomorrow's Skilled Workforce,* Reading, MA: Perseus Book, 1997; D. Stern, M. Raby, and C. Dayton, *Career Academies: Partnerships for Restructuring American High Schools,* San Francisco, CA: Jossey Bass, 1992).

9 Secretary's Commission on Achieving Necessary Skills (1991). This argument has also been advanced by individual authors such as William J. Wilson and the former Secretary of Labor, Robert Reich (W. Wilson, *When Work Disappears: The World of the New Urban Poor*, New York, NY: Vintage, 1996; R. Reich, *The Work of Nations*, New York, NY: Vintage Books, 1991.)

10 See H. Holzer, *What Employers Want: Job Prospects for Less Educated Workers*, New York, NY: Russell Sage, 1996.

11 For discussions of the positive effects of vocational education see A. Kerkhoff and L. Bell, "Hidden capital: vocational credentials and attainment in the United States," *Sociology of Education* 71, 1998, 152–174; R. Arum and M. Hout, *Educational Qualifications and Occupational Destinations,* Cambridge, MA: Oxford University Press, 1997; N. Grubb, "The long-run effects of proprietary schools on wages and earnings: implications for federal policy," *Educational Evaluation and Policy Analysis* 15, 1993, 17–33; N. Grubb, "Postsecondary vocational education and the sub-baccalaureate labor market: new evidence on economic returns," *Economics of Education Review* 11, 1992, 225–248; S. Kang and J. Bishop, "Vocational or academic coursework in high school: compliments or substitutes?," *Economics of Education Review* 8, 1989; R. Rumberger and T. Daymont, *Youth and the Labor Market: Analysis of the National Longitudinal Survey,* Kalamazoo, MI: W. E. Upjohn Institute for Employment Research, 1984; R. Arum and Y. Shavit, "Secondary vocational education and the transition from school to work," *Sociology of Education* 68, 1995, 187–204; L. Hotchkiss and L. Dorsten, "Curriculum effects on early post-high school outcomes," *Research in the Sociology of Education and Socialization* 7, 1987, 191–219; E. Woods and W. Haney, *Does Vocational Education Make a Difference? A Review of Previous Research and Reanalyses of National Longitudinal Data Sets,* Washington, DC: National Institute of Education, 1981; J. Grasso and J. Shea, *Vocational Education and Training: Impact on Youth*, Berkeley, CA: The Carnegie Foundation for the Advancement of Teaching, 1979.

12 Studies that have found positive outcomes of post-secondary vocational education include Kerkhoff and Bell, Dougherty (1994) and Grubb. (A. Kerkhoff and L. Bell, "Hidden capital: vocational credentials and attainment in the United States," *Sociology of Education* 71, 1998, 152–174; Grubb, op. cit.)

13 W. Mueller and Y. Shavit, *Educational Qualifications and Occupational Destinations,* Cambridge, MA: Oxford University Press, 1997.

14 For discussion of school to work transitions in Japan see Rosenbaum and Kariya and in Germany see Hamilton and Hurrelmann and Vickers (1995). (J. Rosenbaum and T. Kariya, "From high school to work: market and institutional mechanisms in Japan," *American Journal of Sociology* 94, 1989, 1334–1366; S. Hamilton and K. Hurrelmann, "The school-to-career transition in Germany and the United States," *Teachers College Record* 96, 1994, 329–344.)

15 For examples and discussion of United States partnerships see N. Maxwell

and V. Rubin, *Improving the Transition from School to Work: Assessing the Impact of Old and New Strategies,* Kalamazoo, MI: W. E. Upjohn Institute for Employment Research, 1998; D. Stern, M. Raby, and C. Dayton, *Career Academies: Partnerships for Restructuring American High Schools,* San Francisco, CA: Jossey Bass, 1992; R. Poczik, *Learning to Work: Employer Involvement in School-to-Work Transition Programs,* Washington, DC: Brookings, 1995.

16 W. Mueller and Y. Shavit, *Educational Qualifications and Occupational Destinations,* Cambridge, MA: Oxford University Press, 1997; researchers from a "new" institutionalist perspective, such as Scott and Meyer, argue that public schools are situated in a common organizational field with little variation in public school outcomes. In this paper, the institutionalist label is used to refer to an alternative institutional approach which focuses attention on variation in the environment of schools as organizations. (R. Scott and J. Meyer, "Environmental linkages and organizational complexities: public and private schools," in James and Levin (eds) *Comparing Public and Private Schools, Vol. I: Institutions and Organizations*, Brighton: Falmer Press, 1988, 128–52.)

17 See J. Rosenbaum, T. Kariya, R. Settersten, and T. Maier, "Market and network theories of the transition from high school to work," *Annual Review of Sociology* 16, 1990, 263–299 for a thorough review of theories associated with organizational linkeages.

18 For examples of when organizations may not be rational see DiMaggio and Powell (1991) and P. England and G. Farkas, *Industries, Firms and Jobs*, New York, NY: Aldine de Gruyter, 1988. For discussion of lower transactions costs and reducing uncertainty during the hiring process see Williamson and March and Olson, respectively. (P. England and G. Farkas, *Industries, Firms and Jobs*, New York, NY: Aldine de Gruyter, 1988; O. Williamson, *Markets and Hierarchies: Analysis and Antitrust Implications*, New York, NY: Free Press, 1975; J. March and J. Olson, *Ambiguity and Choice in Organizations*, New York, NY: Oxford University Press, 1980).

19 W. Powell, "Neither market nor heirarchy: network forms of organization," *Research in Organizational Behavior* 12, 1990, 304.

20 M. Granovetter, "The strength of weak ties," *American Journal of Sociology* 78, 1973, 1360–1380.

21 J. Kirschenman and K. Neckerman, "'We'd love to hire them, but ...': the meaning of race for employers," in C. Jencks and P. Peterson, *The Urban Underclass.* Washington, DC: Brookings Institute, 1991.

22 Rosenbaum and Binder excluded secondary labor market firms, such as restaurants and small stores, which hire youth for low wage jobs with no opportunities for advancement. (J. Rosenbaum and A. Binder, "Do employers really need more educated youth?," *Sociology of Education* 70, 1997, 68–85.)

23 J. Rosenbaum and A. Binder, "Do employers really need more educated youth?," *Sociology of Education* 70, 1997, 78.

24 For a review of the literature on job search and network ties see Granovetter, afterward. Also for research on differential returns see Elliott for class and Way for gender. (M. Granovetter, *Getting a Job* (2nd edn), Chicago, IL: University of Chicago Press, 1995; J. Elliott, "Class, race, and job matching in contemporary urban labor markets," *Social Science Quarterly* 81, 2000, 1036–1052; S. Way, "Gender and job search methods: the effects of high school job placement services on the school-to-work transition," paper presented at American Sociological Association Meetings, San Francisco, CA, August 1998.

25 Rosenbaum and colleagues qualitative study of vocational teachers indicates that many teachers maintain trusted ties with employers in their field. These teachers also spend significant time with students who are potential employees.

26 N. Grubb, T. Dickinson, L. Giordano, and G. Kaplan, *Betwixt and Between:*

Education, Skills and Employment in Sub-Baccalaurate Labor Markets, Berkeley, CA: National Center for Research in Vocational Education, 1992, 44–46.

27 Collins provides a detailed discussion of how educational degrees grant individuals access to certain occupations. (R. Collins, *The Credential Society: A Historical Sociology of Education and Stratification,* New York, NY: Academy Press, 1979.)

28 For overview of the use of informal channels in job search see Granovetter afterward. For additional information on gender difference in networks see, Corcoran, Datcher, and Duncan, Fischer and Oliker, Moore. (M. Granovetter, *Getting a Job (2nd ed.)*, Chicago, IL: University of Chicago Press, 1995; M. Corcoran, L. Datcher, and G. Duncan, "Information and influence networks in labor markets," *Five Thousand American Families: Patterns of Economic Progress* 7, 1980, 1–37; C. Fischer, and S. Oliker, "A research note on friendship, gender, and the life cycle," *Social Forces* 62, 1983, 124–133; G. Moore, "Structural determinants of men's and women's personal networks," *American Sociological Review* 55, 1990, 726–735.)

29 H. Holzer, *What Employers Want: Job Prospects for Less Educated Workers*, New York, NY: Russell Sage, 1996, 50–88.

30 Non-college new hires for craft, operative and laborer occupations by race and gender represented: 43 percent of jobs for white males, 40 percent for black males and 57 percent for Hispanic males; compared to 6 percent for white females, 10 percent for black females and 19 percent for Hispanic females.

31 Arum and Hout, op. cit.

32 For a discussion of changes over time see Ragan and Bratsberg, and Coleman. (J. Ragan and B. Bratsberg, "Earnings inequality narrows for young workers despite a widening wage structure," *Quarterly Review of Economics and Finance* 35, 1995, 387–395; M. Coleman, "Movements in the earnings-schooling relationship, 1940–88," *Journal of Human Resources* 28, 1993, 660–689.)

33 C. Jencks and P. Peterson, *The Urban Underclass*, Washington, DC: Brookings, 1991, 28–102; P. Osterman, *Adolescence and Work: Influence of Social Structure, Labor Markets, and Culture,* Hillsdale, NJ: Lawrence Erlbaum Associates Publishers, 1989.

34 R. Layard, S. Nickell, and R. Jackman, *Unemployment: Macroeconomic Performance and the Labor Market,* New York, NY: Oxford University Press, 1991.

35 An extended analysis of the determinants of school assisted job placement would suggest that the practice was also more prevalent due to other individual characteristics and social and school settings. African-Americans are also more likely to receive school assistance; individuals located in urban areas, who attend schools with more disadvantaged students, or who live in Northcentral and Northeast states are more likely to rely on this practice. In addition, high school graduates are more likely to receive school assistance than high school dropouts, as well as students who receive vocational or academic post-secondary degrees. We refrain from an extended examination of these other weaker determinants to avoid distraction from the larger conceptual aims of the work.

36 All differences noted in the text are statistically significant at the $p < 0.05$ level.

37 See Arum and Shavit, op. cit. and Vetter (1989) for examples.

38 The differences, however, are close to $p < 0.05$ levels of statistical significance. A t-test on the difference between men who took 10 or greater percent coursework and those with less than 10 percent coursework in the percentage of clerical first jobs is 1.92; the difference for those using school assisted job placement and the entire sample is 1.82. The marginal significance level of these findings is related to the small number of men overall who use school assisted placement to find their first jobs after high school.

39 Results discussed here are based on Table 8.A.2, Model 1.

40 Results discussed here are based on Table 8.A.2, Model 2. The coefficient for business coursework decreases 12 percent in magnitude. As noted above, school assisted job placements are much rarer for men than women. Thus while estimates of the effect of school assisted job placement on the likelihood of male unemployment are not significant, this is likely due to the small number of cases observed. In fact, the coefficient estimate for men approaches significance at the $p < 0.10$ level, and is not significantly different than the coefficient for regressions run on women ($t = 1.19$).

41 See Table 8.A.2, Models 3 and 4.

42 In pooled male-female analysis (not shown), estimates of the effects of school assisted job placement on unemployment had a coefficient (and standard error) of –0.042 (0.025) at the $p<0.10$ level.

43 See results in Table 8.A.3, Model 1.

44 In Model 4, the coefficient for school assisted job placement is only 37 percent as large as Model 2 (0.087 compared to 0.237) and is also insignificant. Comparing results to a regression model similar to Model 2 but also including high school work experience, the magnitude of the school assisted job placement effect drops roughly in half (from 0.177 to 0.087).

45 Men increase their earnings through both additional high school work experience and post high school work experience. An additional year of high school work experience increases earnings by 9.2 percent; an additional year of post high school work experience increases earnings by 14.7 percent.

46 Relevant statistics from a regression run similar to Model 3 but with the addition of the interaction between clerical first job and school assisted job placement are: for women, clerical first job 0.198 (0.056)**, school assisted job placement 0.225 (0.146), and clerical first job* school assisted job placement –0.057 (0.191); for men, clerical first job 0.018 (0.088), school assisted job placement 0.127 (0.096), and clerical first job* school assisted job placement –0.705 (0.273)**. The reader is cautioned, however, that these statistically significant differences are based on data with relatively few observations.

47 For discussion of occupational sex-segregation see England (1981, 1992).

48 For example see Bailey, T., *Learning to Work: Employer Involvement in School-to-Work Transition Programs*, Washington, DC: Brookings, 1995.

49 J. Rosenbaum, *Beyond College for All: Career Paths for the Forgotten Half*, New York, NY: Russell Sage Foundation, 2001.

50 Arum and Hout, op. cit.

51 Individual background variables include the following: *test score* (the number answered correctly on a tenth grade battery of cognitive tests including reading, vocabulary and math sections); dummy variables for *African-American* and *Hispanic* individuals; measures of *mother's years of education* and *father's years of education*; status of *parent's occupation* (coded as the Duncan SEI score for the highest scoring occupation of either parent); number of *siblings* in 1980; dummy variable for *two parent family* (not necessarily biological); and *family income* of student during high school (average of reported family income for 1980 and 1982, logged). We further control for three family status factors associated with gender differences in occupational attainment: an individual's marital status, the number of children, and an interaction between marital status and number of children (measured in 1986). Social context variables consist of: the 1982 *local unemployment rate* for the local labor market where the respondent's school was located; dummy variables for region and residential area (*rural, urban*, and suburban). School context variables are included to control for variation in educational experience due to school composition and student–teacher ratios. *School composition* is a composite measure based on

school administrator reports of the percentage of tenth graders who drop out of high school, the percentage of economically disadvantaged students at the school, and the percentage of non-white students at the school (see C. Fischer, M. Hout, M. Sanchez Jankowski, S. Lucas, A. Swidler, and K. Voss, *Inequality by Design: Cracking the Bell Curve Myth*, Princeton, NJ: Princeton University Press, 1996.) The *student–teacher ratio* is based on school administrator reports and calculated as the square-root of the product of the number of students at the school divided by the number of teachers at the school.

52 In unreported analysis, we included a variable measuring whether the student attended a private instead of a public high school. School sector, however, was not significantly related to any of the outcomes studied.

53 See Arum and Hout, op. cit., and Arum and Shavit, op. cit. for examples.

54 See R. Carr, J. Wright, and C. Brody, "Effects of high school work experience a decade later: evidence from the national longitudinal study," *Sociology of Education* 69, 1996, 66–81; W. Marsh, "Employment during high school: character building or subversion of academic goals," *Sociology of Education* 64, 1991, 172–189; and D. Stern and Yoshi-Fumi Nakata, "Characteristics of high school students' paid jobs, and employment experience after graduation," in D. Stern and D. Eichorn (eds), *Adolescence and Work: Influences of Social Structure, Labor Markets, and Culture.* Hillsdale, NJ: Lawrence Erlbaum Associates, 1989, for examples.

Bibliography

Achenbach, T. M. and C. S. Edelbrock, "Behavioral problems and competencies reported by parents of normal and disturbed children aged four through sixteen," *Monographs of the Society for Research in Child Development* 46, 1981, No. 188.

Achenbach, T. M. and C. S. Edelbrock, "Psychopathology of childhood," *Annual Review of Psychology* 35, 1984, 227–256.

Acock, A. C. and D. H. Demo, *Family Diversity and Well-Being,* Thousand Oaks, CA: Sage, 1994.

Adler, A., *The Individual Psychology of Alfred Adler: A Systematic Presentation in Selections From His Writings*, H. Ansbacher and R. Ansbacher (ed and annotated), New York, NY: Basic Books, 1959.

Ahituv, A., M. Tienda, L. Xu, and V. J. Hotz, "Initial labor market experiences of Black, Hispanic and White men," in *Population Research Center Discussion Paper Series, Working Paper* 94–5, Chicago, IL: University of Chicago, 1994.

Ainsworth, M., M. C. Blehar, E. Waters, and S. Wall, *Patterns of Attachment*, Hillsdale, NJ: Lawrence Erlbaum, 1978.

Ainsworth-Darnell, J. and D. B. Downey, "Assessing the oppositional culture explanation for racial/ethnic differences in school performance," *American Sociological Review* 63, 1998, 536–553.

Alba, R. D., J. Logan, and B. Stults, "How segregated are middle-class African Americans?," *Social Problems* 47, 2000, 543–558.

Alderman, H., J. R. Behrman, V. Lavy, and R. Menon, "Child nutrition, child health, and school enrollment: a longitudinal analysis," *Journal of Human Resources* 36, 2001, 185–205.

Alderman, H., J. R. Behrman, D. Ross, and R. Sabot, "Decomposing the gender gap in cognitive skills in a poor rural economy," *Journal of Human Resources* 31, 1996a, 229–254.

Alderman, H., J. R. Behrman, D. Ross, and R. Sabot, "The returns to endogenous human capital in Pakistan's rural wage labor market," *Oxford Bulletin of Economics and Statistics* 58, 1996b, 29–55.

Alderman, H., J. R. Behrman, S. Khan, D. Ross, and R. Sabot, "The income gap in cognitive skills in rural Pakistan," *Economic Development and Cultural Change* 46, 1997, 97–122.

Alexander, K. L. and B. K. Eckland, "School experiences and status attainment," in S. E. Dragastin and G. H. Elder Jr. (eds) *Adolescence in the Life Cycle*, New York, NY: Wiley, 1975.

Alexander, K. L. and D. R. Entwisle, "Educational tracking during the early years: first grade placements and middle school constraints," in A. C. Kerckhoff (ed.) *Generating Social Stratification: Toward a New Research Agenda*, New York, NY: Westview Press, 1996.

Alexander, K. L. and D. R. Entwisle, "Schools and children at risk," in A. Booth and J. F. Dunn (eds) *Family-School Links: How Do They Affect Educational Outcomes*, Mahwah, NJ: Lawrence Erlbaum Associates, 1996, 67–88.

Alexander, K. L., D. R. Entwisle, and S. D. Bedinger, "When expectations work: race and socioeconomic differences in school performance," *Social Psychology Quarterly* 57, 1994, 283–299.

Alexander, K. L., D. R. Entwisle, and S. L. Dauber, "First grade classroom behavior: its short- and long-term consequences for school performance," *Child Development* 64, 1993, 801–814.

Alexander, K. L., D. R. Entwisle, and L. S. Olson, "Schools, achievement and inequality: a seasonal perspective," *Educational Evaluation and Policy Analysis* 23, 2001, 171–191.

Alwin, D. F., "Trends in parental socialization values: Detroit, 1958–1983," *American Journal of Sociology* 90, 1984, 359–382.

Alwin, D. F. and A. Thornton, "Family origins and the schooling process: early versus late influence of parental characteristics," *American Sociological Review* 49, 1984, 784–802.

Amato, P., "More than money? Men's contribution to their children's lives," in A. Booth and A. C. Crouter (eds), *Men In Families: When Do They Get Involved? What Difference Does It Make?*, London: Lawrence Erlbaum Associates, 1998, 241–278.

Anastasi, A., "Intelligence and family size," *Psychological Bulletin* 53, 1956, 187–209.

Andrews, S. R., J. Blumenthal, D. L. Johnson, A. J. Kahn, J. C. Ferguson, T. M. Lasater, P. E. Malone, and D. B. Wallace, "The skills of mothering: a study of parent child development centers," *Monographs of the Society for Research in Child Development* 47, 1982, No. 198.

Anh, T. S., J. Knodel, D. Lam, and J. Friedman, "Family size and children's education in Vietnam," *Demography* 35, 1998, 57–70.

Anyon, J., *Ghetto Schooling: A Political Economy of Urban Educational Reform*, New York, NY: Teachers College Press, 1997.

Armor, D. J., "The evidence on busing," *Public Interest* 28, 1972, 90–126.

Arnove, R., P. Altbach, and G. Kelly (eds), *Emergent Issues in Education: Comparative Perspectives*, Albany, NY: State University of New York Press, 1992.

Arum, R., "Schools and communities: ecological and institutional dimensions," *Annual Review of Sociology* 26, 2000, 395–418.

Arum, R. and M. Hout, "The early returns: transitions from school to work in the United States," in W. Mueller and Y. Shavit (eds), *Educational Qualifications and Occupational Destinations,* Cambridge, MA: Oxford University Press, 1997.

Arum, R. and Y. Shavit, "Secondary vocational education and the transition from school to work," *Sociology of Education* 68, 1995, 187–204.

Ashenfelter, O. and A. Krueger, "Estimates of the economic return to schooling from a new sample of twins," *American Economic Review* 84, 1994, 1157–1174.

Ashenfelter, O. and C. Rouse, "Income, schooling and ability: evidence from a new sample of identical twins," *Quarterly Journal of Economics* 113, 1998, 253–284.

Ashenfelter, O. and D. J. Zimmerman, "Estimates of the returns to schooling from sibling data: fathers, sons and brothers," *The Review of Economics and Statistics* 79, 1997, 1–9.

Astone, N. and S. McLanahan, "Family structure, parental practices and high school completion," *American Sociological Review* 56, 1991, 309–320.

Atoh, M., "Family change and education," *The Journal of Educational Sociology* 48, 1991, 21–41.

Ayalon, H. and A. Yogev, "The alternative worldview of state religious high schools in Israel," *Comparative Education Review* 40, 1996, 7–27.

Bailey, T., *Learning to Work: Employer Involvement in School-to-Work Transition Programs*, Washington, DC: Brookings, 1995.

Baker, A. J., C. S. Piotrkowski, and J. Brooks-Gunn, "The effects of the home instruction program for preschool youngsters (HIPPY) on children's school performance at the end of the program and one year later," *Early Childhood Research Quarterly* 13, 1999, 571–588.

Baker, D. P., "In comparative isolation: why comparative research has so little influence on American sociology of education," *Research in Sociology of Education and Socialization* 10, 1994, 53–70.

Baker D. P. and G. LeTendre, "Comparative sociology of classroom processes, school organization, and achievement," in M. Hallinan (ed.), *Handbook of the Sociology of Education*, New York, NY: Kluwer Academic/Plenum Publishers, 2000, 345–364.

Bankston III, C., "Family structure, schoolmates, and racial inequalities in school achievement," *Journal of Marriage and the Family* 60, 1998, 715–723.

Barnard, K. E., "Developing, implementing, documenting interventions with parents and young children," in L. J. Berlin (ed.), *Opening the Black Box: Understanding How Early Intervention Programs Work* [Special Issue], *Zero to Three* 18, 1998, 23–29.

Barnett, W. S., "Long-term effects of early childhood programs on cognitive and school outcomes," *The Future of Children* 5, 1995, 25–50.

Barnett, W. S. and S. S. Boocock, *Early Care and Education for Children in Poverty: Promises, Programs, and Long-Term Results*, Albany, NY: SUNY Press, 1997.

Barrera, M. E., P. L. Rosenbaum, and C. E. Cunningham, "Early home intervention with low-birth weight infants and their parents," *Child Development* 57, 1986, 20–33.

Barros, R. and D. Lam, "Income and educational inequality in children's schooling attainment," in N. Birdsall, and R. H. Sabot (eds), *Opportunity Foregone: Education in Brazil*, Baltimore, MD: The Johns Hopkins University Press for the Inter-American Development Bank, 1996, 337–366.

Battle, J., "What beats having two parents? Educational outcomes for African American students in single- versus dual-parent families," *Journal of Black Studies* 28, 1998, 783–801.

Baumrind, D., "Effects of authoritative control on child behavior," *Child Development* 37, 1966, 887–907.

Bauserman, R., "Child adjustment in joint custody versus sole-custody arrangements: A meta-analytic review," *Journal of Family Psychology* 16, 2002, 91.

Baydar, N., J. Brooks-Gunn, and F. F. Furstenberg, "Early warning signs of functional illiteracy: predictors in childhood and adolescence," *Child Development* 64, 1993, 815–829.

Becker, G. S., *Human Capital*, Cambridge, MA: Harvard University Press, 1964.

Becker, G. S., 1967, "Human capital and the personal distribution of income: an analytical approach," Ann Arbor, MI: University of Michigan, Woytinsky Lecture, republished in Gary S. Becker, *Human Capital*, New York, NY: NBER, 2nd edition 1975, 94–117.

Becker, G. S., *A Treatise on the Family*, Cambridge, MA: Harvard University Press, 1981.

Becker, G. S., *A Treatise on the Family* (2nd edn), Cambridge, MA: Harvard University Press, 1991.

Becker, G. S. and N. Tomes, "Child endowments and the quantity and quality of children," *Journal of Political Economy* 84, 1976, 143–162.

Becker, G. S. and N. Tomes, "Human capital and the rise and fall of families," *Journal of Labor Economics* 4, 1986, S1–S139.

Behrman, J. R., *Women's Schooling and Child Education: A Survey*, Philadelphia, PA: University of Pennsylvania, mimeo, 1997.

Behrman, J. R., *Targeting Social Protection to the Poor: What are the Tradeoffs?,* Philadelphia, PA: University of Pennsylvania, prepared for Inter-American Development Bank, mimeo, 2001.

Behrman, J. R. and N. Birdsall, "The quality of schooling: quantity alone is misleading," *American Economic Review* 73, 1983, 928–946.

Behrman, J. R. and N. Birdsall, "The quality of schooling: reply," *American Economic Review* 75, 1985, 1202–1205.

Behrman, J. R. and N. Birdsall, "Implicit equity–productivity tradeoffs in the distribution of public school resources in Brazil," *European Economic Review* 32, 1988, 1585–1601.

Behrman, J. R., N. Birdsall, and R. Kaplan, "The quality of schooling and labor market outcomes in Brazil: some further explorations," in N. Birdsall and R. Sabot (eds), *Opportunity Foregone: Education in Brazil*, Baltimore, MD: The Johns Hopkins University Press for the Inter-American Development Bank, 1996, 245–266.

Behrman, J. R., A. Foster, M. R. Rosenzweig, and P. Vashishtha, "Women's schooling, home teaching, and economic growth," *Journal of Political Economy* 107, 1999, 682–714.

Behrman, J. R., Z. Hrubec, P. Taubman, and T. J. Wales, *Socioeconomic Success: A Study of the Effects of Genetic Endowments, Family Environment and Schooling*, Amsterdam: North–Holland Publishing Company, 1980.

Behrman, J. R. and J. C. Knowles, *How Strongly is Child Schooling Associated with Household Income?,* Philadelphia, PA: University of Pennsylvania, mimeo, 1997.

Behrman, J. R. and J. C. Knowles, "Household income and child schooling in Vietnam," *World Bank Economic Review* 13, 1999, 211–256.

Behrman, J. R. and M. R. Rosenzweig, "The returns to schooling: new evidence from twins data," *Economics of Education Review* 18, 1999, 159–167.

Behrman, J. R. and M. R. Rosenzweig, "Does increasing women's schooling raise the schooling of the next generation?," *American Economic Review* 92, 2002, 323–334.

Behrman, J. R. and M. R. Rosenzweig, "Returns to birthweight,' *Review of Economics and Statistics*, forthcoming 2004.

Behrman, J. R., M. R. Rosenzweig, and P. Taubman, "Endowments and the allocation of schooling in the family and in the marriage market: the twins experiment," *Journal of Political Economy* 102, 1994, 1131–1174.

Behrman, J. R., M. R. Rosenzweig, and P. Taubman, "College choice and wages: estimates using data on female twins," *Review of Economics and Statistics* 73, 1996, 672–685.

Behrman, J. R., D. Ross, and R. Sabot, "Improving the quality versus increasing the quantity of schooling: evidence from rural Pakistan,' Topics in the Economics and Growth of Developing Areas of the B.E., *Journals of the Economics and Growth of Developing Areas*, forthcoming 2004.

Behrman, J. R. and P. Taubman, "Intergenerational transmission of income and wealth," *American Economic Review* 66, 1976, 436–440.

Behrman, J. R. and P. Taubman, "Birth order, schooling and earnings," *Journal of Labor Economics* 4, 1986, S121–S145.

Behrman, J. R. and P. Taubman, "Is schooling 'mostly in the genes'? Nature–nurture decomposition with data on relatives," *Journal of Political Economy* 97, 1989, 1425–1446.

Behrman, J. R. and P. Taubman, "The intergenerational correlation between children's adult earnings and their parents' income: results from the Michigan Panel Survey of Income Dynamics," *The Review of Income and Wealth* 36, 1990, 115–127.

Behrman, J. R. and B. L. Wolfe, "Investments in schooling in two generations in pre-revolutionary Nicaragua: the roles of family background and school supply," *Journal of Development Economics* 27, 1987, 395–420.

Bell, T. H., "Reflections one decade after *A Nation At Risk*," *Phi Delta Kappan* 74, 1993, 592–597.

Belsky, J., "The determinants of parenting: a process model," *Child Development* 55, 1984, 83–96.

Belsky, J. and J. Cassidy, "Attachment: theory and evidence," in M. Rutter, D. Hay, and S. Baron-Cohen (eds), *Developmental Principles and Clinical Issues in Psychology and Psychiatry*, Oxford: Blackwell, 1994, 373–402.

Benasich, A. A., J. Brooks-Gunn, and B. C. Clewell, "How do mothers benefit from early intervention programs?," *Journal of Applied Developmental Psychology* 13, 1992, 311–362.

Benavot, A., Y. Cha, D. Kamens, J. Meyer, and S. Wong, "Knowledge for the masses: world models and national curricula, 1920–1986," *American Sociological Review* 56, 1991, 85–100.

Bennis, W. G., "A new role for the behavioral sciences: effecting organizational change," *Administrative Science Quarterly* 8, 1963, 125–165.

Ben-Porath, Y., "The f-connection: families, friends, and firms and the organization of exchange," *Population and Development Review* 6, 1980, 1–30.

Berlin, L. J., C. R. O'Neal, and J. Brooks-Gunn, "What makes early intervention programs work? The program, its participants, and their interaction," in L. J. Berlin (ed.), *Opening the Black Box: What Makes Early Child and Family Development Programs Work*? [Special Issue] *Zero to Three* 18, 1998, 4–15.

Bestor, A., *Educational Wasteland: The Retreat from Learning in Our Public Schools,* Urbana, IL: University of Illinois Press, 1953.

Bianchi, S., "Maternal employment and time with children: dramatic change or surprising continuity?," *Demography* 37, 2000, 401–414.

Bickel, R, "Post high school opportunities and high school completion rates in an

Appalachian state: a near-replication of Florida research," *Youth & Society* 21, 1989, 61–84.

Bickel, R. and G. J. Papagiannis, "Post high school prospects and district-level dropout rates," *Youth & Society* 20, 1988, 123–147.

Bielby, W. T., R. M. Hauser, and D. L. Featherman, "Response errors of non-black males in models of the stratification process," in D. A. Aigner and A. S. Goldberger (eds), *Latent Variables in Socio-Economic Models*, Amsterdam: North Holland, 1977.

Bielicki, T. and A. Szklarska, "The stratifying force of family size: urbanization and parental education in socialist-era Poland," *Journal of Biosocial Science* 31, 1999, 525–536.

Biller, H. B., *Fathers and Families: Paternal Factors in Child Development*, Westport, CT: Auburn, 1993.

Billingsley, A., *Climbing Jacobs Ladder: The Enduring Legacy of African American Families*, New York, NY: Simon and Schuster, 1992.

Birdsall, N., "A cost of siblings: child schooling in urban Columbia," *Research in Population Economics* 2, 1980, 115–150.

Birdsall, N., "Public inputs and child schooling in Brazil," *Journal of Development Economics* 18, 1985, 67–86.

Bishop, J., "Occupational training in high school: when does it pay off?," *Economics of Education Review* 8, 1989, 1–15.

Blake, J., "Family size and the quality of children," *Demography* 18, 1981, 1096–1101.

Blake, J., "Number of siblings, family background, and the process of educational attainment," *Social Biology* 33, 1986, 5–21.

Blake, J., *Family Size and Achievement,* Berkeley, CA: University of California Press, 1989.

Blau, F. D. and A. J. Grossberg, "Maternal labor supply and children's cognitive development," *Review of Economics and Statistics* 74, 1992, 474–481.

Blau, P. M. and O. D. Duncan, *The American Occupational Structure*, New York, NY: Wiley, 1967.

Bledstein, B., *The Culture of Professionalism: The Middle Class and the Development of Higher Education in America*, New York, NY: W. W. Norton and Company, 1976.

Boocock, S., "Early childhood programs in other nations: goals and outcomes," *Future of Children* 5, 1995, 94–114.

Bornstein, M. H., "Between caretakers and their young: two models of interaction and their consequences for cognitive growth," in M. H. Bornstein and J. S. Bruner (eds), *Interactions in Human Development*, Hillsdale, NJ: Lawrence Erlbaum, 1989, 197–214.

Bossard, J. H. S. and E. S. Boll, *The Large Family System*, Philadelphia, PA: The University of Pennsylvania Press, 1956.

Bound, J. and A. B. Krueger, "The extent of measurement error in longitudinal earnings data: do two wrongs make a right?," *Journal of Labor Economics* 9, 1991, 1–24.

Bound, J. and G. Solon, "Double trouble: on the value of twins-based estimation of the return to schooling," *Economics of Education Review* 18, 1999, 169–182.

Bourdieu, P., *Reproduction in Education, Society and Culture*, Beverly Hills, CA: Sage, 1977.

Bourdieu, P., "Le capital social: notes provisoires," *Actes Research Science Social* 31, 1980, 2–3.

Bourdieu, P., "The forms of capital," in J. Richardson (ed.), *Handbook of Theory and Research for the Sociology of Education*, New York, NY: Greenwood Press, 1986, 241–260.

Bowen, W. and D. Bok, *The Shape of the River*, Princeton, NJ: Princeton University Press, 1998.

Bowlby, J., "The nature of the child's ties to his mother," *International Journal of Psychoanalysis* 39, 1958, 350–373.

Bowlby, J., *Attachment and Loss*, vol. 1, New York, NY: Basic Books, 1969.

Bowles, S. and H. Gintis, *Schooling in Capitalist America*, New York, NY: Basic Books, 1976.

Bowles, S. and H. M. Levin, "The determinants of scholastic achievement – an appraisal of some recent evidence," *Journal of Human Resources* 3, 1968, 3–24.

Bradley, K. and F. Ramirez, "World polity and gender parity: women's share of higher education: 1965–1985," *Research in the Sociology of Education and Socialization* 11, 1996, 63–91.

Bradley, R. H., "Environment and parenting," in M. H. Bornstein (ed.), *Handbook of Parenting,* Mahwah, NJ: Lawrence Erlbaum Associates, 1995, 235–261.

Bradley, R. H., B. M. Caldwell, S. L. Rock, C. T. Ramey, K. E. Barnard, C. Gray, M. A. Hammond, S. K. Mitchell, A.W. Gottfried, L. Siegel, and D. L. Johnson, "Home environment and cognitive development in the first three years of life: a collaborative study involving six sites and three ethnic groups in North America," *Developmental Psychology* 25, 1989, 217–235.

Brennan, P. A., C. Hammen, M. J. Andersen, W. Bor, J. M. Najman, and G. M. Williams, "Chronicity, severity, and timing of maternal depressive symptoms: relationships with child outcomes at age 5," *Developmental Psychology* 36, 2000, 759–766.

Broaded, C. M., "The limits and possibilities of tracking: some evidence from Japan," *Sociology of Education* 70, 1997, 36–53.

Brody, G., Z. Stoneman, D. Flor, C. McCrary, L. Hastings and O. Conyers, "Financial resources, parental psychological functioning, parent co-caregiving, and early adolescent competence in rural two-parent African-American families," *Child Development* 65, 1994, 590–605.

Broman, S. H., P. L. Nichols, and W. A. Kennedy, *Preschool IQ: Prenatal and Early Developmental Correlates*, London: Earlbaum, 1975.

Bronfenbrenner, U., *Two Worlds of Childhood: U.S. and U.S.S.R.,* New York, NY: Basic Books, 1970.

Bronfenbrenner, U., "Contexts of child rearing: problems and prospects," *American Psychologist* 35, 1979a, 844–850.

Bronfenbrenner, U., *The Ecology of Human Development: Experiments by Nature and Design*, Cambridge, MA: Harvard University Press, 1979b.

Bronfenbrenner, U., "Ecological systems theory," in R. Vasta (ed.), *Annals of Child Development – Six Theories of Child Development: Revised Formulations and Current Issues*, Greenwich, CT: JAI Press, 1989.

Brooks-Gunn, J., L. J. Berlin, and A. S. Fuligni, "Early childhood intervention programs: What about the family," in J. P. Shonkoff and S. J. Meisels (eds), *Handbook on Early Childhood Intervention,* (2nd edn), New York, NY: Cambridge University Press, 2000, 549–588.

Brooks-Gunn, J. and G. J. Duncan, "The effects of poverty on children," *The Future of Children* 7, 1997, 55–71.

Brooks-Gunn, J., G. J. Duncan, and L. L. Aber, *Neighborhood Poverty: Contexts and Consequences for Children*, New York, NY: Russell Sage Foundation, 1997.

Brooks-Gunn, J., G. J. Duncan, P. K. Klebanov, and N. Sealand, "Do neighborhoods influence child and adolescent development?," *American Journal of Sociology* 99, 1993, 353–395.

Brooks-Gunn, J., G. J. Duncan, T. Leventhal, and J. L. Aber, "Lessons learned and future directions for research on neighborhoods in which children live," in J. Brooks-Gunn, G. J. Duncan, and J. L. Aber (eds), *Neighborhood Poverty: Vol. 1. Context and Consequences for Children*, New York, NY: Russell Sage Foundation, 1997, 279–297.

Brooks-Gunn, J., G. Guo, and F. F. Furstenberg, Jr., "Who drops out of and who continues beyond high school? A 20-year follow-up of black urban youth," *Journal of Research on Adolescence* 3, 1993, 271–294.

Brooks-Gunn, J., P. K. Klebanov, and G. J. Duncan, "Ethnic differences in children's intelligence test scores: role of economic deprivation, home environment, and maternal characteristics," *Child Development* 67, 1996, 396–408.

Brooks-Gunn, J., C. M. McCarton, P. H. Casey, M. C. McCormick, C. R. Bauer, J. C. Berenbaum, J. Tyson, M. Swanson, F. C. Bennett, D. T. Scott, J. Tonascia, and C. L. Meinert, "Early intervention in low birth weight, premature infants: results through age 5 years from the Infant Health and Development Program," *Journal of the American Medical Association* 272, 1994, 1257–1262.

Brooks-Gunn, J., M. C. McCormick, S. Shapiro, A. A. Benasich, and G. W. Black, "The effects of early education intervention on maternal employment, public assistance, and health insurance: the Infant Health and Development Program," *The American Journal of Public Health* 84, 1994, 924–931.

Brown, F., "Assessment and evaluation of urban schools," *The Journal of Negro Education* 44, 1975, 377–384.

Bruce, J. and C. Lloyd, "Finding the ties that bind: beyond headship and household," in L. Haddad, J. Hiddinott, and H. Alderman (eds), *Intrahousehold Resource Allocation in Developing Countries,* Baltimore, MD: Johns Hopkins University, 1997, 213–228.

Bryant, D. M. and K. L. Maxwell, "The effectiveness of early intervention for disadvantaged children," in M. J. Guralnick (ed.), *The Effectiveness of Early Intervention*, Baltimore, MD: Brookes, 1997, 23–46.

Bryk, A. and S. Raudenbush, *Hierarchical Linear Models*, Newbury Park, CA: Sage, 1992.

Bryk, A., S. Raudenbush, Y.F. Cheong, and R. Congdon, *HLM 5: Hierarchical Linear and Nonlinear Modeling*, Lincolnwood, IL: Scientific Software International, Inc., 2000.

Bryson, K. and L. Kasper, "Coresident grandparent and grandchildren," *Current Population Reports*, 1999, 23–198.

Büchel, F. and G. J. Duncan, "Do parents' social activities promote children's school attainments? Evidence from the German Socio-Economic Panel," *Journal of Marriage and the Family* 60, 1998, 95–108.

Büchel, F. and G. Wagner, "Soziale Differenzen der Bildungschancen in Westdeutschland – unter besonderer Berücksichtigung von Zuwandererkindern," in

W. Zapf, J. Schupp, and R. Habich (eds), *Lebenslagen in Wandel: Sozialberichterstattung im Längsschnitt*, Frankfurt: Campus, 1996.

Büchel, F., K. Spiess, and G. Wagner, "Bildungseffekte vorschulischer Kinderbetreuung," *KölnerZeitschrift für Soziologie und Sozialpsychologie* 49, 1997, 528–539.

Buchmann, C., "The state and schooling in Kenya: historical developments and current challenges," *Africa Today* 46, 1999, 95–117.

Buchmann, C., "Family structure, parental perceptions and child labor in Kenya: what factors determine who is enrolled in school?," *Social Forces* 78, 2000, 1349–1379.

Buchmann, C. and B. Dalton, "Interpersonal influences and educational aspirations in twelve countries: the importance of institutional context," *Sociology of Education* 75, 2002, 99–122.

Buchmann, C. and E. Hannum, "Education and stratification in developing countries: review of theories and research," *Annual Review of Sociology* 27, 2001, 77–102.

Burbules, N. and C. Torres (eds), *Globalization and Education: Critical Perspectives*, New York, NY: Routledge, 2000.

Burchinal, M. R., F. A. Campbell, D. M. Bryant, B. H. Wasik, and C. T. Ramey, "Early intervention and mediating processes in cognitive performance of children of low-income African-American families," *Child Development* 68, 1997, 935–954.

Butcher, K. and A. Case, "The effect of sibling sex composition on women's education and earnings," *Quarterly Journal of Economics* 109, 1994, 531–563.

Caldwell, B. M. and R. H. Bradley, "*Home observation for measurement of the environment*," Little Rock, AR: University of Arkansas at Little Rock, 1984.

Caldwell, J., *A Theory of Fertility Decline*, New York, NY: Academic Press, 1982.

California Achievement Test, *Technical Bulletin 1, Forms C and D, Levels 10–19*, Monterey, CA: McGraw-Hill, 1979.

Callahan, Raymond, *Education and the Cult of Efficiency*, Chicago, IL: University of Chicago Press, 1962.

Card, D., "New developments in the economics of schooling," in O. Ashenfelter and D. Card (eds), *Handbook of Labor Economics*, Vol. 4, Amsterdam: North Holland Publishing Co., 1999.

Card, D. and A. B. Krueger, "Does school quality matter? Returns to education and the characteristics of public schools in the United States," *Journal of Political Economy* 100, 1992, 1–40.

Card, D. and A. B. Krueger, "School resources and student outcomes: an overview of the literature and new evidence from North and South Carolina," *Journal of Economic Perspectives* 10, 1996, 31–50.

Carr, R. V., J. D. Wright, and C. J. Brody, "Effects of high school work experience a decade later: evidence from the National Longitudinal Survey," *Sociology of Education* 69, 1996, 66–81.

Center for Human Resource Research, *NLS Users' Guide: 1995*, Columbus, OH: Center for Human Resource Research, The Ohio State University, 1995.

Center for Human Resource Research, *NLSY97 Users' Guide*, Columbus, OH: Center for Human Resource Research, The Ohio State University, 1998.

Chase-Lansdale, P. L., R. A. Gordon, J. Brooks-Gunn, and P. K. Klebanov, "Neighborhood and family influences on the intellectual and behavioral competence of preschool and early school-age children," in J. Brooks-Gunn, G. J.

Duncan, and J. L. Aber (eds), *Neighborhood Poverty: Vol. 1. Context and Consequences for Children*, New York, NY: Russell Sage Foundation Press, 1997, 79–118.

Chase-Lansdale, P.L., F. L. Mott, J. Brooks-Gunn, and D. A. Phillips, "Children of the National Longitudinal Survey of Youth: a unique research opportunity," *Developmental Psychology* 27, 1991, 918–931.

Cherlin, A. and F. F. Furstenberg Jr., *The New American Grandparent: A Place in the Family, A Life Apart*, New York, NY: Basic Books, 1986.

Church, R. L., M. B. Katz, H. Silver, and L. A. Cremin, "Forum: the metropolitan experience in American education," *History of Education Quarterly* 29, 1989, 419–446.

Clewell, B. C., J. Brooks-Gunn, and A. A. Benasich, "Evaluating child-related outcomes of teenage parenting programs," *Family Relations* 38, 1989, 201–209.

Cohen, D. K., "Origins," in A. Powell, E. Farrar, and D. K. Cohen (eds), *The Shopping Mall High School: Winners and Losers in the Educational Marketplace*, Boston, MA: Houghton Mifflin, 1985, 233–308.

Coleman, J., *Equality and Achievement in Education*, Boulder, CO: Westview, 1990.

Coleman, J. S., "Social capital in the creation of human capital," *American Journal of Sociology* 94, 1988, 95–120.

Coleman, J. S., *Foundations of Social Theory,* Cambridge, MA: Harvard University Press, 1990.

Coleman, J. S., E. Campbell, C. Hobson, J. McPartland, A. Mood, F. D. Weinfeld, and R. York, *Equality of Educational Opportunity*, Washington, DC: Department of Health, Education and Welfare, 1966.

Coleman, M., "Movements in the earnings-schooling relationship, 1940–88," *Journal of Human Resources* 28, 1993, 660–689.

College Board, *Reaching the Top: A Report of the National Task Force on Minority High Achievement*, 1999. http://www.collegeboard.org/press/html9900/html/ReachingTheTop.pdf.

Collins, R., *The Credential Society: A Historical Sociology of Education and Stratification,* New York, NY: Academy Press, 1979.

Collins, S., "The Making of the Black Middle Class," *Social Problems* 30, 1983, 369–382.

Collins, W. A., E. E. Maccoby, L. Steinberg, E. M. Hetherington, and M. H. Bornstein, "Contemporary research on parenting: the case for nature and nurture," *American Psychologist* 55, 2000, 218–232.

Coltrane, S. and K. Allan, "New fathers and old stereotypes: representations of masculinity in 1980s television advertising," *Masculinities* 2, 1994, 1–25.

Conger, R. D., K. J. Conger, and G. H. Elder Jr., "Family economic hardship and adolescent adjustment: mediating and moderating processes," in G. J. Duncan and J. Brooks-Gunn (eds), *Consequences of Growing Up Poor,* New York, NY: Russell Sage Foundation, 1997, 288–310.

Conger, R. D. and G. H. Elder Jr., *Families in Troubled Times: Adapting to Change in Rural America*, New York, NY: Aldine de Gruyter, 1994.

Conger, R. D., G. R. Patterson, and X. Ge, "It takes two to replicate: a mediational model for the impact of parents' stress on adolescent adjustment," *Child Development* 66, 1995, 80–97.

Conger, R. D., M. A. Rueter, and G. H. Elder Jr., "Couple resilience to economic pressure," *Journal of Personality and Social Psychology* 76, 1999, 54–71.

Conger, R. D., K. J. Vonger, G. H. Elder, F. O. Lorenz, R. L. Simons, and L. B. Whitebeck, "A family process model of economic hardship and adjustment of early adolescent boys," *Child Development* 63, 1992, 526–541.

Conley, D., *Being Black, Living in the Red: Race, Wealth, and Social Policy in America*, Los Angeles, CA: University of California Press, 1999.

Conley, D., "A room with a view or a room of one's own? Housing and stratification," *Sociological Forum* 16, 2001, 263–280.

Conley, D., "Capital for college: parental assets and postsecondary schooling," *Sociology of Education* 74, 2001, 59–72.

Conley, D. and N. G. Bennett, "Is biology destiny? Birth weight and life chances," *American Sociological Review* 65, 2000, 458–467.

Cooksey, E. C. and M. M. Fondel, "Spending time with his kids: effects of family structure on fathers' and children's lives," *Journal of Marriage and the Family* 58, 1996, 693–707.

Cookson, P. W. and C. H. Persell, *Preparing for Power: America's Elite Boarding Schools*, New York, NY: Basic Books, 1985.

Coons, J. E., W. H. Clune III, and S. D. Sugarman, *Private Wealth and Public Education*, Cambridge, MA: Harvard University Press, 1970.

Corcoran, M., L. Datcher, and G. Duncan, "Information and influence networks in labor markets," *Five Thousand American Families: Patterns of Economic Progress,* Ann Arbor, MI: Institute for Social Research 7, 1980, 1–37.

Corcoran, M., R. Gordon, D. Laren, and G. Solon, "The association between men's economic status and their family and community origins," *Journal of Human Resources* 27, 1992, 575–601.

Cremin, L. A., *American Education: The Metropolitan Experience, 1876–1980*, New York, NY: Harper and Row, 1988.

Crowell, J. A. and S. S. Feldman, "Mothers' internal models of relationships and children's behavioral and developmental status: a study of mother-child interactions," *Child Development* 59, 1988, 1273–1285.

Crul, M., "Success factors in school careers of second-generation Turkish and Moroccan youth," *Tijdschrift voor Sociologie* 17, 1996, 403–420.

Crul, M., "Turkish and Moroccan sibling support and school achievement levels: an optimistic view," *Netherlands Journal of Social Sciences* 35, 1999, 110–127.

Cummings, E. M. and A. W. O'Reilly, "Fatherhood in family context: effects of marital quality on child adjustment," in M. E. Lamb (ed.), *The Role of the Father in Child Development*, New York, NY: Wiley, 1997, 49–65.

Currie, J. and J. Gruber, "Saving babies: the efficacy and cost of recent changes in the medicaid eligibility of pregnant women," *Journal of Political Economy* 104, 1996, 1263–1296.

Currie, J. and R. Hyson, "Is the impact of health shocks cushioned by socioeconomic status? The case of low birthweight," *American Economic Review* 89, 1999, 245–250.

D'Amico, R., "Does employment during high school impair academic progress?," *Sociology of Education* 57, 1984, 152–164.

Datcher, L., "Effect of community and family background on achievement," *Review of Economics and Statistics* 64, 1982, 32–41.

Datcher-Loury, L. and D. Garman, "College selectivity and earnings," *Journal of Labor Economics* 13, 1995, 289–308.

David, J. "Follow through summer study: a two-part investigation of the impact of exposure to schooling on achievement growth," Ed. D. Dissertation, Harvard Graduate School of Education, 1974.

David, J. and S. H. Pelavin, "Secondary analysis: in compensatory education programs," *New Directions for Program Evaluation* 4, 1978, 31–44.

Davis, P. T. and E. M. Cummings, "Marital conflict and child adjustment: an emotional security hypothesis," *Psychological Bulletin* 116, 1994, 387–411.

Davis-Kean, P. E. and J. S. Eccles, "It takes a village to raise a child: an executive function and community management perspective," working paper, University of Michigan 2002.

Dawson, I., "The schools history project: A study in curriculum development," *The History Teacher* 22, 1989, 221–238.

DeGraff, D., R. Bilsborrow, and A. Herrin, "Children's education in the Phillipines: does high fertility matter?," *Population Research and Political Review* 15, 1996, 219–247.

Desai, S., "When are children from large families disadvantaged? Evidence from cross-national analyses," *Population Studies* 49, 1995, 195–210.

Desai, S., "Children at risk: the role of family structure in Latin America and West Africa," *Population and Development Review* 18, 1992, 689–717.

Dewey, J., *John Dewey on Education: Selected Writings*, Chicago, IL: The University of Chicago Press, 1964.

Dickstein, E. B., "The development of self-esteem: theory and measurement," unpublished doctoral dissertation, The Johns Hopkins University, 1972.

DiMaggio, P., "Cultural capital and school success: the impact of status cultures participation on the grades of U. S. high school students," *American Sociological Review* 47, 1982, 189–210.

Downey, D. B., "When bigger is not better: family size, parental resources, and children's educational performance," *American Sociological Review* 60, 1995, 746–761.

Downey, D. B., "Number of siblings and intellectual development: the resource dilution explanation," *American Psychologist* 56, 2001, 497–504.

Downey, D. B. and S. Neubauer, "Is resource dilution inevitable? The association between number of siblings and educational outcomes across subgroups," presented at Annual Meetings of the American Sociological Association, San Francisco, CA, 1998.

Downey, D. B. and B. Powell, "Do children from single-parent families fare better living with same-sex parents?," *Journal of Marriage and the Family* 55, 1993, 55–71.

Downey, D. B., B. Powell, L. C. Steelman, and S. Pribesh, "Much ado about siblings: change models, sibship size, and intellectual development," *American Sociological Review* 64, 1999, 193–198.

Downey, G. and J. C. Coyne, "Children of depressed parents: an integrative review," *Psychological Bulletin* 108, 1990, 50–76.

Dumont, A., *Population et Civilisation*, Paris: Elsevier, 1890.

Duncan, G. J. and J. Brooks-Gunn (eds), *Consequences of Growing Up Poor,* New York, NY: Russell Sage Foundation Press, 1997.

Duncan, G. J., J. Brooks-Gunn, and P. K. Klebanov, "Economic deprivation and early childhood development," *Child Development* 65, 1994, 296–318.

Duncan, G. J. and D. H. Hill, "An investigation of the extent and consequences of measurement error in labor-economic survey data," *Journal of Labor Economics* 3, 1985, 508–532.

Duncan, G. J., W. J. Yeung, J. Brooks-Gunn, and J. Smith, "How much does childhood poverty affect the life chances of children?," *American Sociological Review* 63, 1998, 406–423.

Duncan, O. D., "Inheritance of poverty or inheritance of race," in D. Moynihan (ed.), *On Understanding Poverty*, New York, NY: Basic Books, 1969.

Dunifon, R., G. J. Duncan, and J. Brooks-Gunn, "As ye sweep, so shall ye reap," *American Economic Review* 91, 2001, 150–154.

Duyme, M., *Focus on Naturally Occurring Changes in Development After Varied Early Life Circumstances,* paper presented at the Well-Being and Dysfunction Across the Generations: Change and Continuity Conference, Zurich, Switzerland, 2001.

Early Head Start Research and Evaluation Project, *Building Their Future: How Early Head Start Programs are Enhancing the Lives of Infants and Toddlers in Low-Income Families*, Princeton, NJ: Mathemetica Policy Research, Inc., 2001.

Eble, K. E. and W. J. McKeachie, *Improving Undergraduate Education Through Faculty Development: An Analysis of Effective Programs and Practices*, San Francisco, CA: Jossey-Bass, 1985.

Eccles, J. S., D. Early, K. Fraser, E. Belansky, and K. McCarthy, "The relation of connection, regulation, and support for autonomy to adolescents' functioning," *Journal of Adolescent Research* 12, 1997, 263–286.

Eccles, J. S., A. Wigfield, and U. Schiefele, "Motivation," in N. Eisenberg (ed.), *Handbook of Child Psychology*, vol. 3, New York, NY: Wiley, 1997, 1017–1095.

Echols, F., A. McPherson, and D. Willms, "Parental choice in Scotland," *Journal of Education Policy* 5, 1990, 207–222.

Edin, K., "Single mothers and absent fathers: the possibilities and limits of child support policy," Center for Urban Policy Research Report, New Brunswick, NJ: Rutgers University, 1994.

Educational Policies Commission, *Education for All American Youth*, Washington, DC: National Educational Commission, 1944.

Egeland, B., M. Kalkoske, N. Gottesman, and M. F. Erikson, "Preschool behavior problems: stability and factors accounting for change," *Journal of Child Psychology and Psychiatry* 31, 1990, 891–909.

Elder Jr., G. H., *Children of the Great Depression: Social Change in Life Experience*, Chicago, IL: University of Chicago Press, 1974.

Elder Jr., G. H., *Life Course Dynamics*, Ithaca, NY: Cornell University Press, 1995.

Elder Jr., G. H. and C. Bowerman, "Family structure in childrearing patterns: the effect of family size and sex composition," *American Sociological Review* 28, 1963, 891–905.

Elliot, D. S., W. J. Wilson, D. Huizinga, R. J. Sampson, A. Elliott, and B. H. Rankin, "The effects of neighborhood disadvantage on adolescent development," *Journal of Research in Crime and Delinquency* 33, 1996, 389–426.

Elliott, J., "Class, race, and job matching in contemporary urban labor markets," *Social Science Quarterly* 81, 2000, 1036–1052.

El–Sanabary, N., "Determinants of women's education in the Middle East and North Africa: illustrations from seven countries," PHTEE Background Paper Series, Washington, DC: World Bank, 1995.

Emirbayer, M., "Beyond structuralism and voluntarism: the politics and discourse of progressive school reform, 1890–1930," *Theory and Society* 21, 1992, 621–664.

England, P. and G. Farkas, "Economic and sociological views of industries, firms and jobs," in G. Farkas and P. England (eds), *Industries, Firms and Jobs*, New York, NY: Aldine de Gruyter, 1988.

Entwisle, D. R. and K. L. Alexander, "Beginning school math competence," *Child Development* 61, 1990, 454–471.

Entwisle, D. R. and K. L. Alexander, "Summer setback: race, poverty, school composition, and mathematics achievement in the first two years of school," *American Sociological Review* 57, 1992, 72–84.

Entwisle, D. R. and K. L. Alexander, "Entry into schools: the beginning school transition and educational stratification in the United States," in *Annual Review of Sociology*, Palo Alto, CA: Annual Reviews, Inc., 1993.

Entwisle, D. R. and K. L. Alexander, "Winter setback: school racial composition and learning to read," *American Sociological Review* 59, 1994, 446–460.

Entwisle, D. R. and K. L. Alexander, "A parent's economic shadow: family structure versus family resources as influences on early school achievement," *Journal of Marriage and the Family* 57, 1995, 399–409.

Entwisle, D. R. and K. L. Alexander, "Family type and children's growth in reading and math over the primary grades," *Journal of Marriage and the Family* 58, 1996, 341–355.

Entwisle, D. R., K. L. Alexander, and L. S. Olson, *Children, Schools and Inequality*, Boulder, CO: Westview Press, 1997.

Eppenshade, T., "Investing in children: new estimates of parental expenditures," Washington, DC: Urban Institute, 1984.

Erickson, M. F., J. Korfmacher and B. Egeland, "Attachments past and present: implications for therapeutic intervention with mother-infant dyads," *Development and Psychopathology* 4, 1992, 495–507.

Ernst, C. and J. Angst, *Birth Order: Its Influence on Personality*, Berlin, Germany: Springer–Verlag, 1983.

Farkas, G., *Human Capital or Cultural Capital: Ethnicity and Poverty Groups in an Urban School District*, New York, NY: Aldine de Gruyter, 1996.

Fauman, S. J. and H. Sharp, "Presenting the results of social research to the public," *Public Opinion Quarterly* 22, 1958, 107–111.

Featherman, D. and R. Hauser, *Opportunity and Change*, New York, NY: Academic Press, 1978.

Featherman, D. L. and K. I. Spenner, "Class and the socialization of children: constance, change, or irrelevance?," in E. Hetherington, R. Lerner, and M. Perlmutter (eds), *Child Development in Life-Span Perspective*, Hillsdale, NJ: Lawrence Erlbaum Associates, 1988.

Featherman, D. L. and G. Stevens, "A revised socioeconomic index of occupational status: application in analysis of sex differences in attainment," in R. M. Hauser, D. Mechanic, A. O. Haller, and T. Hauser (eds) *Social Structure and Behavior: Essays in Honor of William Hamilton Sewell*, New York, NY: Academic Press, 1982.

Feinberg, W. and H. Rosemont Jr., *Work, Technology, and Education: Dissenting Essays in the Intellectual Foundations of American Education*, Urbana, IL: University of Illinois Press, 1975.

Feldman, S., "Promises to keep: where we stand," http://www.aft.org/stand/previous/2001/0101.html, 2001.

Feldman, S. S. and S. C. Nash, "Interest in babies during young adulthood," *Child Development* 49, 1978, 617–622.

Feldstein, M., *Tax Avoidance and the Deadweight Loss of the Income Tax*, Cambridge, MA: National Bureau of Economic Research Working Paper No. 5055, 1995.

Fergusson, D. M., M. T. Lynskey, and L. J. Horwood, "The effort of maternal depression on maternal ratings of child behavior," *Journal of Abnormal Child Psychology* 21, 1993, 245–269.

Feuer, L. S., "John Dewey and the back to the people movement in American thought," *Journal of the History of Ideas* 20, 1959, 545–568.

Field, T. M., S. M. Widmayer, S. Stringer, and E. Ignatoff, "Teenage, lower-class, black mothers and their preterm infants: an intervention and developmental follow-up," *Child Development* 51, 1980, 426–436.

Field, T. M., S. M. Widmayer, R. Greenberg, and S. Stoller, "Effects of parent training on teenage mothers and their infants," *Pediatrics* 69, 1982, 245–269.

Filmer, D. and L. Pritchett, "The effect of household wealth on educational attainment: evidence from 35 countries," *Population and Development Review* 25, 1999, 85–120.

Fine, M. and P. Rosenberg, "Dropping out of high school: the ideology of school and work," *Journal of Education* 165, 1983, 257–272.

Fischer, C., M. Hout, M. Sanchez Jankowski, S. Lucas, A. Swidler, and K. Voss, *Inequality by Design: Cracking the Bell Curve Myth*, Princeton, NJ: Princeton University Press, 1996.

Fischer, C. and S. Oliker, "A research note on friendship, gender, and the life cycle," *Social Forces* 62, 1983, 124–133.

Forehand, R., N. Long, G. H. Brody, and R. Fauber, "Home predictors of young adolescents' school behavior and academic performance," *Child Development* 57, 1986, 1528–1533.

Forgione, P. D., "Third international mathematics and science study," National Center for Educational Statistics, U.S. Department of Education, Washington, D. C., 1999.

Foster, A. and M. R. Rosenzweig, "Learning by doing and learning from others: human capital and technical change in agriculture," *Journal of Political Economy* 103, 1995, 1176–1209.

Frazier, F., *Transition from School to Work: Linking Education and Worksite Training*, Washington, DC: General Accounting Office; GAO/HRD, 1991, 91–105.

Freud, S., "Analysis of a phobia in a five-year-old boy," in *The Sexual Enlightenment of Children*, New York, NY: Collier, 1909.

Freud, S., "The passing of the Oedipus complex," in *Collected Papers*, vol. 2, London: Hogarth, 1924.

Frodi, M., A. D. Murray, M. Lamb, and J. Steinberg, "Biological and social determinants of responsiveness to infants in 10- to 15-year-old girls," *Sex Roles* 10, 1984, 639–649.

Frodi, M. and M. E. Lamb, "Sex differences in responsiveness to infants: a developmental study of psychophysiological and behavioral responses," *Child Development* 49 1978, 1182–1188.

Fuchs, V. and D. Reklis, "America's children: economic perspectives and policy options," *Science* 255, 1992, 41–46.

Fuligni, A. S. and J. Brooks-Gunn, "The healthy development of young children: SES disparities, prevention strategies, and policy opportunities," in B. D. Smedley and S. L. Syme (eds), *Promoting Health: Intervention Strategies From Social and Behavioral Research*, Washington, DC: National Academy Press, 2000.

Fuller, B., "What school factors raise achievement in the Third World?," *Review of Educational Research* 57, 1987, 255–292.

Fuller, B. and R. Rubinson (eds), *The Political Construction of Education: The State, School Expansion, and Economic Change*, New York, NY: Praeger, 1992.

Furstenberg Jr., F. F. "Good dads–bad dads: two faces of fatherhood," in A. J. Cherlin (ed.), *The Changing American Family and Public Policy*, Washington, DC: Urban Institute, 1988, 193–218.

Furstenberg Jr., F. F. "Social capital and the role of fathers in the family," in A. Booth and A. C. Crouter (eds), *Men in Families: When Do They Get Involved? What Difference Does It Make?*, Mahwah, NJ: Lawrence Erlbaum Associates, 1998, 295–301.

Furstenberg Jr., F. F., J. Brooks-Gunn, and S. P. Morgan, *Adolescent Mothers in Later Life*, Cambridge: Cambridge University Press, 1987.

Furstenberg Jr., F. F., and A. Cherlin, *Divided Families: What Happens to Children When Parents Part?* Cambridge, MA: Harvard University Press, 1991.

Furstenberg Jr., F. F., and M. E. Hughes, "Social capital and successful development among at-risk youth," *Journal of Marriage and the Family* 57, 1995, 580–593.

Gailbraith, R., "Sibling spacing and intellectual development: a closer look at the confluence model," *Developmental Psychology* 18, 1982, 151–174.

Galton, F., *English Men of Science: Their Nature and Nurture*, London: MacMillan, 1874.

Gamoran, A., "The stratification of high school learning opportunities," *Sociology of Education* 60, 1987, 135–155.

Gamoran, A. and M. Berends, "The effects of stratification in secondary schools: synthesis of survey and ethnographic research," *Review of Educational Research* 57, 1987, 415–435.

Gamoran, A. and R. Mare, "Secondary school tracking and educational inequality: reinforcement, compensation, or neutrality?," *American Journal of Sociology* 94, 1989, 1146–1183.

Garfinkel, I. and S. S. McLanahan, *Single Mothers and Their Children: A New American Dilemma*, Washington, DC: Urban Institute Press, 1986.

Gerber, T., "Family structure and educational careers in Russia: the single/step model vs. evolutionary psychology," presented at the Semi-Annual Meetings of the Research Committee on Social Stratification (RC 28) of the International Sociological Association, Berkeley, CA, 2001.

Geronimus, A. T., S. Korenman, and M. M. Hillemeier, "Does young maternal age adversely affect child development? Evidence from cousin comparisons in the United States?," *Population and Development Review* 20, 1994, 585–609.

Gerson, K., *No Man's Land: Men's Changing Commitments to Family and Work,* New York, NY: Basic Books, 1993.

Gittell, M., "Urban school reform in the 1970s," *Education and Urban Society* 1, 1968, 9–20.

Glewwe, P. and Jacoby, H., "An economic analysis of delayed primary school enrollment and childhood malnutrition in a low income country," *Review of Economics and Statistics* 77, 1995a, 156–169.

Glewwe, P. and H. Jacoby, *School Enrollment and Completion in Viet Nam: An Investigation of Recent Downward Trends*, Washington, DC: World Bank, mimeo, 1995b.

Glewwe, P., H. Jacoby, and E. M. King, "Early childhood nutrition and academic achievement: a longitudinal data analysis," *Journal of Public Economics* 81, 2001, 345–368.

Goering, J., J. Kraft, J. Feins, D. McInnis, M. J. Holin, and H. Elhassan, *Moving to Opportunity for Fair Housing Demonstration Program: Current Status and Initial Findings*, Washington, DC: U.S. Department of Housing and Urban Development, 1999.

Goldscheider, F. K. and L. J. Waite, *New Families, No Families?* Berkeley and Los Angeles, CA and Oxford: University of California Press, 1991.

Gomes, M., "Family size and educational attainment in Kenya," *Population and Development Review* 10, 1984, 647–660.

Gordon, L. (ed.), *Women, the State, and Welfare*, Madison, WI: University of Wisconsin Press, 1990.

Gornick, J., M. Meyers, and K. Ross, "Supporting the employment of mothers: policy variation across fourteen welfare states," *Journal of European Social Policy* 7, 1997, 45–70.

Gornick, J., M. Meyers, and K. Ross, "Public policies and the employment of mothers: a cross-national study," *Social Science Quarterly* 79, 1999, 35–54.

Gottfried, A. E., J. S. Fleming, and A. W. Gottfried, "Role of cognitively stimulating home environment in children's academic intrinsic motivation: a longitudinal study," *Child Development* 69, 1998, 1448–1460.

Graham, J. W., A. H. Beller, and P. M. Hernandez, "The effects of child support on educational attainment," in I. Garfinkel, S. S. McLanahan, and P. K. Robins (eds), *Child Support and Child Well-being*, Washington, DC: The Urban Institute, 1994, 317–354.

Granovetter, M., "The strength of weak ties," *American Journal of Sociology* 78, 1973, 1360–1380.

Granovetter, M., *Getting a Job* (2nd edn), Chicago, IL: University of Chicago Press, 1995.

Grant, G., *The World We Created at Hamilton High,* Cambridge, MA: Harvard University Press, 1988.

Grasso, J. and J. Shea, *Vocational Education and Training: Impact on Youth*, Berkeley, CA: The Carnegie Foundation for the Advancement of Teaching, 1979.

Gray, S. W. and K. Ruttle, "The family-oriented home visiting program: a longitudinal study," *Genetic Psychology Monographs* 102, 1980, 299–316.

Green, A. D. and K. A. Moore, "Predictors of father involvement and the consequences for children," paper presented at NICHD Family and Child Well-Being Network's Conference on Father Involvement, Washington, DC, 1996.

Greenberg, D. and H. Halsey, "Systematic misreporting and effects of income maintenance experiments on work effort: evidence from the Seattle–Denver experiment," *Journal of Labor Economics* 1, 1983, 380–407.

Greenberg, D., R. Moffitt, and J. Friedmann, "Underreporting and experimental effects on work effort: evidence from the Gary income maintenance experiment," *Review of Economics and Statistics* 63, 1981, 581–589.

Greenberger, E. and L. D. Steinberg, *When Teenagers Work: The Psychological and Social Costs of Adolescent Employment*, New York, NY: Basic Books, 1986.

Greenhalgh, S., "Sexual stratification: the other side of 'growth with equity' in East Asia," *Population and Development Review* 11, 1985, 265–314.

Greenhalgh, S., Z. Chuzhu, and N. Lin, "Restraining population growth on three Chinese villages, 1988–93," *Population and Development Review* 20, 1994, 365–395.

Griffiths, C., "Social development and women in Africa – the case of Morocco," *Journal of Gender Studies* 5, 1996, 630–679.

Griliches, Z., "Sibling models and data in economics: beginning of a survey," *Journal of Political Economy* 87, 1979, S37–S64.

Grissmer, D. W., A. E. Flanagan, J. H. Kawata, and S. Williamson, *Improving Student Achievement: What State NAEP Test Scores Tell Us,* Santa Monica, CA: RAND, 2000.

Griswold, R. L., *Fatherhood in America: A History*, New York, NY: Basic Book, 1993.

Grogger, J., "Does school quality explain the recent black/white wage trend?," *Journal of Labor Economics* 14, 1996, 231–253.

Gross, A. C., "On engineering education and engineering students," *The Journal of Higher Education* 40, 1969, 520–533.

Grotevant, H., S. Scarr, and H. Weinberg, "Intelligence and development in constellations with adopted and natural children: a test of Zajonc and Markus Model," *Child Development* 48, 1977, 1699–1703.

Grubb, N., "Postsecondary vocational education and the sub-baccalaureate labor market: new evidence on economic returns," *Economics of Education Review* 11, 1992, 225–248.

Grubb, N., "The long-run effects of proprietary schools on wages and earnings: implications for federal policy," *Educational Evaluation and Policy Analysis* 15, 1993, 17–33.

Grubb, N., T. Dickinson, L. Giordano, and G. Kaplan, *Betwixt and Between: Education, Skills and Employment in Sub-Baccalaurate Labor Markets*, Berkeley, CA: National Center for Research in Vocational Education, 1992.

Guo, G. and K. M. Harris, "The mechanisms mediating the effects of poverty on children's intellectual development," *Demography* 37, 2000, 431–448.

Guo, G. and L. Van Wey, "Sibship size and intellectual development: is the relationship causal?," *American Sociological Review* 64, 1999a, 169–187.

Guo, G. and L. Van Wey, "The effects of closely spaced and widely spaced sibship size on intellectual development," *American Sociological Review* 64, 1999b, 199–206.

Guthrie, J. W., G. B. Kleindorfer, H. M. Levin, and R. T. Stout, *Schools and Inequality*, Cambridge, MA: MIT Press, 1971.

Haddad, L., J. Hodnicott, and H. Alderman (eds), *Intrahousehold Resource Allocation in Developing Countries*, Baltimore, MD: Johns Hopkins University Press, 1997.

Haller, E. J., "Pupil influence in teacher socialization: a socio-linguistic study," *Sociology of Education* 40, 1967, 316–333.

Hallinan, M., "Equality of educational opportunity," *Annual Review of Sociology* 14, 1988, 49–68.

Hallinan, M., "Tracking: from theory to practice," *Sociology of Education* 67, 1994, 79–91.

Hamilton, S. and K. Hurrelmann, "The school-to-career transition in Germany and the United States," *Teachers College Record* 96, 1994, 329–344.

Hammen, C., D. Burge, and C. Adrian, "Timing of mother and child depression in a longitudinal study of children at risk," *Journal of Consulting and Clinical Psychology* 59, 1991, 341–345.

Hammond, P. A. and J. A. Frechtling, "Twelve, nine and three month achievement gains of low and average achieving elementary school students," paper presented at AERA Annual Meeting, San Francisco, CA, 1979.

Hannum, E. and Y. Xie, "Trends in educational gender inequality in China: 1949–1985," *Research in Social Stratification and Mobility* 13, 1994, 73–98.

Hanushek, E., "The economics of schooling," *Journal of Economic Literature* 24, 1986, 1141–1177.

Hanushek, E. A., *Making Schools Work: Improving Performance and Controlling Cost,* Washington, DC: Brookings Institution Press, 1994.

Hanushek, E. A., "Interpreting recent research on schooling in developing countries," *The World Bank Research Observer* 10, 1995, 227–246.

Hanushek, E. A., *Improving America's Schools: The Role of Incentives*, Washington, DC: National Academy Press, 1996.

Hanushek, E. A., "School resources and student performance," in G. Burtless, *Does Money Matter? The Effect of School Resources on Student Achievement and Adult Success*, Washington, DC: Brookings Institution Press, 1996, 43–73.

Hanushek, E. A. and S. G. Rivkin, "Understanding the twentieth century growth in U.S. school spending," *The Journal of Human Resources* 32, 1997, 35–68.

Hanushek, E. A., S. G. Rivkin, and L. L. Taylor, "Aggregation and the estimated effects of school resources," *The Review of Economics and Statistics* 78, 1996, 611–627.

Harbison, R. W. and E. A. Hanushek, *Educational Performance of the Poor: Lessons from Rural Northeast Brazil,* New York, NY: Oxford University Press for the World Bank, 1992.

Harris, K. M. and J. K. Marmer, "Poverty, paternal involvement, and adolescent well-being," *Journal of Family Issues* 17, 1996, 614–640.

Harris, K. M. and S. P. Morgan, "Fathers, sons, and daughters: differential paternal involvement in parenting," *Journal of Marriage and the Family,* 53, 1991, 531–544.

Harter, S., *Manual for the Social Support Scale for Children*, Denver, CO: University of Denver, 1985.

Hauser, P. M., "The chaotic society: product of the social morphological revolution," *American Sociological Review* 34, 1969, 1–19.

Hauser, R. and D. Featherman, "Trends in the occupational mobility of U.S. Men, 1962–1970," *American Sociological Review* 38, 1973, 302–310.

Hauser, R. and D. Kuo, "Does the gender composition of sibships affect women's educational attainment?," *The Journal of Human Resources* 33, 1998, 644–657.

Hauser, R. and W. Sewell, "Birth order and educational attainment in full sibships," *American Educational Research Journal* 22, 1985, 1–23.

Hauser, R. M., "Current population surveys: uniform October files, 1968–1990," Washington, DC: U.S. Dept. of Commerce, Bureau of the Census [producer], 1990: Ann Arbor, MI: Inter-university Consortium for Political and Social Research [distributor], 1993.

Hauser, R. M. and T. N. Daymont, "Schooling, ability, and earnings: cross-sectional findings 8 to 14 years after high school graduation," *Sociology of Education* 50, 1977, 182–206.

Haveman, R. H., *Poverty Policy and Poverty Research: The Great Society and the Social Sciences*, Madison, WI: University of Wisconsin Press, 1987.

Haveman, R. H. and B. S. Wolfe, "Children's prospects and children's policy," *The Journal of Economic Perspectives* 7, 1993, 153–174.

Haveman, R. H. and B. S. Wolfe, *Succeeding Generations: On the Effects of Investments in Children*, New York, NY: Russell Sage Foundation, 1994.

Haveman, R. H. and B. S. Wolfe, "The determinants of children's attainments: a review of methods and findings," *Journal of Economic Literature* 33, 1995, 1829–1878.

Haveman, R. H., B. S. Wolfe, and J. Spaulding, "Childhood events and circumstances influencing high school completion," *Demography* 28, 1991, 133–157.

Hawkins, A. J., S. L. Christiansen, K. P. Sargent, and E. J. Hill, "Rethinking fathers' involvement in child care: a developmental perspective," in W. Marsiglio (ed.), *Fatherhood: Contemporary Theory, Research, and Social Policy*, Thousand Oaks, CA: Sage, 1995.

Hawkins, A. J. and D. C. Dollahite, *Generative Fathering: Beyond Deficit Perspectives*, Thousand Oaks, CA: Sage, 1997.

Hawkins, A. J. and R. Palkovitz, "Beyond the ticks and clicks: the need for more diverse and broader conceptualizations and measures of father involvement," *Journal of Men's Studies* 8, 1999, 11–32.

Hawkins, H., *Between Harvard and America: The Educational Leadership of Charles W. Eliot*, New York, NY: Oxford University Press, 1972.

Hayes, D. P. and J. Grether, "The school year and vacations: when do students learn?," paper presented at the annual meetings of the Eastern Sociological Association, New York, 1969. Subsequently published in *Cornell Journal of Social Relations* 17, 1983, 56–71.

Hayes, D. P. and J. P. King, *The Development of Reading Achievement Differentials During the School Year and Vacations*, Ithaca, NY: Cornell University, 1974, mimeo.

Heberle, J., "PACE: parent and child education in Kentucky," in T. G. Sticht, M. J. Beeler, and B. A. McDonald (eds), *The Intergenerational Transfer of Cognitive Skills: Vol. I. Programs, Policy, and Research Issues,* Norwood, NJ: Ablex, 1992, 136–148.

Heckman, J. J. and V. J. Hotz, "The sources of inequality for males in Panama's labor market," *Journal of Human Resources* 21, 1986, F507–F542.

Heckman, J., "Shadow prices, market wages, and labor supply," *Econometrica* 42, 1974, 679–694.

Heer, D., "Effects of sibling number on child outcomes," *Annual Review of Sociology* 11, 1985, 27–47.

Heer, D., "Effect of number, order and spacing of siblings on child and adult outcomes," *Social Biology* 33, 1986, 1–4.

Heise, D. and E. P. M. Roberts, "The development of role knowledge," *Genetic Psychology Monographs* 82, 1970, 83–115.

Heiss, J., "Effects of African American family structure on school attitudes and performance," *Social Problems* 43, 1996, 246–267.

Henderson, J., "Two are better than one: the fact that a husband and wife break up doesn't make either of them less a parent," in *Global and Mail*, 1988, A7.

Hermalin, A., J. Seltzer, and C. Lin, "Transitions in the effect of family size on female educational attainment: the case of Taiwan," *Comparative Educational Review,* 26, 1982, 254–270.

Hertzog, C. and M. Rovine, "Repeated measures analysis of variance in developmental research: selected issues," *Child Development* 56, 1985, 787–809.

Hetherington, E. M., "Coping with family transitions: winners, losers and survivors," *Child Development* 60, 1989, 1–14.

Heuvel, A., "The timing of parenthood and intergenerational relations," *Journal of Marriage and the Family* 50, 1988, 483–491.

Heyneman, S. and W. Loxley, "The effect of primary-school quality on academic achievement across twenty-nine high- and low-income countries," *American Journal of Sociology* 88, 1983, 1162–1194.

Heyns, B., *Summer Learning and the Effects of Schooling*, New York, NY: Academic, 1978.

Heyns, B., "Educational effects: Issues in conceptualization and measurement," in J.C. Richardson, *Handbook of Theory and Research in the Sociology of Education*, New York, NY: Greenwood, 1986.

Heyns, B., "Schooling and cognitive development: is there a season for learning?," *Child Development* 58, 1987, 1151–1160.

Higgins, J. V., E. W. Reed, and S. C. Reed, "Intelligence and family size: a paradox resolved," *Eugenic Quarterly* 9, 1962, 84–90.

Hill, A. M. and E. M. King, "Women's education and economic well-being," *Feminist Economics* 1, 1995, 21–46.

Hill, M. A. and J. O'Neill, "Family endowments and the achievement of young children with special reference to the underclass," *Journal of Human Resources* 29, 1994, 1064–1100.

Hill, M. S. and G. J. Duncan, "Parental family income and the socioeconomic attainment of children," *Social Science Research* 16, 1987, 39–73.

Hochschild, A. and A. Machung, *The Second Shift: Working Parents and the Revolution at Home*, New York, NY: Viking, 1989.

Hochschild, J. L., *Facing Up to the American Dream: Race, Class and the Soul of the Nation*, Princeton, NJ: Princeton University Press, 1995.

Hofferth, S. L., P. E. Davis-Kean, J. Davis, and J. Finkelstein, "The child development supplement to the panel study of income dynamics 1997 User Guide," 1997. http://www.isr.umich.edu/src/child-development/usergd.html.

Hofferth, S. L., P. Davis-Kean, J. Davis, and J. Finkelstein, "User guide for the child development supplement of the panel study of income dynamics," 1998.

Hofferth, S. L. and J. F. Sandberg, "Changes in American children's time, 1981–1997," in T. J. Owens and S. L. Hofferth (eds), *Children at the Millennium: Where Have We Come From, Where Are We Going? Advances in Life Course Research, Volume 6*, New York, NY: Elsevier Science, 2001, 193–229.

Hofferth, S. L., W. J. Yeung, and F. P. Stafford, "Panel study of income dynamics," *Inter-University Consortium for Political and Social Research Bulletin* 15, 1996, 6–22.

Holzer, H., *What Employers Want: Job Prospects for Less Educated Workers*, New York, NY: Russell Sage, 1996.

Hotchkiss, L. and L. Dorsten, "Curriculum effects on early post-high school outcomes," *Research in the Sociology of Education and Socialization* 7, 1987, 191–219.

Howell, W. G. and P. E. Peterson, *The Education Gap: Vouchers and Urban Schools*, Washington, DC: Brookings Institution Press, 2002.

Hox, J. J., *Applied Multilevel Analysis*, Amsterdam: TT-Publikaties, 1995.

Huston, A. C., "Children in poverty: designing research to affect policy," Social Policy Report, *Society for Research in Child Development* 8, 1994, 1–12.

Hwang, C. and M. E. Lamb, "Father involvement in Sweden: a longitudinal study of its stability and correlates," *International Journal of Behavioral Development* 21, 1997, 621–632.

Ihinger-Tallman, M., K. Pasley, and C. Buehler, "Developing a middle-range theory of father involvement postdivorce," *Journal of Family Issues* 14, 1993, 550–571.

Lynn, I. and P. Moock, "School attributes, household characteristics, and demand for schooling: a case study of rural Peru," *International Review of Education* 37, 1991, 429–451.

Infant Health and Development Program (IHDP), "Enhancing the outcomes of low-birth-weight, premature infants," *Journal of the American Medical Association* 263, 1990, 3035–3042.

Israel, G. D., L. L. Beaulieu, and G. Hartless, "The influence of family and community social capital on educational achievement," *Rural Sociology* 66, 2001, 43–68.

Iwaki, H., "Educational and structural changes in demography as they relate to educational policy," *The Journal of Educational Sociology* 48, 1991, 78–101.

Jackson, A. P., J. Brooks-Gunn, C. Huang, and M. Glassman, "Single mothers in low-wage jobs: financial strain, parenting, and preschoolers' outcomes," *Child Development* 71, 2000, 1409–1423.

Jacoby, H., "Borrowing constraints and progress through school: evidence from Peru," *Review of Economics and Statistics* 76, 1994, 151–160.

Jaynes, G. and R. Williams, *A Common Destiny: Blacks and American Society*, National Research Council, Washington, DC, 1989.

Jencks, C., "Is the American underclass growing?," in C. Jencks and P. Peterson (eds), *The Urban Underclass*, Washington, DC: Brookings, 1991, 28–102.

Jencks, C. S., S. Bartlett, M. Corcoran, J. Crouse, D. Eaglesfield, G. Jackson, K. McClelland, P. Mueser, M. Olneck, J. Schwartz, S. Ward, and J. Williams, *Who Gets Ahead? The Determinants of Economic Success in America*, New York, NY: Basic Books, 1979.

Jencks, C. S., M. Smith, M. Bane, D. Cohen, H. Ginits, B. Heyns, and S. Michelson, *Inequality: A Reassessment of the Effect of Family and Schooling in America*, New York, NY: Basic Books, 1972.

Jencks, C. and M. Phillips, *The Black/White Test Score Gap*, Washington, DC: Brookings Institution Press, 1999.

Johnson, M. S., "Alternate possibilities in education reform: the impact of non-school programs on school performance," unpublished manuscript, Department of Sociology, New York University, 2002.

Josselyn, I. M., "Cultural forces, motherliness and fatherliness," *American Journal of Orthopsychiatry* 26, 1956, 264–271.

Juster, F. T. and F. P. Stafford, "Time, goods, and well-being," Institute for Social Research, University of Michigan, 1985.

Juster, F. T., "The validity and quality of time use estimates obtained from recall diaries," in T. F. Juster and F. P. Stafford (eds), *Time, Goods, and Well-Being*, Ann Arbor, MI: Institute for Social Research, 1985.

Juster, F. T. and F. P. Stafford, "The allocation of time: empirical findings, behavioral models, and problems of measurement," *Journal of Economic Literature* XXIX, 1991, 471–522.

Kablaoui, B. N. and A. J. Paulter, "The effects of part-time work experience on high school students," *Journal of Career Development* 17, 1991, 195–211.

Kamens, D., J. Meyer, and A. Benavot, "Worldwide patterns in academic secondary education curricula," *Comparative Education Review* 40, 1996, 116–138.

Kane, T., "Racial and ethnic preferences in college admissions," in C. Jencks and M. Phillips, *The Black-White Test Score Gap*, Washington, DC: Brookings Institution Press, 1998, 431–456.

Kang, S. and Bishop, J., "Vocational or academic coursework in high school: compliments or substitutes?," *Economics of Education Review* 8, 1989, 133–148.

Keenan, K., D. S. Shaw, B. Walsh, E. Delliquadri, and J. Giovannelli, "DMS-III-R disorders in preschool children from low-income families," *Journal of the American Academy of Child and Adolescent Psychiatry* 36, 1997, 620–627.

Keister, L., "Family structure, race, and wealth ownership: A longitudinal exploration of wealth accumulation processes," Department of Sociology, The Ohio State University, 2000, working paper No. 304.

Kember, D. and J. McKay, "Action research into the quality of student learning: a paradigm for faculty development," *Journal of Higher Education* 67, 1996, 528–554.

Kerckhoff, A., "Institutional arrangements and stratification processes in industrial societies," *Annual Review of Sociology* 15, 1995, 323–347.

Kerckhoff, A. C., "Education and social stratification in comparative perspective," *Sociology of Education* 1, 2001, 3–18.

Kerkhoff, A. and L. Bell, "Hidden capital: vocational credentials and attainment in the United States," *Sociology of Education* 71, 1998, 152–174.

King, E. M. and L. A. Lillard, "Education policy and schooling attainment in Malaysia and the Philippines," *Economics of Education Review* 6, 1987, 167–181.

King, V., "Nonresident father involvement and child well-being: can dads make a difference?," *Journal of Family Issues* 15, 1994, 78–96.

King, V. and G. Elder, "Education and grandparenting roles," *Research on Aging* 20, 1998, 450–474.

Kingston, P. W. and J. C. Smart, "The economic pay-off of prestigious colleges," in P. W. Kingston and L. S. Lewis, *The High-Status Track: Studies of Elite Schools and Stratification,* Albany, NY: State University of New York Press, 1990.

Kirschenman, J. and Neckerman, K., "'We'd love to hire them, but …': the meaning of race for employers," in C. Jencks and P. Peterson (eds), *The Urban Underclass.* Washington, DC: Brookings Institute, 1991.

Klebanov, P. K., J. Brooks-Gunn, P. L. Chase-Lansdale, and R. Gordon, "Are neighborhood effects on young children mediated by features of the home environment?," in J. Brooks-Gunn, G. Duncan, and J. L. Aber (eds), *Neighborhood Poverty: Context and Consequences for Children,* New York, NY: Russell Sage Foundation Press, 1997, 119–145.

Klebanov, P. K., J. Brooks-Gunn, C. M. McCarton, and M. C. McCormick, "The contribution of neighborhood and family income to developmental test scores over the first three years of life," *Child Development* 69, 1998, 1420–1436.

Klebanov, P. K., J. Brooks-Gunn, and M. C. McCormick, "Maternal coping strategies and emotional distress: results of an early intervention program for low birth weight young children," *Developmental Psychology* 37, 2001, 654–667.

Klibanoff, L. S. and S. A. Haggart, *Report # 8: Summer Growth and the Effectiveness of Summer School,* technical report to the Office of Program Evaluation, U.S. Department of Education, Mountain View, CA: RMC Research Corporation, 1981.

Knodel, J., "Fertility decline and children's education in Thailand: some macro and micro effects," in C. Lloyd (ed.), *Fertility, Family Size and Structure,* New York, NY: Population Council, 1993, 268–296.

Knodel, J., "The closing of the gender gap in schooling: the case of Thailand," *Comparative Education* 33, 1997, 61–86.

Knodel, J. and M. Wongsith, "Family size and children's education in Thailand: Evidence from a national sample," *Demography* 28, 1991, 119–131.

Knox, V. W. and M. Bane, "Child support and schooling," in I. Garfinkel, S. S. McLanahan, and P. K. Robins (eds), *Child Support and Child Well-being*, Washington, DC: Urban Institute, 1994, 285–316.

Kohn, M. and C. Schooler, "Job conditions and personality: A longitudinal assessment of their reciprocal effects," *American Journal of Sociology* 87, 1982, 1257–1286.

Kozol, J., *Savage Inequalities: Children in America's Schools,* New York, NY: Crown Publishers, 1991.

Krueger, A. B. and D. Whitmore, "Would smaller classes help close the black-white achievement gap?," in J. Chubb and T. Loveless (eds), *Bridging the Achievement Gap*, Washington, DC: Brookings Institution Press, 2002.

Krueger, A. B. and P. Zhu, "Another look at the New York City school voucher experiment," Working Paper #1, Education Research Section, Princeton University, 2003.

Krug, E. A., *The Shaping of the American High School, Volume I, 1880–1920*, New York, NY: Harper and Row, 1964.

Krug, E. A., *The Shaping of the American High School, Volume II, 1920–1941*, Madison, WI: University of Wisconsin Press, 1972.

Kuo, H. D. and R. Hauser, "Trends in family effects on the education of black and white brothers," *Sociology of Education* 68, 1995, 136–160.

Kuo, H. D. and R. Hauser, "How does size of sibship matter? Family configuration and family effects on educational attainment," *Social Science Research* 26, 1997, 69–94.

Lamb, M. E., *The Role of the Father in Child Development*, New York, NY: Wiley, 1976.

Lamb, M. E., "The changing roles of fathers," in M. E. Lamb (ed.), *The Fathers' Role: Applied Perspectives*, New York, NY: Wiley, 1986, 3–27.

Lamb, M. E., "Paternal involvement: levels, sources, and consequences," in M. E. Lamb (ed.), *The Role of the Father in Child Development*, New York, NY: John Wiley & Sons, Inc., 1997.

Lamb, M. E., "The history of research on father involvement: an overview," *Marriage and the Family Review,* 29, 2000, 23–42.

Lamb, M. E., J. H. Pleck, E. L. Charnov, and J. A. Levine, "Paternal behavior in humans," *American Zoologist* 25, 1985, 883–894.

Lamb, M. E., J. H. Pleck, and J. A. Levine, "A biosocial perspective on paternal behavior and involvement," in B. Lahey and A. Kazdin (eds), *Advances in Clinical Child Psychology*, vol. 8, New York, NY: Plenum, 1987, 229–266.

Lamb, M. E. and M. B. Stevenson, "Father–infant relationships: their nature and importance," *Youth and Society* 9, 1978, 277–297.

Lamont, M. and A. Lareau, "Cultural capital: allusions, gaps, and glissandos in recent theoretical developments," *Sociological Theory* 6, 1988, 153–168.

Lareau, A., *Home Advantage: Social Class and Parental Intervention in Elementary Education*, London: Falmer Press, 1989.

Lareau, A. and E. Horvat, "Moments of social inclusion and exclusion: race, class and cultural capital in family–school relationships," *Sociology of Education* 72, 1999, 37–53.

LaRossa, R., "Fatherhood and social change," *Family Relations* 37, 1988, 451–458.

Larson, C. P., "Efficacy of prenatal and postpartum home visits on child health and development," *Pediatrics* 66, 1980, 191–197.

Lavigne, J. V., R. D. Gibbons, K. K. Christoffel, R. Arend, D. Rosenbaum, H. J. Binns, N. Dawson, H. Sobel, and C. Isaacs, "Prevalence rates and correlates of psychiatric disorders among preschool children," *Journal of the American Academy of Child and Adolescent Psychiatry* 35, 1996, 204–214.

Layard, R., S. Nickell, and R. Jackman, *Unemployment: Macroeconomic Performance and the Labor Market,* New York, NY: Oxford University Press, 1991.

LeClere, F. B. and B. M. Kowalewski, "Disability in the family: the effects on children's well-being," *Journal of Marriage and the Family* 56, 1994, 457–468.

Lee, J.C., "Cash for hash? Explaining the relationship between adolescent employment and substance abuse," unpublished manuscript, Department of Sociology, University of Minnesota, 2001.

Leslau, A., E. Krausz, and S. Nussbaum, "The education of Iraqi and Romanian immigrants in Israel," *Comparative Education Review* 39, 1995, 178–194.

Leventhal, T. and J. Brooks-Gunn, "Moving on up: neighborhood effects on children and families," in M. Bornstein and R. H. Bradley (eds), *Socioeconomic Status, Parenting, and Child Development*, Mahwah, NJ: Erlbaum, 2003.

Leventhal, T. and J. Brooks-Gunn, "The neighborhoods they live in: the effects of neighborhood residence upon child and adolescent outcomes," *Psychological Bulletin* 126, 2000, 309–337.

Liaw, F. and J. Brooks-Gunn, "Cumulative familial risks and low-birthweight children's cognitive and behavioral development," *Journal of Clinical Child Psychology* 23, 1994, 360–372.

Lieberman, A. F., D. R. Weston, and J. H. Pawl, "Preventive intervention and outcome with anxiously attached dyads," *Child Development* 62, 1991, 199–209.

Lillard, L. and R. Willis, "Intergenerational educational mobility: effects of family and state in Malaysia," *Journal of Human Resources* 29, 1994, 1126–1166.

Lin, N., "Social networks and status attainment," *Annual Review of Sociology* 25, 1999, 467–487.

Lin, N., W. Ensel, and J. C. Vaughn, "Social resources and strength of ties: structural factors in occupational attainment," *American Sociological Review* 46, 1981, 393–405.

Linver, M. R. and J. Brooks-Gunn, "Parenting as mediating early intervention effects upon young children," unpublished manuscript, 2001.

Linver, M. R., J. Brooks-Gunn, and D. E. Kohen, "Family processed as pathways from income to young children's development," *Developmental Psychology* 38, 2002, 719–734.

Lloyd, C. (ed.), *Fertility, Family Size and Structure*, New York, NY: Population Council, 1993.

Lloyd, C. and A. Blanc, "Children's schooling in sub-Saharan Africa: the role of fathers, mothers, and others," *Population and Development Review* 22, 1996, 265–298.

Lloyd, C. and A. Gage–Brandon, "Does sibsize matter? The implications of family size for children's education in Ghana," in C. Lloyd (ed.), *Fertility, Family Size and Structure*, New York, NY: Population Council, 1993, 482–519.

Lortie, D. C., "Teacher socialization: the Robinson Crusoe model," in *The Real World of the Beginning Teacher*, National Commission on Teacher Education and Professional Standards, Washington, DC: National Education Association, 1966.

Love, J. M., E. E. Kisker, C. M. Ross, P. Z. Schochet, J. Brooks-Gunn, K. Boller, D. Paulsell, A. S. Fuligni, and L. J. Berlin, *Building Their Futures: How Early Head Start Programs are Enhancing the Lives of Infants and Toddlers in Low-Income Families*, Washington, DC: US Department of Health and Human Services, 2001.

Lucas, S. R., "Effectively maintained inequality: educational transitions, track mobility, and social background effects," *American Journal of Sociology* 106, 2001, 1642–1690.

Lyons-Ruth, K., D. Zoll, D. B. Connell, and H. U. Grunebaum, "The depressed mother and her one-year-old infant: environmental context, mother–infant interaction and attachment, and infant development," in E. Tronick and T. Field (eds), *Maternal Depression and Infant Disturbance*, San Francisco, CA: Jossey Bass, 1986, 61–82.

Madden, J., J. O'Hara, and P. Levenstein, "Home again: effects of the mother–child home program on mother and child," *Child Development* 55, 1984, 636–647.

Mangione, S., "Asthma in Philadelphia minorities: prevalence among middle-school children and the assessment of a multi-intervention self-management program," project funded by Shering-Plough, 1998–2000.

March, J. and J. Olson, *Ambiguity and Choice in Organizations*, New York, NY: Oxford University Press, 1980.

Mare, R. and M. Tzeng, "Fathers' ages and the social stratification of sons," *American Journal of Sociology* 95, 1989, 108–131.

Marjoribanks, K., *Families and Their Learning Environments*, London: Routledge, 1979.

Marjoribanks, K., "Sibling correlates of young adults' status attainment: ethnic group differences," *The Journal of Psychology* 123, 1989, 507–516.

Marsh, W., "Employment during high school: character building or subversion of academic goals," *Sociology of Education* 64, 1991, 172–189.

Marsiglio, W., P. Armato, R. D. Day, and M. E. Lamb, "Scholarship on fatherhood in the 1990s and beyond," *Journal of Marriage and Family Review* 62, 2000, 1173–1191.

Massey, D.A. and N.A. Denton, *American Apartheid: Segregation and the Making of the Underclass*, Cambridge, MA: Harvard University Press, 1996.

Maxwell, N. and V. Rubin, *Improving the Transition from School to Work: Assessing the Impact of Old and New Strategies,* Kalamazoo, MI: W. E. Upjohn Institute for Employment Research, 1998.

Mayer, S. E., *What Money Can't Buy: Family Income and Children's Life Chances,* Cambridge, MA: Harvard University Press, 1997.

McCammon, H., "The politics of protection: state minimum wage and maximum hours laws for women in the United States, 1870–1930," *Sociological Quarterly* 36, 1995, 217–249.

McCormick, M. C., C. M. McCarton, J. Brooks-Gunn, P. Belt, and R. T. Gross, "The Infant Health and Development Program: interim summary," *Journal of Developmental and Behavioral Pediatrics* 19, 1998, 359–370.

McDonald, J. and R. Moffitt, "The uses of tobit analysis," *Review of Economics and Statistics* 62, 1980, 318–321.

McGroder, S. M., M. J. Zaslow, K. A. Moore, and J. L. Brooks, *Impacts of a Mandatory Welfare-to-Work Program on Children at School Entry and Beyond: Findings from the NEWWS Childs Outcomes Study*, Washington, DC: Child Trends, 2002.

McGuire, G., "Gender, race, ethnicity and networks: the factors affecting the status of employees' network members," *Work and Occupations* 27 (4), 2000, 500–523.

McLanahan, S. S. and G. Sanddefur, *Growing Up With A Single Parent,* Cambridge, MA: Harvard University Press, 1995.

McLanahan, S. S., J. A. Seltzer, T. L. Hanson, and E. Thomson, "Child support enforcement and child well-being," in I. Garfinkel, S. S. McLanahan, and P. K. Robins (eds), *Child Support and Child Well-Being*, Washington, DC: The Urban Institute, 1994, 239–256.

McLoyd, V. C., "Socialization and development in a changing economy: the effects of paternal job and income loss on children," *American Psychologist* 44, 1989, 293–302.

McLoyd, V. C., "The impact of economic hardship on black families and children: psychological distress, parenting, and socioemotional development," *Child Development* 61, 1990, 311–346.

McNeal Jr., R. B., "Are students being pulled out of high school? The effect of adolescent employment on dropping out," *Sociology of Education* 70, 1997, 206–220.

McPartland, J. M., *The Segregated Student in Desegregated Schools: Final Report to the Center for the Study of the Social Organization of Schools*, Baltimore, MD: Johns Hopkins University Press, 1968.

Mellow, W. and H. Sider, "Accuracy of response in labor market surveys: evidence and implications," *Journal of Labor Economics* 1, 1983, 331–344.

Mercy, J. and L. C. Steelman, "Familial influence on the intellectual attainment of children," *American Sociological Review* 47, 1982, 532–543.

Mettler, S., *Dividing Citizens: Gender and Federalism in New Deal Public Policy*, Ithaca NY: Cornell University Press, 1998.

Meyer, J. and D. P. Baker, "Forming American educational policy with international data: lessons from the sociology of education," *Sociology of Education* 69, 1996, 123–130.

Meyer, J., W. R. Scott, D. Strang, and A. L. Creighton, "Bureaucratization without centralization: changes in the organizational system of U.S. public education, 1946–1980," pp. 450–462 in R. Arum and I. R. Beattie (eds), *The Structure of Schooling*, Mountainview, CA: Mayfield, 2000.

Meyer, R. and D. Wise, "High school preparation and early labor force experience," in R. Freeman and D. Wise, *The Youth Labor Market Problem: Its Nature, Causes, and Consequences,* Chicago, IL: University of Chicago Press, 1982, 277–339.

Michael, R. T. and N. B. Tuma, "Youth employment: does life begin at 16?," *Journal of Labor Economics* 2, 1984, 464–476.

Miller, J., C. Schooler, M. Kohn, and K. Miller, "Women and work: The psychological effects of occupational conditions," *American Journal of Sociology* 85, 1979, 66–94.

Miller, P., C. Mulvey, and N. Martin, "What do twins studies tell us about the economic returns to education? A comparison of U.S. and Australian findings," *American Economic Review* 85, 1995, 586–599.

Miller, P., C. Mulvey, and N. Martin, "Family characteristics and the returns to schooling: evidence on gender differences from a sample of Australian twins," *Economica* 64, 1997, 119–136.

Milne, A. M., D. E. Myers, A. S. Rosenthal, and A. Ginsburg, "Single parents, working mothers, and the educational achievement of school children," *Sociology of Education* 59, 1986, 125–139.

Mintz, S., "Children, families, and the state: American family law in historical perspective," *Denver University Law Review,* 69, 1992, 639–640.

Mintz, S., "From patriarchy to androgyny and other myths: placing men's family roles in historical perspective," in A. Booth and N. Crouter (eds), *Men in Families: When Do They Get Involved? What Differences Does It Make?*, New Jersey, London: Lawrence Erlbaum Associates, 1998, 3–30.

Mirowsky, J., "Age and the sense of control," *Social Psychology Quarterly* 5, 1995, 31–43.

Misra, J., "Mothers of workers? the value of women's labor: women and the emergence of family allowance policy," *Gender and Society* 12, 1998, 376–399.

Miyaji, N. and M. Lock, "Monitoring motherhood: sociocultural and historical aspects of maternal and child health in Japan," *Daedalus* 123, 1993, 87–112.

Montgomery, M. R. and A. Kouzme, *Fertility and Child Schooling in Cote d'Ivoire: Is There a Tradeoff?,* Stony Brook, NY: SUNY, mimeo, 1993.

Moock, P. R. and J. Leslie, "Childhood malnutrition and schooling in the Terai region of Nepal," *Journal of Development Economics* 20, 1986, 33–52.

Moore, G., "Structural determinants of men's and women's personal networks," *American Sociological Review* 55, 1990, 726–735.

Morales-Gómes, D. and C. Torres (eds), *Education, Policy, and Social Change: Experiences from Latin America*, Westport, CT: Praeger, 1992.

Morris, P. A., "Effects of welfare reform policies on children," *Social Policy Report* 16, 2001, 1–20.

Mortimer, J. T. and M. D. Finch, "The effects of part-time work on adolescent self-concept and achievement," in K. Borman and J. Reisman (eds), *Becoming a Worker*, Norwood, NJ: Ablex Publishing Corp., 1986, 66–89.

Mortimer, J. T., J. Staff, and S. Oesterle, "Adolescent work and the early socioeconomic career," in J. T. Mortimer and M. Shanahan (eds), *Handbook of the Life Course*, New York, NY: Kluwer Academic/Plenum Publishers, 2003, 437–459.

Mosteller, F., *The Tennessee Study of Class Size in the Early School Grades*, Somerville, MA: The American Academy of Arts and Sciences, 1995.

Mosteller, F. and D. P. Moynihan, "A pathbreaking report," in F. Mosteller and D. P. Moynihan, *On Equality of Educational Opportunity*, New York, NY: Random House, 1972, 3–66.

Mueller, W. and Y. Shavit, "The institutional embeddedness of the stratification process: a comparative study of qualifications and occupations in thirteen countries," forthcoming in W. Mueller and Y. Shavit (eds), *Educational Qualifications and Occupational Destinations*, Cambridge, MA: Oxford University Press.

Mulkey, L., R. Crain and A. Harrington, "One-parent households and achievement: economic and behavioral explanation of a small effect," *Sociology of Education* 65, 1992, 48–65.

Müller, W. and D. Haun, "Bildungsungleichheit im sozialen Wandel," *Kölner Zeitschrift fuer Soziologie und Sozialpsychologie* 46, 1994, 1–42.

Murnane, R. J., *The Impact of School Resources on the Learning of Inner City Children*, Cambridge, MA: Ballinger, 1975.

Mwamwenda, T., "Women and education in Africa," *The South African Journal of Sociology* 25, 1994, 143–147.

Nash, J., "The father in contemporary culture and current psychological literature," *Child Development* 36, 1965, 262–297.

Nathan, R. P., *Social Science in Government: Uses and Misuses*, New York, NY: Basic Books, 1988.

National Center for Education Statistics, *High School and Beyond, 1980: Sophomore Cohort and Second Follow-Up (1984)*, Washington, DC: U.S. Department of Education, 1986.

National Center for Education Statistics, *National Educational Longitudinal Study of 1988: Second Follow-Up, Student Component, Data File Users Manual*, Washington, DC: U.S. Department of Education, 1994.

National Commission on Excellence in Education, *A Nation at Risk: The Imperative for Educational Reform,* Washington, DC: Government Printing Office, 1983.

National Opinion Research Center, *Eighth Grade Questionnaire NELS:88,* prepared for U.S. Department of Education, Center for Education Statistics, Chicago, IL: University of Chicago, 1988.

NICHD Early Child Care Research Network, "Chronicity of maternal depressive symptoms, maternal sensitivity, and child functioning at 36 months," *Developmental Psychology* 35, 1999, 1297–1310.

Nord, C. W., D. Brinhall, and J. West, "Fathers' involvement in their children's schools," National Center for Education Statistics, U.S. Department of Education, Office of Educational Research and Improvement, 1997.

Oakes, J., *Keeping Track: How Schools Structure Inequality*, New Haven, CT: Yale University Press, 1985.

Oakes, J., A. Gamoran, and R. N. Page, "Curriculum differentiation: opportunities, outcomes, and meanings," in P. W. Jackson (ed.), *Handbook of Research on Curriculum*, New York, NY: Macmillan, 1992, 570–608.

Olds, D. L., C. R. Henderson Jr., R. Chamberlin, and R. C. Tatelbaum, "Improving the life-course development of socially disadvantaged mothers: a randomized trial of nurse home visitation," *American Journal of Public Health* 78, 1988, 1436–1445.

Olds, D. L., C. R. Henderson Jr., and H. J. Kitzman, "Does prenatal and infancy nurse home visitation have enduring effects on qualities of parental caregiving and child health at 25–50 months of life?," *Pediatrics* 93, 1994, 89–98.

Olds, D. L., C. R. Henderson Jr., H. J. Kitzman, J. J. Eckenrode, R. E. Cole, and R. C. Tatelbaum, "Prenatal and infancy home visitation by nurses: recent findings," *The Future of Children* 9, 1999, 44–65.

Olds, D. L. and H. J. Kitzman, "Review of research on home visiting for pregnant women and parents of young children," *The Future of Children* 3, 1993, 53–92.

Oliver, M. and T. Shapiro, *Black Wealth/White Wealth: A New Perspective on Racial Inequality*, New York, NY: Routledge, 1995.

Olson, L., *The School-to-Work Revolution: How Employers and Educators are Joining Forces to Prepare Tomorrow's Skilled Workforce,* Reading, MA: Perseus Books, 1997.

Orfield, G., *Schools More Separate: Consequences of a Decade of Resegregation*, The Civil Rights Project, Cambridge, MA, 2001.

Osofsky, J. D., A. M. Culp, and L. M. Ware, "Intervention challenges with adolescent mothers and their infants," *Psychiatry* 51, 1988, 236–241.

Osterman, P., "The job market for adolescents," in D. Stern and D. Eichorn (eds), *Adolescence and Work: Influence of Social Structure, Labor Markets, and Culture,* Hillsdale, NJ: Lawrence Erlbaum Associates Publishers, 1989.

Oswald, H., D. P. Baker, and D. L. Stevenson, "School charter and parental management in West Germany," *Sociology of Education* 61, 1988, 255–265.

Page, E. and G. Grandon, "Family configuration and mental ability: two theories contrasted with U.S. data," *American Educational Research Journal* 16, 1979, 257–272.

Palkovitz, R., "Reconstructing 'involvement,' expanding conceptualizations of men's caring in contemporary families," in A. J. Hawkins and D. C. Dollahite (eds), *Generative Fathering: Beyond Deficit Perspectives*, Thousand Oaks, CA: Sage, 1997.

Pallas, A. M., D. R. Entwisle, K. L. Alexander, and P. Weinstein, "Social structure and the development of self-esteem in young children," *Social Psychology Quarterly* 53, 1990, 302–315.

Papagiannis, G. J., R. N. Bickel, and R. H. Fuller, "The social creation of school dropouts," *Youth & Society* 14, 1983, 363–392.

Parcel, T. L. and E. G. Menaghan, *Parental Jobs and Children's Lives*, New York, NY: de Gruyter, 1994.

Parish, W. and R. Willis, "Daughters, education, and family budgets: Taiwan experiences," *Journal of Human Resources* 28, 1993, 863–898.

Parke, R. D., "Father involvement: a developmental psychological perspective," *Marriage and Family Review* 29, 2000, 43–58.

Pascarella, E. T. and P. Terenzini, *How College Affects Students: Findings and Insights from Twenty Years of Research,* San Francisco, CA: Jossey Bass, 1991.

Patterson, G. R. and T. J. Dishion, "Multilevel family process models: traits, interactions and relationships," in R. A. Hinde and J. Stevenson-Hinde (eds), *Relationships With Families: Mutual Influences*, Oxford: Clarendon Press, 1988, 283–310.

Pattillo-McCoy, M., *Black Picket Fences: Privilege and Peril Among the Black Middle Class,* Chicago, IL: University of Chicago Press, 1999.

Pattillo-McCoy, M. and C. M. Heflin, "Poverty in the family: siblings of the black and white middle class," paper presented at the Annual Meeting of the American Sociological Association, Chicago, IL, 1999.

Pavalko, E. and J. Artis, "Women's caregiving and paid work: casual relationship in late midlife," *Journal of Gerontology: Social Sciences* 52B, 1997, S170–S179.

Pelavin, S. H. and J. L. David, *Evaluating Long-Term Achievement: An Analysis of Longitudinal Data from Compensatory Educational Programs,* prepared for Office of the Assistant Secretary for Education, Department of Health,

Education and Welfare, EPRC 4537–15, Washington, DC: SRI International Educational Policy Research Center, 1977.

Pettigrew, T. F. and R. T. Riley, "Race and the outcomes of schooling," in F. Mosteller and D. P. Moynihan, *On Equality of Educational Opportunity*, New York, NY: Vintage, 1972.

Philliber, W. W., R. E. Spillman, and R. King, "Consequences of family literacy for adults and children: some preliminary findings," *Journal of Adolescent and Adult Literacy* 39, 1996, 558–565.

Phillips, M., J. Brooks-Gunn, G. J. Duncan, P. K. Klebanov, and J. Crane, "Family background, parenting practices, and the black-white test score gap," in C. Jencks and M. Phillips (eds), *The Black-White Test Score Gap*, Washington, DC: Brookings Institution Press, 1998, 103–145.

Pleck, J. H., "Husbands' paid work and family role: current research issues," in *Research in the Interweave of Social Roles*, vol. 3, *Families and Jobs*, H. Lopata and J. H. Pleck (eds), Greenwich, CT: JAI, 1983, 231–233.

Pleck, J. H., "Changing fatherhood," unpublished manuscript, Wellesley, MA: Wellesley College Center for Research on Women, 1984.

Pleck, J. H., *Working Wives, Working Husbands*, Beverly Hills, CA: Sage, 1985.

Pleck, J. H., "Paternal involvement: levels, sources, and consequences," in *The Role of the Father in Child Development*, New York, NY: John Wiley & Sons, 1997.

Poczik, R., "Work-based education and school reform," in T. Bailey (ed.), *Learning to Work: Employer Involvement in School-to-Work Transition Programs*, Washington, DC: Brookings Institution Press, 1995.

Pollak, R. A., "A transaction cost approach to families and households," *Journal of Economic Literature* 23, 1985, 581–608.

Pong, S., "School participation of children from single-mother families in Malaysia," *Comparative Educational Review* 40, 1996, 231–249.

Pong, S., "Sibship size and educational attainment in Peninsular Malaysia: do policies matter?," *Sociological Perspectives* 40, 1997, 227–242.

Popenoe, D., *Life Without Father*, New York, NY: The Free Press, 1996.

Portes, A., "Social capital: its origins and applications in modern sociology," *Annual Review of Sociology* 24, 1998, 1–24.

Post, D., "Educational stratification, school expansion, and public policy in Hong Kong," *Sociology of Education* 67, 1994, 121–138.

Post, D. and S. Pong, "The waning effect of sibship composition on school attainment in Hong Kong," *Comparative Education Review* 42, 1998, 99–117.

Powell, B. and D. Downey, "Living in single-parent households: an investigation of the same-sex hypothesis," *American Sociological Review* 62, 1997, 521–539.

Powell, B. and L. C. Steelman, "The liability of having brothers: paying for college and the sex composition of the family," *Sociology of Education* 62, 1989, 134–147.

Powell, B. and L. C. Steelman, "Beyond sibship size: sibling density, sex composition, and educational outcomes," *Social Forces* 69, 1990, 181–206.

Powell, B. and L. C. Steelman, "The educational benefits of being spaced out: sibship density and educational progress," *American Sociological Review* 58, 1993, 367–381.

Powell, B. and L. C. Steelman, "Feeling the pinch: child-spacing and constraints on parental economic investments in children," *Social Forces* 73, 1995, 1465–1486.

Powell, B., L. C. Steelman, and R. Carini, "Advancing age, advancing youth: parental age and the flow of resources to progeny," Nashville, TN: Annual Meetings of the Southern Sociological Society, 1999.

Powell, M. A. and T. Parcel, "Parental work, family size, and social capital effects on early educational outcomes: the United States and Great Britain," *Comparative Research in the Sociology of Work* 7, 1999, 1–30.

Powell, W., "Neither market nor heirarchy: network forms of organization," *Research in Organizational Behavior* 12, 1990, 295–336.

Powers, J., *The Girl Question in Education*, London: Falmer Press, 1992.

Pritchett, L., "Desired fertility and the impact of population policies," *Population and Development Review* 20, 1994, 1–55.

Psacharopoulos, G., "Returns to investment in education: a global update," *World Development* 22, 1994, 1325–1344.

Putnam, R. D., "The prosperous community: social capital and public life," *American Prospect*, 1993, 35–42.

Putnam, R. D., "Bowling alone: America's declining social capital," *Journal of Democracy* 6, 1995, 65–78.

Quadagno, J., *The Color of Welfare*, New York, NY: Oxford University Press, 1994.

Raftery, J. R., *Land of Fair Promise: Politics and Reform in Los Angeles Schools, 1885–1941*, Stanford, CA: Stanford University Press, 1992.

Ragan, J. and B. Bratsberg, "Earnings inequality narrows for young workers despite a widening wage structure," *Quarterly Review of Economics and Finance* 35, 1995, 387–395.

Rankin, R., A. Gaite and T. Heiry, "Cultural modification of the effects of family size on intelligence," *Psychological Reports* 45, 1979, 391–397.

Ravitch, D., *The Great School Wars*, New York, NY: Basic Books, 1974.

Ray, C. A. and R. A. Mickelson, "Restructuring students for restructured work: the economy, school reform, and non-college-bound youths," *Sociology of Education* 66, 1993, 1–20.

Reich, R., *The Work of Nations*, New York, NY: Vintage Books, 1991.

Retherford, R. and W. Sewell, "Birth order and further tests of the confluence model," *American Sociological Review* 56, 1991, 141–158.

Richardson, D. C. and M. Brown, *Family Intergenerational Literacy Model: Fact Sheet and Impact Statements,* Oklahoma City, OK: National Diffusion Network, 1997.

Rodgers, J. L., "What causes birth order-intelligence patterns," *American Psychologist* 56, 2001, 505–510.

Roncek, D., "Learning more from tobit coefficients: extending a comparative analysis of political protest," *American Sociological Review* 57, 1992, 503–507.

Roscigno, V., "Race and the reproduction of educational disadvantage," *Social Forces* 76, 1998, 1033–1060.

Roscigno, V., "The black-white achievement gap, family-school links, and the importance of place," *Sociological Inquiry* 69, 1999, 159–186.

Roscigno, V. and J. Ainsworth-Darnell, "Race, cultural capital and educational resources: persistent inequalities and educational returns," *Sociology of Education* 72, 1999, 157–177.

Rosenbaum, J., *Beyond College for All: Career Paths for the Forgotten Half*, New York, NY: Russell Sage Foundation, 2001.

Rosenbaum, J. and A. Binder, "Do employers really need more educated youth?," *Sociology of Education* 70, 1997, 68–85.

Rosenbaum, J. and T. Kariya, "From high school to work: market and institutional mechanisms in Japan," *American Journal of Sociology* 94, 1989, 1334–1366.

Rosenbaum, J., T. Kariya, R. Settersten, and T. Maier, "Market and network theories of the transition from high school to work," *Annual Review of Sociology* 16, 1990, 263–299.

Rosenzweig, M. R. and K. I. Wolpin, "Evaluating the effects of optimally distributed public programs," *American Economic Review* 76, 1986, 470–487.

Rosenzweig, M. R. and K. I. Wolpin, "Natural 'natural experiments' in economics," *Journal of Economic Literature* 38, 2000, 827–874.

Ross, D., *G. Stanley Hall: The Psychologist as Prophet,* Chicago, IL: University of Chicago Press, 1972.

Ross, G. S., "Home intervention for premature infants of low-income families," *American Journal of Orthopsychiatry* 54, 1984, 263–270.

Rothstein, R., "Out of balance: our understanding of how schools affect society and how society affects schools' paper presented at The Spencer Foundation 30th Anniversary Conference: Traditions of Scholarship in Education, 2002.

Rouse, C., "Further estimates of the economic return to schooling from a new sample of twins," *Economics of Education Review* 18, 1999, 149–157.

Rowe, D. C., *The Limits of Family Influence: Genes, Experience, and Behavior*, New York, NY: Guilford Press, 1994.

Rowe, D. C. and J. L. Rodgers, "Poverty and behavior: are environmental measures nature and nurture?," *Developmental Review* 7, 1997, 358–375.

Rowe, D. C., K. C. Jacobson, and E. Van den Oord, "Genetic and environmental influences on vocabulary IQ: parental education level as moderator," *Child Development* 70, 1999, 1151–1162.

Ruggles, S. and M. Sobek, "Integrated public use microdata series: version 2.0," Minneapolis, MN: Historical Census Projects, University of Minnesota, 1997.

Rumberger, R. W., "Dropping out of high school: the influence of race, sex, and family background," *American Educational Research Journal* 20, 1983, 199–220.

Rumberger, R. and T. Daymont, "The economic value of academic and vocational training acquired in high school," in M. E. Borus (ed.), *Youth and the Labor-Market: Analysis of the National Longitudinal Survey,* Kalamazoo, MI: W. E. Upjohn Institute for Employment Research, 1984, Chapter 6.

Rury, J., *Education and Women's Work*, Albany, NY: State University of New York Press, 1991.

Sameroff, A. J., R. Seifer, R. Barocas, M. Zax, and S. Greenspan, "Intelligence quotient scores of 4-year-old children: social and environmental risk factors," *Pediatrics* 79, 1987, 343–350.

Sameroff, A. J., R. Seifer, A. Baldwin, and C. Baldwin, "Stability of intelligence from preschool to adolescence: the influence of social and family risk factors," *Child Development* 64, 1993, 80–97.

Sampson, R. J., "The embeddedness of child and adolescent development: a community-level perspective on urban violence," in J. McCord (ed.), *Violence and Childhood in the Inner City*, New York, NY: Cambridge University Press, 1997, 31–77.

Sandberg, J. F. and S. L. Hofferth, "Changes in children's time with parents, U.S. 1981–1997," *Demography* 38, 2001, 423–436.

Sapiro, V., "The gender basis of American social policy," in L. Gordon (ed.),

Women, the State, and Welfare, Madison, WI: University of Wisconsin Press, 1990.

Sathar, Z. and C. Lloyd, "Who gets primary schooling in Pakistan: inequalities among and within families?," *Pakistan Development Review* 33, 1994, 103–134.

Saxe, G. B., S. R. Guberman, and M. Gearheart, "Social processes in early number development," *Monographs Social Research Child Development* 52, 1987, No. 216.

Schneider, B. and J. Coleman (eds), *Parents, Their Children, and Schools,* Boulder, CO: Westview Press, 1993.

Schneider, B. and D. Stevenson, *The Ambitious Generation,* New Haven, CT: Yale University Press, 1999.

Schoenhals, M., M. Tienda, and B. Schneider, "The educational and personal consequences of adolescent employment," *Social Forces* 77, 1998, 723–762.

Schultz, T. P., "Returns to women's education," in E. M. King and M. A. Hill (eds), 1993, *Women's Education in Developing Countries: Barriers, Benefits, and Policies*, Baltimore, MD and London: The Johns Hopkins University Press, published for the World Bank, 1993, 51–99.

Schumacker, R. E. and R. G. Lomax, *A Beginner's Guide to Structural Equation Modeling*, Mahwah, NJ: Lawrence Erlbaum Associates, 1996.

Schweinhart, L. J., H. V. Barnes, D. P. Weikart, W. S. Barnett, and A. S. Epstein, *Significant Benefits: The High/Scope Perry Preschool Study Through Age 27,* Ypsilanti, MI: High/Scope Press, 1993.

Scott, R. and J. Meyer, "Environmental linkages and organizational complexities: public and private schools' in T. James and H. Levin (eds), *Comparing Public and Private Schools, Vol. I: Institutions and Organizations*, 1988, 128–152.

Seitz, V. and N. H. Apfel, "Parent-focused intervention: diffusion effects on siblings," *Child Development* 65, 1994, 677–683.

Seltzer, J. A., "Father by law: effects of joint legal custody on nonresident fathers' involvement with children," *Demography* 35, 1998, 135–146.

Semel, S. F., *The Dalton School: The Transformation of a Progressive School*, New York, NY: Peter Lang, 1992.

September, R., "How does it work, and who benefits: the distribution of scientific knowledge in South Africa," *International Review of Education* 36, 1990, 469–484.

Settersten Jr., R. A. and J. U. Mayer, "The measurement of age, age structure, and the life course," *Annual Review of Sociology* 23, 1997, 233–266.

Sewell, W.H. and R. M. Hauser, *Education, Occupation, and Earnings: Achievement in the Early Career*, New York, NY: Academic Press, 1975.

Shafer, M., "International nongovernmental organizations and Third World education in 1990: a cross-national study," *Sociology of Education* 72, 69–88.

Shapira, R. and P. Cookson (eds), *Autonomy and Choice in Context: An International Perspective*, New York, NY: Elsevier, 1997.

Shavit, Y., "Expansion and inequality of opportunity in higher education," presented at the Annual Meetings of the American Sociological Association, Anaheim, CA, 2001.

Shavit, Y. and W. Müller, *From School to Work*, Oxford: Clarendon Press, 1998.

Shavit, Y. and J. Pierce, "Sibship size and educational attainment in nuclear and extended families: Arabs and Jews in Israel," *American Sociological Review* 56, 1991, 321–330.

Shonkoff, J. P. and D. A. Phillips (eds), *From Neurons to Neighborhoods: The*

Science of Early Childhood Developmental Science, Washington, DC: National Academies Press, 2000.

Shreeniwas, S., "Family size, structure and children's education: ethnic differentials over time in Peninsular Malaysia," in C. Lloyd (ed.), *Fertility, Family Size and Structure*, New York, NY: Population Council, 1993, 332–372.

Simms, M. C. and J. M. Maleveaux, *Slipping Through The Cracks: The Status of Black Women*, New Brunswick, NJ: Transaction Books, 1986.

Smith, J. R., J. Brooks-Gunn, and P. K. Klebanov, "Consequences of living in poverty for young children's cognitive and verbal ability and early school achievement," in G. J. Duncan and J. Brooks-Gunn (eds), *Consequences of Growing Up Poor*, New York, NY: Russell Sage Foundation, 1997, 132–189.

Smith, M. S., "Equality of educational opportunity: the basic findings reconsidered," in F. Mosteller and D. P. Moynihan (eds) *On Equality of Educational Opportunity*, New York, NY: Vintage Books, 1972.

Smith, R., "Making village women into 'good wives and wise mothers' in prewar Japan," *Journal of Family History* 8, 1983, 70–84.

Snarey, J., *How Fathers Care for the Next Generation*, Cambridge, MA: Harvard University Press, 1993.

Snow, C. E., "Conversations with children," in P. Fletcher and M. Garman (eds), *Language Acquisition: Studies in First Language Development,* Cambridge, UK: Cambridge University Press, 1986, 69–89.

Sobel, M. E., "Asymptotic confidence intervals for indirect effects in structural equation models," in S. Leinhart (ed.), *Sociological Methodology 1982,* San Francisco, CA: Jossey Bass, 1982, 290–312.

Solon, G. R., "Intergenerational income mobility in the united states," *American Economic Review* 82, 1992, 393–408.

Solon, G., "Intergenerational mobility in the labor market," in O. Ashenfelter and D. Card (eds), *Handbook of Labor Economics*, North Holland, Amsterdam, forthcoming.

Solon, G., M. Corcoran, R. Gordon, and D. Laren, "A longitudinal analysis of sibling correlations in economic status," *Journal of Human Resources* 26, 1991, 509–534.

Somit, A., A. Arwine, and S. Peterson, *Birth Order and Political Behavior*, Lanhan, MD: University Press of America, 1996.

Spiker, D., J. C. Ferguson, and J. Brooks-Gunn, "Enhancing maternal interactive behavior and child social competence in low birth weight, premature infants," *Child Development* 64, 1993, 754–768.

Spring, J., *The Sorting Machine: National Educational Policy Since 1945*, New York, NY: David McKay Company, Inc., 1976.

SPSS, *SPSS for Windows Advanced Statistics*, Chicago, IL: SPSS, 1993.

SPSS, *SPSS for Windows Base System User's Guide*, Chicago, IL: SPSS, 1993.

Stack, C., *All Our Kin: Strategies for Survival in a Black Community*, New York, NY: Harper and Row, 1974.

Stafford, F. P. and G. J. Duncan, "The use of time and technology by households in the United States," in T. F. Juster and F. Stafford (eds), *Time, Goods, and Well-being*, Ann Arbor, MI: Institute for Social Research, University of Michigan, 1985.

Steelman, L. C., "A tale of two variables: a review of the intellectual consequences of sibship size and birth order," *Review of Educational Research* 55, 1985, 353–386.

Steelman, L. C. and J. Mercy, "Unconfounding the confluence model: a test of sibship size and birth order effects on intelligence," *American Sociological Review* 45, 1980, 571–582.

Steelman, L. C. and B. Powell, "Acquiring capital for college: the constraints of family configuration," *American Sociological Review* 54, 1989, 844–855.

Steelman, L. C. and B. Powell, "Sponsoring the next generation: parental willingness to pay for college," *American Journal of Sociology* 96, 1991, 1505–1529.

Steelman, L. C. and B. Powell, "The family devalued: the treatment of the family in the small groups literature," *Advances in Group Processes* 13, 1996, 211–236.

Steelman, L. C., B. Powell, R. Werum, and S. Carter, "Reconsidering the effects of sibling configuration: recent advances and challenges," *Annual Review of Sociology* 28, 2002, 243–269.

Steinberg, L. D. and S. M. Dornbusch, "Negative correlates of part-time employment during adolescence: replication and elaboration," *Developmental Psychology* 27, 1991, 304–313.

Steinberg, L. D., S. Fegley, and S. M. Dornbusch, "Negative impact of part-time work on adolescent adjustment: evidence from a longitudinal study," *Developmental Psychology* 29, 1993, 171–180.

Stern, D., M. Raby, and C. Dayton, *Career Academies: Partnerships for Restructuring American High Schools,* San Francisco, CA: Jossey Bass, 1992.

Stern, D. and Y. Nakata, "Characteristics of high school students' paid jobs, and employment experience after graduation," in D. Stern, and D. Eichorn (eds), *Adolescence and Work: Influences of Social Structure, Labor Markets, and Culture,* Hillsdale, NJ: Lawrence Erlbaum Associates, 1989.

St. Pierre, R. G., A. Ricciuti, and C. L. Creps, *Synthesis of State and Local Even Start Evaluations: Draft,* Cambridge, MA: Abt Associates, 1998.

St. Pierre, R. G. and J. P. Swartz, "The even start family literacy program," in S. Smith (ed.), *Advances in Applied Developmental Psychology: Vol. 9. Two Generation Programs for Families in Poverty: A New Intervention Strategy,* Norwood, NJ: Ablex Publishing Corporation, 1995, 37–66.

St. Pierre, R. G., J. P. Swartz, B. Gamse, S. Murray, D. Deck, and P. Nickel, *National Evaluation of the Even Start Family Literacy Program: Final Report,* Washington, DC: U.S. Department of Education, 1995.

Strom, R., P. Collingsworth, S. Strom, and D. Griswold, "Strengths and needs of black grandparents," *International Journal of Aging and Human Development* 36, 1993, 255–268.

Sullivan, M., *"Getting Paid:" Youth Crime and Work in the Inner City,* Ithaca, NY: Cornell University Press, 1989.

Szymanski, A., "International foundations in Latin America," *Revista Mexicana de Sociologia* 35, 1973, 801–817.

Tanguy, L., "Academic studies and technical education: new dimensions of an old struggle in the division of knowledge," *Sociology of Education* 58, 1985, 20–33.

Tansel, A., "School attainment, parental education and gender in Cote d'Ivoire and Ghana," *Economic Development and Cultural Change* 45, 1997, 825–856.

Tao, F., B. Gamse, and H. Tarr, *National Evaluation of the Even Start Family Literacy Program: 1994–1997 Final Report*, Washington, DC: U.S. Department of Education, Planning and Evaluation Service, 1998.

Tao, F., J. Swartz, R. St. Pierre, and H. Tarr, *National Evaluations of the Even Start Family Literacy Program,* Washington, DC: U.S. Department of Education, 1997.

Taubman, P. and J. Behrman, "Effects of number and position of siblings and adult outcomes," *Social Biology* 33, 1986, 22–33.

Taylor, H. F., "Playing the dozens with path analysis: methodological pitfalls in Jencks *et al., Inequality*," *Sociology of Education* 46, 1973, 433–450.

Teachman, J., "Family background, educational resources and educational attainment," *American Sociological Review* 52, 1987, 548–557.

Teachman, J., K. Paasch, and K. Carver, "Social capital and the generation of human capital," *Social Forces* 75, 1997, 1343–1359.

Thomas, D., R. F. Schoeni, and J. Strauss, *Parental Investments in Schooling: The Roles of Gender and Resources in Urban Brazil*, Santa Monica, CA: RAND, mimeo, 1996.

Thomas, G. E. and F. Brown, "What does educational research tell us about school desegregation effects?," *Journal of Black Studies* 13, 1982, 155–174.

Thompson, M., K. L. Alexander, and D. R. Entwisle, "Household composition, parental expectations, and school achievement," *Social Forces* 67, 1988, 424–451.

Thompson, R. A., "Sequelae of early attachment experiences," in J. Cassidy and P. Shaver (eds), *Handbook of Attachment Theory and Research*, New York, NY: Guilford Press, 1998.

Tienda, M., "Poor people and poor places: deciphering neighborhood effects on poverty outcomes," in J. Huber (ed.), *Macro-Micro Linkages in Sociology,* Newbury Park, CA: Sage Publications, 1991, 244–262.

Tikly, L. and T. Mabogoane, "Marketisation as a strategy for desegregation and redress: the case of historically white schools in South Africa," *International Review of Education* 43, 1997, 159–178.

Timmer, S. G., J. S. Eccles, and K. O'Brien, "How children use time," in T. F. Juster and F. P. Stafford (eds), *Time, Goods, and Wellbeing*, Ann Arbor, MI: Institute for Social Research, The University of Michigan, 1985.

Tomeh, A., "Birth order and dependence patterns of college students in Lebanon," *Journal of Marriage and the Family* 34, 1972, 361–374.

Torres, C., "The state, nonformal education, and socialism in Cuba, Nicaragua, and Grenada," *Comparative Education Review* 35, 1991, 110–130.

Townsend, N. W., "Fathers and sons: men's experience and the reproduction of fatherhood," in K. V. Hansen and A. I. Garey (eds), *Families in the U.S.: Kinship and Domestic Politics*, Philadelphia, PA: Temple, 1998.

Trace, A., *What Ivan Knows That Johnny Doesn't*, New York, NY: Random House, 1961.

Tremblay, R. E., "The development of aggressive behaviour during childhood: what have we learned in the past century?," *International Journal of Behavioral Development* 24, 2000, 129–141.

Tyack, D. B., *The One Best System: A History of American Urban Education,* Cambridge, MA: Harvard University Press, 1974.

Tyack, D. B. and E. Hansot, *Managers of Virtue: Public School Leadership in America, 1820–1980,* New York, NY: Basic Books, 1982.

Tyack, D. and E. Hansot, *Learning Together: A History of Coeducation in American Schools*, New Haven: Yale University Press, 1990.

Urban, W., "Organized teachers and educational reform during the progressive era: 1890–1920," *History of Education Quarterly* 16, 1976, 35–52.

U.S. Bureau of the Census, "Series H, Table 599: high school graduates, by sex: 1870 to 1970," *Historical Statistics of the United States: Colonial Times to 1970, Bicentennial Edition, Part 1,* Washington, DC: U.S. Bureau of the Census, 1975.

U.S. Bureau of the Census, *Census of Population: 1980 Vol. 1. Characteristics of the Population*, Washington, DC: U.S. Government Printing Office, 1983.

U.S. Bureau of the Census, "Current population reports, Series P60–187," Washington, DC: U.S. Government Printing Office, 1992.

U.S. Commission on Civil Rights, *Racial Isolation in the Public Schools*, Vol. 1, Washington, DC: Government Printing Office, 1967.

U.S. Department of Education, *A Nation at Risk: The Imperative for Educational Reform.* http://www.ed.gov/pubs/NatAtRisk/index.html, 1983.

U.S. Department of Education, *America's Kindergarteners: Findings from the Early Childhood Longitudinal Study, Kindergarten Class of 1998–99, Fall 1998,* NCES 2000–070 by J. West (Project Officer), K. Denton and E. Germino-Hausken, Washington, DC: U.S. Department of Education, National Center for Education Statistics, 2000.

U.S. Department of Labor, *Employment Experience of Youths: Results from a Longitudinal Survey*, USDL 00–353, Washington, DC: U.S. Department of Labor, Bureau of Labor Statistics, 2000a.

U.S. Department of Labor, *NLS Handbook, 2000*, Washington, DC: U.S. Department of Labor, Bureau of Labor Statistics, 2000b.

Useem, E., "Middle schools and math groups: parents' involvement in children's placement," *Sociology of Education* 65, 1992, 263–279.

Valenzuela, A. and S. Dornbusch, "Familism and social capital in the academic achievement of Mexican origin and Anglo adolescents," *Social Science Quarterly* 78, 1994, 713–719.

Van de Walle, D. and K. Nead (eds), *Public Spending and the Poor: Theory and Evidence*, Baltimore, MD and London: The Johns Hopkins Press for the World Bank, 1995.

Van Zanten, A., "Market trends in the French school system: overt policy, hidden strategies, and actual changes," *Oxford Studies in Comparative Education* 6, 1996, 63–75.

Vetter, L., "The vocational education option for women," in S. Harlan and R. Steinberg, *Job Training for Women: The Promise and Limits of Public Policies*, Philadelphia, PA: Temple University Press, 1989.

Violas, P. C., *The Training of the Urban Working Class: A History of Twentieth Century American Education,* Chicago, IL: Rand McNally, 1978.

Volling, B. L. and J. Belsky, "Multiple determinants of father involvement during infancy in dual-earner and single-earner families," *Journal of Marriage and the Family,* 53, 1991, 461–474.

Wagner, M. M. and S. L. Clayton, "The parents as teachers program: results from two demonstrations," *The Future of Children* 9, 1999, 91–115.

Warren, J. and R. M. Hauser, "Social stratification across three generations: new evidence from the Wisconsin longitudinal study," *American Sociological Review* 62, 1997, 561–572.

Warren, J. R., "Reconsidering the relationship between student employment and academic outcomes: a new theory and better data," *Youth & Society* 33, 2002, 366–393.

Warren, J. R. and E. F. Cataldi, "Trends in the selectivity and consequences of adolescent employment, 1966–1997," unpublished manuscript, Department of Sociology, University of Minnesota, 2003.

Warren, J. R. and J. C. Lee, "The impact of adolescent employment on high school dropout: differences by individual and labor market characteristics," *Social Science Research*, 32, 2003, 98–128.

Warren, J. R., P. C. LePore, and R. D. Mare, "Employment during high school: consequences for students' grades in academic courses," *American Educational Research Journal* 37, 2000, 943–969.

Watson, J. and S. Koblinksy, "Strengths and needs of working class African-American and Anglo-American grandparents," *International Journal of Aging and Human Development* 44, 1997, 149–165.

Way, S., "Gender and job search methods: the effects of high school job placement services on the school-to-work transition," paper presented at American Sociological Association Meetings, San Francisco, CA, August 1998.

Weinberg, R. A., "Intelligence and IQ: landmark issues and great debates," *American Psychologist* 44, 1989, 98–104.

Weiss, C. H., "Nothing as practical as a good theory: exploring theory-based evaluation for comprehensive community initiatives for children and families," in J. P. Connell, A. C. Kubisch, L. B. Schorr, and C. H. Weiss (eds), *New Approaches to Evaluating Community Initiatives: Vol. 1. Concepts, Methods, and Contexts,* Washington, DC: The Aspen Institute, 1995, 65–92.

Wenglinsky, H., "How money matters: the effect of school district spending on academic achievement," *Sociology of Education* 70, 1997, 221–237.

Werum, R., "It's not what you know but whom you know: adult social capital and track placement of ethnic groups in Germany," paper presented at American Sociological Association Meeting, Washington, DC, 2000.

Werum, R., "Does one shoe fit all? How parental social capital affects track placement of Caucasians and Latinos," paper presented at American Sociological Association Meeting, Anaheim, CA, 2001.

Werum, R., "Matching youth and jobs? Gender dynamics in new deal job training programs," *Social Forces* 81, 2002, 473–502.

Whitehurst, G. J., D. S. Arnold, J. N. Epstein, A. L. Angell, M. Smith, and J. E. Fischel, "A picture book reading intervention in day care and home for children from low-income families," *Developmental Psychology* 30, 1994, 679–689.

Whitehurst, G. J. and C. J. Lonigan, "Child development and emergent literacy," *Child Development* 69, 1998, 848–872.

Will, G. F., "Broken families and school performance," *Washington Post*, p. B07, 2002 (January 6).

William T. Grant Foundation, *The Forgotten Half: Pathways to Success for America's Youth and Young Families,* Washington, DC: William T. Grant Foundation, 1988.

Williamson, O., *Markets and Hierarchies: Analysis and Antitrust Implications*, New York, NY: Free Press, 1975.

Willms, D. and M. Chen, "The effects of ability grouping on the ethnic achievement gap in Israeli elementary schools," *American Journal of Education* 97, 1989, 237–257.

Willms, D. and F. Echols, "Alert and inert clients: the Scottish experience of parental choice of schools," *Economics of Education Review* 11, 1992, 399–450.

Wilson, M. N., "Child development in the context of the Black extended family," *American Psychologist* 44, 1989, 380–385.

Wilson, W., *When Work Disappears: The World of the New Urban Poor*, New York, NY: Vintage, 1996.

Winer, B. J., *Statistical Principles in Experimental Design*, New York, NY: McGraw-Hill, 1971.

Woods, E. and W. Haney, *Does Vocational Education Make a Difference? A Review of Previous Research and Reanalyses of National Longitudinal Data Sets,* Washington, DC: National Institute of Education, 1981.

Woodward-Lopez, G., J. Ikeda, and P. Crawford, "Improving children's academic performance, health, and quality of life: a top policy commitment in response to children's obesity and health crisis in California," report written for the California Elected Women's Association for Education and Research, 1999, 13. http://www.cnr.berkeley.edu/cwh/PDFs/CewaerPaper_Research.pdf.

Wrigley, J. (ed.), *Education and Gender Equality*, London: Falmer Press, 1992.

Yeung, W. J., "How multiple domains of paternal involvement affect children's well-being," paper presented in American Sociological Association Annual Meeting, Chicago, IL, 2001.

Yeung, W. J., G. J. Duncan, and M. S. Hill, "Putting fathers back in the picture," *Journal of Marriage and Family Review* 4, 2000a, 97–114.

Yeung, W. J., M. Linver, and J. Brooks-Gunn, "How money matters for young children's development: parental investment and family processes," *Child Development* 73, 2002, 1861–1879.

Yeung, W. J., J. F. Sandberg, P. E. Davis-Kean, and S. L. Hofferth, "Children's time with fathers in intact families," *Journal of Marriage and Family Review* 63, 2001, 136–154.

Yoshikawa, H., "Long-term effects of early childhood programs on social outcomes and delinquency," *The Future of Children* 5, 1995, 51–75.

Zahn-Waxler, C., R. J. Iannotti, E. M. Cummings, and S. A. Denham, "Antecedents of problem behaviors in children of depressed mothers," *Development and Psychopathology* 2, 1990, 349–366.

Zajonc, R., "Family configuration and intelligence," *Science* 192, 1976, 227–236.

Zajonc, R., "The family dynamics of intellectual development," *American Psychologist* 56, 2001, 490–496.

Zajonc, R. and G. Markus, "Birth order and intellectual development," *Psychological Review* 82, 1975, 74–88.

Zill, N., "American children: happy, healthy, and insecure," report on Foundation for Child Development's National Survey of Children, New York, NY: The Foundation for Child Development, 1981.

Zimmerman, D. J., "Regression toward mediocrity in economic stature," *American Economic Review* 82, 1992, 409–429.

Index

www.ingramcontent.com/pod-product-compliance
Lightning Source LLC
LaVergne TN
LVHW011111300926
849160LV00008B/347
9780415645768